THE GREAT DIDACTIC

OF

JOHN AMOS COMENIUS

British Library Cataloguing-in-Publication Data
A catalogue record for this book is available from the
British Library

IOHAN-AMOS COMENIVS, MORAVVS. Aᵒ AETAT. 50. 164

Exſump: M. S: G Glouer fc.

Loe, here an Exile! who to ſerue his God,
Hath ſharely taſted of proud Paſturs Rod.
Whoſe learning, Piety, & true worth, being knowne
To all the world, makes all the world his owne.
                                    F. Q:

THE

GREAT DIDACTIC

OF

JOHN AMOS COMENIUS

NOW FOR THE FIRST TIME ENGLISHED

WITH INTRODUCTIONS, BIOGRAPHICAL AND HISTORICAL,

BY

M. W. KEATINGE, B.A.

LATE EXHIBITIONER OF EXETER COLLEGE, OXFORD

PREFACE

THE present version of the *Didactica Magna* is a close paraphrase from the original Latin in the Advocates' Library, Edinburgh. The Introductions are based upon original research and on the best German authorities. They embody a fuller account of Comenius' life and works than has hitherto been accessible to the English reader; while a part of their contents is, I believe, a fresh contribution to the biography and the historical environment of the great School Reformer.

The portrait is a reproduction of the frontispiece to Hartlib's *A Reformation of Schooles*, published in 1642.

My best thanks are due to my friend and colleague, Dr. J. S. Mackay, who read over a large portion of the work in manuscript, and gave me valuable assistance on many points.

M. W. K.

THE EDINBURGH ACADEMY,
February 1896.

CONTENTS

INTRODUCTION

I

BIOGRAPHICAL

JOHN AMOS COMENIUS (in Bohemian Komensky) was born on the 28th of March 1592, in the village of Nivnitz,[1] near Ungarisch-Brod in Moravia. His father, Martin Komensky, was a miller in fairly prosperous circumstances and belonged to the religious body known as the Moravian Brethren.[2] This community had been organised in 1547; it carried on, with modifications, the traditions of John Hus, and took a position midway between the Utraquists, his followers, and the Roman Catholics. Though the ideas of the Lutherans had not been without a decided influence, the Moravians differed from that body on certain fundamental points, such as the Doctrine of Works, and, at one period, the celibacy of the clergy. Their chief

---

[1] In the Introduction to *De cultura ingeniorum oratio* (*Op. Did. Omn.* iii. 72) he calls himself Hunno Brodensis Moravus; but, as he was known at Herborn as John Amos Niwnizensis, was inscribed in the Matriculation book at Heidelberg as Joannes Amos Nivanus Moravus, and wrote his name "Johannes Amos Nivanus" on the manuscript of Copernicus' *De revolutionibus orbium cælestium* that he bought from a widow Christman at Heidelberg, it seems probable that Nivnitz was his birthplace and that he refers to Ungarisch-Brod as the spot where his childhood was spent.

[2] By contemporary writers they are also termed the *Bohemian Brethren* and *The Unity*.

I

characteristic was extreme simplicity, and their great desideratum to lead a pure life, and one as far as possible in accordance with the commands of Scripture, which they interpreted in their most literal sense.

It was in this atmosphere of free Biblical inquiry that Comenius was brought up, and the result of early training can be seen in his habit of appealing to the Scriptures on every possible occasion, and of proving his most technical propositions directly from their pages.

Shortly after his son's birth, Martin Komensky left Nivnitz and moved to Ungarisch - Brod, where he died in 1602. His wife did not survive him more than a couple of years, and shortly afterwards his two daughters Ludmilla and Susanna died also. Comenius was thus left an orphan at an early age, and his guardians appear to have robbed him of any small fortune that his father had bequeathed. This was not the only manifestation of his evil star. During the two following years, while attending the elementary school at Strasnic, he made the acquaintance of Nicolaus Drabik. It was a strange irony of fate that a wanderer like Comenius, when only eleven years old and in his native land, should commence the intimacy that was to embitter his old age in Amsterdam.

From the point of view of positive instruction this early training was unproductive, and the Latin school at Prerau, to which he was not sent till his sixteenth year,[1] appears to have been even less efficient than the other secondary schools of the age. Comenius however, who, as we shall see, was rather inclined to underestimate the educational activity of contemporary Europe, assures us that his experience was nothing exceptional, and that he was but one of the thousands whose youth was wasted in these "slaughter-houses" of the young.[2] Often did his eyes fill

---

[1] Admodum enim puer parente utroque orbatus, tutorum supinitate ita fui neglectus ut demum ætatis anno decimo sexto Latina elementa gustare contigerit.—J. A. Comenius, *Opera Didactica Omnia*, Amsterdam, 1657, i. 442.

[2] Millibus e multis ego quoque sum unus, miser homuncio, cui

with tears when thinking of his wasted childhood, often did he vainly wish that he might live those years over again and employ them more profitably.

Viewed differently, the defects in his early education were the seeds from which sprang the whole of his didactic efforts. Considerably older than his schoolfellows, he was able to criticise the methods in use, and speedily arrived at the conclusion that the lack of progress was due more to the inefficiency of the teachers than to the idleness of their pupils. From this time onwards, full of pity for the sufferings of his fellows, he began to devise new methods of class instruction and better schemes of study. From the vivid memory of the horrors through which he had passed, of the thousand-and-one rules that had to be learned by rote before they were understood, of the monotonous study of grammar, only diversified by the maddening effort to translate Latin authors without the assistance of suitable dictionaries or commentaries, sprang that intense sympathy with beginners which characterises his whole life and gives practical worth to every precept that he enunciated.

In the Latin school he only remained for two years. He had definitely made up his mind to seek ordination as a minister of the Moravian Brethren, and needed a more advanced education than could be obtained in Bohemia. Not that the University of Prague was in any way below the standard of the age, but it was in the hands of the Utraquists, whose attitude towards the "Brethren" was by no means friendly. It was therefore to Herborn in Nassau that Comenius, then eighteen years old, turned his steps. A university had been founded in this town in 1584, and enjoyed a very high reputation. The range of subjects taught was wide, as, though great prominence was given to Theology, ample provision was made for the "Humanities" as well; and in addition it was possible to learn music and the French and Italian languages.

amœnissimum vitæ totius ver, florentes juventutis anni, nugis scholasticis transmissi, misere perierunt.—*Did. Mag.* xi. 13.

It was under the Rectorship of Wolfgang Ficinus that Comenius matriculated in March 1611. Of his residence at the University we unfortunately know very little; but he can scarcely have remained there for two years without coming under the influence of John Henry Alsted, and the similarity of their views and dispositions renders it probable that the two men were brought into very close contact. Although only twenty-six years old, Alsted had already a very considerable reputation, and in point of attainments was undoubtedly one of the most remarkable men of his time. His industry was so great that his contemporaries christened him *Sedulitas*,[1] an anagram on the Latinised form of his name. As an etymologist he took a high place, as a writer on Didactic he ranks historically with Ratke as the immediate forerunner of Comenius, and his *Encyclopædia Scientiarum Omnium*, published at Herborn in 1630, proves him to have been a master in every branch of learning. The range of knowledge was limited, and to write with authority *de omni scibili* was not the impossibility that it now is, but a glance through the pages of this Encyclopædia shows that its author obtained a marvellous grip of every subject that he studied, and had a very unusual power of co-ordinating the mass of erudition that he possessed. Nor did his many-sidedness end here. His *Triumphus Biblicus*, in which he attempts to lay the foundation of all positive knowledge in the literal interpretation of Scripture, displays an aspect of his character that we do not meet in the Encyclopædia, and gives evidence of a mind imbued with the most intense mysticism.

Of the exact nature of the intercourse between Comenius and Alsted we have no direct information, but, as Alsted was in the habit of maintaining the closest relations with his pupils and is afterwards found in correspondence with Comenius, we may take it for granted

[1] Sedulus in libris scribendis atque legendis
Alstedius nomen sedulitatis habet.
Encyclopædia Scientiarum Omnium, Leyden, 1649
(2nd Ed.), ad init.

that the great similarity of the views held by the two men should not be attributed to accident. The only point on which they were at actual variance was the constitution of the elementary or vernacular school. This Alsted would have restricted to the use of girls, and of boys destined for a handicraft, while Comenius insists on the necessity of giving a distinct primary education to those who are afterwards to enter a learned profession. With the exception of this difference of opinion, a large number of the most striking precepts that figure in the Great Didactic might have been taken direct from Alsted's Encyclopædia. The man who declared that instruction in the mother tongue should precede the study of Latin, who thought that grammar was the least effective instrument in teaching a language,[1] who proclaimed, almost in Baconian language, the doctrine of "Experience,"[2] and who believed in method to such an extent that he drew up time-tables of the most intricate description for a day, a week, a month, and a year, assuredly played the part of a kindly foster-father to the callow educational zeal of the Herborn student.

That Comenius, while at Herborn, devoted much attention to the study of educational method, we know from his own words. Wolfgang's Ratke's essay on the Reformation of schools had been authorised and approved by the Universities of Jena and of Giessen in 1612, and a tractate on the new method, probably that by the Giessen professors Helwig and Jung, rapidly found its way into Comenius' hands.[3] To this he gratefully acknowledges his debt and attributes his efforts to reform the school at Prerau.

From Herborn he proceeded to Heidelberg, where he matriculated in June 1613. Here he appears to have

---

[1] Nulla lingua docetor ex grammatica. — *Encyc. Scient. Omn.* ii. 287.

[2] Experientiæ nulla authoritas præjudicet.—*Ibid.*

[3] Statim ut Wolphgangii Ratichii de Studiorum rectificanda methodo consilium, ab Academiis Jenensi et Gissena scripto publico laudatum, Anno 1612, prodierat, fama hæc meas quoque ad aures studiis tunc Herbornæ Nassoviorum operam dantis pervenit.—*Op. Did. Omn.* i. 3.

devoted some attention to the study of astronomy, as we find him purchasing the original manuscript of one of Copernicus' works. This, however, is the solitary incident that is known of his residence here.

After a journey through Europe, in the course of which he visited Amsterdam for the first time, he went back to Heidelberg. A short illness followed, possibly the result of exposure on his travels, and in 1614 he returned to Moravia on foot. He was now twenty-two years old, and, as he could not be ordained for two years, undertook the management of the school at Prerau. This was one of the many schools established by the "Unity" for the education of those of their own persuasion, and must have been rather more than an elementary school, as Comenius, who now for the first time came into contact with the practical difficulties of instruction, began to evolve an easier method for teaching Latin. To this he devoted a great deal of attention [1] and produced a small book for beginners,[2] afterwards printed at Prague in 1616, but which has not been preserved. This was not his first literary effort. As early as 1612, while at Herborn, he had begun to collect the materials for a Bohemian dictionary with the twofold object of purifying his native tongue and of mastering it thoroughly. As he was now old enough to commence his ministry in the Moravian Church, he was ordained in April 1616, in company with his old schoolfellow Drabik. The two following years he probably spent at Olmütz.

Of the next few years, as of the whole of the earlier portion of his life, the information to be obtained is fragmentary. In 1618 he was sent to Fulneck, where he acted as pastor to the Moravian community and was at the same time inspector of the school. During the three years that followed he devoted himself entirely to the spiritual and bodily welfare of his flock, sparing no pains to further the prosperity of the town. He even tried to introduce bee-culture, and sent to Hungary for bees, then

---

[1] Multa igitur et multum animo volvebam.—*Op. Did. Omn.* i. 442.
[2] Facilioris grammaticæ præcepta.—*Ibid.* i. 3.

unknown in Fulneck.[1]   His married life now began, and in the society of his wife, a Hungarian lady, Comenius spent what were probably his happiest years.

The year in which he entered upon his pastorate at Fulneck is memorable for the outbreak of the Thirty Years' War, and from this time onwards the position of the non-Catholic bodies, exposed as they were to the relentless persecution of Pope Paul V. and the Jesuits, was most precarious.   Their hopes were finally overthrown by the battle of the White Mountain in November 1620, and by the execution of the chief Bohemian Protestants, which followed at Prague in June 1621.

Comenius' wanderings were now to begin.   In 1621 Fulneck was plundered and burned by Spanish troops.   On this occasion he lost everything that he possessed, including the greater part of his library and the manuscript of some Didactic works on which he had been engaged, and took refuge, in company with many others of the Brethren, on the estate of Karl von Zerotin.   Here he remained for three years, during which time he occupied himself in reading books on education,[2] and wrote besides several religious works in the Czech language.   To this period must also be ascribed his metrical translation of the Psalms, a composition of great poetic merit; his *Labyrinth of the World*, an allegorical description of life, dedicated to Karl von Zerotin; and a map of Moravia that was for a long time the best in existence.[3]

It was doubtless in this literary activity that he sought relief for the sorrow caused him by the death of his wife and his two children,[4] who were carried off in 1622 by an epidemic that was raging through Moravia.   He was thus once more left alone in the world.

In 1624, with startling rapidity, if we consider the cir-

[1] J. A. Comenius, *Grosze Unterrichtslehre* (Julius Beeger und Franz Zoubek), p. 14.

[2] *Op. Did. Omn.* i. 442.

[3] It had gone through twenty editions by 1695.

[4] *Ep. ad Montanum*, p. 77.   Quoted by Kvacsala in *Johann Amos Comenius.   Sein Leben und seine Schriften.*   Notes, p. 12.

cumstances and the forlorn condition of the Brethren, he married again. His bride was Maria Dorothea Cyrill, the daughter of John Cyrill, a Moravian pastor and a former senior of the Consistory at Prague. The members of the Unity cannot have been left entirely destitute by the persecution to which they were subjected, as Maria brought her husband a small fortune. The sequel proved that marriage at such a time had been far from prudent. In the same year the order was issued that all non-Catholic preachers and pastors were to leave Bohemia within six weeks, and a few months later another mandate expelled them from Moravia as well. Karl von Zerotin had great influence with Ferdinand II., but the Jesuits were too strong for him. He received a personal injunction to cease harbouring non-Catholics on his estate, and the twenty-four ministers whom he was sheltering had to conceal themselves as best they could in caves and forests.

The Brethren now recognised that all hope of remaining in their fatherland must be relinquished, and in 1625 sent Comenius and two companions to Poland to report on the advisability of their removing thither in a body. On the way the messengers made the acquaintance of Christopher Kotter, a native of Sprottau. Kotter was a prophet, and his visions and the announcements that he had to make concerning the future of the Evangelical Church were full of interest to the Brethren. Comenius, to whom anything of a prophetic nature was always an attraction, gave a proof of his remarkable energy by translating the whole of Kotter's prophecies into Czech, a task which took him sixteen days. After a short visit to Berlin, where there were a number of Bohemian exiles, he returned to Moravia. During the next two years the Brethren held themselves in readiness to fly at a moment's notice. The only incident of any interest is the appearance on the scene of a prophetess, Christina Poniatowska. Christina was an hysterical girl, only sixteen years old, and her visions, like those of Kotter, dealt with the speedy restoration of the Evangelic Church, and the cessation of

the persecutions to which it was being subjected. Needless to say, Comenius displayed as great an interest in her
as he had done in Kotter. Already the visionary tendencies, out of which his enemies made such capital in
later years, were getting possession of him.

In 1627 a few of the Evangelical Pastors, preparatory
to their final departure, took refuge on the estate of George
Sadowski at Slaupna, and here Comenius again took up
the threads of his didactic efforts. As a slight return for
the protection afforded him, John Stadius, one of the
pastors, had undertaken the education of Sadowski's three
sons, and asked Comenius, whose interest in the subject
was well known, to draw up a few rules for his guidance.[1]
The request was gladly complied with, and the return
to his former pursuit was accentuated by the following
incident.

One summer day Comenius and a few of the other pastors
walked over to the castle of Wilcitz to look at the library
there. Among other works of interest they found the
Didactic of Elias Bodinus, which had recently been brought
from Germany. The perusal of this fired Comenius to
attempt a work on a similar scale in his own language.
True, his Church and the institutions that it supported were
falling into ruin before his eyes, but, if he might believe
the prophecies of Kotter and of Poniatowska, the day
was not distant when the Brethren would be restored to
their native land, and then his first task would be the
reorganisation of the schools. "With this end in view,"
he writes, "I entered on the work with fervour, and completed as much of it as I could while I still remained in
my native land."[2]

His efforts were soon interrupted. In 1628 all who
shared the evangelic faith had definitely to leave Bohemia.
Comenius, accompanied by his wife, his father-in-law, and
the prophetess Poniatowska, set out for Poland, and on
the 28th of March reached Lissa, a town in the province
of Posen. Here, under the powerful protection of Count

[1] *Op. Did. Omn.* i., 3. [2] *Ibid.*

Raphael of Lissa, he was destined to find a home for the next twelve years, and it is to this period that his chief educational activity belongs. Though to the end of his days he never ceased to devise fresh plans for the easier instruction of the young, most of the works that made his name famous were written before 1641. There were many reasons why these years should be especially fruitful. Now for the first time since his ordination he took to teaching as a means of earning his livelihood, and, as a master of the Gymnasium at Lissa, of which he became Rector in 1636,[1] he had ample means of putting his theories into practice, and of bringing them into harmony with the dust and friction of the class-room. To these years of actual work in a large institution is due much of the practical character of his writings, and the very faults of the Gymnasium (it had to be completely remodelled in 1635, in order to bring it into harmony with his ideas) served to show him more clearly what should be avoided. In addition to this he had far more time to devote to educational theory than at any later period of his life. Though the welfare of the Unity already absorbed a large share of his energy, he had not that weight of responsibility that made him, as its bishop, look on all else as a subsidiary task. His pansophic conceptions, that afterwards took such hold of him, were only in their infancy, and more important than all, his spirit was still unbroken. He still believed that the Evangelical religion would be restored in his native land, and that the happy days of his early ministry would be repeated. He still believed that the prophecies of Kotter and of Poniatowska would be fulfilled, and in his efforts to reform the Gymnasium at Lissa and to write suitable school-books for it, he saw nothing but a preparation for the future reformation of schools in Bohemia, and a means by which the youth of his own country might be brought up with minds well tempered to fight for their country and their Church. He accordingly applied himself to his task with great vigour. The

[1] Zoubek, p. 28.

Gymnasium at Lissa consisted of four classes, and instruction was given for five hours daily. All the time that remained to him he devoted to the working out of his ideas. The Great Didactic, his *Magnum Opus*, for which he had already begun to make notes at Slaupna, now began to assume a definite shape, and in order that it might embody the views of those whose opinion was most worth having, he attempted to place himself in communication with Ratke, first ascertaining that he was still alive. But Ratke, who in his characteristics resembled a vendor of quack medicines, returned no answer to Comenius' letter.[1] Again he wrote adjuring him, by all that was sacred, not to keep him in suspense any longer, but to give him some details of the true method that he was reported to have discovered. Again he waited in vain for an answer, and it was not till three years later that a letter from George Wincler, pastor of Goldbergen in Silesia, explained the silence. The fact was that Ratke made as great a mystery of his method as was possible, and hoped, by judiciously concealing its details and advertising its merits, to sell it for a high price to some prince or noble. Without gold he resolutely refused to speak. "What hopes," writes Wincler, "did not the pompous eulogy of Ratke's method by Helwig and Jung arouse? But our friend Ratke preserves his silence, and will continue to do so. Mr. Moser, the chief assistant in our school, actually went to live with him in the hope of finding out the basis of his method, but came away empty-handed."[2]

As a matter of fact, Comenius was acquainted with many points of the method that was so carefully shrouded, and, though he cannot resist a sneer at the system and its pretensions,[3] never forgets to acknowledge that it was Ratke who first fired him to attempt school-reform.

Getting no answer from Ratke he now addressed a

[1] *Op. Did. Omn.* ii. 282.
[2] *Ibid.* ii. 282.
[3] Hæc summa est Ratichianæ illius vulgo decantatæ methodi.—*Ibid.* ii. 81.

letter to John Valentine Andreae,[1] whose works, both religious and educational, he had read with great interest. Andreae, who was then pastor of the church at Calva in the Duchy of Wittemberg, sent a prompt reply, but only to the effect that he was too old to pronounce an opinion on such matters. Greatly disappointed, Comenius wrote again, but, though the answer that he elicited was long and sympathetic, it contained nothing that could help him to put his ideas into shape.

Of greater use were the didactic works of Rhenius, Ritter, and Glaum [2] that now came into his hands.[3] These writers were loud in their complaints of contemporary education, and turned a search-light on the defective arrangements that Comenius saw daily in the Gymnasium. Less stimulating, perhaps, but of more definite assistance, were the writings of Eilhard Lubin and of C. Vogel. Lubin, a friend of Andreae's, had been elected Professor of Theology at Rostock in 1605, and had brought out a parallel edition of the New Testament in Latin and Greek, to which he had prefixed some hints on the teaching of Latin to boys.[4] Vogel, who was head-master of the Paedagogium at Göttingen, had drawn up a scheme of instruction in Latin in which he had specified the daily task for twelve months. The student was to commence by learning a list of simple words, arranged in alphabetical order with the German meanings attached, and was then to aid his memory by combining these words into sentences. In this way he claimed that a boy of moderate intelligence, by working only two hours daily, could easily learn the whole Latin language in one year. The system was probably in Comenius' thoughts when he devised the

---

[1] *Op. Did. Omn.* ii. 283.

[2] In 1628 Gabriel Holstein had expounded Glaum's method under the title "Divinæ Glaumianæ Methodi Specimina," and claimed that any language could, by its aid, be learned in six months. "But," says Comenius, "hanc methodum prodiise [*sic*] non vidimus," ii. 86, 87.

[3] Comenius ad Palatinum Belzensem.—*Ep. Com. Mus. Boh.* [Kvacsala.]

[4] Consilium de latina lingua compendiose a pueris addiscenda.

Janua Linguarum ; the claim has been made with equal assurance by all the inventors of infallible language-methods, from that day to this.

More original, and full of sound common-sense, were the ideas of J. Cecilius Frey, a physician residing in Paris. He had brought out a work on education in 1629,[1] and this must have come into Comenius' hands shortly after publication. According to Frey, all languages should be learned colloquially, and attention should be given to arithmetic, geography, drawing, and mechanics. In this upholder of " real studies " Comenius must have hailed a kindred spirit.

With these works before him Comenius applied himself to the double task of creating a more comprehensive and philosophically-based scheme of education than had ever before been devised, and of compiling a series of class-books suited to the various stages of scholars. These books, while carefully adapted to the capacity of the school-boy, were written in accordance with the philosophic principles set forth in *The Great Didactic,* and thus to a remarkable degree combined theory and practice. The class-books were written for the practical teacher, the *Didactic* was intended for the schoolmaster whose interest in his work was not confined to the school-room, and for nobles, statesmen, and philosophers who wished to reform the schools of their country, but found no scheme ready to hand that was both practical and comprehensive.

Comenius' aims were revolutionary, and his didactic principles were capable of changing by slow degrees the aspect of civilisation, but the philosophic basis on which they rested was that of harmonious development from existing institutions. Children were to learn their lessons in less time and with less trouble. This had been suggested by previous writers. The time thus gained was to be

---

[1] *J. C. Frey, Medici, Paris. Opuscula varia nusquam edita,* Parisiis, 1646, pp. 327-331. Frey recommends " Coenobia," or continuous conversation in a boarding-school, as the best means of learning a language.

devoted to a thorough grounding in morality and religion. This again had been frequently urged, though not so weightily or so systematically. But when we come to the introduction of " real studies," the rudiments of which are to be taught in the nursery, and when his views on this subject gradually merge into " Pansophia " or " Universal Knowledge," we feel that a really new element has been introduced. This element, however, contains nothing subversive. Nothing could be further removed from the method of Rousseau. Comenius starts with no fundamental condemnation of society. No brilliant paradoxes fill his pages. His reform is to be a gradual development of what already exists, and, that his suggestions may be practicable and may pave the way for a transition with as little friction as possible, he bases them on the writings of his predecessors. With some of these he was not familiar. As we shall see, in our general view of the educational systems of the age, there were writers of whom he had not heard ; but, be that as it may, he had done all in his power to analyse the tendencies actually at work, and his Didactic is an endeavour to embody all that was good in existing schemes, while adding many features that were new.

From the first day of his residence in Lissa, Comenius never ceased to work at his comprehensive treatise *The Great Didactic.* Written in Czech, and probably completed in 1632, it remained in manuscript till 1849, when it was printed at Prague. A Latin translation, however, with several additional chapters, was published at Amsterdam in 1657, and occupies the first ninety-eight pages of the *Opera Didactica Omnia.*

Even before his final departure from Bohemia, Comenius had probably sketched out his educational scheme, in which he provides for the education of a child from the very hour of its birth. Six years in what he calls the Mother School, six years in the Vernacular School, and six years in the Latin School enable a young man to proceed to the University at eighteen, having had a training, though necessarily a somewhat superficial one, in every subject that possesses educational value. In accordance with this scheme Comenius prepared several guides and class-books for the use of the teachers and pupils in the various classes. The first of these, the *Informatorium Skoly Materske*, or *Informatory of the Mother School*, was written in Czech, in which language it was not published till 1858. A German translation was issued at Lissa in 1633 for the Palatine of Belz.[1] This work, which appears in the folio of 1657 as *Schola Infantiæ*, or *The School of Infancy*, was primarily intended for parents, and treats at length some of the points touched on in *The Great Didactic*, and more particularly in chap. xxviii., *Sketch of the Mother School*. It is written in the voluminous style characteristic of the author, and the chapters treat of the following subjects :—

1. The greatest care should be taken of children, God's most precious gift.
2. Why God sends so many children into the world.
3. Children stand in great need of a good education.
4. In what subjects children should be instructed.
5. How their safety and health can be attained.
6. How they can be taught to take an intelligent interest in what they see around them.
7. How they should be habituated to the actualities of life.
8. How they should be taught eloquence and the proper use of language.
9. How they can be brought up in the paths of morality.
10. How they can be imbued with piety.
11. How long they are to be detained in the Mother School.
12. How they are to be prepared for the Public Schools.

No mean scheme this for children under six years of age. Here was a great truth that Comenius was the first to enunciate. Education begins on the mother's knee.

[1] *Op. Did. Omn.* i. 197.

The schools for older boys may be as good as possible, but they can never be thoroughly effective unless the children come to them possessed of an elementary grounding in each subject taught, a grounding that can only be given by the patient mother.

In this stage education cannot be organised in any cut-and-dried fashion. What is necessary is a suggestive hand-book that shall tell parents what is required of them, and how these requirements can be met. It was to meet this need that the *Informatory of the Mother School* was com-posed. For the Mother School class-books were un-necessary, as the instruction given was naturally of an informal character. The children who go to the Vernacular School, however, are old enough to be arranged in definite classes, and to meet their wants Comenius wrote six class-books, one for each class. These books, like the *Informa-tory of the Mother School*, were composed with a view to the reorganisation of Evangelist schools in Bohemia.[1] This occasion did not come, and the books were never published. The Czech language, in which they were written, appealed to a very small audience, while the books dealing with the Latin School were of universal interest. Under pressure of other work, therefore, their author never found time to correct them, and no trace remains but their titles trans-lated into Latin and a short description of each given by Comenius himself.[1] The first, intended for boys in their seventh year, is the *Violet-bed of the Christian Youth*, containing "the pleasantest flowerets of scholastic in-struction."

The second is the *Rose-bed of the Christian Youth*, containing "nosegays of the most fragrant flowers of knowledge."

For the third year of attendance a more ambitious work was provided, to be called *The Garden of Letters and of Wisdom*. This was to embody a pleasantly-written account of "everything necessary to be known in heaven and earth."

[1] *Op. Did. Omn.* i. 248, 249.

For the fourth year's work the *Labyrinth of Wisdom* was provided. This consisted largely of questions and answers of a subtle description, and was intended to sharpen the intellect. Next followed the *Spiritual Balsam-bed of the Christian Youth*, in which the use of all sciences and arts is demonstrated, while the series is terminated by the *Paradise of the Soul*, which comprised an abstract of Scripture History, together with the principal Church hymns and prayers.

It is much to be regretted that this series of books has not been preserved, but the titles enable us to gather an adequate idea of their contents. The scholar enters the vernacular school, having received a grounding in the elements of knowledge. This groundwork is developed in a definite manner by means of regular class instruction, and thus, by the time he reaches his twelfth year, the boy possesses a fair acquaintance with the realities of the world in which he lives. This acquaintance is the more extensive, because his attention has been exclusively devoted to " real studies," and Latin has been completely deferred to the next stage.

In particular should be noticed the way in which the principle of gradation is applied. Each class-book is suited to the age of the pupils. The very name of the first, *The Violet-bed*, is intended to attract the child who comes to school for the first time, and is apprehensive that the process of learning will be dull and distasteful, while the course of instruction for the fifth year is but a more advanced edition of that for the third.

In spite of the practical tendency of the age, a tendency strongly exemplified by Comenius himself, the study of Latin still remained the chief factor in the school curriculum. Nor was this altogether without reason. Apart from its philological value, Latin was the gate through which alone the world of letters could be entered, and the student who could talk and write in the tongue of Cicero possessed a means of communication with kindred spirits throughout the world, unequalled in universality by any

language of the present day. It is true that Latin no
longer tyrannised over the intercourse of the learned to
such an extent as in the previous century. The Reformation had ousted Latin from the services of the Reformed
Church. In every country the vernacular was beginning
to assert itself, and the establishment of the Academia
della Crusca at Florence in 1582, and of the Académie
Française in 1637, showed that the instinctive movement
in this direction was becoming thoroughly self-conscious.

But this modernising breeze had not yet stirred the
dust on the school-room benches. Latin was still the
chief subject taught, though the high estimation in which
it stood was shown more by the time devoted to it than
by any successful efforts to teach it rapidly and well.
Attempts had been made, and many of them, to render
the path of the beginner easier, and it was no longer
necessary for him to sit down to the task of finding his
way through Terence with no other assistance than that
given by an ignorant usher; but none of these attempts
had attained any genuine result, and there was still no
suitable class-book from the study of which could be
obtained a fairly comprehensive vocabulary and a knowledge of the structure of sentences sufficient to enable a
boy to attack a classic author on his own account.

To the composition of such a class-book Comenius
applied himself in 1628,[1] and the result of his efforts was
the publication in 1631 of his *Janua Linguarum Reserata*,
or *Seminarium Linguarum et Scientiarum Omnium*. This
book, as an introduction to the study of Latin, was an
immense advance on anything that had yet appeared. Its
method of construction, however, was not original, as the
idea had already suggested itself to two pedagogues, the
one Elias Bodinus, and the other William Bateus, a member of the Jesuit College at Salamanca.

With Bodinus' scheme Comenius had been familiar
since 1627, and from it he doubtless borrowed the essential features of the *Janua*. Bodinus' suggestion was as

[1] *Op. Did. Omn.* ii. 82.

follows : seventeen hundred of the most useful words were to be skilfully arranged in sentences of a kind calculated to impress themselves indelibly on the memory of the student, and by a careful perusal of these a comprehensive knowledge of the language was to be obtained before any classic author was attempted. Such a book, says Bodinus, would be of great use, and he expresses a wish that some competent scholar may undertake the task.

Of the existence of the other work Comenius only became aware after the plan of his own *Janua* had taken a definite shape in his mind. On acquainting his friends with the scheme, one of them told him that such a book, under the title *Janua Linguarum*, had already been written by some Jesuit priests in Spain.[1] He lost no time in procuring the work, but found that while it proceeded much on the lines proposed by him, its execution was so imperfect as to minimise its educational value.

Of this contribution made by Spain towards the scholastic needs of the day, Comenius gives a full account,[2] and the book itself is worthy of notice. Originally conceived by William Bateus, it had been written by him in conjunction with his brother, John Bateus, and an Irishman named Stephen. William Bateus died at Madrid in 1614, but his work survived him. A Prussian nobleman, when travelling in Spain in 1605 in the company of some Englishmen of good birth, had made the acquaintance of Stephen, who displayed to him his new and infallible method of teaching Latin. Struck by the merit of the book, he took a copy with him, and, on the return of the party to England, had it published in 1615 with a French and an English translation attached. Though imperfect, it supplied a manifest demand, and was shortly afterwards republished at Strasburg by Isaac Habrecht with the addition of a German translation. Still finding favour, it was again brought out by Gaspar Scioppius at Milan in 1627

---

[1] *Op. Did. Omn.* i. 250.   [2] *Ibid.* ii. 81.

in Latin and Italian under the title of *Mercurius Bilinguis*, and again at Basle in 1636 under the title of *Mercurius Quadrilinguis*, the latter edition being in Latin, German, Greek, and Hebrew.

The work carried into effect the scheme suggested by Bodinus. All the principal words in Latin were arranged in 1200 sentences. Each word, with the exception of auxiliary verbs and connecting particles, only occurred once, and, by a careful study of the whole, Latin was to be learned in an incredibly short time. As Isaac Habrecht remarked, the book was a kind of Noah's Ark, in which all the important words were grouped together, and the necessity of reading voluminous authors in order to find them was obviated.

The book was so very faulty that its undoubted success points to the very great demand that existed for a practical method of teaching beginners. Many of the most import-ant words were altogether omitted, and others that were included were uncommon and quite unsuited for beginners. No care was taken to use the words in their root-significa-tion, and the sentences themselves, far from possessing any educational value, were so ill-conceived[1] as to make it scarcely credible that the book had been translated into eight languages by 1629.[2]

From this work, therefore, Comenius borrowed nothing but its name, the *Gate of Languages*, and, indeed, his own attempt showed so much originality that it would be unfair to hint that he was indebted to his predecessors for the chief points in its construction.

The Grammar School, as Comenius found it, was as far removed as possible from the spirit of scientific observation. Boys were set to translate crabbed authors by the help of still more crabbed commentaries, and might easily acquire

---

[1] Comenius gives the following examples :

623. Vadem in ergastulo clam confectum comperi.
953. Has dictionum telas posthumus nevit.

Op. Did. Omn. i. 252.

[2] *Ibid.*

a fair knowledge of Latin without having any acquaintance with the objects to which the Latin words referred. The professed object of Comenius was to write a book for beginners in Latin, but the bent of his mind was too practical, and his love of the "real" too pronounced, to allow him to work out in detail a class-book that could produce nothing but superficial literary knowledge. With Spencer and the modern Realists he believed that for training of any kind—intellectual, moral, or religious—the study of surrounding phenomena was immensely superior to the study of grammars and lexicons.[1] But grammar could not be ousted from the schools, and the study of the classics, that even now takes the giant's share of the energy devoted to secondary education, was the only subject to which any serious attention was given. A compromise had therefore to be made, and the elements of Latin became the medium through which an accurate knowledge could be obtained of the world and of the function played by the various objects met with in daily life.

The material with which he started was about 8000 of the most common Latin words, which he arranged so as to form 1000 sentences. At the beginning of the book these were short and simple to suit the stumbling efforts of the beginner, gradually becoming complex and involving more difficult constructions towards the end. Each word was used in its root-signification, and, with the exception of particles like *et*, *sed*, *quia*, etc., only occurred once in the whole work. In the formation of the sentences care was taken to bring out the differences that existed between the vernacular, Czech in the first instance, and Latin, while no grammatical construction of importance was omitted.

The scientific side of the work was accentuated by its division into one hundred sections or chapters, each dealing with some one class of phenomena in nature, art, or society, such as fire, diseases, trade, arithmetic, learned conversation, and angels.

---

[1] Spencer, *Education*, ch. i.

Sec. 36. *Of Gardening* gives a good idea of the nature of these sentences.

36. *De Hortorum Cultura*

379. Hortus, vel pomarium est vel viridarium vel vivarium.

380. Sepitur vel aggere, vel macerie, vel plancis, vel sepe palis [sudibus] longuriis aliisque vitilibus plexa.

381.   Hortulanus [olitor] ligone, et rutro, bipalioque fodit, et per pulvinos semina spargit.

382. Arborator seminario vel taleis vel viviradicibus consisto [concinnitas est et elegantia si per quincuncem digerantur] surculos inserit et rigat, scalproque germi germina putat, stolones amputat.

383. Oleum ex olivis exprimitur ; subtus amurca fidit, fraces abjiciuntur.

384. Aviarius alvearia curat, ceramque liquat.

The sec. *Of Constancy* shows how abstract subjects are treated.

92. *De Constantia*

897. In honesto instituto immoti persistere, constantiæ est, non perseverare levitatis.

898. Sed heus tu, aliud est constantem, aliud pervicacem esse.

899. Si quis ergo meliora suadet aut dissuadet, adhortatur vel dehortatur, ne sis contumax, ne præfracte repugna, nec obstinate contradic, sed obsequere.

900. Verum si quis te in bono labefactat, obfirma animum et obstina, usque dum perrumpas obstacula : rata enim irrata reddere dedecet.

The reader will at once ask himself if it could be possible to teach a boy Latin from a book constructed on such a plan.   The first of the illustrations given above contains a number of words by no means easy to remember, and each of these is only used once.   If the student found that a word or a construction did not stick in his memory. his only resource was to go over the sentence again ; and to learn the same word repeatedly in the same juxtaposition would wear out the patience of the most diligent pupil. A modern writer who wished to construct a book of this kind would proceed on the assumption that a very limited number of words must be repeated as often as possible, so that each, by dint of its perpetual recurrence, may impress itself on the mind. Of the great principle of iteration Comenius was well aware; indeed he lays special stress upon it,[1] and it is therefore the more surprising that in this instance his practice runs directly contrary to his theory.

Whatever the shortcomings of the book may have been, and Comenius fully realised that it had many,[2] its success was extraordinary. No one was more surprised than the author himself at the triumphal procession that it made through Europe.[3] It was translated into twelve European languages — Latin, Greek, Bohemian, Polish, German, Swedish, Belgian, English, French, Spanish, Italian, and Hungarian, and even travelled as far eastward as Asia, where it appeared in Arabic, Turkish, Persian, and Mongolian. For the existence of many of these translations we have only the author's word,[4] but it is an undoubted fact that in every European country generations of children thumbed the *Janua* and no other book until they were sufficiently advanced to begin Terence or Plautus, and that for years after its publication Comenius' name was familiar in every school-room.[5] Even Bayle, who is little disposed to sympathise with Comenius, confesses that the

---

[1] *Did. Mag.* chap. xviii. sec. 43.

[2] Hic, inquam, scopus fuit, quem attigisse tantum abest ut glorier, ut primus etiam defectus agnoscam et confitear.—*Op. Did. Omn.* i. 254.

[3] Factum est, quod futurum imaginari non poteram, ut puerile istud opusculum universali quodam eruditi Orbis applausu fuerit acceptum.—*Ibid.* iii. 381.

[4] *Ibid.* iii. 381. Beeger says that a manuscript translation into Turkish by Ali Beg, and dating from 1650, exists in Paris.

[5] *Evelyn's Diary*, 27th January 1658 : "My deare son Richard died. He had before the fifth yeare learned out Puerilis, got by heart almost the entire vocabulary of Latin and French primitives and words, could make congruous syntax, turn English into Latin . . . and had made a considerable progress in Comenius' Janua."

Janua met with marvellous success. "Had Comenius written no other book than this he would have rendered himself immortal. The work was reprinted countless times, and was translated into I know not how many languages. There are several polyglot editions. I do not doubt that Comenius speaks sincerely when he admits that the success of the work surpassed anything that he anticipated, for who would not be surprised that such a book should have been translated into twelve European languages." [1]

The approval bestowed on the *Janua* was not quite universal. Some critics refused to believe that the new method of teaching Latin was a whit superior to the old, or, quite overlooking the educational value of the matter, directed their remarks against the style, which they said was bad, and the Latinity, which they considered faulty.

Milton in his *Tractate on Education* dismisses the book with a contemptuous remark, [2] and Adelung, writing a hundred years later, quotes with approval the criticism, " In vain will the beginner look for the result that its author claims from the use of the Janua." [3]   Adelung himself goes so far as to assert that its universal use would have been the surest way of restoring the barbarous Latin of the Middle Ages (die Barbarey der mittleren Zeiten).[4]

In truth, these criticisms of Comenius' Latinity are beside the point. Granted that he was no great scholar (in comparison with men like the Scaligers and Casaubon he was none at all), his claim on the historian of education lies in the fact that he rescued the boys of his generation from the sterile study of words and introduced them to the world of mechanics, politics, and morality.

---

[1] Bayle, *Dictionnaire historique et critique*, Rott. 1697, i. 882.

[2] "To tell you therefore what I have benefited herein among old re-nowned Authors, I shall spare ; and to search what many modern Janua's and Didactics more than ever I shall read, have projected, my inclination leads me not."

[3] Adelung's *Geschichte der menschlichen Narrheit*, Leipzig, 1785 ; p. 205.

[4] *Ibid.* p. 222.

The publication of the *Janua* and the success with which it met brought Comenius into contact with many of the most striking and influential men of the day. In England in particular the book had been well received, and an English version, brought out shortly after its publication at Lissa in 1631 under the title *Janua Linguarum Trilinguis*, at once attracted the attention of Samuel Hartlib.[1] Of German origin, Hartlib resided in London, and took a keen interest in everything that savoured of intellectual progress. The friend of Milton and of Evelyn, he formed the centre of a circle of thinkers to which any foreigner who arrived in England readily found access, and, in spite of his many engagements at home, contrived to keep up a correspondence with men of mark in Europe. At the beginning of 1632, greatly struck by Comenius' didactic venture, and especially by its Encyclopædic features, he sent him a friendly message with a copy of Streso's *Of the use and abuse of reason*. He also hinted that it might be possible to procure him some monetary aid in England to enable him to carry on his work with greater ease.

Comenius, in answering, expressed his satisfaction at the approval with which his efforts had been received. Any pecuniary assistance would be useful. At the moment he was being aided by the Palatine of Belz, but, as he was travelling, the funds came in but slowly. He was getting on with his didactic works as fast as possible, as there would be much to do when the Brethren were allowed to return to their labours in Bohemia.

As a matter of fact his scholastic work was to be interrupted. A Latin Grammar that he wrote in 1631 [2] had not satisfied him, and for the next few years he devoted himself to history and physics. The Synod of the Brethren that sat in 1632 asked him to write an account of the events that had befallen the "Unity," and this request caused him to compose his *History of the Bohemian Brethren* and

---

[1] For information about Hartlib I am indebted to *Samuel Hartlib, a biographical memoir*, by H. Dircks, 1865.
[2] 'Grammatica latina legibus vernaculæ concinnata.' Not preserved.

his *History of the persecutions of the Bohemian Church*, the latter of which was not published till 1648.

But most of his attention was given to the composition of his treatise on physics. This work, which appeared at Leipzig in 1633,[1] is a most curious publication, and, as Comenius always based his didactic laws on the operations of nature and on the fundamental principles that underlie the constitution of the universe, it is on this account worthy of special attention.

The scope of the work will be best illustrated by the headings of the individual chapters, twelve in number.

1. Sketch of the creation of the world.
2. Of the invisible principles of the world.
3. Of motions.
4. Of the qualities of things.
5. Of the changes of things.
6. Of the elements.
7. Of vapours.
8. Of concrete substances.
9. Of plants.
10. Of animals.
11. Of man.
12. Of angels.

In writing a Christian Cosmogony, Comenius was to a large extent following precedent. Valesius, Lambartus, Levinus, Oscalus, Kasmannus, and his own tutor Alsted had done so before him, and had made the same effort to combine the desire for scientific progress on inductive lines and the belief that the truth on every subject, scientific or otherwise, is to be found in the Scriptures.

For the production of works of this kind the curious conflict of ideas at the close of the sixteenth century was responsible. The spirit of free inquiry introduced by the reformed religion had to a large extent overthrown the authority of Aristotle, but the Christian philosophers of the

---

[1] 'Physicæ ad lumen divinum reformatæ synopsis philodidactorum et theodidactorum censuræ exposita.'

period merely substituted the Bible for the Aristotelian physics, based their theories on arguments drawn from the Mosaic account of the Creation, and, while they were half awake to the value of experimentation, had but little dealing with it in the actual development of their hypotheses.

The great representatives of these conflicting strains of thought were Campanella and Bacon, for both of whom Comenius had a profound admiration.[1] The two books of the *Novum Organum* had appeared in 1620, and in the same year Campanella's *De sensu rerum et magia* was published at Frankfort, where his *Prodromus Philosophiæ* had been published three years previously. These three works were read with great interest by Comenius ; but, while he had a great regard for Bacon and alludes to him continually, he remained in reality little affected by the Inductive Philosophy. Though dimly conscious that Bacon was on the right path, and attracted by the notion of penetrating to the inmost essence of things,[2] he was but slightly impressed by the experimental side of the question. In his *Great Didactic*, which professes to be founded on an analysis of natural processes, he never mentions Bacon's name, and his method of procedure is based almost entirely on analogy, often of a far-fetched nature.

While Bacon was not free from the fantastic notions of his age, Campanella is their representative, and with him Comenius has far more in common. " I could easily show that our Prometheus stole a large part of his false beacon-lights from Campanella's heaven," wrote Des Marets in 1668,[3] and, though he was no friendly critic, it must be confessed that his appreciation was a just one. We need not be surprised, therefore, to find Comenius dealing with essences, principles, and similar monstrosities of Physics.

[1] Campanellam et Verulamium, philosophiæ restauratores gloriosos. Pansophici Libri Delineatio.—*Op. Did. Omn.* i. 442.

[2] Verulamius mirabili suo organo rerum naturas intime scrutandi modum infallibilem detexit.—*Ibid.* i. 426.

[3] Facile ostenderem nostrum Prometheum magnam partem suorum ignium fatuorum ex illius cœlo suffuraturum fuisse.—*Antirrheticus*, p. 37 (quoted by Bayle).

For his cosmogony he rests on the authority of Genesis. The world is created out of the three principles of Matter, Spirit, and Light. The qualities of things are Consistency (salt), Oleosity (sulphur), and Aquosity (mercury). Plants are endowed with "vital spirit," while animals are distinguished from them by the power of originating movement and by the possession of "animal spirit." Man consists of Body, Spirit, and Soul.

Comenius wrote his Physics under the inspiration of Campanella; but he differs from his master on certain points. As substratum for his philosophy Campanella had taken the existence of two principles, cold and heat. Alsted also had imagined two principles, heaven and earth, the first active and the second passive. According to Comenius this duality is inconsistent with the harmony that exists in nature. Whenever two opposing principles meet we find nothing but strife, and a Trinity of cosmic principles is therefore necessary to account for the peaceful working of the universe. In introducing this Trinity he was doubtless influenced by a desire to make the Christian Trinity harmonise with the basis of natural phenomena, but in reality he is only returning to the fancies of Paracelsus, who had already originated the conception of salt, sulphur, and mercury as a Cosmic Triad. What part Comenius made these principles play in the Astronomy [1] that he published at the same time as the Physics, it is impossible to say, as the book has unfortunately been lost.

The writing of school-books was now once more to occupy his attention. The *Janua* had proved too difficult for the boys who entered the Latin School, and to meet their wants the *Vestibulum* or *Entrance Hall* to the *Janua* was composed. [2] His first intention was to write some dialogues for boys to make them familiar with the Latin language, [3] but he decided to preserve the form of the

---

[1] 'Astronomia ad lumen physicum reformanda.'

[2] 'Januæ Linguarum reseratæ Vestibulum quo primus ad Latinam Linguam aditus Tirunculis paratur.'

[3] *Op. Did. Omn.* i. 303.

Janua that the book might serve the better as an introduction to it.   He selected about 1000 of the most common ·Latin words, and out of them constructed 427 sentences. These are very simple throughout, as the following examples will show :—

Chapter I

De accidentibus rerum

6. Deus est æternus, mundus temporarius.
7. Angelus immortalis, homo mortalis.
8. Corpus visibile, spiritus invisibilis, anima itidem.
9. Cœlum est supremum, Aer medius, Terra infima.

Chapter IV

De rebus in Schola

246. Scholasticus sponte frequentat scholam, quo in artibus erudiatur.
247. Initium est a literis.
248. Ex syllabis voces componuntur, e dictionibus sermo.
249. Ex libro legimus tacite, aut recitamus clare.
250. Involvimus eum membranæ et ponimus in pulpito.
251. Atramentum est in atramentario.

The preface contains instructions for the book's use.   It is first to be read through twice, and then the boy is to commit the sentences to memory, learning two or three in an hour and repeating them to the master.   Each sentence is to be translated to the pupil before he reads it, that he may have no difficulty in making it out.   The declension of nouns is to be taught as the boy makes his way through the book; nouns and adjectives should be declined together as *Deus æternus ; Mundus temporarius*.   As a help to recollecting the case-meanings the following table is given :—

1. Ecce Tabula nigra.
2. Pars Tabulæ nigræ.
3. Addo Partem Tabulæ nigræ.
4. Video Tabulam nigram.
5. O tu Tabula nigra.
6. Video aliquid in Tabula nigra.

The *Vestibulum* met with considerable success, and, though never as popular as the *Janua*, was published in English, German, Hungarian, and Swedish.

Having once started theorising about the physical constitution of the universe, Comenius carried his train of thought still farther than in the *Physics*. He had already enabled the "studious youth" to take an external survey of natural objects by means of the *Janua Linguarum*, he would now introduce him to their essential nature,[1] and with this end in view began to compose a *Gate of phenomena or doorway to wisdom;*[2] the work to be a kind of small Encyclopædia or hand-book of universal knowledge.[3] Some friends with whom he had discussed this project now visited England, and excited so much interest by the reports that they brought of the Pansophistic work on the stocks, that a "worthy man" (~~probably~~ Hartlib) wrote to him and asked for a slight sketch of the projected treatise. Comenius obligingly complied with the request and sent him a short manuscript entitled *Outline of my work on Universal Wisdom.*[4]

Imagine his surprise, when the manuscript intended for his friends' eyes alone was returned to him in print.[5] Still, though publication had been far removed from his intention, he could not but recognise the advantage of sounding public opinion and seeing what the learned world thought of the issue of a work on such ambitious lines. As a feeler,

---

[1] Quid per essentiam suam res quæque sit.—*Pansophici Libri Delineatio*, i. 403.

[2] Janua rerum sive Sapientiæ porta.—*Ibid.*

[3] Encyclopædiolam seu Pansophiolam.—*Ibid.*

[4] 'Pansophici Libri Delineatio.'

[5] 'Conatuum Comenianorum Præludia. Oxoniæ, excudebat Gulielmus Turnerus.'

the *Prelude to the efforts of Comenius* served its purpose
admirably. "Every corner of Europe is filled with this
pansophic ardour," wrote John Adolphus Tassius, Professor
of Mathematics at Hamburg, in a letter to Hartlib; "if
Comenius were to do no more than stimulate the minds of
all men in this way he might be considered to have done
enough."[1] On all sides opinions were freely expressed.
Some went so far as to say that no greater benefit had
been bestowed on the human race since the revelation of
God's Word, and called upon Comenius to finish his work.
Others said that the task was too great for one man, that
collaborators must be found for him, and that a Pansophic
College should be established. In some quarters, on the
other hand, the book was openly derided, and in Poland it
met with strong disapproval from those who said that it
was a dangerous experiment to mix things divine with
things human, Theology with Philosophy, Christianity with
Paganism.

This conflicting criticism made Comenius a little uncertain, and for the moment he discontinued his work.
First, however, he wrote a further *Explanation of my Pansophic efforts*,[2] to reassure those who saw any impiety in his
design.[3]

In the conception of a comprehensive Encyclopædia
there was nothing new. As early as 1264 Vincent of
Beauvais had collected the entire knowledge of the Middle
Ages in three volumes, while Alsted's great work, published
in 1630, performed the same office for the seventeenth century. Even while Comenius was engaged on his *Delineatio*,
a new Encyclopædia, that of Peter Laurenberg, appeared,
under the title *Pansophia*. Needless to say, he obtained
and read it eagerly, but found that it was not the kind of
work he had in view, "since it said nothing of Christ, the
fount of true wisdom, and nothing of the life to come."[4]

---

[1] *Op. Did. Omn.* i. 455.

[2] 'Dilucidatio Conatuum Pansophicorum.'

[3] An English translation of the *Delineatio* and *Dilucidatio* was brought
out by Hartlib in 1642, under the title 'A reformation of schooles,
designed in two treatises.' [4] *Op. Did. Omn.* i. 458.

The *Janua Rerum* was in the first instance to give a synopsis of natural phenomena in the same way that the *Janua Linguarum* did of the Latin language, but its construction was to be quite different from that of the Encyclopædias in use. "Even the best-arranged Encyclopædias that I have so far seen have been more like a chain containing many links well fastened together than like an automaton whose wheels are cunningly contrived so that the whole can set itself in motion." [1] This defect can be obviated by disposing the arts and sciences in such a manner that we may begin with what we know best and proceed by slow degrees to what is less familiar. In this way the first chapter will throw light on the second, the second on the third, and so on. [2] The essential point is that the universal laws of thought be taken as a basis, and that then, by sound processes of reasoning, some universal way be opened to ascertaining the truth of things. [3] It is by neglecting to find this universal principle and by limiting themselves to one subject that physicists and philosophers in general have fallen into so many errors and contradictions. The hypotheses of Copernicus are plausible, it is true, but quite inconsistent with the laws of physics. Gilbert, totally absorbed in the study of magnetism, has tried to base his whole philosophy upon it, and here again has offended against the true principles of nature. [4] Campanella's views met with some approval, but were overthrown by the telescope of Galileo Galilei. These contradictions cannot be avoided "unless the rays of truth that are scattered through all things meet together in one spot, so that the same symmetry may be evident in all that appertains to the senses, to the intellect, and to divine

[1] *Delineatio*, sec. 39.

[2] *Ibid.* sec. 24.

[3] *Ibid.* sec. 26. Ut per universalissima cognoscendi principia, eosque ad ultimas usque conclusiones rite deducendi modos, universalem aliquam veritati rerum cognoscendæ aperiret viam.

[4] *Ibid.* Gilbertus magnetis speculatione abreptus totam Philosophiam ex magnete deducere voluit : sed evidentissime cum injuria principiorum Physicorum.

revelation. These are the three channels through which knowledge comes to us, and error will cease if the balance between them be preserved."

For a moment Comenius seems to lay more stress on the materialistic side, and tells us that "Universal Wisdom" should reduce all things to number, measure, and weight; a process of meting out nature with a foot-rule for which he dutifully finds authority in Scripture (Wisdom ii. 20).[1] But he soon recedes from the common-place conception of accurate measurements. Bacon, he says, seems to have discovered the necessary method of separating the true from the false by his system of "artificial induction"; but this process takes too long, requiring generations of effort, and, besides, it is useless for the construction of Pansophia, since it deals only with natural phenomena, while Pansophia treats of the whole universe.[2]

Very different are the laws or norms by which universal knowledge is to be obtained, and these Comenius proceeds to enunciate in eighteen aphorisms :—

1. Universal knowledge, so far as it can be obtained by man, has as its objects God, nature, and art.

2. A perfect knowledge of these three is to be sought. '

3. The knowledge of things is perfect when it is full, true, and ordered.

4. Knowledge is true when things are apprehended as they exist in reality.

5. Things are apprehended in their essential nature when the manner in which they have come into existence is understood.

6. Each object comes into existence in accordance with its "idea," that is to say, in relation to a certain rational conception through which it can be what it is.

7. Therefore, all things that come into existence, whether they are the works of God, of nature, or of man, do so in accordance with their "ideas."

8. Art borrows the "ideas" of its productions from nature, nature from God, and God from Himself.

[1] *Delineatio,* sec. 40.   [2] *Ibid.* sec. 63.

9. In fashioning the world, therefore, God produces an image of Himself, so that every creature stands in a definite relation to its creator.

10. As all things share in the "ideas" of the Divine mind, they are also mutually connected and stand in a definite relation to one another.

11. It follows that the rational conceptions of things are identical, and only differ in the form of their manifestation, existing in God as an Archetype, in nature as an Ectype, and in art as an Antitype.

12. Therefore the basis of producing as of apprehending all things is harmony.

13. The first requisite of harmony is that there should be nothing dissonant.

14. The second is that there should be nothing that is not consonant.

15. The third is that the infinite variety of sounds and concords should spring from a few fundamental ones, and should come into being by definite and regular processes of differentiation.

16. Therefore, if we know the fundamental conceptions and the modes of their differentiation, we shall know all things.

17. Such rational conceptions can be abstracted from phenomena by means of a certain method of induction, and must be posited as the norms of phenomenal existence.

18. These norms of truth must be abstracted from those objects whose nature is such that they cannot be otherwise, and which are at every one's disposal for the purpose of making experiments, that is to say, from natural phenomena.

These aphorisms constitute the philosophic basis of Pansophia. The work constructed with reference to them is to be "an accurate anatomy of the universe, dissecting the veins and limbs of all things in such a way that there shall be nothing that is not seen, and that each part shall appear in its proper place and without confusion." Great care is to be taken that terms, especially general terms, be carefully defined. These general terms of Pansophia are, as it were, axioms of physics; ultimate truths that do not admit of demonstration or analysis, but only need to be illustrated by examples. They are given us from heaven; but in selecting from them great care must be taken to avoid error. The particular cases that are brought forward in the system should not introduce any new truth, but should merely consist of a special application of the general conceptions that have preceded. In this way physical investigation is to be conducted on the analogy of geometry, and developed deductively from axioms. It will be seen that Comenius, in spite of his constant praise of Bacon and his sympathy with the more fantastic conceptions of that thinker, has but little in common with his inductive philosophy. His "idea" is an echo of Plato; his "ratio" is a reincarnation of Aristotle's logos; while his general axioms are obtained by intuition and not by any definitely planned method of induction. While granting that Bacon's "artificial induction" may be of use for the investigation of natural objects, he distinctly repudiates it for the purposes of Pansophia, since this deals with the universe, in which the supernatural is included. With the exception of the steam-engine, there are few civilising agencies of the present day that have not been ascribed to Comenius' fertile brain by his continental admirers,[1] and the attempt to link his name with that of Bacon as an inductive philosopher is backed by equally scanty evidence. As a natural philosopher he belongs to the century that preceded him and not to the age of experiment that was to follow, and his didactic principles were due rather to an extraordinary intuition of what was necessary than to patient reasoning on inductive lines.[2]

It is on the conception of the universe as ordered, and of the relations that exist between phenomena as rational,

[1] One commentator actually declares that the rules of Freemasonry have been taken from Comenius' writings.

[2] In the Preface to the *Great Didactic* Comenius expressly says that his principles were arrived at *a priori*.

that any system of education, apart from the mere incul-
cation of facts, must rest, and this is the truth that
Comenius brings out most strongly in his Pansophic
writings.   It is towards this "Universal Wisdom" that
all his didactic efforts tend.   The student is led from
one fact to another, and, as these facts are arranged in
their natural order, he is thus placed in touch with the
actual cosmic processes, can follow up the train of
thought, and enlarge the circle of knowledge by working
on the lines indicated by the operations of nature.   As
result, the mature student is no pedant, crammed to
overflowing with dry and uncoördinated facts, but a man
whose faculty of original thought has been developed and
whose training fits him to be an independent investi-
gator of the universe.   The boldness of the scheme excites
admiration; but the enthusiasm evinced by Hartlib and his
friends can only suggest the thought that these gentlemen
had failed to appreciate that the one important point in
the Baconian philosophy was the insistence on experiment
and verification as a basis for sound induction.

It must not be imagined that this excursion into the
realm of first principles and philosophic abstractions
impeded Comenius in the performance of his practical
duties as a teacher.   During these years (1635-1640) his
activity in school-organisation was as great as ever, and
the leading position that he now took in the Moravian
Fraternity laid an extra burden on his shoulders.   In
1635 the Synod asked him to bring out a Latin-Bohemian
edition of the *Vestibulum* and of the *Janua*, and expressed
its satisfaction at hearing that the learned David Bechner
was working at a *Viridarium Linguæ Latinæ*, an amplifica-
tion of the *Janua*.   Additional labour was given by the
reorganisation of the Gymnasium in accordance with the
plans of Comenius, and we accordingly find him drawing
up *The rules of the renowned Gymnasium at Lissa.*[1]   These
are of an eminently practical character.   Especial stress
is laid on the need of a spirit of piety throughout the

[1] *Leges illustris Gymnasii Lesnensis.*

school.   Rules are laid down for good behaviour in
class, in the streets, and at home.   Playing in the streets
is forbidden, though the boys are urged to go and play
outside the town, first choosing one of their number as a
leader.   Early rising is recommended, and all are advised
to enter in a notebook anything of interest that they may
learn from day to day.   Dancing is strictly forbidden.
"The dance is a circle whose centre is the devil"[1] is the
portentous phrase by which the heinousness of the offence
was impressed on the boys' minds.

In the following year a portion of Bechner's *Viridarium*,
under the title *Proplasma Templi Latinitatis*, was completed,
and was subjected to Comenius' criticism.   As a writer of
school-books Bechner was inferior, and the chief value
of the work lies in its preface.   Comenius, however, must
have thought well of it, as he includes it in the Amsterdam
Folio (i. 318-345).

In his preface Bechner laments that Latin is learned as
a dead and not as a living language.   Themistocles learned
to speak Persian in a short time by going to Persia, and
Ovid picked up Sarmatian rapidly by living at Tomi.
Why do we not bear these examples in mind when we
teach Latin?   A suitable place should be set apart with
its own church, school, workshops, and everything necessary
for carrying on life.   Here boys should be sent to school,
and in this community nothing but Latin should be talked.
A master must accompany each division of boys to see
that the vernacular is completely laid aside.   Pictures and
carved models of every-day objects are to be exposed to
view with their Latin names written under them that the
boys may be given every opportunity of absorbing Latinity,
and, in addition to this, they should act moral and instructive plays in Latin.[2]

With this last suggestion in view he takes section 5 of
the *Janua*, "De Igne," and works it up into a series of
dialogues of increasing difficulty, all illustrative of the

---

[1] Chorea est circulus cujus centrum est Diabolus.
[2] *Op. Did. Omn.* i. 320.

nature of fire. There are five stages, the *Limen*, the *Janua*, the *Atrium*, the *Odeum*, and the *Adytum*. A short extract from the *Atrium* will suffice to show the fantastic nature of the composition. The actors are Uriel, Pyrodes, and Caius Carbo, and they elucidate the subject as follows :—

P. Quis iste concursus hominum et clangor insolens tinnitusque extra numerum ?

C. Incendium excitatum est.

P. Ubi ergo exarsit ?

C. In ædibus nescio cujus ; in platea cui ab arce nomen factum est.

U. Atque hoc quomodo . . . ? etc.

The *Odeum* is more advanced, while the *Adytum* gives, still in dialogue form, a long philosophical and historical disquisition on fire. The idea was not new, having been already employed by the Jesuits, and the dialogues are written with no dramatic power. The work is dedicated to Comenius and his friends and well-wishers—Hartlib in London, Schneider in Leipzig, Evenius in Weimar, Mochinger in Dantzig, and Docemius in Hamburg.

In this year Comenius succeeded Henrici as Rector of the Gymnasium ; but his reforming ardour was damped by the death of his friend and patron Count Raphael, over whose grave he preached a funeral sermon. This was afterwards published under the title "The mirror of good government, in which out of the prophet Isaiah, and from the example of the pious Eliakim, the true qualities of right and praiseworthy government are depicted and set forth as a model to all good rulers."

The death of their patron made no serious difference to the safety of the Brethren, as his son Bohuslaw promised to protect them as his father had done. It was for Bohuslaw that Comenius composed his *Faber Fortunæ, The Moulder of Fortune*. This work starts with the conception of man as a free agent. We are not dependent on circumstances, but control them ; we must first, however, learn to control ourselves and thus to identify our will with

the desire for the true good. Thus the art of moulding
our fortunes consists in depending not on circumstances
but on reason, and not on the reason of another but on
our own; that is to say, on the reason of God that works
in us.

It is impossible to say how much time was devoted to
the *Janua Rerum* during the last few years of Comenius'
stay in Lissa. Apart from his work as a schoolmaster, his
other literary productions were sufficient to fill up any
ordinary man's time, and the claims made on him by
admirers in other towns and countries increased daily.
In 1637 a request was addressed to him from Breslau
asking him to write some hints on school-teaching for the
Gymnasium in that town. With this demand he complied
in his *De sermonis Latini studio dissertatio.* It is interesting
as being the first published work of Comenius that dealt
with school organisation in a philosophic spirit.

The treatise opens with a dedicatory verse by George
Bechner, in which the author is ranked above Epictetus.[1]
After some general remarks on the importance of a
knowledge of facts—"Verba sine rebus, putamina sunt
sine nucleo, vagina sine gladio, umbra sine corpore, corpus
sine anima"—Comenius proceeds to divide the Latin
School into four classes, each of which is to have its own
book. The first and second classes are to be provided with
the *Vestibulum* and the *Janua,* whose acquaintance we have
already made; while for the two more advanced classes he
suggests the compilation of two other books, *The Palatium*
and *The Thesaurus.* The *Palace* is to be divided into
four parts—"The Palace of Letter-writing," "The Palace
of History," "The Palace of Oratory," and "The Palace of
Poetry." "The Palace of Letter-writing" is to contain a
hundred letters corresponding to the hundred divisions of
the *Janua.* The style is to be varied, and a few general
remarks on letter-writing are to be added. "The Palace
of History" is to consist of dialogues embodying historical
information about the objects mentioned in the *Janua.*

[1] Cedat Epictetus nomen tibi, clare Comeni.—*Op. Did. Omn.* i. 348.

"The Palace of Oratory" is to repeat the same material in oratorical form, the phrases used being adapted from Cicero, Quintilian, and Seneca; while the "Palace of Poetry" deals with the same subjects treated in verse. The verses are not to be original, but are to be taken from the classic poets. In this way Rossie [1] in England had written a life of Christ with lines taken from Vergil.

The culminating point in this series of graduated school-books is the *Thesaurus*. This is a collection of extracts from classic writers dealing with the subjects of the *Janua*. For all these books suitable lexicons are to be compiled, and a Latin grammar is to be written for use with the *Janua*. As a further assistance to the use of the *Thesaurus* he proposes a *Clavis Intellectus Humani*,[2] in which the subject-matter is to be arranged in "a certain general proportion" with reference to the relation in which things, the concepts of things, and language, stand to one another.

These books are to be spread over the six years devoted to the Latin School as follows: for the *Vestibulum* six months is sufficient, and for the *Janua* a year; for the *Palatium* a year and a half is allowed, leaving the remaining three years for the study of the authors.

Then follow some general remarks on teaching, after which come some special rules for the use of the class-books.

From the use of the *Vestibulum* the boy must learn to read Latin words with the proper accent and to write what he knows with fluency; he is also to master the rudiments of grammar and syntax. As a help to writing, some of the Latin sentences should be printed faintly (green is recommended as a suitable colour), and over this the boy may write in black ink.

The *Vestibulum* is to be read through ten times, and

---

[1] Rossæus Anglus.—*Op. Did. Omn.* i. 357. I have been unable to obtain any further information about this scholar.

[2] This he further on identifies with the *Janua Rerum.*—*Op. Did. Omn.* i. 362.

'each time stress should be laid on some fresh point. By the ninth reading it should practically be known off by heart. Great stress is laid on the importance of employing the morning hours for learning, and the afternoon for reading and writing. Similarly, the *Janua* is to be read ten times, the tenth reading being a kind of Latin disputation in which the winner gets a prize.[1]

In the following year (1638) an invitation came from Sweden asking Comenius to undertake the reformation of the schools in that country. He refused. The task, he said, was too great for one man, and he foresaw nothing but envious opposition from the local schoolmasters.

But, though not induced to leave Lissa, it was brought home to him how much schools all over Europe were in need of reformation, and he was induced to commence the translation of *The Great Didactic* out of Czech into Latin. The headings of the chapters he communicated to Hartlib, who published them in 1642 as an appendix to his *Reforme of Schooles*. In other directions his literary output was as great as ever. To these years belong two plays, *Diogenes Cynicus redivivus* and *Abrahamus Patriarcha*, which were acted by the students of the Gymnasium.

To the interest excited by his philosophic schemes we have alluded in our account of the *Prodromus*. This interest continued to increase, and Comenius, who had come to Lissa in 1628, known merely as a member of a little band of Bohemian exiles, with sensible views on the teaching of Latin, began to realise that he had achieved European notoriety and that any country would be glad to secure his services. Much of his renown was probably due to the enthusiasm of Hartlib, who was in correspondence with a large number of intellectual men both in England and on the continent. Pell, an English mathematician and the friend of Hartlib, was in communication with Mersenne in France; Mersenne had written to Comenius on the subject of his Pansophic schemes, and Descartes himself, an old school-fellow and friend of

[1] *Op. Did. Omn.* i. 348-393.

Mersenne, had expressed his approval of them, though hitherto he knew of them only by hearsay.[1]

Comenius thus began to feel that the walls of the Lissa Gymnasium formed a limited horizon, and one beyond which his personal influence might with great advantage be extended. Many causes worked together to make him dissatisfied with his position. The death of Count Raphael in 1636 and of his old master Alsted in 1638 had taken from him two of his best friends. Enemies, envious of his success, had worked upon the distrust that his brothers in the faith could not refrain from evincing towards his scientific efforts, and had accused him before the Synod of displaying irreverence in his Pansophic writings. Count Bohuslaw had seceded from the Evangelic party and embraced the Catholic faith, and seems to have given an unsatisfactory reply when Comenius (in 1640) laid before him his further schemes for scholastic and pansophic works. It is therefore not surprising that he yielded to the pressing demands of Hartlib and, having first obtained leave from the Unity, set out for England.

It was after a most unsatisfactory voyage, during which he had been carried by a storm into the Baltic, that he reached London in the September of 1641; but, once there, he was received with open arms by the little band of which Hartlib was the centre.

A man of great enthusiasm but of less judgment, Hartlib knew everybody in England who was worth knowing. "I could fill whole sheets," he wrote to Worthington,[2] "in what love and reputation I have lived these thirty years in England; being familiarly acquainted with

---

[1] De modo autem speculum ejusmodi conficiendi, naturæ maxime consentaneus ille videtur (quem et Comenium hac de re libros mundi utriusque Majoris nimirum et Minoris cum libro Scripturæ, ut audio, potissimum consulentem sibi eligere conjicio) qui Vestigia Creatoris in producendis rebus accuratissime observet, ita ut ex rationis lumine primo probetur; necessario concedendum esse rerum conditorem et Deum, deinde Creaturæ eo pertractentur modo, quo Moses eas in Genesi sua procreatas luculenter descripsit. — Excerpta Literarum, J. Duræi, 1638.   MS. Sloane, Brit. Mus. 417.

[3] Dr. John Worthington, Master of Jesus College, Cambridge.

the best of archbishops, bishops, earls, viscounts, barons, knights, esquires, gentlemen, ministers, professors of both Universities, merchants, and all sorts of learned or in any kind useful men." Himself a voluminous author[1] and translator, he was ever on the look-out for talent in need of assistance, and was rapidly getting through his fortune in the promotion of every Utopian scheme that came under his notice. It was to him and at his request that Milton addressed his essay *Of Education* (1644).

At this time in easy circumstances, he was living in Duke's Place, Drury Lane, an address which we may be sure was the centre of Comenius' London experiences. Here would have met to discuss the intellectual and political problems of the day men like Theodore Haak, John Durie, John Beale, John Wilkins, John Pell, and Evelyn, who had just returned to London after a three months' journey through Europe. Milton was living in London, and must certainly have met and conversed with the illustrious stranger ; while no farther off than at Sevenoaks was Thomas Farnaby, a very remarkable English schoolmaster, who had evinced his interest in the *Janua* by prefixing a short Latin poem to Anchoran's edition of 1631.

It was a strange society to which Comenius was introduced. Haak was a naturalised Englishman who had been ordained deacon in 1634 by Hall, Bishop of Exeter. He it was who in 1648 suggested the meetings of learned men that eventually led to the formation of the Royal Society. To No. 5 of Hooke's philosophical collections he contributed the criticisms of Marin Mersenne and of Descartes upon Dr. John Pell's *An Idea of Mathematics*, and, according to Anthony à Wood, translated half of *Paradise Lost* into High Dutch.

John Durie, the son of Robert Durie, minister of the Scotch Church at Leyden, had been educated for the

---

[1] He wrote among other works 'An essay for the advancement of Husbandry-learning : or proposition for the erecting of a College of Husbandry' (1651); 'The advice of W. P. (Sir William Petty) to Mr. Sam. H. for the advancement of some particular parts of learning'; and a pamphlet entitled 'An invention of Engines of Motion.'

ministry at Sedan under Andrew Melville, and also at
Leyden and Oxford. A great advocate of Evangelical
unity, he was continually employed on semi-religious em-
bassies. Recently ordered out of her country by Christina,
Queen of Sweden, he was now in London without any
definite occupation. Two years later he obtained the post
of Keeper of the books, medals, and manuscripts of St.
James.

John Beale, afterwards rector of Yeovil in Somerset-
shire, and chaplain to Charles I., was, like Hartlib, an
agricultural enthusiast, and wrote, among other things,
Aphorisms concerning Cider. Hartlib, writing to Boyle in
1658, says of him: "There is not the like man in the
whole island nor in the continent beyond the seas so far
as I know it—I mean that could be made more universally
use of to good to all, as I in some measure know and
could direct."

John Wilkins, afterwards Bishop of Chester, was ready
to entertain any absurdity as long as its aim was philan-
thropic. He was the author of some curious works, including *Discovery of a New World* (1638), a description
of communication with the moon by means of flying-
machines, and *Mercury, or the secret and swift messenger,
showing how a man may with privacy and speed communicate
his thoughts to a friend at any distance.*

Last comes Dr. John Pell, a mathematician of no mean
order. He had published his *Commentationes in Cosmo-
graphiam Alstedii* in 1631, and had doubtless many a
conversation with Comenius about the character and parts
of his old master.

Such was the circle in the midst of which Comenius
found himself, and much further our acquaintance with the
details of his visit does not go. He was delighted with
London. To his friends in Lissa he writes with enthusiasm
of the preachers, the libraries, and the anxiety displayed
for school reform.

"I live," he says in a letter dated the 18th of October,
"as a friend among friends; though not so many visit me as

would do so if they knew that I could speak English, or if they had more confidence in their own Latin, or if they had not such a high opinion of me."

This shyness on the part of callers gave him plenty of time to talk over plans with his friends. He had not arrived at a fortunate moment; the king had gone to Scotland, Parliament had risen for three months, and nothing remained but to stay in London for the winter and unfold to Hartlib and his circle[1] the sketch, such as it was, of his Pansophic system. His leisure time he employed in the composition of a new work, entitled *Via Lucis*,[2] which was, however, not published until the year 1668 in Amsterdam.

Uppermost in the minds of Hartlib and his friends was the formation of a Universal College for physical research, on the lines suggested by Bacon in the *New Atlantis*. Now at last in Comenius they thought they had discovered a man competent to found a "Solomon's House," if only sufficient assistance were given him by Parliament. This was their chief object in urging him to come to England, and it was on the establishment of the college that the conversation turned. As we have seen, Comenius was totally unfitted to organise a collection of laboratories for physical research—for that was what the proposal practically amounted to. He was, as he himself confesses, primarily a theologian, and, though he could talk glibly and attractively of enlarging the boundaries of human knowledge, he had no conception of the tedious processes of experimentation that were necessary, and flew off to vague generalisations at every opportunity. If proof was necessary, he supplied it from the Scriptures, and as a means for verification valued a text from Genesis more than all the paraphernalia of the chemist and the physicist.

The *Via Lucis*, while much of it is of that fantastic

[1] Amicis apparatum Pansophicum (quam tenuis fuit) lustrantibus.— *Op. Did. Omn.* ii. preface.

[2] 'Via Lucis. Hoc est, Rationabilis disquisitio, quomodo intellectualis animorum lux, Sapientia, tandem sub mundi vesperam per omnes mentes et gentes feliciter spargi possit.'

nature that we have already noticed in Comenius' Pan-sophic writings, contains some points that are both new and interesting.   The term "light" is taken to signify the millennium of learning to be attained by Pansophic methods, though at the same time the physical phenomenon of light is dealt with and its nature declared to consist of waves or motion (chap. ix.)   This "light" is to be obtained by means of four things—universal books, universal schools, a universal college, and a universal language (chap. xv.)   The universal college is to consist of men chosen from the whole world.   These must be gifted, industrious, and pious, and their task is to further the welfare of mankind and extend the limits of knowledge in every way.   England is a suitable place in which to found this college, partly because its position renders communication easy with the whole world, partly in memory of Bacon, and partly because it has offered to found the college and supply it with funds.

More important than all is the foundation of a universal language.   Vives had suggested Latin, but Comenius thinks otherwise.   Latin is too difficult, and is at the same time a poor language.   A new tongue must be devised, at the same time easier and more complete than other languages.   With this end in view, it is important to investigate the relation of sounds to objects and to harmony.

A new language can be formed in two ways, from the languages that exist or from things themselves.   The latter is the method approved by Comenius.[1]   This universal language is not to abolish others.   Learned men may still use Latin, Greek, and Hebrew, and nations their vernaculars (chap. xix.)   A golden age is then to set in, in which the conversion is to take place, first of the Mohammedans, then of the heathen, and finally of the Jews (chap. xxi.)

In the conception of a new language, on which he lays so much stress, he was not alone.   Dalgarno, a Scotsman, published a sketch of a *Lingua Philosophica* in 1661, and

[1] Cujus singulæ voces loco definitionum essent, ad rerum ipsarum numeros, mensuras, et pondera factæ.

Bishop Wilkins, at the request of the Royal Society, brought out an elaborate scheme of a similar nature in 1668. Wilkins' scheme does not deal with the relations of sounds to things. "The first thing in such an institution," he says, "is to assign several letters and sounds for the forty genuses."[1] This is done arbitrarily, and·on this substratum the language is built up. It was to be written in a kind of shorthand, the signs for which are rather clumsily chosen. The universal language must have been one of the topics of conversation between Wilkins and Comenius, and it is difficult to say which, if either, borrowed it from the other.

Parliament now sat again, but had too much work on its hands to devote any attention to Comenius, and told him to wait. In the meantime he was assured that the intention was to give over to him some college with its income for the carrying into effect of his schemes. In London the Savoy or Chelsea College, and in the country Winchester College, were suggested as suitable institutions, so that, as Comenius remarks, "nothing seemed more certain than that the scheme of the great Verulam, of opening in some part of the world a universal college, whose one object should be the advancement of the sciences, would be carried into effect."[2]

But trouble had broken out in Ireland, and in England it was evident that affairs were working up to civil war. Comenius soon perceived that amid so much turmoil there was little chance of these suggestions being carried into practice, and began to think of returning home.[3] His position was unpleasant. On the strength of Hartlib's invitation and assurance that funds would be forthcoming, he had given up his post in Lissa. Hopes of universal colleges and pecuniary support were now vanishing into thin air, and he found himself with baffled expectations,

[1] 'An Essay towards a real character and a philosophical language,' by John Wilkins, D.D., Dean of Ripon and Fellow of the Royal Society. London, 1668. P. 414.

[2] *Op. Did. Omn.* ii, preface.

[3] ' De novis studia didactica continuandis occasionibus.'

a wife and daughters to support, and a rapidly emptying purse.

It was at this juncture that a new patron, Ludwig de Geer, appeared on the scene. De Geer belonged to an aristocratic Dutch family, and had realised an enormous fortune in commerce. The centre of his business transactions, which he left to his agent Hotton, was Amsterdam. He himself resided on his estates at Finspong and Norköping in Sweden. It was through Hotton that he first heard of Comenius, in whose projects he began to take a keen interest as soon as his attention was directed to them. A letter sent to Lissa through Hotton's agency arrived too late, and it was not till he had been in London for some time that Comenius received it. Feeling that Hartlib had perhaps promised more than he could bring about, he wrote to de Geer saying that if he had received his letter before leaving Lissa he would now be not in London but in Sweden.

This letter elicited another pressing invitation from de Geer, and to this Comenius sent an answer in December, explaining that he was not quite a free agent; his Church had the first claim on him, and he must consult his superiors before taking any fresh step.

Hartlib, who was aware of the correspondence with de Geer, now did his best to induce Comenius to stay in London, and brought out an English translation of the *Prodromus* under the title *A Reformation of Schooles*, in the hope of attracting renewed attention to the Pansophic schemes. But the unsettled state of affairs and his growing need of money made Comenius daily more anxious to get away. Fresh correspondence with de Geer followed, in which he pointed out that, if he was to make any real progress with his Pansophic books, he must have the assistance of some fellow-workers. Alone, he would find the task too great. De Geer, however, seems to have demurred to the proposal, and objected to Joachim Hubner, one of the proposed colleagues, on the ground of his religious opinions.

These negotiations occupied the spring of 1642, during which time Comenius employed himself by composing his *Pansophiae Diatyposis*, published two years later at Amsterdam.

He now, quite unexpectedly, received an invitation to go to France, but, having already made up his mind to visit Sweden, left London for Holland in June.

In August he reached Norköping and had his first interview with de Geer. On the subject of Pansophia the new patron preserved a discreet silence, but after several days' conversation an understanding appears to have been arrived at, and nothing remained but to fix on a suitable spot in which Comenius might settle down to his labours.

Partly with the object of getting suggestions on this point he went to Stockholm by de Geer's advice to see Oxenstierna, the Swedish Chancellor, and Skythe the Rector of the University at Upsala. The fact was that what de Geer wanted was not Pansophic works, but school-books for the Swedish schools, and in sending Comenius to call on Oxenstierna he was doubtless carrying out a preconcerted scheme.

Arrived at Stockholm, Comenius had to undergo a running fire of interrogation. Oxenstierna in particular plied him with the most searching questions, and his remarks seem to have made a deep impression on the worthy pedagogue, since, in one of the brief biographical notices that are scattered up and down his works, he devotes more space to this interview than to any other event in his life. For two days the Chancellor discussed the Didactic works. From his youth, he confessed, he had felt that the common methods of instruction were contrary to nature, but had been unable to say exactly what the defect was. At last, when on an embassy to Germany, some learned men with whom he discussed the subject told him that Wolfgang Ratke had devised a new method. He immediately put himself into communication with him; but Ratke absolutely refused to give him a personal interview, and sent him instead a ponderous quarto volume, the contents of which did not come up to his expectation and appeared to be of less practical worth than the suggestions of Comenius. Comenius modestly replied that he had done what he could in this branch of reform and was now busy with his Pansophic schemes. To which Oxenstierna rejoined that he was aware of this, as he had read the *Prodromus*, and that he would discuss the subject on the following day.

The morrow's interview was far less pleasing to Comenius. The hard-headed Chancellor was not nearly so disposed to be enthusiastic over the Pansophia and the visionary schemes connected with it as were Hartlib and his circle. "Can you stand contradiction?" he asked. Comenius replied that the one object of publishing the *Prodromus* had been to obtain criticism of any kind, while that of a man like Oxenstierna would be doubly valuable. The Chancellor then began to bring forward objections to the whole scheme of regenerating the world by means of Pansophia. Some of these objections were political, others rested on the Scriptural assurance that darkness rather than light was to be man's lot on earth, but to all Comenius gave such satisfactory replies that he imparted some of his enthusiasm even to the sceptical critic, who exclaimed, "I do not believe that any one ever had ideas like yours. Continue to build on the foundations that you have laid." Wiser judgment then returned, and he strongly advised him to leave his Pansophic schemes alone for the moment, to devote himself to the improvement of schools, and to elaborate his improved method of teaching Latin, since thus he would pave the way for more ambitious efforts in the future.

To Comenius, who was heartily sick of what he calls his *spinosa didactica*, this advice must have been a bitter potion, but, as Skythe echoed Oxenstierna's opinion, and further suggested that Elbing in Prussia would be a suitable place for him to settle in with his family, he gulped it down with the best grace possible.

Comenius now returned to Norköping, and, on communicating the result of the interview to de Geer, found to his disgust that his patron viewed Oxenstierna's advice with the highest approval. He had, therefore, no resource but to submit, and consoled himself with the hope that the task would only take him a couple of years, after which he might again devote himself to philosophy.[1]

Preparations for the move, and a preliminary visit to Elbing, occupied the next few months. In Lissa he had to take final leave of his scholastic and clerical duties and engage some assistants to help him with the philological work in view.

At this return to philology his friends in England were indignant, and did their best to recall him to his former projects. "You have devoted sufficient attention to school-books," they wrote; "others can carry on the work you have begun. The world will gain far more advantage from having the paths of true wisdom opened to it than from any study of Latin." "Quo moriture ruis? minoraque viribus audes?" added Hartlib, more disappointed than any of them at the dissipation of their Pansophic dreams of the previous winter.

Comenius wavered. He still hankered after Pansophia, and sent Hartlib's letter to Sweden in the hope that it might cause de Geer and Oxenstierna to alter their views. But a stern reply, bidding him to persist in his undertaking and complete the school-books, was all that he obtained, and with great unwillingness he set to work.

In the history of great renunciations surely none is stranger than this. We have a man little past the prime of life, his brain teeming with magnificent if somewhat visionary plans for social reform, a mighty power in the community that shared his religious ideas, and an object of interest even to those who may have shrugged their shoulders at his occasional want of balance. Suddenly he flings his projects to the winds, consigns his darling plans to the dust-heap of unrealisable ideas, and retires to a small sea-side town—not to meditate, not to give definite form to latent conceptions or to evolve new ones, not to make

---

[1] 'De novis studia didactica continuandis occasionibus.'

preparations for the dazzling of intellectual Europe with an octavo of fantastic philanthropy or of philosophic mysticism, but—to write school-books for the little boys in Swedish schools.   True, he was paid.   He was bartering his inclinations against coin of the realm, against the good gold that streamed from de Geer's Dutch counting-house. He was going to do useful work.   Europe gained far more advantage from his school-books than from the Pansophia that did but impart a certain dignity and finish to his didactic method.   None the less, Comenius was martyrising himself.   Money, sufficient for his daily wants, he could always obtain, and with ease.   Of school-books he had written enough, and of school method he was sick unto death.   It was the old story.   The old inability, on the part of a versatile man, to realise his true vocation.

Musicians have hankered after brushes and palate, states-men have grudged to public affairs the energy filched from literary pursuits, and Comenius, the inspired schoolmaster, wished to shut up his dictionaries and grammars and to philosophise about things in general.   His Pansophia may have been useless ; to the progress of exact thought it may even have been harmful; he may have been totally unfitted to attempt the welding together of a philosophic system ; but this it was, and nothing else, that he wished to do, and this it was that he determined to renounce.

The reason is not far to seek.   It was his stead-fast belief, backed up by the prophecies of Kotter and of Christina Poniatowska, that his co-religionists would one day triumph over their enemies and be restored to their native land, and the agent that was to bring this about was Sweden, the great Protestant power of Europe. By thus linking himself with Sweden, by carrying out the wishes of de Geer, Oxenstierna, and Skythe, he was establish-ing a powerful claim upon the generous treatment that he believed the Swedes destined to accord to his countrymen, and making straight the path along which his Church was to march home in triumph.   This was why he held him-self bound to accept de Geer's offer ; this was the ulterior object, to attain which he thought no present sacrifice too great.

It was in the November of 1642 that he reached Elbing. In spite of his eagerness to get to work, the first week was one of enforced idleness, for in the house that he had taken there were neither tables nor chairs; but these material defects were soon remedied. The immediate task was to rewrite the *Janua Linguarum* and to compose the lexicon and grammar that were to accompany it. He was now to have assistance in his labours, and as fellow-workers had brought with him Paul Cyrillus, Peter Figulus, Daniel Petreus, and Daniel Nigrinus. Bechner, whom he had been anxious to secure as a collaborator, was unable to come. Still further to ensure getting through the work with speed, he gave out that he must drop all correspondence with his friends for one year, an intention, needless to remark, that he found impossible to carry out.

The Swedish patron was as good as his word, and as soon as he heard that Comenius was definitely settled at Elbing, and ready to set to work, remitted 1000 thaler for him and for the Brethren. With the letter of thanks that Comenius sent to Wolzogen, de Geer's agent at Finspong, he forwarded also some copies of the *Vestibulum*, and suggested that the Swedish boys should write it out from dictation while waiting for the revised versions on which he was engaged, such an exercise being an essential part of his method.

Elbing had seemed an eminently suitable place to work in, and Comenius had imagined that he would be free from any great interruption. Unfortunately Bartholomew Nigrin, formerly minister of the Reformed Church at Dantzig, had settled there, and his presence appears to have been a continual source of disturbance to Comenius. Nigrin had been imbued with the notion, shared, as we have seen, by John Durie, Hartlib, and many others, that a union of Christendom was possible. With the apparent object of furthering this end, he tried to induce Comenius to throw up his contract with de Geer and withdraw himself from all connection with Sweden. Comenius, who saw in Sweden the future protector of the Evangelic Faith, had made his engagement with open eyes, so that it is difficult to see why these overtures on the part of Nigrin should have caused him so much annoyance. At any rate, Nigrin soon went over to the Roman Catholic faith, and from that time gave Comenius little trouble.

Resolutions notwithstanding, philological works were very far from getting Comenius' undivided attention. His *Pansophiæ Diatyposis* [1] had been commenced in England, and, in his anxiety to get it into print and thus give his friends in England some earnest that his Pansophic activity was only dormant, he devoted a great part of his time to its completion. In the summer of 1643 we find him in Dantzig making arrangements for its publication, which followed shortly after.

He now made a vigorous effort to devote himself wholly to the revision of the *Janua*. Latin authors had to be gone through with minute care to ensure that no important word was being omitted, and, the more labour Comenius and his assistants bestowed on their task, the farther it seemed to be from completion. It was impossible to say how many months would pass before the end was reached, and more than once, while suffering from the irritation induced by his somewhat pettifogging occupation, he was on the point of throwing up his engagement and returning to his *Universal Knowledge.* But the Brethren had to be considered, and de Geer was helping them liberally. In June a fresh subsidy was sent, and Comenius, by way of showing some sign of life, sent letters to his patron, to Bishop Matthiae of Sweden,

[1] ' J. A. Comenii, Pansophiæ Diatyposis Ichnographia et Orthographia delineatione Totius futuri Operis amplitudinem, dimensionem, usus adumbrans.' This work was translated into English in 1651 by Jeremy Collier, Fellow of St. John's College, Cambridge (father of the non-juror), under the title ' A Patterne of Universall Knowledge in a plaine and true draught : or a diatyposis or model of the eminently learned and pious promoter of science in generall, Mr. J. A. Comenius, shadowing forth the largeness and use of the intended work in an ichnographicall and orthographicall delineation.'

and to Oxenstierna. To the latter he also forwarded a copy of his *Via Lucis*, in the hope of stimulating the slight interest in the Pansophia that the statesman had evinced in the previous year. In particular he asked him for a criticism of the didactic principles contained in chap. xvi. This letter shows what extravagant expectations he entertained of the part that Oxenstierna was to play in the support of Evangelism. " Since we live in hope," he wrote, " that the fall of Babylon will give an opportunity for the restoration of Zion, and since we see that the time is drawing near, I am of opinion that you ought not to remain in ignorance of our views on this matter, since you are one of those in whose hands the rod of judgment has been placed."

These expectations were increased by his old school-companion Drabik, of whom he had, for a long time, heard nothing. Drabik, who was living in Hungary, sent a copy of fourteen revelations that had been made him from heaven. These spoke of the brilliant future in store for the Evangelical Church, and in particular of the exaltation of Comenius, who was destined to make the good news known to all nations. Comenius had already had an unfortunate experience with the prophecies of Kotter and of Poniatowska, whose weak point was their unfulfilment. This time he was more wary, and replied that, before he accepted any prophecies as true, he must examine them, as well as the prophet, carefully. In the meantime he would pray God to give him light.

It now began to dawn on de Geer that the scholar whom he was paying to write class-books for Sweden was spending his time over matters philosophical and theological. In answer to a remonstrance from Wolzogen, who complained that time was passing and that nothing had been produced, Comenius answered that it was too soon to expect any result. He was writing books and not copying them ; his work was on a totally new plan, and needed time and labour to make it harmonious in all its details. If the Swedish children had no school-books, let them employ themselves in learning their own language, Scripture history, piety, and good manners. They would soon make up for lost time when the Latin text-books were completed. With this assurance de Geer had, for the moment, to be content.

But, in spite of his promise to get on with his philological works as quickly as possible, we find Comenius still busied with philosophic plans. Under the circumstances, it is not surprising to find that de Geer strongly objected to a Dr. Kozak of Bremen, whom Comenius suggested as a collaborator, since Kozak's interests were purely scientific. At the same time an effort was made to induce the Hamburg professors, Jung and Tasse, to join him in his Pansophic work, but they refused to leave their present positions unless a high salary could be guaranteed them, and for this Comenius knew that it would be useless to ask de Geer.

It is possible that, had he been able to arrange a meeting with his patron in the summer of 1644, he would have attempted to withdraw from an engagement that he found so irksome, but travel was rendered dangerous by the war that had broken out between Sweden and Denmark in the preceding year. The claims on his time remained as numerous as ever. In this year (1644) he published a religious work, *Absurditatum Echo ;* and, at the request of the Elbing Town Council, undertook to lecture at the Gymnasium on the *Janua Rerum* four times weekly, from one till three o'clock. For this he was to receive a salary of 400 florins. As if he were not already sufficiently occupied, he found himself compelled by his position as an elder in the Moravian Church to attend an Evangelical meeting at Orla in Lithuania.

It may appear like dishonesty on Comenius' part that he so persistently dissipated his energies on other work while in de Geer's pay for one definite purpose, but to any such accusation two very strong rejoinders may be made.

In the first place, he was undoubtedly devoting to his school-books a very great deal if not quite the whole of his time ; and, in the second, he had shown to what extent he considered himself bound to carry out his engagement, by refusing two offers of a far more congenial character.

In 1643, George Rakoczy, Count of Transylvania, had asked him to accept the professorship formerly held by Alsted, and at the same time to undertake a general reform of the school system in Hungary. Count Radziwill of Lithuania had gone further, and had actually proposed to give him a residence on his estate and endow him with the quarter of his income that he might carry on his Pansophic studies in peace. Both these suggestions Comenius had rejected, and he therefore felt that, while practically fulfilling his promise, he was not called upon to become an utter slave to de Geer's desire for school-books.

De Geer, however, did not see matters in the same light, and, on his return from Orla to Elbing, Comenius found himself compelled to write a dutiful letter to Hotton, each line of which shows that the chains that bound him to philology were galling his flesh. "O that it had pleased God," he writes, "to instil these thoughts into another, to implant these intellectual desires in another's mind! O that I might have either greater powers or fewer desires! But with every forward step that I make, a further insight is granted me, and I find it impossible not to strive after what is deeper and better. The consequence is that my former work always seems imperfect, and though I correct and improve in a thousand ways and without intermission, I arrive at no definite result. The task that I have undertaken is a great one, and my efforts are like a stream whose volume of water increases as it gets farther from its source. You see that I have something in my mind greater than a Vestibulum, a Janua, a Dictionary, or leading-strings for boys of that description."

But neither this letter nor one of a later date received any answer, and Comenius wrote again (November 1644) imploring de Geer, in God's name, not to desert him, since he had refused help from other quarters. In proof of this he copied several passages from Count Radziwill's letter and sent them to Hotton, that de Geer might see if he had really been guilty of inconstancy. He must at this time have been in serious pecuniary distress, only slightly alleviated by the authorities at Elbing, who provided him with a house rent-free.

At last the long-expected letter from Sweden arrived. Hotton had made peace with de Geer, and the result was a remittance of 400 thaler.   In his letter of acknowledgment, Comenius, with that simplicity which is his strongest characteristic, speaks out of his inner consciousness and assures his patron that what hinders him in his work is the novelty of his Pansophic system, and the effort to lay the foundations of truth without any sophistry.

It must indeed have been small comfort to de Geer, who was impatiently waiting for his school-books, to be told that their composer was engaged on a work destined to reform human affairs, and of which the Pansophia was only the seventh part.

In the following year (1645) Wladislaw IV. of Poland summoned a great religious conference at Thorn, and invited the various religious bodies to send representatives. The union of Catholics and Protestants had been one of Comenius' favourite notions, but, on hearing that Dantzig proposed to send to the Synod two Lutherans, who had little in common with the Moravian Brethren, he decided to have nothing to do with it.   Though the Brethren at Lissa had been very anxious that he should represent them, they excused him at his earnest request.   " May all these sects and their supporters perish," he wrote.   " Christ, whom I serve, knows no sect."   In order, however, that he might have some reason for absenting himself from such a representative gathering, he wrote to de Geer, asking him to send a summons to Sweden and thus free him from the pressure to which he was being subjected. But de Geer dissuaded him from coming to Sweden until the war between that country and Denmark was at an end.

Deprived, therefore, of this excuse, and continually urged by his friends to attend the conference, Comenius gave way, and set out for Thorn.   On his arrival (August 1645) he received a friendly communication from Hotton, warning him that de Geer's patience was exhausted, that he wished for completed works and not new plans, and that an angry letter from him was on its way.

This news made Comenius anxious, and, as the conference progressed but slowly and promised to be a long affair, he determined to return to Elbing. Just before leaving Thorn he received from de Geer the letter that had been heralded by Hotton. It was violent and full of accusations. He had better get those for whom he worked to support him. The three years at Elbing had been fruitless, since he had published nothing. Descending to particulars, de Geer complained that the salary of 400 thaler promised to a Dr. Cyprian Kinner was far too high.

At first, Comenius was completely overcome by this attitude on the part of his patron, but, by the time he returned to Elbing, he had recovered his self-possession, and wrote de Geer a calm justification of his conduct. He pointed out that his works, which, as a matter of fact, were nearly completed, formed a harmonious whole, so that one could not be published before the other ; that the distracting occupations, that de Geer cast in his teeth, were no more than was necessary to give his mind needful relaxation after its arduous labours. Coming to the incident of Kinner, he pointed out that a captain in the army received more pay than the salary that was considered too high, and that, if de Geer wanted the books finished at all, it was absolutely essential that he should supply competent assistance. If he wished, he might withdraw his support. "Were I not beset with applications on every side," he concludes, "and, in addition, threatened by approaching old age, I should desire nothing better than to retire into some solitude and there give myself up to my favourite investigations. I should seek no patron, but rather strive with all my might to stand in need of none."

Comenius' friends in Lissa now came to the rescue, not with funds, for money was a very scarce commodity among the Moravian Brethren, but with what was, from their point of view, the soundest advice under the circumstances.

"Finish your school-books as quickly as you can," they said, "and then devote yourself to your clerical duties." So Comenius set to work once more, and this time in earnest. There was still a good deal to be done. The *Janua* had to be completely rewritten, in accordance with a new principle of arrangement, and the composition of the grammar and lexicon demanded patience. He had hoped from assistance from Kinner, but for the moment Kinner was detained in Schleswig-Holstein, and, though we find him working with Comenius later on, he seems to have been partly engaged on a Didactic of his own.[1]

De Geer was mollified by Comenius' letter and by his evident intention to complete his task. At the beginning of 1646 he sent him 500 thaler for himself and the same sum for the Brethren. At the end of the year we find Comenius in Sweden, where a commission of three men examined the school-books, now almost completed, and reported favourably on them. It only remained to put the finishing touches.

But poverty and trouble pursued Comenius relentlessly. Any money that came into his hands soon found its way to the pockets of the needy scholars and exiles who clustered round him. At this time he was especially anxious to aid Ritschel, a former collaborator, now in great distress. Himself in need of assistance, he made urgent applications on Ritschel's behalf to the Reformed Church in Belgium, and managed to collect the sum of 50 thaler. Importuning for charity, even though he himself was not its object, was greatly against the grain ; "Better die than beg," he wrote to Hartlib.

In former years Hartlib might have helped him, but he had already spent the greater part of his fortune in the promotion of experiments of various kinds, and, though

---

[1] A sketch of this 'D. Cypriani Kinneri Cogitationum Didacticarum Diatyposis Summaria' was translated by Hartlib, under the title : 'A Continuation of J. A. Comenius' School Endeavours, or a Summary Delineation of Dr. Cyprian Kinner . . . his Thoughts concerning Education, or the way and method of Teaching. London, 1648.'

Cromwell had awarded him a pension of £100 yearly, it is doubtful if he received it regularly. Certain it is that, after the Restoration, he was in great distress. He was now busily engaged with the project of a "Correspondence Agency," which he wished to see established in London. This was to be a kind of Information Office, where any one might seek advice (gratis, if he were poor) on any subject. In addition, it was to further correspondence and learned intercourse between men of talent within and without England, and by this means the realisation of Bacon's scientific and of Comenius' pedagogic schemes was to be rendered easier. The scheme, however, a somewhat visionary one, was not carried out, and remained one of the blind alleys into which so many enthusiasts in England were led before their efforts culminated in the actual formation of the Royal Society in 1660.

A considerable portion of the school-books was now actually ready, and was despatched to Sweden at the beginning of 1647. This included the *Methodus Linguarum Novissima*, with its index and dedication, and part of the *Janua*. More Comenius refused to send until definite arrangements for publication had been made. The *Janua* was to be illustrated, and this caused additional delay. Considering that Comenius was now engaged on his treatise, *Independentia confusionum origo*, a work directly aimed against the sectarian tendency of religious bodies in England, it is difficult to imagine how he found time to busy himself with business arrangements at all.

A fresh page in his life was now to be turned, and, had the bulk of de Geer's books not been completed, the chances are that they would have remained unfinished. The aged Bishop of the Unity, L. Justinius, had died at Ostrorog, and Comenius was elected to fill his place. His acquiescence in this choice meant that the connection with de Geer must to a large extent be broken, as pastoral duties would now take up much of his time. In spite, therefore, of his expectations from Sweden, he at length made up his mind to turn his back upon that country, and, leaving his retreat at Elbing, once more took up his residence at Lissa. De Geer and Hartlib were both anxious that he should leave the books to be published by Elzevir in Amsterdam, but he thought it better to see them printed under his own eyes, and insisted on entrusting them to a local printer at Lissa.   He was now settling for the second time in the town where his spurs as a schoolmaster and as an educationist had been won, and many things combined to make him enter on this new stage of his career with that melancholy to which the Slavonic temperament is ever prone.   He was fifty-six years old.   His life had been spent in exile and in the continual struggle against poverty. His hopes that the Evangelic religion would ultimately prosper must, by this time, have been a good deal shaken. The Pansophia was not completed, and, at his age, with his duties, and in a century when the duration of life was much shorter than at the present day, he could scarcely hope to finish it.   True, he had produced his school-books, his Great Didactic, and his Treatise on language, but these were to him nothing but *spinosa didactica*.   His life-work, the work for which he had wished to be remembered, existed but in his own fancy and in the loose sheets of uncoördinated information that he had been collecting for years.   In addition, the death of his wife, for whose weak state of health the journey to Lissa had proved too much, made him more than ever in need of the sympathy that, as a Bishop, he was expected to extend to others.

To leave the author for a moment, and return to his writings.   The printer at Lissa proved unsatisfactory, and, in 1650, Comenius sent the manuscripts to Amsterdam, washed his hands of them, and left their publication to de Geer.   The works written between 1642 and 1650 constitute the second part of the *Opera Didactica Omnia*.   Here we find the *Methodus Linguarum Novissima*, a couple of pages of the *Vestibulum*, in Latin and in German, and the same amount of the *Janua*, both left unfinished because, as he tells us,[1] he brought out an improved edition later on, in

---

[1] *Op. Did. Omn.* ii. 297.

Hungary, and preferred to print this version in Part III. of the Folio. The grammar for the *Janua*, under the title *Januæ Linguarum novissima clavis, Grammatica Latino-Vernacula*, he gives in full, because, though also revised in Hungary, the two works are practically distinct. The grammar written at Elbing proved too long for young boys (it occupies over 100 folio pages), and is more suited to the master than to the pupil,[1] while that written in Hungary is much shorter.

Following the grammar are some *Annotationes super Grammaticam novam Janualem ;* additional information for teachers and hints as to the spirit in which the grammar should be used. "This is a grammar that I have given you," he says, in a few concluding words, "but one that is to serve as a prelude to logic, rhetoric, and the sciences themselves. Do we wish to train up boys so that they may always remain boys? Nay, it is to higher things that they must be · advanced." The *Lexicon Januale* is not printed in the folio, since an edition of it was brought out by Thomas Gölz at Frankfort in 1656,[2] while the publication of the *Atrium* was hindered by Comenius' call to Hungary in 1650.

We thus see that the series of works composed for de Geer consisted of a philosophic treatise on Language, its nature, its functions, and the laws to be observed in teaching it, followed by a set of graduated reading-books and lexicons based on these laws. The *Methodus Novissima* deserves special notice, more indeed than can be given to it here. Its scope is not so wide as that of the *Great Didactic*, since it deals primarily with language, but in breadth of thought it is fully equal to it. Its great drawback is its bulk (it is half as long again as the *Great Didactic*). As a writer Comenius lacked the instinct of limitation, and in the *Methodus*, as in much that he wrote, allowed his pen to run away with him.

The work contains thirty chapters, and these fall naturally under seven heads.

I. cc. i.-iv. Theory of Language.—Philosophic dis-

---

[1] *Op. Did. Omn.* ii. 304.   [2] *Ibid.* 455.

cussion of the nature of language, the differences and resemblances that exist between various languages, and their respective defects and advantages.

II. cc. v.-viii.   Historical.—Especial attention should be paid to one language in particular.   Why this language should be Latin.   The method of teaching it hitherto in vogue.   Brief account of the efforts that have been made to improve upon that method.

III. cc. ix., x.   Didactic.—A new method, based upon true didactic principles, is needed.   Thorough exposition and analysis of these principles.

IV. cc. xi.-xiii.   General description of the *Methodus Novissima*, with special reference to the principle of gradation involved.

V. cc. xiv.-xvii.   This principle as applied to Latin. Description of the *Vestibulum, Janua, Atrium,* and *Thesaurus.*

VI. cc. xviii.-xxviii.   Universal application of the method, not only to the teaching of Latin, but to the vernaculars as well; to polyglotty, to scientific ends, to the better understanding of the Scriptures, to the improvement of schools, and to the education of rude peoples.

VII. cc. xxix., xxx.   Appeal to learned men, theologians, and rulers, to further the principles involved.

With a large portion of the detail in this work the reader has already been made familiar, and about one-sixth (chap. x.) is an abstract of the Great Didactic; but scattered through the earlier chapters there are a number of suggestive remarks that illustrate the author's versatility and breadth of mind, and these we will briefly indicate.

It must be confessed that some of Comenius' philosophising on the nature of language is sorry stuff.   The remark that language is derived from thought and thought from objects (*rebus*), has a plausible air, but is not developed.   Of far greater interest is his description of a perfect language.   For this, four things are necessary: (1) a complete nomenclature of objects, (2) no ambiguity in the meaning of words, (3) explicit laws for the proper construction of sentences, (4) the nomenclature should not be redundant, each object being represented by one word and no more.

While such a conception of language is of logical value, it is evident that it could only seriously recommend itself to one who lacked all appreciation of literary style. Objects are limited, but the ways in which they may be viewed are indefinite, and it is the possession of several words of varying etymological significance to express different aspects of the same conception that lends a language its charm.

In the domain of comparative philology we find Leibnitz to a large extent anticipated. The similarities between the chief languages of Europe prove beyond a doubt that they have a common origin, and this can be none other than Hebrew. In proof of this assertion he purposes, so he tells us, to write a comparative lexicon of the five chief languages of Europe. It is scarcely necessary to say that the choice of Hebrew as a root-language is suggested by religious associations and by the Scriptural account of the manner in which diversity of language originated. The difficulty of intercourse between nation and nation, for which the Tower of Babel is answerable, can be overcome by the adoption of some one language as a medium of communication. Here Comenius forgets his former decision in favour of a philosophical language, and casts his vote for Latin. After giving at length the arguments of Vives, he adds a few of his own. Latin is easy to pronounce, and in this respect possesses an advantage over most modern tongues. It is free from the difficulties of the Hebrew *ham* and of the Arabic *hha*. It has no *th* like English, no nasal vowels like Polish, and its consonants are not sometimes hard and sometimes soft, as in the Slavonic languages. Hungarian words are monstrously long, Chinese and, to a large extent, German words are too short, and have to be joined agglutinatively; but Latin vocables are of a medium and practicable length.

This prominence given to Latin as a link between nation and nation is not to discourage the cultivation of modern languages. On the contrary, it is of great importance that each people should learn its own language thoroughly, and try to preserve it pure and free from admixture with others. A thorough knowledge of any tongue can be obtained by means of translations of the *Vestibulum*, the *Janua*, and the *Atrium*, and the desire to introduce foreign words will be diminished as the resources of the vernacular become better known. In this respect some nations are great offenders, and particularly the Bohemians, who continually borrow foreign words and expressions although their own language is an exceptionally rich one. The best method of maintaining the purity of a language is the inception of Academies, such as the Society della Crusca at Florence, or the Fruchtbringende Gesellschaft at Weimar. Some such society should exist in every country, and its first object should be to analyse the syntax and grammar of the vernacular, and to reduce them to definite rules. The conditions of those nations who are not sufficiently civilised to do this for themselves, exercises Comenius greatly. The task obviously falls to the lot of the neighbouring people. Thus, the language of the Laps must be set in order by the Swedes, Welsh by the English, and the American dialects by the Spaniards, Belgians, and English that live in America.

Such are a few of the interesting points, buried as usual beneath a mass of verbosity and repetition, that are raised in the *Novissima Methodus*. A short quotation from the fragment of the *Vestibulum* that immediately follows it in the folio edition of 1657, will show how closely the German was fitted to the Latin—

Invitatio.	Einladung.
Veni puer	Kom [her du] Knab
aut quisquis es	oder wer du seyst
qui cupis discere	der du begehrst zu lernen
Latinam linguam :	die Lateinische Sprach :
quae pulchra est	welche schön ist
communisque populis	und gemein den Völkern
et facit doctos	und macht gelehrte [Leut]

It was only in the introduction to the *Vestibulum* that the material was worked up into sentences. Comenius' didactic principles had led him to think that it was a mistake to begin with sentences, no matter how simple. The body of the work, therefore, consisted of lists of words, arranged under the various headings of the *Vestibulum*, and these the child had to learn, preparatory to employing them later on. The *Janua* did not undergo so much alteration. In its new form the plan of not repeating individual words was abandoned; it was not written, as was the first edition, with special reference to the Bohemian language, and some fresh chapters, embodying an account of the world's chief religions, were added.

The grammar composed for the *Janua* does Comenius little credit. It is far too long (it occupies sixty-three folio pages), it abounds in divisions, subdivisions, and such-like complications, and is thus totally at variance with the rules laid down in the *Great Didactic*. It is followed by some notes for the teachers who used it.

In the midst of his varied activity Comenius had ever kept his eyes fixed on one beacon light, and this was the triumphant return of the Bohemian Protestants to their fatherland. To this end he had devised plans for school-organisation, church discipline, social reform, and what not. For this he had courted Sweden and waited in Oxenstierna's antechamber; for this he had buried himself at Elbing, and had spent the best part of six years in doing what he detested, writing school-books; for this he had pocketed his pride and eaten another's bread; for this he had borne de Geer's petulant humours and inconsiderate arrogance. And now it all proved to be in vain. The Thirty Years' War was at an end. In 1648 the Peace of Westphalia had been ratified at Münster and at Osnabrück, and, while religious toleration had been granted to the Protestants in general, it had not been extended to the Bohemian Brethren. These found themselves as far as ever from the return to their beloved country.

To the whole Unity the blow was tremendous, but to none more than to its bishop. The revulsion of feeling caused by the overthrow of all his hopes was sufficient to strain the mental equilibrium of a man more evenly balanced than Comenius, and it is from this juncture that he commenced to give way to those prophetic tendencies that made him the butt of every academic scoffer in Europe, and contributed more than anything else to neutralise the influence that his life should have had on the immediate future of school-organisation.

Hard work, the most easeful of anodynes, came to his rescue. The bond by which the Brethren had been kept together was loosened, and the Unity was fast dispersing. Comenius' energies were divided between resisting this tendency and finding places as teachers for those who were leaving Lissa to seek their fortunes elsewhere. The Gymnasium had greatly declined since the days of his Rectorship, and the effort to bring it up to its former pitch of excellence laid an additional burden upon him. It was in literature, however, that he found the most complete refuge from the dull disappointments of life. His solicitude for the purity of modern languages was not confined to the general propositions laid down in the *Methodus Novissima*. In this year (1649) a German Dictionary from his pen was published,[1] followed by a translation of the eighth book of Lasici's *History of the Bohemian Brethren ;* a last effort to keep the Unity together and excite the sympathy of Europe in its behalf. In cheerfulness his family history contrasted favourably with his political outlook. He had married again, now for the third time, and in the same year two of his daughters, Dorothea and Elizabeth, were married, the first to his literary collaborator Figulus, and the second to a young Hungarian, Molitor by name. It is to be regretted that we get no glimpse into the interior of the household, as, in the absence of definite information, it is difficult to imagine anything but a some-

---

[1] ‘Index plenus Germanicarum vocum,’ *Op. Did. Omn.* ii. 457.

what dreary environment of depressed theologians and needy compilers of school-books.

In the following year (1650) he addressed to his flock a curious document entitled *The Will of the Dying Mother*. The "dying mother," needless to say, is the Bohemian Church, who exhorts her children and divides among them her spiritual treasures. The title alone speaks of a morbidly sensitive state on the part of the author, and it was well that his activity was soon to find an outlet into a channel healthier than any provided by the somewhat moribund Lissa.

Attracted by the *Methodus Novissima*, which was printed at Lissa at the same time as a work of his own, Christopher von Bnin, the Palatine of Posen, had already asked Comenius to assist him in founding a three-class Gymnasium at Sirakow.[1] This offer he was unable to accept, since he was already in communication with the son of George Rakoczy, his former well-wisher. Sigismund Rakoczy and his mother, the Countess Susanna, had read the Pansophia, some of which appears to have been published by this time,[2] and invited its author to come to Hungary and open a school on the lines laid down in it. Several circumstances made Comenius anxious to go to Hungary. There he would find a large portion of the Moravian Church, and there lived Nicolas Drabik, in whose revelations of the future he took more interest daily. He accordingly set out for Saros-Patak, where he arrived in May (1650). A short journey to Tokai with his patrons, during which he discussed the matter, gave him time to make up his mind, and he accepted the offer on the following conditions. Count Rakoczy was to provide a well-built school-house with seven class-rooms, adjoining which there was to be boarding accommodation for as many pupils as possible. There were to be some scholarships by means of which poor students, of whom a certain number were to be Bohemians, might receive board and education for a nominal fee; a sufficient number of masters to allow one for each class;

---

[1] *Op. Did. Omn.* ii. 458.
[2] Visa enim illis et lecta, eatenus edita.—*Ibid.* iii. 3.

and lastly, but probably, in Comenius' eyes, the most important of all, a printing-press, well supplied with type, and some printers to work it.[1]

To these conditions the Count agreed, and Comenius then proceeded to draw up and submit to him a detailed scheme for the school, which he published in the following year under the title *Sketch of the Pansophic School*.[2] This sketch, of which we give a full description elsewhere, proves Comenius to have been a master of organisation. In scope and breadth of view, the scheme was centuries in advance of its time, while many of the suggestions that it contains are but imperfectly carried into effect at the present day.

Leaving his wife, his son Daniel, and his daughter Susanna at Lissa,[3] Comenius, accompanied by his son-in-law Figulus, settled definitely at Saros-Patak in October (1650), and set about his task without any delay. With the object of exciting the sympathy of the residents in the town, he commenced a course of lectures on Education. The first of these, *On the cultivation of the intellect*,[4] was delivered in the lecture-room of the school on the 24th of November, and was followed, four days afterwards, by another on *Books as the chief instrument of culture*.[5] But his ingrained tendency to theorise was as displeasing to his Hungarian friends as it had been to de Geer. "Your schemes," they said, "are too ambitious. While you lecture to us and talk about your seven-class Gymnasium, the education of our sons is neglected. Make a modest commencement and open a few classes at once."

Under this pressure, therefore, Comenius wrote a short sketch of a three-class Gymnasium,[6] which he dedicated to Sigismund Rakoczy, and in accordance with this sketch the lowest or Vestibular class was opened on the 13th of

---

[1] *Op. Did. Omn.* iii. 5.
[2] 'Scholæ Pansophicæ Delineatio.'
[3] Kvacsala, p. 329.
[4] 'De cultura ingeniorum oratio,' *Op. Did. Omn.* iii. 72.
[5] 'De primario Ingenia colendi instrumento, Libris,' *Ibid.* 106.
[6] 'De Schola Latina, tribus classibus divisa,' *Ibid.* 114.

February (1651). On this occasion he delivered his *Panegyric of the true method.*[1] The second, or Janual class, followed on the 14th of March, and was inaugurated in turn by a lecture *On the advantage of an exact nomenclature of objects.*[2] The opening of the Atrial class, occasion for a lecture on *The elegant study of style*, had to be postponed until the January of 1652.

In spite of the enthusiasm with which he had been welcomed on his arrival at Saros-Patak, Comenius' path of reform was a thorny one. In asking for a seven-class Gymnasium, he had, like a practical man, probably asked for a good deal more than he expected to get, but he experienced great difficulty in obtaining that even the three classes opened should be arranged in accordance with his didactic principles. The teachers of the school, who had been vaguely anxious for an improved method that promised to make their work lighter, were mutinous when they understood the details of the scheme. The introduction of so much orderliness meant for them regular attendance and continuous application, and to this they objected strongly. Chosen from " the crowd of students," accustomed to attend the lectures of professors and to come into class only in their spare hours, and then with their minds full of other matters, it is small wonder that reform was more congenial to them in principle than in practice.[3] " The task of a schoolmaster needs the whole man, since it consists in fashioning and refashioning the countenance, the hands, the minds, and the hearts of the little ones "; but how could this be expected from men who only intended to remain in the profession for one year,[4] who looked on their occupation as degrading, and meant to leave it as soon as they could find any more lucrative employment?[5] It need scarcely cause surprise

---

[1] ' Methodi veræ encomia,' *Op. Did. Omn.* iii. 739.
[2] ' De utilitate accuratæ Rerum nomenclaturæ Oratiuncula,' *Ibid.* 745.
[3] ' Methodi veræ encomia,' preface, *Ibid.* 736.
[4] Nemo ultra annum perduraturus.—*Ibid.*
[5] ' Leges Præceptorum,' xvi. *Ibid.* 796.

that masters of this stamp were little in sympathy with the most striking features of the new method. "Of what use is a complete nomenclature of objects to us? we are not going to be philosophers," they said, when the *Janua* was placed in their hands. "Of what use is style to us? we are not going to be Ciceros,"[1] they remarked, when they saw the *Atrium*. With such unpromising material it needed a stronger man than Comenius to achieve success.

He was probably at a loss to know how to treat their opposition. The publication at this time of the *De Ratione Studii* of Joachim Fortius, and of the similarly named treatise of Erasmus, seems due to his desire to avoid odium by sheltering himself behind the authority of former writers. These treatises, however, produced no effect, so he followed them up by a pamphlet of his own, entitled *Fortius redivivus, sive de pellenda Scholis ignavia*, and, that he might enlist the sympathy of the boys on his side, began to sketch out the work that he called the *Vestibuli et Januæ Lucidarium* or the *Ocular demonstration of the nomenclature of Objects*, afterwards famous as the *Orbis Pictus* or *World in pictures*, and to write his dramatic arrangement of the *Janua*, published later as the *Schola Ludus*.

But this brings us back to the text-books. Count Rakoczy had provided a printing-press and other requisites. Their publication was thus rendered a matter of comparative ease, and some of the masters in the school fitted a Hungarian version to the Latin text. They appear in Part III. of the Amsterdam Folio, arranged in order of usage.

First comes the *Vestibulum*, remodelled as already described. This is followed by a very simple and practical child's grammar, occupying only thirteen folio columns, after which comes a complete index to the *Vestibulum*, referring each word to the number of the section in which it occurs. A few hints to the teacher express Comenius' views as to the method to be adopted. The boy is first

---

[1] 'De Studii Pansophici Impedimentis,' *Op. Did. Omn.* iii. 735.

to learn, in the vernacular, the names of all the objects mentioned; an hour's instruction being arranged as follows. In the first quarter of an hour, the master reads over a portion of the *Vestibulum* to his class, and makes the boys read it aloud in turn. In the second, they copy out what he has read to them. In the third, the master explains the meaning of each word and examines the boys to see if they understand. In the fourth they learn the portion off by heart.

Two months should suffice for learning the whole of the *Vestibulum* in the vernacular, and then the Latin version may be placed in the pupils' hands. The same method as before may be adopted, and it is estimated that in four months the class should know their task thoroughly. The grammar may then be commenced, care being taken to translate each rule into the vernacular before the boys learn it. For this, three months are allotted, after which the pupils proceed to the lexicon or index. This should be read through in a fortnight, and with a fourfold object: (1) the boys will thus become accustomed to the abbreviations that they will find in the lexicon of the *Janua*; (2) it will be an excellent opportunity for seeing how well they know the meaning of the words; (3) by referring to the text from the words that they do not know, they will learn the numbers up to 500; (4) an examination in grammar can be instituted by asking them to parse each word as they come to it.[1]

The pupil is now sufficiently advanced to leave the Vestibular and enter the Janual class. In the method that he suggests for this class, Comenius by no means rises to his own level, making the extraordinary proposal that the lexicon (100 folio pages) should be learned first, that then the grammar (twenty-five folio pages) should be mastered, and that then only should the text of the *Janua* be given to the boys.

Of course he had his reasons for this method, though

---

[1] ' De instituendis e Latinæ Linguæ Vestibulo exercitiis ad Præceptorem commonefactio,' *Op. Did. Omn.* iii. 206.

they are scarcely convincing. Under the old system, he says, when the beginner was introduced straight to the *Janua*, he had three difficulties to contend with, ignorance of the words, of their constructions, and of the objects to which many of them referred.   These difficulties he hopes to overcome by adopting the order indicated.   "First, rising from its roots, comes the forest of Latin words, the lexicon.   Then we give you the tools for cutting this forest down, sawing the trees into planks, and fastening these together, namely, the grammar.   Finally we place before you a short universal history of objects, fashioned out of all the words in Latin properly fitted together, namely, the text of the *Janua*."

This is a good example of Comenius' habit of running a fanciful illustration to death.   It is quite true, as he points out, that in making any construction it is necessary to have, first the materials, and then the tools to work them into shape ; but the result of his reasoning on these lines is grotesque.   He places a ponderous dictionary in the child's hand, saying, "Learn this and I will let you read Latin."   The older grammarians, with their seven genders and their multitudinous rules, never attained this pitch of absurdity.

The grammar, if not quite a model, from the modern standpoint, is yet extremely good.   It is far shorter than that written in Elbing, and the rules are terse and to the point.   It may interest the reader to see how Comenius introduces the prepositions that govern the ablative.

Præpositiones Ablativi.

Cum lupus nollet cedere de i via, nec ille fugere posset ab 2 eo, aut stare diu coram 3 eo, et sic fuit haud procul 4 morte, nisi pugnaret pro 5 vita : licet esset sine 6 socio (absque 7 socio) vibravit tamen hastam cum 8 impetu et transverberavit lupum, distractasque ex 9 illo exuvias ostentat, præ 10 gaudio, palam omnibus.

The edition of the *Janua*, that follows, is considerably

enlarged. It occupies fifty folio pages, and treats at some length of everything in heaven and earth, as the following extracts indicate :—

Sec. 518 (Geometria). Ex concursu linearum fit angulus qui est vel rectus, quem linea incidens perpendicularis efficit, ut est (in subjecto schemate) angulus ACB ; vel acutus, minor recto, ut BCD ; vel obtusus, major recto, ut ACD.

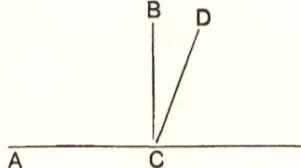

Sec. 578 (Chronologia cum Historia). Circa A. ch. 1300, coepit innotescere vis magnetis, qua se obvertit ad polos mundi ; quod dedit ansam fabricandi Pyxidem nauticam, cujus ope detectum est alterum hemispherum orbis, totusque mundus navigationibus factus pervius ; ut gentes (prius seclusæ et ignoratæ sibi invicem), jam possint colere communicationem utilitatum.

Sec. 717 (Theologia). Theologia tota fundatur super Revelationes Dei ; quarum nihil ignorare, universalem sensum tenere catholice et posse vindicare qua inde torquentur hæretice, Theologica est exactio.

The pupil of the Janual class had thus the opportunity of acquiring a very fair knowledge of the world in which he lived. Armed with this, he proceeded to the study of the *Atrium*, and turned his attention to "style." Commencing with a *Grammatica Elegans*, which presupposes a knowledge of the rudiments of grammar and deals with subjects such as the transposition of sentences and prosody, he is then introduced to the *Atrium Latinitatis*. This is the *Janua* writ large (it covers eighty folio pages), and is composed with a view to illustrating the ornate capacities of the Latin language. The lexicon, written for use with it, was not printed in Hungary, and was first published by

Janson at Amsterdam in 1657. It was a Latin-Latin and not a Latin-Vernacular dictionary, as, by the time he reached the Atrial class, the pupil was supposed to possess a competent knowledge of the language. The Saros-Patak class-books, with the exception of the grammars for the *Vestibulum* and the *Janua*, were all inferior to the first editions previously published at Lissa. In his effort to be scientific Comenius fell into the very trap that he wished to avoid, and became complicated and tedious. But this relapse was more than compensated for by the celebrated *Orbis Pictus*, or *World in Pictures*.[1] It was impossible to publish this work at the printing-office of the Patak Gymnasium, as no engraver competent to execute the illustrations could be found, and it was therefore sent to Nuremberg, where it was brought out at the cost of Michael Endter in 1658. In the preface, Comenius states the philosophic principles by which he was guided in the composition of the work. "There is nothing in the intellect that has not first existed in the senses," says he, with an airy assumption of the materialistic standpoint that he rejects whenever he philosophises about things in general, but which yet plays such a living part in his pedagogy. "It is because schools commonly neglect this truth, and give the pupils things to learn that they do not understand and which have never been properly placed before their organs of sense-perception, that the tasks of the teacher and of the learner are so irksome, and that so little result is produced." When dealing with objects that are in the school-room it is easy enough to point them out to the beginner, but, when the range of the boys' vocabulary becomes more extended, the "object-lesson" process can only be effected by means of a picture-book. Such a book will serve several purposes. Small boys generally imagine that the operations of the school-room must necessarily be of a most dismal character. "Now it is well known that, from their

---

[1] 'Orbis sensualium pictus, hoc est Omnium fundamentalium in mundo rerum, et in vita actionum, Nomenclatura, ad ocularem demonstrationem deducta.'

earliest childhood, boys delight in pictures and feast their eyes upon them greedily. If we can thus free the gardens of wisdom from their terrors, our labour will have been well employed." In the second place, the book will excite the boy's interest and help him to fix his attention; and, thirdly, it will serve as a stepping-stone to the *Vestibulum* and the *Janua*, with which end in view it was primarily written.

Imagine the *Janua Linguarum* considerably shortened, simplified, and illustrated, and you have before you the *Orbis Pictus*. Each section has a picture corresponding to it, and numbers, affixed to individual words in the text, enable the boy to pick out in the picture the exact object to which the word refers. For example :—

AËR

Aura (1), spirat leniter; *Ventus* (2), flat valide; *Procella* (3), sternit arbores; *Turbos* (4), agit se in gyrum; Ventus *subterraneus* (5), excitat *Terræ motum*; *Terræ motus* facit *Labes* (et ruinas), 6.

Translated into the vernacular, it was to serve as a first reading-book. Even the letters and the manner of pronouncing them might be learned from a kind of picture

alphabet by which the text is preceded, and which suggests
a connection between the sound of the letter and the cry
of an animal.

Cornix cornicatur,	*à à*	A *a*
Agnus balat,	*bé è è*	B *b*
Cicada stridet,	*cì cì*	C *c*
Upupa dicit,	*du du*	D *d*
Infans ejulat,	*è è è*	E *e*

The success of this book was even more extraordinary
than that of the *Janua Linguarum*. It went through
numberless editions, and was bought by thousands of
parents who knew little of Comenius, and cared less

for his didactic principles. They found that children liked the pictures and picked up their alphabet, and a few words, easier in that way than in any other. That was sufficient for them, and they paid no attention to pedantic detractors who insisted that pictures should have been given only of those objects that could not be submitted to direct inspection. The *Orbis Pictus* was the first picture-book ever written for children, and exercised a softening influence on the harshness with which, in an unsympathetic age, the first steps in learning were always associated. For years it remained unequalled. Basedow's *Elementarwerk mit Kupfern* (1773) was the first attempt, not altogether successful, to improve upon it. "Apart from the *Orbis Pictus* of Amos Comenius," wrote Goethe, "no book of this kind found its way into our hands."[1]

It is impossible to pass such a favourable criticism on the *Schola Ludus*, or dramatised form of the *Janua*. These plays were to be acted at the end of each term, and put the subject-matter of the *Janua* into the mouths of the *dramatis personæ*. These were generally about fifty in number, so that the greater part of the school could take part in the performances. The plays were intended to interest the pupils, but, if the boys of Saros-Patak in the seventeenth century were like those of the present day, they must have looked upon them as an unmitigated nuisance, and have objurgated the name of Comenius when they had to get up the dreary screed. In one of them, the mathematical section of the *Janua* is worked into a dialogue between *Mathematicus*, *Metrito*, and *Trytanio*.

Math. And so you are seized with a desire to learn mathematics?

Num. We are, sir. We seek for information, and promise you our gratitude.

Mathematicus then proceeds, in the most stilted manner, to expound the elements of mathematics, occasionally interrupted by expressions of wonder on the part of his pupils. Were it not wholly contrary to Comenius' character

[1] *Aus meinem Leben,* pt. i. bk. i.

to jest with a subject so sacred as education, we might almost suspect that the following was intended to be humorous :—

"This demonstration," says Mathematicus, referring to Archimedes' calculation dealing with the sand on the sea-shore, "is very accurate. But I am unwilling to waste time."

"Marvellous, marvellous!" breaks in Numeriano, evidently afraid that Mathematicus may think better of it, and enter on a long discourse. "*Let us proceed to addition.*"

The plays occupy 100 folio pages, and are dismal stuff. If the audiences were as delighted with them as Comenius assures us they were, they must have been easily satisfied.[1]

Of more interest are the hints as to their production, by which they are preceded.

Great care is to be taken that all the boys are present at the performances (attendentibus decurionibus ne quis absit). The actors are to be praised, if they acquit themselves successfully, and any of the poorer students who are among them may be presented with a prize of books. Finally, he adds, evidently mindful of reluctance on the part of all concerned, it will be a great stimulus if the actors and their masters are invited to supper after the play.

Of the Patak publications it only remains to mention the little tract *On Manners*,[2] and the *Laws of a well-ordered School*.[3]

These are both so full of interest that we greatly regret that lack of space prevents our giving them in full. Comenius, in this respect in accord with William of Wykeham, was evidently a great stickler for good manners. "He who excels in learning, but lacks manners, is deficient rather than proficient," he writes at the head of his precepts. These treat of dress, of how to stand and how to walk, of speech, of manners toward the master and toward school-fellows, of behaviour in school, in church, at table, and in the playground. The following are some of the rules for behaviour at meals.

---

[1] Peractis cum applausu hisce Ludis.—*Op. Did. Omn.* iii. 1042.
[2] 'Præcepta morum, in usum juventutis collecta.'
[3] 'Leges scholæ bene ordinatæ.'

It is ill-mannered for boys :—

To lean their elbows on the table,
Or to hold their hands beneath the table.
To place morsels of excessive size in their mouths.
To gnaw bones with their teeth,
Or to hand on to others food that they have half-
eaten.
To take food out of their mouths.
To scratch their heads, or chatter and laugh while
eating.
To drink with their mouths full, or to make a noise
while drinking.
To pick their teeth with their nails or with their
forks.
At table a boy should not speak until first spoken to.

In the playground, boys are urged to run, to jump, and
to play games with balls, since it is necessary to put the
body in motion and allow the mind to rest. Forbidden
pastimes are games played with dice, wrestling, boxing, and
swimming, since these are either useless or dangerous.

On getting up in the morning, a boy is first to say his
prayers, then to comb his hair, wash his hands and face,
and dress neatly. He must remember to wish good morning to all whom he may meet. At night, he is to go
straight to bed after evening prayers, and should not
forget his private devotions. Once in bed, he should take
care not to lie on his back, but must sleep half the night
lying on his right and the other half lying on his left side.
If several boys are sleeping in one room, there must be no
talking after a given hour, and in any case all conversation
out of school must be carried on in Latin.[1]

The *Laws of a well-ordered School* repeat many of what
we may call the commonplaces of the Comenian method,
but also contain much that is new and to the point.
Each class must have a separate class-room, and this
should contain a raised desk for the master and a suffi-

[1] *Op. Did. Omn.* iii. 776-784.

cient number of seats for the boys, so arranged that the master can see all his pupils at once. The boys should sit with their backs to the window, that the light may fall on the master as he works at the blackboard. In addition to the class-rooms there must also be a big school for dramatic performances and speech-days. Once a month the headmaster, accompanied by the clergyman of the parish or by one of the school-managers, should examine the class to see if fitting progress has been made. At the end of the year an examination on a larger scale is to be held, but, as it is impossible to examine the whole class, boys should be selected haphazard and questioned on their year's work. Promotions must be arranged in accordance with this examination.

Flogging is allowed, but with certain restrictions. On the first hour of Sunday, the whole school shall be called together, and, after the headmaster has read the rules, each master shall chastise those of his own pupils who have broken any of them during the previous week.

Comenius had evidently been a sufferer at the hands of that scourge of schoolmasters, the unreasoning parent. Before any boy is admitted to the school, his father must sign a document by which he undertakes to abide by the rules of the institution, and promises that his son's attendance shall be as regular as possible.

In the boarding-house, no meals are allowed out of hours, and such a thing as a tuck-shop is evidently not to be tolerated for a moment. Boys go to bed at eight o'clock and get up at four, and must make their own beds as soon as they rise.

The masters are reminded that their position is one of dignity and of great importance. For the headmaster, in particular, special duties are laid down. He should be a model to the whole school of virtue, piety, and diligence. As he has no class of his own he ought to go through all the classes daily, "as the sun courses through the heavens." He is to look after the school archives, and to keep an exact record of each boy's entrance to and departure from the school. He is to be hospitable, and should give testimonials of good conduct to deserving boys who leave the school. If other schools or cities send to him for masters, he may send them some of his best pupils.[1]

It may seem surprising that Comenius remained for any length of time in Hungary. With his colleagues he was not a *persona grata.* His patron, Sigismund Rakoczy, died in 1652, and there was no prospect that the Gymnasium would be increased beyond the three classes already in existence. The Protestants in Lissa were continually urging him to return to them, and enemies whispered that his only object in staying at Saros-Patak was to line his own purse.

The Countess Susanna herself, a lady of a thrifty disposition and not particularly enthusiastic about Comenius, was the best refutation of this latter charge, and any disinclination to return to Poland must probably be ascribed to the influence of his evil genius Drabik.

Drabik, though living at Lednic, was in constant correspondence with Comenius and paid several visits to Saros-Patak, with the object of inducing the Rakoczy family to take some interest in his prophecies. In this he was not very successful, although Comenius did his best to impress on George Rakoczy that the revelations deserved careful attention, if not credence.

Were it not that Sludge is still with us and that scientific men of our own day still fall victims to the spirit-rapper, it would be difficult to understand how a man of Comenius' practical gifts, and not Comenius only but a host of Protestants throughout Europe, could for one minute have given any credence to this wretched impostor. Kotter may possibly have believed in his own revelations; Christina Poniatowska was a weak-minded and weak-bodied girl, subject to genuine fits of hysteria; but Drabik was a cunning calculator, who took stock of the material with which he had to deal and saw that, in

[1] *Op. Did. Omn.* iii. 784.

their present state of despair combined with superstitious expectation, the struggling Protestant communities would swallow almost any prophetic farrago that he chose to deliver to them. Count Rakoczy was to overthrow the house of Hapsburg, and Comenius was to anoint him king at Pressburg. In combination with Sweden, the Count was then to make Protestantism the faith of Europe. In this operation the Turks, of all people in the world, were to assist him, and, by the translation of the Bible into Turkish, for which the Countess Susanna was to supply the funds, were to be made cognisant of the exact grounds of dispute between the Reformed and the Catholic Church.

The transparency of Drabik's motives was only equalled by his brazen-facedness. In ignorance of the events that were taking place in the Rakoczy family, he continued to receive and to impart revelations concerning the future actions of Sigismund Rakoczy for months after his death. The shout of laughter that the scoffers raised at this unfortunate mistake would have been sufficient to induce most prophets to retire from business, but Drabik, with the greatest calmness, created George Rakoczy his brother's prophetic heir, and had the impudence to announce repeatedly that in a few weeks—so he was informed from heaven—he would be summoned to Saros-Patak, and taken on by the Rakoczys as a kind of family seer; a hint that produced no effect of the kind intended.

Comenius was as yet indisposed to give these revelations full credence, but he thought them well worth considering, and, as events of a peculiarly startling character were foretold for the year 1653, he remained in Hungary, thinking that it might be as well to encounter a social upheaval under the protection of the powerful Rakoczy family. Needless to say, nothing remarkable occurred at the prescribed date, and, as the Church in Lissa needed his presence urgently, he finally (1654) made up his mind to leave Saros-Patak. The non-fulfilment of the prophecies had, strange to say, not diminished his interest in Drabik, whose hold upon him grew firmer daily.

On the 2nd of June he delivered a farewell oration in the great hall of the Gymnasium. All the circumstances that had led to friction between himself and his colleagues were forgotten, and, in an eloquent speech, he wished prosperity to the school, and reminded its governors and patrons of the golden rules by which it might be attained.[1] Shortly afterwards he left Saros-Patak.

He did not, however, go straight back to Lissa, but stayed for a few weeks at Lednic, where he was in daily communication with Drabik. During the last few months of his residence in Hungary he had redoubled his efforts to induce George Rakoczy to take an interest in the Revelations, and had actually been invited to go to Siebenbürgen and expound them in person. This he had been unable to do, but, with the object of retaining the Count's interest, he wrote the tractate *Gentis felicitas*, in which, after discussing the general essentials of good and successful government, he treats of Hungary in particular, and urges the Count, as the perfect ruler and saviour of the Hungarian nation, to place himself in opposition to the house of Hapsburg and uphold the cause of Evangelism.

Under the fire of so much exhortation, George Rakoczy was unable to make up his mind. From a letter to Count Jonas Mednyanszky it appears that he did not attach very much importance to the prophecies, though, for other reasons, he was decidedly disposed to take the line suggested by them. To Comenius he wrote that his difficulties were immense, as he had to cope with the Emperor, the king of Poland, the Turks, and the fickleness of his own subjects. If, however, another defender of Evangelism were to arise, he would be quite willing to assist him.

The occasion was not far to seek. The succession of Charles Gustavus to the throne of Sweden introduced a new element into the political situation, and may have induced Rakoczy to think that Drabik's forecast of striking events in the near future was, after all, a divine communication. That he was greatly tempted to abandon the cautious pro-

[1] 'Oratio valedictoria,' *Op. Did. Omn.* iii. 1041.

cedure of diplomacy, and show his hand with the careless indifference of a passionate enthusiast, seems beyond a doubt.   In sending an ambassador to the young king he was acting in conjunction with and under the direct influence of Comenius.   Constantine Schaum, to whom the task of conducting the negotiations with Charles and with Oxenstierna was entrusted, had orders to go to Lissa on his way to Sweden, and the Count begged Comenius to give his envoy what advice he could.

For the Protestant exiles in Lissa the position was now greatly altered.   Though Count Bohuslaw, on embracing the Catholic faith, had not withdrawn his protection from Comenius and the Brethren under his spiritual charge, it was evident that, in case of war, their situation was precarious.   The undisguised sympathy that they displayed for Sweden did not mend matters, and, when Charles Gustavus, in the August of 1657, actually crossed the Polish frontier and marched as a victor on Warsaw and Cracow, danger stared them daily in the face.   It was distinctly the moment when Comenius should have preserved a discreet silence, and have suffered himself and his compatriots to remain screened by their political insignificance; instead of this, with his habitual simplicity, he published a *Panegyric on Charles Gustavus*, in which he hailed him as "the liberator of humanity, the comfort of the afflicted, and the pattern for kings."   The work, which had a considerable vogue, cannot have failed to embitter the feelings of the Poles against the aliens in their midst, and, as Comenius' enemies afterwards declared, may have been partly responsible for the calamities that befell Lissa.

During his victorious march through Poland, Charles had spared a town that contained so many non-Catholics, and merely left a Swedish garrison to maintain the footing that he had acquired in the district.   On the 17th of April, a large body of Polish troops came down unexpectedly, compelling the garrison to withdraw and leave Lissa at the mercy of the infuriated Poles.   A large number of Protestants sought safety by fleeing into the forests on the

Silesian frontier, but Comenius and some of his friends scorned this course, and, with confidence inspired by Drabik's prophecies, calmly awaited the development of events. They were not left long in suspense. On the 29th of April, the Poles burst once more into the defenceless town, sacked it, and reduced it to ashes. It was with the greatest difficulty that any of the Protestants who had remained there saved their lives. Comenius succeeded in escaping to Silesia, where he took refuge with a wealthy nobleman, the Freiherr of Budova. He was once more homeless, and his worldly assets consisted of the clothes in which he stood, a few good friends, and a reputation somewhat damaged by the fanatical views to which he had committed himself.

Some days afterwards, his host sent Comenius' amanuensis over to Lissa with an escort to see if anything had escaped the conflagration; nothing could be found, however, but a few pages of the *Pansophia* that he had buried before his flight. Amongst other things he had lost his library, and promissory notes to the value of 1000 thaler; though these he valued but little in comparison with his precious manuscripts, into which he had put the best part of his energy, and with which his fondest hopes were bound up. His *Sylva Pansophiæ*, containing "the definitions of all things"; his *Dictionary of the Bohemian Language*, on which he had been engaged for thirty years; his *Harmony of the Evangelists;* his refutations of Descartes and of the Copernican theory, and his collected sermons of forty years, all had been devoured by the flames,[1] and he filled the air with his lamentations. "Had God only spared me the *Sylva Pansophiæ*," he cried, "all else would have been easier to bear, but even this is destroyed." [2] Was ever such irony? With the exception of the Bohemian dictionary, the works that were lost could have elicited little but contempt from subsequent generations. Those, on which his fame to a large extent rests, were already in the hands of half the

---

[1] *Op. Did. Omn.* iv. 5.
[2] Letter to Harsdörfer, Zoubek, p. 90.

school-boys in Europe, and beyond the reach of any casual conflagration.

A letter of Pell's,[1] dated July 17th, shows that Comenius' friends in England were kept well informed as to the state of his affairs. "Five days ago," writes Pell, "I received a letter dated Dantzig, June 17th, containing a letter from Mr. Comenius, dated 22nd of May, wherein he describes the sad estate of those Protestants that escaped from Lesna, where he, for his own part, besides his writings, lost in money, books, and household stuff, above 3000 reichs-dalers (about £700 sterling). He had with incredible labour and no small journeys gotten the favour of some liberal persons, and hoped perhaps to leave his children £200 apiece, which among so many poor exiles would have seemed great riches. I hear he is sixty-five years old, and, it seems, hath nothing left but the clothes on his back. Those papers which have been found in the ashes and rubbish of Lesna are little worth in comparison of those which he accounts irrevocably lost. . . I should have been willing to read over his refutations of the Copernicans and Cartesians, but with that prejudice that I do not believe him to be a competent judge of all the differences between them and other writers. And therefore of all his papers, there is none for whose loss I am less sorry, though he say of them, 'Me valde dolet, siquidem in iis multum posueram operæ et diligentiæ.'

"I have caused his letter to be fairly written out and have sent it to the divines (pastors and professors) of Zurich, who esteem him and have introduced his *Janua* into their higher school some years ago. I make no question but they will do something for him."[2]

The terrible calamity that had befallen the Protestant community at Lissa excited the sympathy of non-Catholics throughout Europe. On every side collections were made

[1] Probably to Hartlib.
[2] *The Protectorate of Oliver Cromwell*, by Robert Vaughan, D.D. London, 1839. Vol. ii. p. 431. From Lansdowne Coll. of MS. in Brit. Mus.

in aid of the homeless exiles. From Dantzig as much as 3000 thaler was contributed to the fund, and in England it was even suggested that a grant of land should be made to them in Ireland. For Comenius, Silesia was but a temporary refuge, and on leaving it his first movements were unfortunate. His effort to settle at Frankfort on the Oder was frustrated by an outbreak of the plague, and in Hamburg, his next resting-place, the old man, worn out by the fatigues to which he had been subjected, underwent a severe illness.

As regards money he had no cause for anxiety. Laurence de Geer, the son of his former patron, came to the rescue and insisted that he should settle permanently in Amsterdam, under his immediate protection. Laurence had long been a passionate admirer of Comenius, though more from the religious and philosophical than from the educational standpoint. The hard-headed old merchant, his father, had refused to listen to Pansophic schemes and prophetic rhapsodies, and had sternly insisted that school-books and nothing else were what he wanted for his money; but the younger de Geer would place no such restriction upon his friend. Comenius might still dabble in education, if he wished; but he was to be left free to rewrite the Pansophic works that had been destroyed by the flames, and thus to complete what he regarded as the great work of his life.

As soon as he was well enough to travel, he set out with his family to Amsterdam, and here he found himself in the midst of friends. "Mr. Drury has returned to Amsterdam," writes Hartlib to Pell, "and promises with all speed to hasten unto us, and it is very like Mr. Comenius will come along with him." [1] But the invitation to England was not accepted. Comenius' time was fully occupied in getting together a library to replace that lost at Lissa, and in arranging for the publication of his collected works on education, and of the prophecies of Kotter, Poniatowska, and Drabik. At the printer's

[1] Lansdowne Coll. of MS. Quoted by Vaughan, ii. 423.

de Geer seems to have given him unlimited credit. Indeed, his literary renown was so great, that a profit was actually expected from the sale of the *Didactic Works*, and with this his patron offered to finance a new translation of the Bible into Polish.

It is impossible to say if the magnificent folio, in which the *Didactic Works* appeared, sold as well as was anticipated. The edition must have been a small one, as the book was very rare a few years after Comenius' death. To the modern student it is invaluable on account of the numerous autobiographical notices of the author that it contains; but there is no doubt that it can have done little to further Comenius' renown as a theoretic educationist. The school-books, that appear in chronological order, were already well known, and their collected mass is so great that it quite swamps the *Great Didactic*. Had this work been published separately it could scarcely have failed to go through several editions, and might have been the means of rescuing the Comenian method from the oblivion into which it afterwards fell.

In itself the volume is a fine one, over 1000 folio pages in length, well printed and well bound. Under the title *The Complete Didactic Works of J. A. Comenius*,[1] it comprises works written, in Part I., between 1627 and 1642; in Part II., between 1642 and 1650; in Part III., between 1650 and 1654; in Part IV., between 1654 and 1657.

With the contents of the first three parts the reader is already acquainted. Part IV., which is comparatively short, consists of works written in Amsterdam. A collection of sentences based on the *Vestibulum*, arranged in alphabetical order and entitled *Vestibuli Auctarium*, is the only section of it that forms an essential part of the Comenian series of school-books. It is dedicated to a Dr. Rulice of Amsterdam, with whom Comenius was in daily

---

[1] 'J. A. Comenii Opera Didactica Omnia, variis hucusque occasionibus scripta, diversisque locis edita; nunc autem non tantum in unum, ut simul sunt, collecta, sed et ultimo conatu in Systema unum mechanice constructum, redacta. Amsterdami. Impensis D. Laurentii de Geer, Excuderunt Christophoros Cunradus et Gabriel a Roy. Anno 1657.'

intercourse. Of greater interest is the work that follows, *An Apology for the Latinity of the Janua.* On his arrival in Amsterdam, Comenius had been asked by some influential citizens to open a small school, and try the efficacy of his method on the Dutch boys. This suggestion seems to have made the established schoolmasters of the town apprehensive that the stranger, with his new methods, would make a bid for their teaching connection, and thus render their position insecure. They therefore brought against him the only charge that would hold water, namely, that his scholarship was poor and likely to lead boys astray.[1] To this Comenius replied in his *Apologia Latinitatis*, and, anxious to leave his enemies no case against him, he followed this up by his *Ventilabrum Sapientiæ*,[2] in which he subjects his own method to a critical examination and points out his own shortcomings so unsparingly as to leave nothing for the ill-disposed to say.

He had now finished with the Latin school-books, "from which he had so often turned in disgust,"[3] and was free to devote himself to the Pansophia. "Mr. Comen," writes Hartlib to Pell, "to retire himself to give himself wholly to his Pansophia goes this spring to be at Monsieur de Gerre's house for a certain time, where he is provided for as a prince, but nobody knows he is there but we three and one of Comen's amanuenses."[4] It would have been well had de Geer's sympathy stopped short at the Pansophia. Unfortunately he took quite as much interest in the Revelations and in the cognate doctrine of Chiliasmus, or the one thousand years' reign of peace on earth to be inaugurated by Christ at His second coming, and even invited Drabik to come to Amsterdam.[5] The year 1656, so fateful to the Unity, had been foretold as that in which

---

[1] *Op. Did. Omn.* iv. 6.

[2] 'Ventilabrum Sapientiæ sive sapienter sua retractandi ars. Cum adjuncta authoris omnium Didacticarum suarum cogitationum retractatione brevi.'

[3] Latinitatis studia mihi toties nauseata.—*Op. Did. Omn.* iv. 6.

[4] Hartlib to Pell, quoting a letter of Rulice, Vaughan, ii. 448.

[5] *Ibid.*

the reign of peace was to commence, and, this expectation falsified, 1671 or 1672 was the next date to which
Comenius, inspired by Drabik, had given his entire confidence.   The alliance of Rakoczy with Charles Gustavus,
and the death of Ferdinand II., had given a passing air of
plausibility to Drabik's ravings, and poor Comenius finally
threw common-sense scruples to the wind and definitely
identified himself with the party of prophecy.   The publication by him of *Lux in Tenebris*, or the collected prophecies
of Kotter, Poniatowska, and Drabik, may have been largely
due to de Geer's influence, but it must be borne in mind
that men like Thomas Burnet and William Whiston were
staunch adherents of the doctrine of Chiliasmus, and that
both on the continent and in England a large number of
Protestants had no doubt whatever that Drabik was directly
inspired from heaven.   "This last week I have twice read
the book of Drabicius," writes Beale to Hartlib, "and cannot doubt but, in the main, God is in it."   Comenius was
now leaving the legitimate paths of Churchmanship and
pedagogy, and entering upon the trackless maze of vati-
cination.   Revelation succeeded revelation.   "About three
weeks ago," writes Hartlib to Pell in 1658, " Mr. Comen
did impart unto me a copy of the last three visions of
Drabicius from March 8th to September 1st, wherein he
says again that the king of France is to be the German
emperor."   In the following year appeared the *History of
the Revelations ;* in 1663, the more recent visions of Drabik
were given to the public ; and, two years later, a complete
illustrated edition of all the prophecies up to date, under
the title *Lux e Tenebris*, was issued.

In spite of the popularity of these works, murmurs of
disapproval were heard in many quarters.   Nicholas
Arnold, a professor at Franecker, gave vent to his feelings
in his *Discursus Theologicus contra Comenium*, and Samuel
Des Marets, Professor of Theology at Groningen, published
several brochures, in which, however, he was careful to
state that the object of his attack was not Comenius, but
the Revelations fathered by him.   Even in his own

family he met with opposition. We learn from letters of Figulus to Arnold, that his son-in-law had disapproved of the publication of *Lux in Tenebris* in 1657.

It is difficult to understand how Comenius found it possible to do much more work at his Pansophia during these years, since to edit the prophecies and fight their battles with the sceptical must have taken up nearly as much time as to write school-books at Elbing. De Geer, however, seems to have made every arrangement in his power to ensure that the *Universal Knowledge* should be carried to a successful issue. "I still more and more admire the zeal and piety of that admirable man," wrote Rulice to Hartlib in 1658. "I must tell you *in aurem*, if Comen do not mention it, he hath called also Figulus, with his family, hither, and will maintain him only to assist his father-in-law and to know all concerning Pansophia, that if Comen should die or be carried away, he may finish it."

De Geer, in fact, was willing to spend his money on any object that commended itself to his evangelical friends. The Rakoczy family had refused to finance the translation of the Bible into Turkish, but he came to the rescue with his inexhaustible purse. The work was undertaken by a certain Warner, who had travelled in Turkey, and was to be revised by Golius, the well-known orientalist. Hartlib announces this in triumph to Boyle and Worthington. At last the *Deus ex machina*, destined to interpose and strike the final blow at Catholicism, would be instructed in the part that he was called upon to play.

With the publication of the *Opera Omnia Didactica*, Comenius had not entirely ceased to take an interest in matters educational. In 1658 we find him giving practical instruction in his method to Jacob Redinger, master of the Latin School at Frankenthal. Redinger had heard of him from afar, and was not satisfied till he came to Amsterdam to consult the great oracle of school-craft. Comenius' magic influence, that enthralled every school-master with a disinterested love for the profession of education, made a deep impression on him. He became the most devoted adherent of the new method, and, in his young enthusiasm, brought out an edition of the *Vestibulum* and a German translation of the *Schola Ludus*. A follower of Comenius in one direction, he soon became his disciple in another, embraced the doctrine of Chiliasmus, and joined the crowd of Protestants who, throughout Europe, were eagerly awaiting the fulfilment of the Drabician prophecies.

That the Pansophia made but slow progress need cause little surprise, as, in addition to his occupations of a purely theological nature, Comenius had undertaken the task of managing the finances of the Bohemian Brethren. The sympathy of friends in England had not been confined to words, but had led to collections on a large scale. In 1658 £5900, and in the following year £3000, were sent to the Continent in aid of the exiled victims of Catholicism. At the same time, collections were made in Holland and in Switzerland, and the whole sum of money had to pass through Comenius' hands. Applications for assistance poured in from every side, and the aged Bishop had to tear himself from his philosophic labours and undertake the duties of a paymaster-general. From England supplies continued to come in until, in 1661, Charles II., alarmed at the removal of so much money from the country, put a stop to the collection, and impounded the money that was ready for transmission. Needless to say, an indignant letter from Amsterdam remained ineffective and unanswered. In the midst of so many distractions it is remarkable that Comenius, whose health was rapidly failing, found time to conduct some physical experiments on the nature of heat and cold, and to correspond with Robert Dalgarno in England on the subject of a complicated clockwork construction that the latter was devising.[1]

Of the last ten years of Comenius' life our information, never very direct or very full, is extremely scanty. His correspondence with Hartlib ceases in 1662, and we are

---

[1] *The works of the Hon. Robert Boyle.* London, 1772. Vol. vi. p. 99.

thus deprived of an important source of information.[1]   In
1665 death took from him his wife, his friend Dr. Rulice,
and his patron Laurence de Geer, and, though the place of
the latter was, to a certain extent, supplied by his brother
Gerard, who continued to support him in comfort, he must
have led but a forlorn existence, an exile from his native
land, and the survivor of most of his friends.   In his
loneliness he devoted himself to his metaphysical writings
with all the energy that a feeble old man, whose life had
been a perpetual hoping against hope, could muster.   His
Janua Rerum appears to have been completed in 1666,
though, if this was identical with a work of the same name
that he mentions previously as being in print,[2] it is impossible to say.   The only edition known was published at
Leyden in 1681.[3]   Of this treatise it suffices to say that it
is a deductive metaphysic, totally unlike the *Janua Rerum*
that he anticipated in his younger days, and that it bears
no trace of Bacon's influence.   The same may be said of
his Pansophic writings, some of which were completed in
the same year.   Under the title of *A general deliberation
for the improvement of the human race*[4] were comprised six
parts, named respectively, *Panegersia, Panaugia, Pantaxia* or
Pansophia, Panpædia, Panglottia, and *Panorthosia,* concluded
by a seventh consisting of a general exhortation.   If the
first two were published during Comenius' lifetime, the
editions must have been limited to a few copies, as
Buddaeus, in 1702, had to edit the *Panegersia* from the
original manuscript,[5] and of the *Panaugia* there only exists
one copy—in the museum at Prague.[6]   The *Panegersia*
excited the admiration of Herder,[7] but it is unnecessary

[1] Hartlib had been in ill-health for some time, and probably died in
this year.
[2] In his letter to the bookseller Montanus (Van den Berge) in 1661.
[3] 'Janua Rerum reserata, hoc est Sapientia prima (quam vulgo metaphysicam vocant).   Authore J. A. Comenio.   Lugduni Batavorum ; apud
heredes Jacobi Heeneman.   Anno 1681.'
[4] 'De rerum humanarum emendatione consultatio catholica.'
[5] There is a manuscript copy of the *Panegersia* in the British Museum.
[6] Kvacsala.
[7] 'Briefen zur Beförderung der Humanität,' No. 41.

for us to say more than that its contents embody a curious admixture of fantastic metaphysic and weak analogies drawn from the processes of nature.   The general drift of the argument is that of the *Via Lucis*, written during his stay in England, and published by Cunrad at Amsterdam in 1668.   Of this work Comenius sent a copy to the Royal Society in London, with a letter in which he implored its members not to deal too exclusively with the physical aspect of the universe to the neglect of the more important metaphysical and supernatural side.

He was now seventy-seven years old, but his desire to write and to publish remained as great as ever.   His *Unum Necessarium*, a religious work, appeared in 1668, and in the following year he again plunged into controversy with a tract [1] directed against Samuel Des Marets, who still persisted in his sceptical attitude towards the prophecies and the chiliastic doctrine.   The result of this brochure was startling.   Des Marets lost his temper completely, and in his reply *Antirrheticus* [2] he quits the ground of argument and assails Comenius' personal character in a manner quite unjustifiable, if the age and failing strength of his antagonist be considered.   After terming Comenius "a fanatic, a visionary, and an enthusiast in folio," he proceeds, "I would venture to say that by feeding one family, that of de Geer, on pansophic hope, and by nourishing it or rather bewitching it with chiliastic smoke and Drabik's prophecies, he has been able to make a yearly income three or four times as great as the salary that I receive from the government." [3]

The sharp tone of this attack cut Comenius to the quick. Forlorn, and on the verge of the grave, he had neither the force nor the inclination to rebut the insinuations of dishonesty that it contained.   Some consolation in his distress he may. have derived from the society of the aged

[1] ' De Zelo sine scientia et charitate, admonitio fraterna J. A. Comenii ad D. Samuelum Maresium : pro minuendis odiis et ampliandis favoribus.'

[2] I have been unable to find any copy of this tractate.   Bayle quotes it largely.

[3] Bayle, *Dictionnaire historique et critique*.   Vol. ii. p. 884, note.

French prophetess and visionary, Antoinette Bourignon, who had recently come to reside at Amsterdam; but his life was burning low, and not even the fuel of fanaticism was able to revive the flame.   Early in the year 1670 his son-in-law Figulus died, and, on the 15th of November, the last Bishop of the Bohemian Brethren quitted that life in which every ambition that he entertained had been doomed to disappointment.   He was buried at Naarden, near Amsterdam, on the 22nd of November.

It was a strange account on which the ledger had closed.   For himself, Comenius was a failure, and his life bankrupt; not so for mankind.   The despised pedagogy, the "puerilia illa mihi toties nauseata" have laid posterity under an eternal obligation, and have given the deepest possible meaning to the words of Leibnitz,

> "Tempus erit, quo te, Comeni, turba bonorum.
> Factaque spesque tuas, vota quoque ipsa colet." [1]

Of Comenius' descendants little is known.   His son Daniel was ordained, and died in 1694, but these two facts exhaust the material for his biography.   Nor have we much more information about the fate of his literary remains.   Gerard de Geer's interest in the Pansophic writings did not cease with the death of their author, and he entrusted the arrangement and publication of the manuscripts to a certain Nigrinus, who appears to have found his task a difficult one, owing to the complex nature of the plan that Comenius had been trying to work out.   In 1677 he announced that the *Panorthosia* was completed, but no trace of its publication remains.   In 1680 he brought out a *Specilegium Didacticum*,[2] giving the scheme of the didactic works.   If he was responsible for the *Janua Rerum* that appeared in 1681 it is impossible to say.

---

[1] Leibnitz, *Coll. Works.* Ed. Pertz.   Vol. iv. p. 270.

[2] 'Specilegium Didacticum artium discendi aut docendi summam brevibus præceptis exhibens.'

We now approach the question, "What was the effect of the personality and of the theoretic writings of Comenius on the generation that immediately succeeded him, and on the following century?" The answer is somewhat surprising. The man whom we unhesitatingly affirm to be the broadest-minded, the most far-seeing, the most comprehensive, and withal the most practical of all the writers who have put pen to paper on the subject of education, the man whose theories have been put into practice in every school that is conducted on rational principles, who embodies the materialistic tendencies of our "modern side" instructors, while avoiding the narrowness of their reforming zeal, who lays stress on the spiritual aspect of true education while he realises the necessity of equipping his pupils for the rude struggle with nature and with fellow-men—Comenius, we say, the prince of schoolmasters, produced practically no effect on the school organisation and educational development of the following century. His school-books, frequently reprinted, were thumbed for years to come by boys in every corner of Europe; but the theoretic works, *The Great Didactic, The Newest Method of Languages, The Mother School*, remained unknown and ineffective. For all the result that they produced, they might as well have perished in the flames at Lissa.

The cause of this is not far to seek. If we have laid stress on his entanglement with the prophet Drabik, the reason has been less the intrinsic value of that worthy's revelations than their effect on the reputation of his unfortunate dupe. Comenius was not alone in believing them to be heaven-sent. As we have seen, the prophet had a large following. Few members of the Bohemian Church but had followed the example of their bishop, and put their faith in the misty fabrication; and throughout Europe, Protestants, if not convinced of its truth, awaited the future with interest.

Imagine the effect produced, when, eight months after Comenius' death, Drabik formally retracted all the prophecies and went over to the Roman Catholic faith.

The reaction was terrible. The remnant of the Moravian Brethren, who felt they had been duped, laid all the blame upon their spiritual guides. In Hungary, a minister who had been a keen partisan of Drabik's was dismissed from his office. Daniel Comenius, anxious to go to Hungary, was warned by his friends that his life would scarcely be safe there ; while his father's efforts and sacrifices on behalf of his flock were forgotten in the virtuous indignation that was showered on his want of judgment. Worse than this, the dictionary-makers, biographers, and historians, who should have been the guardians of his fair fame, either took their impressions from the hostile tractates of his enemies, or, in ignorance of his theoretic works, measured his value as an educationist by their peddling standard of correct Latinity. "He worked at a *Pansophia*," wrote Morhof, in 1688, "which he left only half finished. He wrote a *Prodromus* to it, and this, together with some other philosophic matter, he published at Amsterdam in folio." "His *Janua* is full of barbarisms, which he tried in vain to defend ; for his Apology stands itself in need of one." He also wrote a *Physic remodelled in accordance with Divine Light.* . . . I praise the man's piety, but piety alone will not do everything."[1]

The whole of his writings on the theory of education alluded to as "some other philosophic matter"! This is bad enough, but worse was to follow. The sceptical Bayle, writing in 1697, gets the greater part of his material from Des Marets' *Antirrheticus*, and treats the angry retort of an antagonist as a reliable estimate of Comenius' character. Des Marets gets a special word of praise. "On ne sauroit assez louer notre Des Marets," he writes, "de sa vigueur contre les Enthousiastes et contre les annonciateurs de grandes révolutions. On a pu voir comme il poussa Comenius."[2] Of the Amsterdam folio he says, "C'est un ouvrage in folio divisé en quatre parties

[1] Morhof, *Polyhistor literarius, philosophicus, et practicus.* Lubecæ, 1688, pp. 119, 120.
[2] Bayle, *Dictionnaire historique et critique.* Rott. 1697, ii. 559.

qui coûta beaucoup de veilles à son auteur, et beaucoup d'argent à d'autres et dont la République de lettres n'a tiré aucune profit ; et je ne crois pas même qu'il y ait rien de practicable dans les idées de cet auteur." [1]

In the eighteenth century Bayle's Dictionary was widely circulated, and ignorant readers readily acquiesced in the estimate given to Comenius' character and merits.   In 1742 a protest was raised by Paul Eugene Layritz, school-director at Nuremburg, under the title *Vindication of the Memory of Comenius*,[2] but this was unable to counteract Bayle's influence, and a still more deplorable fate awaited the unhappy pedagogue.   Adelung, in his *History of Human Folly*,[3] gives him a prominent place, and classes him with magicians, alchemists, and soothsayers—a truly humiliating position for the father of modern education.

To be abused tries one's temper, but need not diminish his self-esteem ; to be misunderstood may embitter a disposition, but need not shatter a sense of merit ; but to be absolutely ignored presents no element of compensation, and this is what befell Comenius at the hands of his successors in the path of school reform.   While the pedagogic writers of the seventeenth century were firm believers in the continuity and organic development of educational theory, those of the eighteenth to a large extent ignored the efforts of their predecessors, and were at no pains to discover if the principles that they enunciated had already been worked out by others.   A. H. Francke mentions the *Unum Necessarium*, but never alludes to the *Great Didactic*.   Had Rousseau been put through a course of Comenian method, his *Emile* might have lost in paradox and in piquancy, but the educationist would have gained, where the lover of polite literature lost.   In *How Gertrude*

---

[1] Bayle, *Dictionnaire historique et critique.*   Rott. 1697, i. 883.

[2] ' Manes Comenii vindicati, ejusque docendi discendique methodus a Petri Baylii injuriis liberata,' 1742.

[3] Adelung's ' Geschichte der menschlichen Narrheit, oder Lebenschreibungen berühmter Schwarzkünstler, Goldmacher, Teufelsbanner, Zeichen- und- Liniendeuter, Schwärmer, Wahrsager, und anderer philosophischen Unholden.'   Leipzig, 1785.

Teaches her Children, Pestalozzi, from a slightly different point of view, enunciates principles almost identical with those of the *School of Infancy,* and, had Pestalozzi been led to study the *Great Didactic,* he would probably have confined himself to the development, on the subjective side, of the objective principles embodied in that treatise. Subsequent writers were wittier than Comenius, none possessed, in combination, his sympathy with children, his power of analysis, and his breadth of mind.

It is only recently that Comenius has been rediscovered. Von Raumer in his *History of Pedagogy* (1843) was the first to attract attention to the surpassing merit of the *Great Didactic,* and since then several translations of that work and a voluminous Comenian literature have appeared in Germany. In 1841 Professor Purkyňe found the manuscript of the Bohemian *Didactic* at Lissa. It was published at Prague in 1849, and has since been twice reprinted. The *School of Infancy* was translated into English by D. Benham in 1858, and more recently Professor Laurie has provided the student with an admirable epitome of the Amsterdam Folio of 1657. In the present volume, the *Great Didactic* is presented to English readers for the first time.

INTRODUCTION

II

HISTORICAL

WE have already traced the growth of Comenius' Educational Theories, and pointed out his debt to contemporary writers, notably in the case of the *Janua Linguarum*. We will now endeavour to show the general relation in which he stands to his predecessors, to bring into greater relief the condition in which he found schools and schoolmasters, and to estimate the worth of his school-books for his own age, and of his theoretical writings for all time.

Against Comenius, as against his predecessors and contemporaries, the accusation may be brought that, in spite of professions of a desire to widen the school curriculum and shake off the more binding traditions of the past, he still retained Latin as the concentration-point of his system, and allowed it to usurp more than its fair share of attention. While this charge is to a certain extent justified, a brief consideration of the circumstances will suffice to show that the blame lies less with Comenius than with the strength, born of tradition, that enabled the Latin language to blockade every avenue that led to polite learning or scientific pursuits.

In mediæval times the schools were in the hands of the

monasteries, and Latin was the language of Christendom. After the Renaissance, Latin was the language of culture and opened the door to a more perfect literature than any that existed in the vernaculars. After the Reformation, though banished from the services of Protestantism, it still remained a most important medium of communication between nation and nation. At the present day great stress is laid on the practical value of modern languages, but in the sixteenth century a man furnished with a good colloquial knowledge of Latin might have travelled over Europe with nearly as great comfort as if he had been thoroughly acquainted with the language of each country through which he passed. To write English fluently and well is now of infinitely more value to a man than to have acquired the same proficiency in Latin; but in the sixteenth century the advantage was greatly on the side of the Latin scholar. By sending his son to learn Latin an uncultured parent immediately raised him into a higher sphere of society and placed in his hands a passport which secured admission where the language of the country invited rebuff.

But the study of Latin in the latter half of the sixteenth century was very different both in manner and method from that of the monkish schools. Up to the time of Comenius, and indeed till very recently, grammar was allowed to usurp far more than its due share of the school programme; but in mediæval schools it was the chief subject taught, sometimes indeed the only one. A slight knowledge of arithmetic sufficed to enable the future monk to make the *computus* or calculation necessary for ascertaining on which days the festivals of the church should fall, and the remainder of his energies he was forced to devote to Priscian or Donatus. The work of the latter, *De partibus orationis pars minor* had been arranged in 2645 leonine hexameters by Alexander de Villa dei in 1199, and under the name of the Doctrinal was the staple grammar for nearly 300 years. The school-books bought for the Dauphin in 1484 consisted of "Ung A, B, C, Ungs sept pseaulmes, Ung Donast, Ungs accidens, Ung Caton, and Ung Doctrinal."[1]

Another famous Grammar was the *Græcism* of Ebrard, written in 1212. It was still in use at Deventer when Erasmus was at school there in 1476,[2] and was popular in the Parisian schools until the end of the fifteenth century.[3] This work,[4] a bulwark of linguistic training in the fourteenth century, commences with a metrical treatise on grammatical forms, each of which is labelled with a Greek name. This is followed by chapters nominally on the declensions and the conjugations, but really on the exact meanings of words that resemble one another. Its editor, Johannes Vincentius Metulinus, who had a high opinion of its merits, introduces it as follows:—

> Hic liber Ebrardi Celebris : doctique magistri
> Græcismus fons est : arida corda fovens.
> Cujus in irriguo tu margine sisteris : a quo
> Sumere grammatices plura fluenta potes.[5]

Here is a sample of the draughts of grammar that he who stands on the brink may quaff. In chap. i., *De figuris*, we are informed that:

> Sincopa de medio tollit quod epenthesis auget :
> Aufert apocope finem quem dat paracope.

Pages of this stuff had to be learned by the unfortunate scholar, nor was his case much better when he came to the grammar proper. In chap. xvi., under the heading *De verbis secundæ conjugationis*, he was given the following information :—

> Hortibus insideo : pius medicus assidet egro ; (sic)
> Subsidet his caro : presidet ille solo.
> Obsidet hic muro : considet ille loco,

---

[1] 'La vie privée d'autrefois ; Écoles et Collèges, par Alfred Franklin,' p. 153.

[2] 'Prælegebatur Ebrardus et Joannes de Garlandia. Vita Erasmi. Erasmo auctore.'

[3] 'Les colloques scolaires du seizième siècle.' Massebieau, p. 21.

[4] 'Libri Ebrardi Greciste.' (Adv. Lib. Edin. No date or place.) Massebieau quotes an edition of 1487. [5] Preface ad init.

and so forth.   The so-called grammar is little more than a vocabulary, in which the words are strung into rude verses illustrating their usage.

The other bugbear of Erasmus' childhood was John de Garlande.   Garlande was the author of a *Compendium Grammaticæ* and of an epic poem entitled *De Triumphis Ecclesiæ.*   The latter may well have been among the works that the student was expected to read, as its subject-matter would have removed any prejudice to which its monkish eccentricities might have given rise.[1]   The main object of learning Latin was to read Ambrose and Hilary.   As late as 1523 we find Vives recommending the poems of Prudentius, Sydonius, Paulinus, Arator, Prosper, and Juvencus, as being · equal to the classics in style and infinitely superior in matter.[2]

The Reformation may have been prejudicial to the advancement of Humanism at the higher seats of learning, but to schools it was the breath of life.   Though a few sensibly-managed institutions were to be found, such as the Collège de Guyenne at Bordeaux, these were great exceptions.   In the schools attached to the monasteries prejudiced monks would have little to say to the new learning, looked on it with suspicion, and deemed it safer to abide by Ebrard and the Doctrinal.

But a more energetic man than Erasmus was to turn upon them and tear their pedantry into shreds.   Martin Luther had been subjected to the mill of scholasticism, and grammar-lessons, flogged in with the customary vigour, had left an iron impression on his soul.   "Instead of sound books," he cries in 1524, "the insane, useless, harmful, monkish books, the Catholicon,[3] the Florista, the Græcista,

[1] It contains "retrogradi Versus," such as :—

> Parisiis proba non pugnat gens parcere clero
> Provida, non curat perfidiam sua lex.
> Lex sua perfidiam curat, non provida clero
> Parcere, gens pugnat non proba Parisiis.

Wright's Ed. p. 41.

[2] 'Jo. Lodovici Vivis Valentini Opera, in duos distincta tomos.   Basileæ, 1555,' i. p. 7.

[3] 'A Grammar and Vocabulary,' by John Balbi, printed by Gutenberg in 1460.

the Labyrinth, the Dormi secure, and such-like stable-refuse
have been introduced by the devil, so that the Latin
tongue has decayed, and in no place is any good school or
instruction or method of study left." [1]

With his wide-minded contempt for petty details he
would have wished to abolish the formal study of grammar
altogether. The books to be used are "the poets and
orators, be they Christian or heathen, Greek or Latin.
From these the grammar must be learned." [2] Now, while
it is certainly a grievous error to sacrifice the whole morning of youth to the study of grammar, it is also evident
that to neglect it altogether could only lead to a slipshod
habit of mind in later years. A corrective for Luther's complete carelessness of academic accuracy was at hand in
Philip Melanchthon, the grammarian of the Reformation
in Germany, whose Latin Grammar appeared in 1525.[3]
Melanchthon, while attaching the utmost importance to
grammar, was fully aware how necessary it was to make
rules as short and concise as possible. Other Grammars,
he tells us, existed, but most of them were neglected on
account of their length, and he had therefore written his
to supply the practical wants of the age.

In truth the Grammar of 1525 is many centuries in
advance of the shibboleth that Erasmus learned at Deventer.
Apart from its intrinsic merit, Melanchthon's name on the
title-page would have secured its widespread use in Protestant schools. It underwent many editions, notably that by
Jacob Micyllus, and was still in use at the beginning of the
eighteenth century. Worthy of notice is the relative importance given to the rules for gender (these take up thirty-
three pages), and the introduction of words like *Halec, Huber,
Lafer,* and *Meninx ;* but the main interest of the work lies
in its preface, which embodies Melanchthon's views on the
study of grammar. "Of what importance it is to Christ's

---

[1] 'An die Rathsherren aller Städte deutschen Landes, dass sie christliche
Schulen aufrichten und halten sollen.'
[2] *Ibid.*
[3] I quote from the Paris edition of 1643.

Church," he says, "that boys be rightly instructed in grammar ! . . . How many grievous errors I might relate that have wrought great havoc in the Church, and that have arisen solely from ignorance of grammar ! " More than this, grammar is made an indispensable preliminary to knowledge of any kind. "A defective grounding in grammar leads to a most impudent misuse of other studies." [1]

Melanchthon was not without competitors. We find Vives [2] (1523) recommending Catherine of Aragon to get Thomas Linacre's Grammar for her daughter Mary ; and elsewhere [3] he says that any one may be selected from among those of Perottus, Aldus, Nebrissensis, Mancinella, Sulpitus, Melanchthon, and Ninivita. The Grammar of the last mentioned, who is better known as Despauter, [4] was for a long time in vogue, both in France and in Germany. An abridged edition was brought out by Sebastian of Duisburg in 1534, and was used in Scotland as late as 1637. [5] It is greatly inferior to Melanchthon's Grammar, and burdens the mind of the student with an inordinate quantity of mnemonic verses. [6] It is surprising to what an extent the notion prevailed that grammar should be made as complex as possible. Few scholars would care to name off-hand the seven genders in Latin, yet this was the number commonly

---

[1] Qui non recte Grammaticen didicerunt, postea cæteras disciplinas audacissime corrumpunt.

[2] *Opera*, vol. i. p. 5. Buchanan also recommended Linacre's Grammar, and brought out a Latin translation of it, printed at Paris in 1533.

[3] *Ibid.* p. 10.

[4] His full name was Joannes Despauterius Ninivita. He flourished in Holland, 1460-1520.

[5] I have before me a copy entitled, ' Joan. Despauterii Ninivitæ, Grammaticæ Institutiones, Lib. vii. Docte et concinne in compendium redacti, per Sebastianum Duisburgensem, multo quam antea castigatiores. Edinburgi. Sumptibus Hæredum Andreæ Hart. Julii 25. Anno 1637.'

[6] The following are good examples, taken from the rules for the 3rd declension :—

> Tertia dat varios fines, dans is genitivo,
> Græcorum patrius vel in os, vel in i vel in us fit.

or

> Em dat et im buris, pelvis cum clave securis
> Et puppis, turris, restis : sic febris, æqualis,
> Sic pestis, navis, tor quis conjunge bipennim.

given in sixteenth-century works. Even in 1633 a Scotch Grammar [1] tells us that "the genders are seven in number: masculine, feminine, neuter, common of two, common of three, promiscuous, and doubtful." At this rate, why stop at seven? It is surprising that the writer did not bring their number up to twenty-one and work them into a mnemonic verse. For the beginner seven genders must have been a more crushing burden than the *As in præsenti* that caused such agony to our grandfathers.

The set of metrical rules beginning with this locution, as well as the *Propria quæ maribus*, were by Lily, one of the first masters at St. Paul's School and afterwards high-master of Wolsey's school at Ipswich, and are often found affixed to his *Brevissima Institutio*, the most popular Grammar ever written and the basis of the Eton Latin Grammar published in 1826.

Lily's work appeared in many forms. The edition of 1577 [2] is in English with a Latin appendix, and is prefaced by an injunction of Elizabeth "Not to teach your youth and scholers with any other Grammar than with this English introduction hereafter ensuing, and the Latine Grammar affixed to the same." The use of the *Brevissima Institutio* was confined to England, but Lily's Syntax met with considerable success on the continent. An edition [3] was brought out by Erasmus at Strasburg in 1515, and was afterwards reprinted at Basle, Paris, Antwerp, and Cologne.

We cannot leave Lily without giving some account of his rules *Ad discipulos de moribus*. These survey the whole field of school morality in elegiac verse.

[1] 'Rudimenta Grammatices in Gratiam juventutis Scotiæ conscripta. Edinburgi. Excudebat Joannes Wrentoun. 1633.'
Quid adfers de genere? Genera sunt numero septem: Masculinum, Fœmininum, Neutrum, Commune duum, Commune trium, Promiscuum, et Dubium.

[2] 'A short introduction of Grammar generally to be used, compyled and set forth for the bringing up of all those that intend to attayne the knowledge of the Latin tongue.' London, 1577.

[3] 'Absolutissimus de octo Orationis partium constructione libellus, nuperrime recognitus. Argentorati, 1515.'

Scalpellum, calami, atramentum, charta, libelli,
Sint semper studiis, arma parata tuis.
At tamen inprimis facies sit lota manusque
Sint nitidæ vestes, comptaque cæsaries.

With Lily, as with the continental educationists, a colloquial knowledge of Latin was highly prized—

Et quoties loqueris, memor esto loquare Latine
Et scopulos veluti barbara verba fuge.

For the boy who prompts in class a terrible punishment is threatened—

Nec verbum quisquam dicturo suggerat ullum
Quod puero exitium non mediocre parit.[1]

Comenius' complaint that the beginner in Latin was compelled to learn the unknown through the medium of the unknown, does not apply with very much force to England.   As early as 1495 we find a black-letter treatise, *Pervula*[2] by name, giving the rules of syntax in English. Nothing could be simpler or more explicit than the proposition with which it starts.   "What shalt thou doo when thou hast an englyssh to be made in latyne?   I shall reherse myn englysshe fyrst ones, twyes, or thryes, and loke out my princypal verbe and aske hym this question, who or what.   And that worde that answeryth to the questyon shall be the nominatyf case to the verbe."

In English is also the curious Grammar and Syntax by M. Holt, entitled *Lac Puerorum.*[3]   On the subject of gender Holt exercises a rare restraint and only inflicts one page on the learner; but his pent-up passion for analysis bursts forth when he comes to the moods, and he introduces us to "the shewynge mode," the "biddynge mode," "the askynge mode," "the wysshynge mode,"

[1] Appendix to Wolsey's *Rudimenta Grammatices*, 1529.
[2] 'Pervula.   Printed at Westmynstre in Caxton's house by Wynkyn de Worde.'
[3] 'Lac Puerorum.   M. Holti.   Mylke for children.   1510.   Emprynted at London by Wynkyn de Worde in Flete Strete in the sygne of the sonne.'

"the potencyal mode," and the "subjunctyf mode." A heavy burden for the boy who cannot yet conjugate *Amo*.

That it is in English and, from the book-fancier's point of view, its rarity claim notice for Linacre's Grammar,[1] but otherwise this work is not superior to other Grammars of the age. In company with those previously mentioned it is scarcely worthy of remark by the side of the Grammar [2] written by Cardinal Wolsey for his school at Ipswich. An almost touching simplicity breathes through the pages of his little volume, showing the great Cardinal in a most pleasing light as the sympathiser with blundering boyhood. In the preface he confesses that Grammars exist in abundance, but he considers them unsuitable for beginners, for whose need he therefore takes it upon himself to cater. "In which lytel boke I have left many thynges out of purpose, consydering ye tendernes and smal capacite of lytell mynds." He then proceeds to state the rudiments of grammar in the simplest way imaginable. *Musa* is declined in full, and the conjugations of the regular verbs are given at length. The inevitable "seven genders" make their appearance, it is true, but no time is wasted over them. This Grammar does not appear to have been as popular as its contemporaries, still it is quite the best written for beginners before the Vestibular Grammar of Comenius.

In Scotland, Latin appears to have been the medium through which the rudiments were learned, though vernacular grammars were not unknown. In 1528 John Vaus, master of the Grammar School at Aberdeen, published a Grammar [3] a large part of which is in Scotch ; and there is in existence

[1] 'Linacri Progymnasmata grammatices vulgaria. Emprynted in London on the sowth syde of paulys by John Rastell, with the privylege of our most suverayn lord Kyng Henry the VIII. graunted to the compyler thereof.'

[2] 'Rudimenta grammatices et docendi methodus, non tam scholæ Gypsuichianæ per reverendissimum Thomam Cardinalem Eborem feliciter institutæ quam omnibus aliis totius Angliæ scholis præscripta. Peter Treveri. 1529.'

[3] 'Rudimenta puerorum in artem grammaticam per Joannem Vaus Scotum.' Paris, 1528.

a fragment of a Donatus written in Scotch, which has been hypothetically placed as early as 1508.[1]

Of mathematics and science, the subjects that form the backbone of a "modern side" curriculum, only the first was in a sufficiently advanced state to be even given consideration as a subject of school instruction, and it is improbable that boys were taught more than the barest elements. Indeed there appears to have been a considerable amount of prejudice against mathematics as a means towards general culture. "Mark all mathematical heads, which be only and wholely bent to those sciences," writes Ascham in the *Scholemaster*, "how solitary they be themselves, how unfit to live with others, and how unable to serve in the world." Many educationists, however, were not of this opinion, and efforts were made by the more far-seeing among them to render the study of numbers more accessible to the beginner. In 1522 Cuthbert Tonstall, afterwards Bishop of London, published his Arithmetic *De arte supputandi*. Written for boys (Tonstall suggests that it may be of use to Sir Thomas More's sons), it is very practical, and well suited for school use,[2] and was far ahead of anything else that had been written on the subject. Sturm thought so highly of it that he brought out a reprint at Strasburg in 1544,[3] and in his preface assured the public that the book was the best in the market, and that any student who mastered it would know all that was to be known on the subject.[4]

It must be confessed that in the sixteenth century the advocates of arithmetic as a study laid more stress on its

---

[1] 'Notes on a leaf of an early Scottish Donatus, printed in Black Letter. By E. Gordon Duff, Edinburgh Bibliographical Society. Session 1892-93.'

[2] It contains a large number of exercises on the various rules given. De Morgan says of it: "For plain common-sense well expressed, Tonstall's book has never been surpassed in the subject of which it treats."—*Arithmetical Books*, p. 13.

[3] 'De arte supputandi, Libri quattuor, hactenus in Germania nusquam ita impressi. Argentorati, 1544.'

[4] Nec abest longe a perfectione, qui ejus præcepta intelligit.—Sturm's preface.

practical and commercial worth than on its value as a factor in the expansion of the mental powers. Cardinal Sadoleto, writing in 1549, points out the necessity of adding arithmetic to the school curriculum, but only because without its aid we cannot tell how many fingers we have or with how many eyes we see.[1]

On this position a great advance is made by Robert Recorde, who published his Arithmetic in 1561 under the title *The Grounde of Artes.* According to Recorde the great claim of arithmetic is that it exercises the mind purely, apart from lines as in geometry and from spheres and axes as in astrology.[2] The capacity for mathematics is the special prerogative of man. "Whoso setteth small price by the witty device and knowledge of numbring, he little considereth it to be the chief point (in manner) whereby men differ from all brute beasts; for as in all other things (almost) beasts are partakers with us, so in numbring we differ cleane from them and in manner peculiarly, sith that in many things they excell us againe." It must not be imagined from this quotation that the *Grounde of Artes* is of a philosophical nature. It is a very practical arithmetic, and is of special interest as being written in English. In his work on algebra also, *The Whetstone of Witte,* published in 1557, Recorde discards Latin in favour of the vernacular.

In France a staunch upholder of mathematics was that many-sided man of learning, Peter Ramus. Himself the author of an Arithmetic,[3] he was at some pains to ascertain the modes of instruction most approved of in other countries. In a letter to John Dee, dated 1565, he begs him to say what old mathematical books he has in his library, who are the teachers of mathematics in English

---

[1] Cujus usus ita necesse est ut videamur absque ea ne quot digitos quidem habeamus in manibus, aut quot oculis intueamur scire posse.— 'De Liberis recte instituendis Liber. Jacobi Sadoleti Opera. Moguntiæ, 1607,' p. 547.

[2] Preface to *The Grounde of Artes.*

[3] 'Petri Rami Arithmetices Libri duo, et Algebræ totidem.' De Morgan says this was published in 1584.

grammar schools, and what method they follow.[1]   In
Germany, at a rather later date, the Arithmetic [2] of Christopher Clavius, a Jesuit priest, went through many editions,
though it is difficult to say if it was used outside the Jesuit
schools.   It is worth noting that Alsted, Comenius' teacher
at Herborn, wrote several works on mathematics,[3] though
these were for more advanced scholars.

The question now arises, "By what method or system
of teaching were these books backed up?   What pains
were taken to ascertain the difficulties of the individual
school-boy and remove them by timely explanation?"

The answer is as simple as it is unsatisfactory.   In
every difficulty or dilemma the one resource of the schoolmaster was the stick.   Between recalcitrant school-boys
and ignorant teachers the friction was great, and the
sturdy use of the cane proved the readiest way to disperse
the evil humours of the master.   Witness the complaint
of Ascham: "The scholar is commonly beat for the
making, when the master were more worthy to be beat for
the mending or rather marring of the same: the master
being many times as ignorant as the child what to say to
the matter."[4]   In France the same complaint was made.
"Those daily and severe floggings," wrote Maturin Cordier,
"deter simple-minded youths from the study of letters to
such an extent that they hate school worse than a dog
or a snake."[5]   From time to time protests were raised
against this process of brutalising children ; but the general
tendency of the age was to believe that a little physical

[1] 'Petri Rami Professoris Regii, Præfationes, etc.   Parisiis, 1577.
P. 204.   Petrus Ramus, Joan. Dio Londinensi.'   "Itaque gemino pig-
nore amoris erga me tui obligatus mihi videbor, si hoc utrumque abs te
impetravero, et qui sunt e veteribus in bibliotheca tua scriptores mathe-
matici, et quinam in vestris gymnasiis, quaque authoritate mathematicas
artes profiteantur."
[2] 'Christopheri Clavii Bambergensis e Societate Jesu, Epitome Arith-
meticæ practicæ,' 1st ed. 1583 (the edition before me is of 1607).
[3] 'Methodus admirandorum Mathematicorum, novem libris exhibens
universam Mathesin.'   Herborn, 1641.   (De Morgan.)
[4] Ascham, *Scholemaster.*
[5] ' De corrupti sermonis emendatione.'   Paris, 1530.   Preface.

pain, judiciously applied, was worth much persuasion of a gentler kind. Instructive in this connection is the conversation between Sir William Cecil and his friends reported by Ascham in the preface to his *Scholemaster.* "I have strange news brought me this evening," says Cecil, "that certain scholars of Eton be run away from the school for fear of beating." To this Mr. Peter replied that "the rod only was the sword that must keep the school in obedience and the scholars in good order"; while Mr. Haddon went so far as to say that the best schoolmaster of their time (Nicholas Udall) was the greatest beater. Small wonder that the boys left the Grammar School "great lubbers, always learning and little profiting!"[1]

Machyn, writing in 1563, quotes a typical case of brutality: "A schoolmaster that had a child to lerne, and for a small fault did bett him so severely with a leden gyrdyll with buckles that he left no skyne on his body." Even for the sixteenth century this seems to have passed the limits of legitimate severity, as we read that "thys master was sett on the pelere and wyped that his blude ran downe."[2] A curious way this of maintaining the doctrine that corporal punishment should be sparingly administered.

The extensive use of Latin as a medium for imparting knowledge was frequently brought forward by reformers, and in particular by Comenius, as the reason why beginners made such slow progress. To a certain extent they were undoubtedly right. Many Grammars and Arithmetics were written in Latin, and though constant exercise in that language may have been of use to the more advanced student, the combination of a new tongue and a new subject must have had a disastrous effect on younger boys whose knowledge of Latin was limited.

It would, however, be an error to lay too much stress on this point, as there is evidence that side by side with the enthronement of Latin there was a strong under-

---

[1] *Scholemaster*, Bk. ii.   [2] *Machyn's Diary*, 1563.

current of feeling in favour of the vernaculars. In England the use of the English language in learned works found a strong upholder in Peter Levins.[1] In the Preface to his *Pathway to Health* (1587) he avers that those who think that such books should be written in an unknown tongue, and thus hide the knowledge of health from the people, are guilty of "malice exceeding damnable and devillish." Some years previously (1570) Levins had brought out an English-Latin dictionary with the title *Manipulus Vocabulorum.* "This," he tells us in his Preface, "I brought out for conscience sake, thinking that when I have bene long conversant with the schooles and have from tyme to tyme lamented to see the youth of our country (in the studies of the Latin tong) lacke such little instruments as this fit and needful for their exercises, and saw no man set his hand to the same, I was bound for the portion of my small talent to do somewhat therein." [2]

If Levins thought that his was the first English-Latin dictionary he was mistaken, as nearly 100 years before (1499) Pynson had printed the *Promptuorium parvulorum sive clericorum.*[3] But the English used in this lexicon was the Norfolk dialect, and the work was more suitable for older students than for boys.

To the Latin grammars written in English reference

---

[1] According to Anthony à Wood, Levins taught a Grammar School.

[2] A quotation from this dictionary may be of interest. It is arranged, not alphabetically, but in accordance with the termination of the words, forming in fact a kind of rhyming dictionary ; *e.g.*

Coste	Sumptus -us
The frost	Gelu -us ; hoc Frigus
A ghoste	Spiritus -us. Larva
An hoste of men	Exercitus
An hoste	Hospes, hospitis, etc.

[3] 'Promptuorium parvulorum sive clericorum. Auctore fratre Galfrido Grammatico dicto. 1440.' A short extract will indicate its nature :—

Byryele	Sepulchrum, tumulus
Byrthe	Nativitus, partus
Byschelle	Modius, chorus, busellus
Bysshope	Episcopus, antistes, pontifex, presul

has already been made, and as regards arithmetic, Tonstall tells us that there was scarcely a nation that did not possess a vernacular treatise on that subject.[1] If further proof is necessary that Latin had never become so fashionable in England as on the continent it can be found in the *Governour* of Sir Thomas Elyot, and in Ascham's *Scholemaster.* Ascham seems to have been apprehensive that scholars on the continent might think an English setting somewhat undignified for so academic a theme as Education, and in a letter to Sturm at Strasburg he instances the uncultured condition of England as his excuse. He was writing "for Englishmen and not for foreigners," [2] and wished to be understood. In France, where the Latin of the Renaissance had taken a far stronger hold, Montaigne had advanced precisely the same reason for writing his essays in French. He was addressing a French and not a European audience. Rabelais had chosen the language that they despised as an instrument for the abuse of pedants and scholastics. In the Collége de France, founded in 1529, Francis I. had ordained that the lectures should be given in French and not in Latin. Peter Ramus (Pierre de la Ramée) Latinised his name and wrote in Latin, but this did not prevent him from bringing out a French Grammar in 1562.[3] A cursory glance at the list of their publications would not lead us to suppose that Robert and Henry Estienne give much thought to their native language. Yet Robert Estienne published his *Traicté de la Grammaire Française* in 1569, and his son Henry gives us to understand that French was already ousting all other languages as a refined medium of expression. "It is proverbial," he tells us, "that the Italians bleat, the Spaniards groan, the Germans howl, and the

---

[1] Nulla pene natio est quæ non eam artem vulgi lingua scriptam habeat.—*De arte supputandi*, Preface.

[2] Et quia meus hic Præceptor non e Græcia, non ex Italia accersitus est, sed in hac barbara insula natus, et domi intra parietes meos altus est, propterea barbare hoc est Anglice loquitur. . . . Nostris non alienis, Anglis non exteris scribo.—Letter to Sturm.

[3] Published by André Weckel at Paris.

French sing." [1]   In 1549 Joachim de Bellay had written
his spirited *Défense et illustration de la langue Française*, in
which he is at pains to prove "que la langue Françoise
n'est pas si pauvre que beaucoup l'estiment." [2]   In his
intense desire that his countrymen shall write in French
he advances the somewhat paradoxical argument that, in
view of the present "literary competition," French writings
have the best chance of surviving.   "Vrai est que le nom
de cesluy cy (*i.e.* the author who writes in Latin) s'estend
en plus de lieux ; mais bien souvent comme la fumée qui
sort grosse au commencement, peu à peu s'esvanouit
parmy le grand espace de l'air, il se perd ou pour estre
opprimé de l'infinie multitude des autres plus renommez, il
demeure quasi en silence et obscurité." [3]

These objections to the encroachments of the Latin
tongue were largely due to a patriotic desire to dethrone a
language whose tendency was to usurp for itself all the
high places in literature.   Another argument on the same
side, the plea of lack of time, had already begun to make
itself heard.   Merchants wanted to give their sons a good
education, but, as they needed their assistance at an early
age, grudged the inordinate length of time that had to be
spent before good scholarship could be attained.   "My
father wished to see my learned education completed in
one year," says the school-boy in Cordier's *Colloquies*, when
told what a long business it is to learn Latin colloquially. [4]

In Germany the vernacular was more backward in assert-
ing itself.   Luther's sermons and hymns were a powerful
factor in the development of German style, but the troubled
state of the country during the following century hindered
any progress towards the refinement of the language.   The
foundation of the Fruchtbringende Gesellschaft, a kind of
"academy" organised at Weimar in 1617 by Ludwig,

[1] Projet du livre intitulé ' De la precellence du langage Français.'   Par
Henri Estienne.   Paris, 1579.   Preface.   "Balant Itali, gemunt Hispani,
ululant Germani, cantant Galli."
[2] Pt. i. ch. 4.
[3] Pt. ii. ch. 12.
[4] Cordier, *Colloquies*, iii. 31.

Prince of Anhalt-Köthen, marks the first effort to purify the German tongue and set it on a firm basis.

It must be confessed that the earlier humanists had not so much wished to impede the use of the vernaculars in Europe, as to add another language to those already in "vogue." "Just as a gem set in a gold ring ornaments it rather than disfigures it," wrote Laurentius Valla in 1450, "so our language (Latin), if added to the vernaculars of other nations, increases rather than diminishes their lustre."[1] Latin, though essentially a scholar's tongue, was not to be treated as a classic language, but was to be placed on exactly the same footing as the vernaculars. To write like Cicero was not sufficient, the accomplished man of letters was also expected to talk like the characters of Terence and Plautus. If the Latin vocabulary of the golden age proved unequal to the heavier demands of sixteenth-century life, it had to be stretched and supplemented by Greek words. Above all, fluency was the great desideratum. In addition to the accuracy that he acquired by a patient study of grammar, of the moods and of the figures, a school-boy had to learn to chatter in Latin without any hesitation and with as much correctness of expression as could be obtained. Some idea of the task thus imposed on teachers may be realised by those who have experienced the difficulty of imparting a colloquial knowledge of French or German through the medium of class instruction. The humanist schools sought to solve the question by making it obligatory that boys should talk Latin and nothing else during their play-hours as well as in school; but this was very difficult to enforce, and, in spite of the usher with his *tabella delatoria*[2] ready to report the slightest lapse into the mother-tongue, they drifted into the vernacular on every possible occasion. "Our boys," wrote Cordier in 1530, "always chatter French with their companions, or if they

---

[1] Laurentii Vallensis, *Elegantia Linguæ Latinæ*, preface.

[2] Pueri . . . tabellis illis delatoriis ad Latinæ linguæ observationem in Gymnasiis adiguntur.—'Commentarius puerorum de quotidiano sermone, qui prius Liber de corrupti sermonis emendatione dicebatur. Maturino Corderio autore. Parisiis, 1541' (1st ed. in 1530). Preface.

try to talk Latin, cannot keep it up for three consecutive words." [1]

It was to remedy this state of things that Cordier compiled, under the title *De corrupti sermonis emendatione*, a French-Latin manual of useful phrases, arranged under a variety of headings. The Latin is not always of the most academic type, but the sentences were doubtless useful to boys whose vocabulary was limited. Thus, in chap. v., under the heading *Beneficiorum, officiorum, et gratificandi*, we find " Tu mas faict ung grand plaisir," "Magno me affecisti beneficio. Vehementer me oblectasti. Pergratum mihi fecisti." Chapter ix., under the heading *Cedendi, concedendi, obsequendi*, gives us a remark that only a very priggish boy could have used—"Je confesse que tu es meilleur grammarien que moy," "Grammaticæ scientiam tibi concedo." More in sympathy with school-boy nature is the joyful announcement, "Le régent nous a rien baillé à estudier," "Præceptor nihil dedit nobis ad studiendum " (chap. xix.) That the most renowned schoolmaster of the sixteenth century should render "Je vouldroye que tu disse cela de bon cœur " by " Ego vellem quod tu istud diceres de bono corde " is startling to those who live in an age when the practice of talking Latin, entailing, as it must, much monkish inaccuracy, has fallen into disuse.

Of more importance than this phrase-book were the Colloquies by various authors, so much used in schools, even as late as the end of the eighteenth century. These represented conversations between school-boys or young students, and were intended to be learned off by heart, and thus to supply the student with a stock of phrases suitable for use in every-day life. Occasionally, indeed, these dialogues outstripped themselves. Those of Erasmus are conversations of great literary and philosophic merit, and are on this account often unsuitable for school-boys. They were, however, extensively used, and, together with the

[1] Nostros autem cum suis condiscipulis aut Gallice semper garrire, aut si Latine loqui tentarent non posse tria verba Latina continuare.— ' Commentarius puerorum,' etc.

dialogues of Vives,[1] were recommended as an extra study in the Pansophic school. This is the only occasion on which Comenius alludes to the Colloquies. It is, indeed, surprising that he makes so little mention of what must have been one of the most important instruments in the process of teaching conversational Latin.

More practical than either of the above-mentioned works were Maturin Cordier's dialogues.[2] Cordier did not publish these till 1564, when he was quite an old man. The choice of words and phrases speaks of a long life spent in intelligent teaching, while the vivid descriptions of the life and conversation of the typical school-boy show that Cordier, kindly and observant, did not confine his interest in his pupils to the hours of class-instruction. The anxious parent or schoolmaster desirous to obtain the best Colloquies possible had indeed a long list to choose from. Sturm, to whom Latin conversation was the most important element in education, published his *Neanisci* in 1570, a set of Dialogues that no longer survives since the burning of the library at Strasburg.[3] Even Mosellanus, Professor of Greek at Leipzig, published a Pedology[4] in 1517, though some persuasion had been necessary before he consented to compose it. "For a long time," he writes in his preface to John Polyander, headmaster of St. Thomas' School, who had asked him to write some colloquies, "I resisted your request, as you know, partly because the importance of my occupations made me disdain this work, doubtless useful, but humble and almost mean in appearance, and partly because, not being used to it, I found it difficult to play the part suitably, since I saw that for this kind of comedy a man must become a child once

---

[1] *Linguæ Latinæ exercitatio.* Pub. in 1539.

[2] 'Colloquiorum scholasticorum libri quattuor ad pueros in sermone Latino paulatim exercendos Maturini Corderii. Lugduni excudebat Thomas de Straton. 1564.'

[3] L. Massebieau, 'Les Colloques Scolaires du seizième Siècle et leurs Auteurs,' p. 61.

[4] 'Pædologia Petri Mosellani Protegensis, jam denuo in puerorum usum diligenter ædita et recognita. Moguntiæ, 1521.' (Mass. p. 81.)

more." [1]   Happily for the Leipzig boys he overcame his contempt for school-book compilation, and has left us a book which, apart from its educational merits at the time, is now invaluable as a record of the student manners and morals of the sixteenth century.

Of a different character are the Colloquies of Schottenius, published in 1535. [2] Schottenius was a private school-master at Cologne, and his dialogues, though written in poor Latin, are more natural than the somewhat stilted phraseology of Mosellanus.   The subject-matter also is different.   Mosellanus treats of the poor student at his wits' end for food and lodging.   The pupils of Schottenius are the sons of rich citizens of Cologne.   They eat and drink, and talk about their food on all occasions, now and then lapsing into expressions of disgust at the spy who carries word to the master that they are not talking Latin, or at the flogging that they know will follow this breach of the rules.

The story of the Colloquies does not end here.   Louvain supplies its quotum in the Dialogues of Barland. [3]   These were partly composed for a gentleman of position who wished to renew his acquaintance with the Latin language, but were doubtless used in schools as well.   Not being written expressly for boys, they deal with scenes out-side school life, and in their pages innkeepers, canons, and merchants figure more largely than pedagogues.

In short, with the exception of England, there is scarcely a country in Europe but made some addition to the library of scholastic conversation.   Even in the newly-conquered Mexico, the Colloquies established themselves as an adjunct of polite learning.   Francis Cervantes Salazar, Professor of Rhetoric in the University of Mexico, published an edition of Vives' *Exercitationes* in 1554, and added to them seven

---

[1] *Pædologia.*   Preface ; quoted by Massebieau, p. 83.

[2] ' Colloquia moralia ex variis philosophorum dictis condita, per quæ stulta juventus sapere possit et eam prosequi prudentiam quam senibus contulit longævitas ' (Mass. p. 116).

[3] ' Dialogi xlii. per Hadrianum Barlandium, ad profligandam e scholis barbariem utilissimi.   Coloniæ apud Eucharium, anno 1530.'   (Mass.)

dialogues of his own composition treating of Mexico and its institutions.[1]

Though Colloquies in the strict sense were lacking, it must not be imagined that the English school-boy of the sixteenth century was without a convenient hand-book of phrases. The Vulgary of Stanbridge [2] gives a list of useful sentences, and these the scholars were doubtless made to learn by heart with a view to using them in their daily conversation :—

Good morowe.	Bonum tibi hujus diei sit primordium.
I was set to schole when I was seven years olde.	Datus eram scholis cum septennis eram.
What part singest thou ?	Qua voce tu cantas ?
It is evyll with us when the master apposeth us.	Male nobiscum est cum præceptor examinat nos.

It is difficult to imagine a boy eulogising one of his "chums" with the remark, "He is born to drink well, both on the faders side and moders side"; but Stanbridge duly provides for the emergency—"Ex utraque parentum parte aptus ad bibendum nascitur." Even for the sententious scholar proverbial expressions are given—

He is an evyl coke that cannot lycke his own lyppes.
Fatuus est coquus qui nescit lambere labra.

Of a more pretentious though less practical nature was the Vulgary of William Horman,[3] headmaster of Eton. Horman cannot be congratulated on the selection of his phrases, which are arranged under thirty-seven heads. "Put not your trust in a bunglar of printer's craft," "Mancipem librariæ officinæ ne sequaris," is not good material for the

---

[1] 'Tres dialogos Latinos que Francisco Cervantes Salazar escribió è imprimió en México en dicho año. Los reimprime, con traducion Castellana y notas, Joaquim Garcia Icazbalceta.' Mexico, 1875. (Mass.)

[2] The copy in the British Museum is bound up with the 'Accidentia ex Stanbrigiana editione, nuper recognita et castigata lima Roberti Whitintoni Lichfeldensis. Wynkyn de Worde. 1528.'

[3] 'Vulgaria viri doctissimi Guil. Hormani Cæsariburgensis. Apud inclytam Londini urbem, 1519.'

daily conversation of a boy, and "Jacent hæc in caliganti vetustatis recessu" is but a clumsy translation of "These matters be out of my mynde."

The foregoing pages give the reader some notion of the books that a good school might have possessed in the century preceding the publication of the *Janua*, and no commentary is necessary on the contrast that they bear to those of Comenius. Grammars are diffuse, complicated, and overburdened with unnecessary matter. Phrase-books are haphazard compilations often ill-suited to the end in view. In every case exclusive attention is paid to form; any actual information about the world in which he lives the scholar may pick up for himself. If he satisfies the spirit of pedantry by mastering the seven genders he is not prevented from using his powers of observation as much as he pleases; but he is not encouraged or helped to do so. The Colloquies, it is true, conveyed some definite information, but they were primarily intended as phrase-books, and between them and the systematised exposition of nature in the *Janua* a very great gulf is fixed.

We should now wish to give a slight sketch, and it must necessarily be a very slight one, of the essays towards the creation and organisation of schools that form the historical background to the life efforts of Comenius. Ours will not be the received method of the comprehensive history of education. Of Rabelais, of Montaigne, of Erasmus, of Vives we shall make no mention. Like Ascham and Locke they dealt with the training of the "young gentleman," and stand in no relation to schemes for the education of the people. For the same reason we shall pass over the great teaching corporation of the Jesuits. In many ways their methods of instruction have never been surpassed. For the organisation of boarding-schools a body of priests starts with a very great advantage, and solves with comparative ease the grave questions of discipline that always confront the directors of such institutions. The usher, who is at the same time an acolyte, gains a degree of dignity to be obtained in no

other way; and in addition to this the priest-usher of one
year developes with ease into the trained teacher of the next.
But though we may grant the Jesuits these and other merits,
we must yet recognise that their mansion stands far away
from the high-road of true educational development.   Leaving out of sight the carefully planned and narrowing one-
sidedness of the training they supplied, we shall only lay
stress on the fact that they excluded the people from any
participation in it.   Among the upper classes the supremacy
of Mother Church was to be promoted by the teacher armed
with the methods of the Jesuit school; among the ranks of
labour by the preacher, whose task was rendered easier by
the prevalence of superstition and the limitation of knowledge.   Very different was the ideal of Comenius.   The
day school open to children of every rank; the large class
managed by a single teacher as the only means by which
such schools were economically possible; the introduction
of every subject of instruction that could free the understanding from sophistic habits and teach men to look
facts squarely in the face—these were the goals towards
which his efforts strove, and his historical antecedents are
bound up with the great democratic movement of which
the Reformation was the most striking manifestation, with
the names of Luther, Sturm, Calvin, and Knox.

The conscience had been installed by the Reformers as
guide, and its counsellor, the understanding, needed education.   Good schools, and nothing else, could remove monkish
ignorance from the land ; and this truth Luther was not slow
to enunciate.   In his stirring letter to the Magistrates
of Germany,[1] he exhorts them to erect and maintain
Christian schools.   " Is it not evident," he cries, "that it
is now possible to educate a boy in three years so that
when he is fifteen or eighteen years old he shall know
more than the whole sum of knowledge of the high
schools and monasteries up to this time ?   Hitherto, in
the high schools, and monasteries, men have only learned to

[1] 'An die Rathsherren aller Städte deutschen Landes, dasz sie christliche Schulen aufrichten und halten sollen,' 1524.

be asses, blocks, and stones. They have studied for twenty and forty years and have learned neither Latin nor German." [1]

Schools must therefore be established for boys and girls, and these must be managed, not by the Church, but by the civil powers. As for the subjects taught, "Had I children," says Luther, "I should make them learn not only languages and history, but also singing, music, and mathematics." To the poor who objected that they needed the services of their children at home and could not afford to bring them up as gentlemen, he answers: "Let them go to school for one or two hours daily, and spend the rest of their time in learning a trade. These few hours they can easily spare; indeed, as it is, they waste far more time in playing at ball." If parents refuse to send their children to school they must be made to do so; "I am of opinion that those in authority should compel their subjects to send their children to school." [2]

Luther did but formulate the charter of national education; its accomplishment he left to other hands, and it must be confessed that the schoolmasters of the Reformation carried out his recommendations in a very half-hearted way. In the then state of Europe, an approximation to the national school could scarcely have been expected, and we accordingly find that the leading reformed schools are of the "Grammar School" type, and intended for the middle class. It is their programme of instruction that is so disappointing. A glance at the curriculum proposed by Sturm at Strasburg in 1539 will show that to read and speak Latin still remained the chief objects. It is not until a boy is sixteen and in the highest class that he commences such useful subjects as arithmetic, history, and geography.

While according to Sturm the object of instruction is

[1] 'An die Rathsherren aller Städte deutschen Landes, dasz sie christliche Schulen aufrichten und halten sollen,' 1524.

[2] 'Ein Sermon oder Predigt, dasz man solle Kinder zur Schule halten'— "Ich halt aber, dasz auch die Obrigkeit hie schuldig sei, die Unterthanen zu zwingen, ihre Kinder zur Schule zu halten."

to instil learning and piety, it is evident that learning is of little use unless we can express it fitly. Therefore, in their early youth children should be taught to speak well.[1] Of the teachers no more is specified than that they should excel other men in learning and piety.[2] Some corporal punishment is necessary, but masters who take actual pleasure in flogging must be removed from their office.[3] Not all boys should be sent to school, but only those who are naturally fitted for the study of letters.[4] A certain number of poor children should be educated, but these must be of exceptional ability, and are to be excluded from the school at once if they give any trouble.[5] In each town there should be one school.[6] In large cities such as Paris more are naturally required; but if possible the educational needs of a town should be met by one Gymnasium of the liberal arts.

This Gymnasium should be divided into nine classes, in each of which the boy remains one year. In this manner, if he goes to school in his sixth year, he will be able to proceed to a university course of five years at the age of sixteen.[7] The removes from one class to another shall take place in October, and shall be made the occasion for an imposing ceremony at which the magistrates, clergymen, parents of boys and their friends should be present, and when prizes should be given to the first two boys in each class.[8]

Sturm then proceeds to give a detailed programme for each class, commencing with the ninth or lowest.

In this class reading and writing are taught. Care must be taken that the pupils learn to form their letters as neatly as possible, and particular attention must be given to reading aloud. Boys must be shown how to moderate their voices and how to speak distinctly. If any time is

---

[1] 'De Literarum Ludis recte aperiendis Liber Joannis Sturmii, emendatus et auctus ab ipso Auctore. Argentorati, 1557' (1st ed. 1538), p. 4.

[2] *Ibid.* p. 5.

[3] Amovendi a literariis ludis sunt quicunque ex verberibus voluptatem capiunt. [4] *Ibid.* p. 9. [5] *Ibid.* p. 12.

[6] *Ibid.* p. 14. [7] *Ibid.* p. 16. [8] *Ibid.* p. 18.

left after these points have been mastered a few of the
easiest of Cicero's letters may be read.[1]

In the eighth class the study of grammar is to be
attacked; but no exceptions should be learned, and not more
than two hours daily should be devoted to the elements.
The rest of the day may be employed in reading Virgil's
Eclogues and Cicero's Letters.[2]   In the seventh class the
pupil may advance to grammar of a more advanced kind,
and to syntax. One hour daily is enough for this. Another
may be devoted to reading Cicero's *De Amicitia* and *De
Senectute*.   During the third hour the poets, such as Virgil,
Catullus, Tibullus, and Horace, the latter only in selections,
may be read. The fourth hour can be employed in exercises
of style.[3]

In these three classes the memory is the chief thing to
be exercised.   Neither boys nor masters should work less
than four or more than five hours daily in school.[4]   The
boy who now enters the sixth class is nine or ten years old
and has mastered the rudiments of Latin.   Cæsar's Commentaries, Plautus, Terence, and Sallust may be added to
the authors already in hand.   One hour daily to be given
to style and composition.[5]

In the next class Greek is commenced.   After a
few months' preliminary grammar Aesop's Fables and the
Olynthiac Orations of Demosthenes may be attempted.[6]

The fourth class adds Homer to the list, and introduces
the pupil to the study of rhetoric.[7]

In the third class dialectic may be commenced, and
should be studied in Aristotle.   Cicero's Topics and Livy
are also recommended.[8]

In the second class the Dialogues of Plato and of Cicero
may be read.   The pupil has now got beyond the stage
when he should spend time in learning rules.   What he
needs is practice.[9]

---

[1] 'De Literarum Ludis recte aperiendis Libe Joannis Sturmii,' etc.,
p. 19.

[2] *Ibid.* p. 20.   [3] *Ibid.* p. 20.   [4] *Ibid.* p. 22.

[5] *Ibid.* p. 23.   [6] *Ibid.* p. 25.   [7] *Ibid.* p. 26.

[8] *Ibid.* p. 30.   [9] *Ibid.* p. 31.

The boy is now fifteen years old, and enters the first class. Here he reads Aristotle's *De Interpretatione*, and should learn some arithmetic, geography, history, and the elements of astrology. In the classics he should continue to read Demosthenes, Homer, and Cicero.[2]

Religious instruction is to be left for Saints' days and Church festivals. Before a boy leaves the school he should be well acquainted with the history of Christ and the Apostles, and with the most important events in the Old Testament. In the first class the Catechism, and in the first two the elements of Hebrew grammar should be taught. The afternoon of the last day in each week should be devoted to music, since this is an essential part of a liberal education.[2]

Such was Sturm's scheme, the model for most of the post-Reformation schools on the continent. Humanist to the back-bone he yet sees the need of real studies, of mathematics, of history, of music. But it is not for these that the school exists. Latin, either written or spoken, is the dish served up for each form. The tardy recommendation of " modern subjects " for the first class, barely saves Sturm from falling into the category of " gerund-grinders."

Of equal celebrity with Sturm's establishment, though even less " modern," was the Latin school reorganised by Calvin at Geneva in 1559. Calvin took the Strasburg school as his model, and the differences to be found in the copy are typical of the man. Great stress is laid on discipline. The boys are to be conducted home from their classes by the masters of the four lowest forms.[3] Each lesson, no matter what the subject be, must commence with prayer,[4] and at every turn we are confronted with the

---

[1] ' De Literarum Ludis recte aperiendis Liber Joannis Sturmii, etc., p. 32.

[2] *Ibid.* p. 34.

[3] ' L'Ordre des Escholes de Genève reveu et augmenté par ordonnance de nos très honnorez Seigneurs, Syndiques, et Conseil, l'an 1576,' sec. 17.

[4] *Ibid.* sec. 16.

order to repeat " L'Oraison Dominicale, la Confession de
Foy qu'on appelle le Symbole et puis les dix commande-
mens de la Loy." All the boys must learn how to sing,
and a master especially appointed for the purpose must
teach them how to intone the Psalms.[1]

In the general organisation of the institution, we find
one remarkable piece of common-sense. The Principal
(who is controlled by the Rector of the University) is not to
be the stern and academic personage generally connected
with the term "headmaster." "Que le principal, estant
de moyen scavoir pour le moins, soit surtout d'un esprit
debonnaire et non point de complexion rude ni apre ; afin
qu'il donne bon exemple aux enfants en toute sa vie, et
aussi qu'il puisse porter tant plus doucement le travail de
sa charge." [2] With its "debonnaire" headmaster and with
Maturin Cordier, grown grey in the service of the young,
to expound his Colloquies in person, the Genevan
school must have been imbued with a genial spirit rare
indeed in this age of pretentious grammarians and flogging
pedagogues.

In the lowest of the eight classes, into which the school
was divided, the boys learned their A B C. In the seventh,
they read Latin and conjugate and decline "selon la formation qui en est dressée"; the sixth is chiefly devoted to
Latin grammar, of a more advanced kind.

The fifth class brings the boys on to the rudiments of
syntax and the Bucolics of Virgil. In the fourth, Cicero's
letters and some Ovid may be read, but the special task
is the elements of Greek. In the next class Greek
grammar is continued, and the Æneid and Cæsar's Commentaries are read.

On reading that in the second class the pupils, who
have only recently commenced Greek, are to study Xeno-
phon, Polybius, Homer, and Hesiod, one is inclined to
wonder if this scheme could ever have been actually enforced. At the same time dialectic, rhetoric, and syllo-

---

[1] 'L'Ordre des Escholes de Genève,' etc., sec. 18.
[2] *Ibid.* sec. 7.

gisms are commenced, and St. Luke's Gospel is read in Greek.

The list of subjects for the first class comprises the Categories, the Topics, and the Elenchi, as well as Cicero and Demosthenes.

We have thus the programme of an eight-class school dealing with nothing but grammar and the classics, relieved by prayers and psalm-singing. Luther's mathematics and history have disappeared altogether.

In England the history of the Reformed Church is not bound up with educational progress to the same extent. Edward VI., it is true, founded a number of Grammar Schools, but with the exception of the regulations for the Cathedral Schools drawn up by Cranmer in his *Reformatio legum Ecclesiasticarum*,[1] we meet with no very definite scheme for school organisation. Nor is the section in the *Reformatio*, "Of the schools to be attached to the Cathedrals," of very great value to the historian of Education. No division of classes is given, and the whole plan is sketchy in comparison with those of Sturm, Calvin, and Buchanan.

A school is to be attached to each Cathedral, that boys who have learned the rudiments from a private tutor may be able to obtain instruction in public classes.[2] These schools are primarily ecclesiastical in character, and exist "that the knowledge of God's word may be maintained in the Church ; which is scarcely possible without a knowledge of languages."[3]

The master is to be chosen by the Bishop, and must be a sincere believer in the Evangelic doctrine, of good character, learned in grammar and humane letters, and sufficiently strong to stand the strain of teaching. The school shall be visited once a year by the Ordinary, who shall expel any boys on whom he thinks education is wasted,

---

[1] 'Reformatio Legum Ecclesiasticarum, ex authoritate primum Regis Henrici 8 inchoata ; deinde per Regem Edovardum 6 provecta adauctaque in hunc modum, atque nunc ad pleniorem ipsarum reformationem in lucem edita auctore T. Cranmero.'

[2] *Ibid.* p. 110.   [3] *Ibid.* p. 109.

shall substitute good school-books for inefficient ones, if
necessary, and summon the master to appear before the
dean if he has neglected his charge.   As for the class-
divisions and methods of teaching, these are left to the
individual judgment of the master.[1]   Special attention is
to be paid to the Catechism, and at the beginning and
end of the day the boys are to repeat the twelve articles of
the faith, the Lord's Prayer, and the Ten Commandments.
Boys are not to be admitted before they are eight, or after
they are fourteen years old, and each, on admission, must
be able to read English, repeat the Catechism in English,
and write his own name.   He must also possess an English
New Testament.[2]   For further information as to the
functions of the master and management of the boys, we
are referred to the "Statutes of the Cathedral, if any such
exist"—a vague statement that does not add much to our
knowledge.

That so little attention should be given to education in
the *Reformatio* is the more remarkable, because in other
respects very minute instructions for the subject under discussion are forthcoming.   In the section on "Matrimony,"
for example, the writer even urges mothers to suckle their
own children.   It is only when he deals with schools that
he leaves the organisation to the man in charge.

It must be confessed that the rules drawn up by
Wolsey for his school at Ipswich,[3] though prior to the
Reformation, are better conceived, and present more points
of interest.

To this establishment boys below a certain standard were
not to be admitted.   "If your chyld can red and wryte Latyn
and Englyshe suffycyently, so that he be able to rede and
wryte his owne lessons, then he shall be admitted into the
schole for a scholer."   An attendance rule is enforced.   "If
he be absent six dayes, and in that meane season ye shewe
not cause reasonable (reasonable cause is only sekeness),

---

[1] *Reformatio Legum Ecclesiasticarum*, p. 111.   [2] *Ibid.* p. 112.
[3] *Rudimenta Grammatices.*

then his rowme to be voyde without he be admytted agayne and pay 4d."

"Also ye shall fynde hym ware in the winter."

"Also ye shall fynde hym convenyent bokes to his lernynge."

The instructions to the masters embody a scheme for an eight-class school. In the lowest class especial attention is to be paid to articulation. In the second, Æsop and Terence may be read, and Lily's gender rules learned; and so on with successive doses of classics throughout the remainder of the classes. Of special interest is the method indicated for reading one of Terence's Comedies in the eighth or highest class. The teacher is to commence by prefacing a short account of the author's life, genius, and manner of writing. He should then proceed to explain the pleasure and profit to be derived from reading a Comedy, and to discourse on the signification and etymology of the word. Next he must give a summary of the story, and an exact description of the metre. Then he should construe in the natural order, and, finally, may indicate to his pupils the more remarkable elegances of style.

Throughout the general scheme no mention is made of arithmetic, though a small concession is made to the mother-tongue. "Sometimes you ought, in the English language, to throw out a slight groundwork for an essay; but let it be somewhat that is elegant."

In Scotland, religious and educational reform went hand in hand, and the necessity for the establishment of the parish schools, that have existed in that country for three hundred years, was definitely formulated by John Knox. Knox, unlike Luther, wished the school to be dependent on the Church and not on the civil magistrate; but in his desire to put education within the reach of the very poorest, he is essentially at one with the German reformer, and endorses the principle of compulsion. "Of necessitie we judge it, that everie severall Churche have a schoolmaister appointed, suche a one as is able, at least, to teache Grammar and the Latine toung, yf the Toun be of any

reputation.   Yf it be Upaland, whaire the people convene
to doctrine but once in the weeke, then must either the
reidar or the minister take cayre over the children and
youth of the Parische, to instruct them in their first rudiments."   " This must be carefully provideit, that no fader,
of what estait or condition that ever he be, use his children
at his awin fantasie, especiallie in thair youth-heade ; but
all must be compelled to bring up their children in
learnyng and virtue."[1]   In addition to these elementary
schools, a secondary school was to be established "in everie
notable toun," while the three Universities of St. Andrews,
Glasgow, and Aberdeen completed the system.   To smaller
details, such as subjects of instruction or class-divisions,
Knox did not condescend ; but the deficiency is supplied
by George Buchanan in his scheme for the "College of
Humanite," to be attached to the University of St. Andrews.
In this scheme,[2] written before 1567, Buchanan gives us
a curriculum which is purely humanist and literary, and
which was possibly modelled on Calvin's school at Geneva.

The school is divided into six classes, divided in turn
into *decuriones*, each in charge of a *nomenclator*.   In the
lowest class the boys begin to read and write Latin through
the medium of Terence.   "In thys classe thay salbe con-
straint to speik Latin ; and dayly to compone sum smal
thyng eftyr thair capacite."

In the fifth and fourth classes they shall read Terence,
Cicero, and Ovid.   The third class commences Greek
grammar, and the study of prosody.   It also attacks
Linacre's Latin Grammar.

In the second and first classes Cicero's Rhetoric and
Orations, as well as the works of Virgil, Horace, Ovid, and
Homer, are read.   The boys are to be exercised every
month in verse, oration, and declamation.

At the end of the year, in August, a kind of examination,

---

[1] *Buke of Discipline.*   Circ. 1560.
[2] ' Mr. George Buchanan's Opinion anent the Reformation of the
Universitie of St. Andros.' (Vernacular writings of George Buchanan,
edited by P. Hume Brown, 1891-92.   Scottish Text Society.)

consisting of theme-writing and disputations, is to be held, and then the school breaks up for holidays. "Heir efter because the maist part of the countrey will be glaid to se thair bairnis and mak thayme clathys, and provid to thair necessiteis the rest of the yeir, thair may be given sum vacans on to the first day of October, on the quhilk day al lessonis begynnis againe in al collegis. At the quhilk day naine salbe promovit to na classe without he be examinat be the principal and regentis committit thairto."

Corporal punishment by inferior masters is forbidden. "Nor yit sal it be leful to the said pedagogis to ding thair desciples, but only to declair the fall to the principal or to thair regent, and refer the punition to thayme."

Of a large portion of this, his academic ancestry, Comenius was unaware, though, as has been shown, he did his best to assimilate and to build upon the efforts of previous workers. It remains to mention three of his contemporaries who exercised an undoubted influence upon him. These are Wolfgang Ratke, John Valentine Andreæ, and John Henry Alsted.

At first sight it would appear as if Ratke (1571-1635) were the chief inspirer and forerunner of the *Great Didactic*, but a little investigation tends to weaken this presumption. It has already been shown that Comenius, while putting his ideas into shape at Lissa, did not know with any exactness in what the method of Ratke consisted, and that the secrecy maintained by the latter hindered his contemporaries from knowing what were the actual suggestions that he had formulated. It was possibly the eulogy of his method by the Giessen professors Helwig and Jung that had reached Comenius at Herborn, and it is more than probable that no more detailed account ever came into his hands. True, he lays stress on the fact that Ratke's examples fired him, in the beginning, to attempt school-reformation, but he speaks with little appreciation of his system of teaching Latin; and, though he can scarcely have been ignorant of the general principles contained in them, does not appear to have been intimately acquainted with his works.[1]

Far more immediate was the influence of Andreæ, to whose Utopia, *Reipublicæ Christiano-Politicæ Descriptio*, and the educational reforms described in it, Comenius' debt is very great.   Andreæ, imbued with the scientific spirit that was awakening throughout Europe, wished to add both mathematics and natural science to the ordinary humanist curriculum, and was undoubtedly a strong factor in the development of Comenius' "modern side" tendencies.

But it is to John Henry Alsted, his friend and teacher at Herborn, that the debt is greatest.   In his *Encyclopædia of all the Sciences*, published in 1630, Alsted included a very complete treatise on Education, and, though many of the propositions brought forward resemble those of Ratke, it does not appear that they were directly borrowed from him. Indeed, in the list of writers on Education at the beginning of Alsted's *Consilarius Academicus*, Ratke's name does not

---

[1] The great similarity between the method of Ratke and of Comenius is well exemplified by the programme submitted by Ratke to a commission at Jena in 1629.   1. Everything is to be preceded by prayer.   2. Everything according to the method of nature.   3. Not more than one thing at a time.   4. And that frequently.   5. Everything first in the vernacular.   6. From the vernacular into other languages.   7. Everything without compulsion.   8. All subjects should be taught on principles that are similar and harmonicus.   9. All effort should be on the side of the teacher.   10. The pupil should maintain a Pythagorean silence, and should not ask questions or talk while the lesson is proceeding.   11. Each language should be taught in accordance with its own genius.   12. The pupil should approach everything with an unbiassed mind.   13. Not more than one teacher in one subject.   14. Form should not precede matter.   15. Education should begin with religion.   16. All the young should be educated.   17. All certainty should be obtained through induction and experiment.   18. Nothing but the subject actually before the class should be discussed.   19. All subjects should be taught in two ways, first superficially, then in detail.   20. The teacher should do nothing but teach.   Discipline must be left to the ushers.   21. All the pupils should sit in a row, in view of the teacher.   22. A pupil must miss no school hour.   23. At home a boy should be subjected to the same discipline as at school.   24. In printing school-books the importance of local memory should be borne in mind.   25. Languages should be taught with a view to conversation.   26. Nothing that can give rise to any evil thought is to be placed before the pupil (*Geschichte der Pädagogik*, Prof. Th. Ziegler, p. 149).

appear. Helwig's *Didactica*, however, is mentioned, and it was doubtless through this work that Alsted was brought into contact with the educational scheme that was causing so much stir at Giessen. A few quotations from his maxims will suffice to show how great must have been the influence of this thinker, an influence that was personal as well as intellectual, as he made a point of maintaining the closest intercourse with his pupils.

1. Not more than one thing should be taught at a time.

2. Not more than one book should be used on one subject, and not more than one subject should be taught on one day.

3. Everything should be taught through the medium of what is more familiar.

4. All superfluity should be avoided.

5. All study should be mapped out in fixed periods.

6. All rules should be as short as possible.

7. Everything should be taught without severity, though discipline must be maintained.

8. Corporal punishment should be reserved for moral offences, and never inflicted for lack of industry.

9. Authority should not be allowed to prejudice the mind against the facts gleaned from experience ; nor should custom or preconceived opinion prevail.

10. The constructions of a new language should first be explained in the vernacular.

11. No language should be taught by means of grammar.

12. Grammatical terms should be the same in all languages.[1]

In restricting the use of the vernacular school to girls, and to boys destined for manual labour,[2] Alsted was less thorough than his disciple ; but in duly valuing the personal influence of the individual teacher, he shows, on this point at least, the sounder judgment. "The teacher," he says,[3] "should be a skilled reader of character, that he may be

---

[1] *Encyclopædia Scientiarum Omnium*, ii. 287.   [2] *Ibid.* ii. 281.
[3] *Ibid.* ii. 273.

able to classify the dispositions of his pupils. . . . Unless he pays great attention to differences of disposition he will but waste all the effort that he expends in teaching." This is the one point of which Comenius sometimes appears to lose sight. He relies too much on the class-book and too little on the class-master. The class becomes a machine, flawless it is true, but lacking spontaneity—the spontaneity that a teacher can only supply if left free to employ his trained faculties according to the dictates of a trained judgment.

The foregoing sketch, brief though it is, will suffice to show in outline the position in which Comenius found the problem of education. His contribution to the material of the school-room we have already discussed in treating of his *Janua Linguarum*, his grammars, his dictionaries, and his other class-books; while the philosophical principles on which his educational precepts are based will be found in the *Great Didactic*. It remains to give, as a pendant to the school programmes of Sturm and Calvin, the scheme, only half carried out, that he drew up for the Pansophic school at Saros-Patak; a scheme which is none the less interesting because it differs in certain details of classification from that contained in the *Great Didactic*.

The most cursory glance at the Patak scheme will suffice to show that Comenius is more than two centuries ahead of his immediate predecessors. His programme is essentially modern, and, even at the present day, is extremely suggestive for those engaged in the practical work of school organisation.

The *Outline of the Pansophic School*[1] is divided into two parts. The first prescribes general rules, while the second takes the classes one by one and gives a detailed description of each.

To a large extent Part I. does but reiterate the general positions with which the reader is already familiar. The scheme of instruction is to be universal, and as much

[1] 'Scholæ Pansophicæ Delineatio,' *Op. Did. Omn.* iii. 10.

attention is to be paid to the formation of character as to the instilling of knowledge. Boys are to be urged to read for themselves out of school-hours, and among the books suggested for private study are the Dialogues of Erasmus and of Vives, since these are easy and require little explanation.

Great care must be taken not to overstrain the minds of the pupils. After each hour's work they are to be allowed half an hour's play, and after dinner and supper should rest for an hour at least. At night eight hours, from eight in the evening till four in the morning, must be set aside for sleep, and twice in the week, on Wednesday and on Sunday, a half-holiday is to be given. At Christmas, Easter, and Whitsuntide the boys may have a fortnight's holiday, and in the Autumn a full month.

Comenius begs the reader not to consider this an excessive allowance of holidays. There still remain forty-two weeks with thirty school-hours in each. This makes a total of 1260 hours, and by employing these rationally an immense amount of knowledge may be acquired in seven years. The general sketch concludes with a time-table to be employed throughout the whole school.

Morning

(i)   6-7.   Hymns, Bible-reading, and prayers.

(ii) 7.30-8.30.   The principal subject of the class, theoretically treated.

(iii) 9-10.   The same, treated practically.

Afternoon

(i)   1-2.   Music, or some other pleasant mathematical exercise.

(ii) 2.30-3.30.   History.

(iii) 4-5.   Exercises of style.

In Part II. we find a detailed account of the seven classes.

Class I.—*The Vestibular*

1. Over the door is placed the inscription :

" Let no one enter who cannot read."

2. The walls of the class-room are to appeal to the senses of the pupils, and should be covered with diagrams, illustrating the subjects taught in the class. These diagrams are to represent: (1) The Latin alphabet, in small and in capital letters. (2 and 3) Types of the declensions and conjugations. The beginner is to be allowed to look at these while repeating his grammar lesson, until he knows them so well that it is less trouble to repeat from memory than to tire his eyes by looking at the wall. (4) Short maxims containing the most important rules of conduct, which will thus be impressed on the memory of the class.

3. The religious exercises consist of the heads of the Catechism, together with a few short hymns and prayers.

4. The class-book is to be the *Vestibulum*, containing the chief matters on which the constitution of the universe hinges, the roots of the words on which language is dependent, the fundamental principles of intelligence, and a course of Moral Philosophy suited to children.

5. In mathematics the boys learn the elements of arithmetic ; but no geometry, except the difference between a point and a line. In music they may learn the scale and the keys.

6. No special history-book is provided for this class. The *Vestibulum* is sufficient.

7. Exercises in style will here consist in the explanation of words, in translation and re-translation, and, near the end of the course, in joining the words together into sentences.

8. The only accessory studies are good hand-writing and drawing.

9. Those games to be allowed that are suitable to the boys' age and nationality.

10. In place of a dramatic performance at the end of a term there is to be an examination, in which each boy is to challenge another, and to ask and answer questions on the subject-matter of the *Vestibulum*.

Class II.—*The Janual*

1. Over the door is the inscription :

" Let no one enter who is ignorant of mathematics,"

that is to say, the elements are supposed to be known.

2. On the walls are to be pictures of the more important objects mentioned in the *Janua* (if the things themselves cannot be procured). On one wall may be drawn those that are natural, on another those that are artificial. On the other two walls grammatical rules may be written.

3. The Catechism is to be thoroughly learned.

4. The class-books are the *Janua*, the Latin Vernacular dictionary, and the Janual grammar.

5. In arithmetic, addition and subtraction are to be taught ; in geometry, plane figures. The music is to be rather more advanced than in the Vestibular class.

6. In history no book other than the *Janua* is to be used.

7. Exercises of style will deal with the structure of phrases, sentences, and periods.

8. No accessory study is prescribed for the boys in this class, as they have already enough to do. It will be sufficient if they learn with exactness the names and natures of external objects.

9. Games to be chosen by the master.

10. In place of a dramatic performance, the boys may ask one another hard questions on the subject-matter of the *Janua*.

Class III.—*The Atrial*

1. Over the door is to be written :

   " Let no one enter who cannot speak."

2. The walls are to be covered with ingenious diagrams, and with select maxims relative to the adornment of speech.

3. In this class the boys should begin to read the Bible ; but not as it stands.   An abridged form, suited to their intelligence, should be given to them, and a portion of this must be expounded daily.

4. The class-books are the *Atrium* of the Latin language, the *Grammar of Elegance*, and the Latin-Latin dictionary, especially written for the *Atrium*.

5. In arithmetic the boys may learn multiplication, division, and the table of Cebes.   In geometry, solid figures.   In music, harmony.   The rudiments of Latin verse may be taught, together with selections from Cato, Ovid, and Tibullus.

6. The history for this class is the famous deeds of the Biblical narrative.

7. Exercises of style consist in making paraphrases and in transposing sentences.   No boy may attempt to write verse until he has been in the class eleven months.

8. It will be sufficient accessory study if the boys read attentively and imitate what they read.   They should be able to read any Latin author, and to talk Latin fluently by the time they leave this class.

9. Recreation to be taken at fixed hours.

10. For dramatic purposes the *Schola Ludus* is provided.

Class IV.—*The Philosophical*

1. Over the door is to be written :

   " Let no one ignorant of history enter here."

2. The walls should be adorned with pictures illustra-

tive of arithmetic, geometry, and statics. Adjoining the class-room there should be a dissecting-room and a chemical laboratory.

3. A special collection of hymns and psalms must be arranged for this class; also an epitome of the New Testament, which should comprise a continuous life of Christ and His Apostles compiled from the four Gospels.

4. The class-book is to be the *Palace of Wisdom*, in which natural phenomena should be described in such a manner as to show how they came into existence.

5. In mathematics the rules of proportion should be learned, and trigonometry and the elements of statics may be commenced. The pupils should now learn instrumental music.

6. The history for this class should be natural history, and may be learned from Pliny and Ælian.

7. Exercises of style may be discontinued, and the time thus gained devoted to the study of Greek.

8. The accessory study is Greek. This is a difficult subject, but need not cause the pupil much alarm for three reasons: (*a*) No learned man is expected to have an exhaustive knowledge of Greek. (*b*) It is comparatively easy to learn enough to read the New Testament, and this is the chief utility of the study. (*c*) Difficulties must be surmounted by a good method, so that in one year, by employing the last hour on four afternoons in the week, the intricacies of the language may be overcome. In addition to the New Testament, suitable selections from Greek authors may be read.

9. In this class serious matters and not games claim the attention of the pupils; but fitting recreation must not be neglected.

10. For dramatic performances, plays that deal with philosophy and philosophers may be acted.

Class V.—*The Logical*

1. Over the door is the inscription :

" Let no one enter who is ignorant of natural philosophy."

2. The walls are to be covered with the rules of logic and ingenious devices of a similar nature.

3. Religious instruction comprises hymns, psalms, and prayers. A Bible manual also, called the *Gate of the Sanctuary*, is to be placed in the pupils' hands. This is to contain the whole of Scripture history in the words of the Bible, but so digested that it may be read in one year.

4. The class-book is a work dealing with the human mind, and consisting of three parts, which are respectively : (*a*) Pansophic, treating of the things that have been discovered and that should be discovered by man. (*b*) A formal logic, in which the whole process of reasoning should be explained, and a description given of the analytic, synthetic, and syncritic methods. (*c*) A repertory of all the problems that can be suggested by the mind.

5. For the afternoon the following studies are advised :

> In arithmetic, the rules of partnership, alligation, and position.[1]
> In geometry, mensuration of heights, distances, and plane surfaces.
> In geography and astronomy, the general description of the earth and the heavens.
> In optics, the most important facts.

6. The history studied should be that of mechanical inventions.

7. With a view to style, historians like Cornelius Nepos, Curtius, Cæsar, and Justin may be read.

8. As an accessory study, attention may be devoted to Greek. Isocrates and Plutarch are recommended.

---

[1] ' Regulæ Societatum, Alligationis, Falsi.'

9. By way of recreation the pupils are advised to ask one another hard questions.

10. A dramatic performance, illustrating the contest between grammar, logic, and metaphysic, and their final reconciliation, may complete the year's work.

Class VI.—*The Political*

1. Over the door is the inscription :

   " Let no one enter who cannot reason."

2. The pictures on the wall should illustrate the necessity of order and limitation. With this in view, the human body may be represented in four ways: (*a*) Lacking certain limbs. (*b*) Supplied with superfluous limbs. (*c*) With its limbs wrongly put together. (*d*) A perfect body, properly constructed and shapely.

3. In theology the whole Bible is to be read.

4. The class-book is to be a work dealing with human society and the laws of economics.

5. In arithmetic *Logistic*, and in geometry *Architectonic* may be learned. Special attention should be given to geography and to that part of astronomy that deals with the theory of the planets and the laws of eclipses.

6. The history should be that of ritual.

7. For the sake of style Sallust, Cicero, Virgil, and Horace may be read.

Compositions in verse are not to be insisted upon. They are extremely difficult, aptitude for them is rare, and the time devoted to them might be more profitably employed on other things. But if a boy shows very great aptitude for verse-writing, he is not to be dissuaded from it.

8. As an accessory study, Thucydides or Hesiod may be read.

9. Suitable recreations may be chosen according to inclination. They should not be dangerous or excessive.

10. A dramatic performance may be given representing the degeneration of Solomon and his moral downfall.

Class VII.—*The Theological*

1. Inscription over the door:

   " Let no one enter who is irreligious."

2. The walls should be covered with mystic symbols illustrating the wisdom hidden in the Scriptures.   On one wall diagrams of Hebrew grammar may be placed.

3. The most devotional psalms and hymns of the Church may be used, as well as prayers of a special nature taken from the Scriptures and from the works of the most inspired theologians and of the sainted martyrs.   In addition a compendium of Christian beliefs, duties, and hopes, written in the phraseology of the Bible, should be read daily.

4. The class-book should be a work dealing with the last stage of wisdom on earth, that is to say, the communion of souls with God, and should consist of three parts :

   (*a*) *The ascent of the mind to God.*   In this a survey should be made of the universe, preserving the order of the *Janua*, and with regard to each fact should be pointed out what God tells us about it in the Scriptures, and how the heaven and the earth and all that in them is tell the glory of God.

   (*b*) The formal part should consist of a key to God's Book; that is to say, practical rules for reading the Scriptures with profit and for duly considering the works of God.   Here a three-fold commentary should be supplied : (1) from Scripture itself; (2) from reason ; (3) from sense-experience.

   (*c*) The third part should be a *Repertory of Theology*, giving a detailed account of the mysteries of Salvation.

5. In arithmetic the sacred and mystic numbers that occur in the Scriptures should be studied ; also sacred architecture, as exemplified by Noah's ark, the Tabernacle, and the Temple.

6. Universal history should be studied, and in particular the history of the Church, for whose sake the world exists.

7. In this class some training should be given in oratory. The future minister must learn how to address a congregation, and should be taught the laws of sacred oratory. The future politician must be taught how to appeal to the reason of his hearers.

8. The accessory study is Hebrew, which must be studied in such a way that before the end of the year the pupil shall be able to read and understand the original text of the Scriptures.

9. Recreation is to be allowed, but must not interfere with the theological studies.

10. Religious plays dealing with the character of, say Abraham or David, may be acted.

Thus ends the detailed description of the Pansophic school. A few general remarks follow. Each class is to have its own master, and in addition there is to be a headmaster, whose duty it will be to enter each class daily, superintend the school, and take the place of any master who may be kept away by illness. The headmaster must be well paid, as indeed should the class-masters, since this is the only way to make them contented with their positions and prevent them from seeking more remunerative work in some other profession.

Comenius then pertinently asks, "Where is the money to come from?" It is not his business, he replies, to answer this question, but he suggests that citizens should give a fixed proportion of their incomes for educational, as they already do for charitable purposes, and that it is the duty of princes and of wealthy citizens to assist schools in every way.

Comenius' title to fame as an educationist rests on the discovery, application, and embodiment in a large-minded treatise on Didactic, of the fundamental principles :

I. That all instruction must be carefully graded.

II. That in imparting knowledge to children the teacher must, to the utmost, appeal to the faculties of sense-perception.

If the reader wishes to realise with any force to what extent the gradation and proper articulation of studies was neglected, or rather unthought of, when Comenius was writing, let him read a few chapters in the *Great Didactic* and then turn to Milton's tractate *Of Education*. In the one he will find a rigorous distribution of the subject-matter of instruction, based on an analysis of the capacity and age of the scholar and on a common-sense estimate of the difficulty of the subject.   In the other he meets with breadth of mind, it is true, but with no scheme of gradation whatever.   Subjects and authors are dumped down in a heap and are declared suitable for educational purposes, but no effort is made to sort them.

Now to construct a solid pile of subjects of instruction that are really suitable instruments with which to educate the young is no easy task ; but a greater difficulty arises when we try to pull the large heap to pieces, and to arrange it in nine or ten smaller heaps, carefully graduated as regards quantity and quality.   Both these tasks Comenius undertook and performed ; the first with as great success as could possibly be expected, if we consider how ill the several branches of knowledge were then defined, and the second in a manner which, even at the present day, can excite nothing but admiration.

By Comenius the principle of gradation is carried into every department of school management, the result being a careful grading of schools, of boys, and of books.   The twenty-four years to be devoted to education are divided into four periods of six years, and to each of these a school is assigned.   The first of these, the Mother School, was a totally new conception, and emphasises the necessity of commencing education from the moment the child leaves the cradle. The next stage, the Vernacular School, lays the foundation of all that is to follow, with the exception of Latin, and grounds the boy thoroughly in one or two modern languages. The next stage, the Latin School, introduces the boy to the classics, continues the modern subjects commenced in the Vernacular School, and corresponds to a present-day secondary school with a good modern side. Finally the University gives the scholar the opportunity of thoroughly mastering any one of the branches of knowledge that he has already learned superficially and in outline.

In the Vernacular and in the Latin School the proper gradation and classification of the boys is attained by a division into six classes, in each of which the scholars must remain one year, and which they must not leave until their fitness to proceed to the next class has been tested by an examination. Throughout the twelve classes of these two schools a properly graded series of schoolbooks is supplied, all, from the lowest to the highest, treating of the same subjects, namely, the entire world of phenomena, and leading the scholar from the rudimentary facts and bare nomenclature acquired in the Mother School to the detailed exposition of them in Latin that awaits him in the higher classes of the Latin School.

But it may be asked, Does Comenius supply a graded method? Is there any essential difference in his manner of presenting knowledge to his most elementary and to his most advanced pupils?

While it is evident that his graded classes and graded books ensured that the beginner should have the subject-matter of his studies presented to him more simply and with less complications than to the advanced pupil, it must be confessed that the same method seems intended to run through all the classes, from the lowest to the highest. Of this method the basis is the presentation of information to the senses first, and then, but not till then, to the understanding. Appeal, that is to say, is to be made to the sight and to the touch, and models or pictures of everything that has to be learned should be given to the pupil.

To Comenius' eternal credit be it that he was the first to realise that the object-lesson was the only way in which any impression could be made on the half-developed thinking powers of the child, that he practically anticipated Pestalozzi, and paved the way for Froebel. Unfortunately he stops here. Up to the highest classes of the Pansophic school, the pictures on the wall and the models in front of the pupils are the prime aids to the teacher in his task of instilling knowledge. Visualisation in all things is the watchword of the Comenian method.

Now while it is evident that this factor is of great value at every stage of education, it is also evident that, at a certain stage, it becomes of secondary importance. By means of pictures, models, and what-not, a boy's progress in acquiring the nomenclature of, let us say a language, may be immensely facilitated; but, when he reaches a certain point, when he is beginning to grapple with syntax, with analysis, with the various modal forms, or, in algebra, when he is attacking the mysteries of quadratic equations, a completely new element is introduced. Visualisation and object-lessons barely touch the fringe of the teacher's difficulties. Between the ages of twelve and sixteen, when the boy is learning, not to see, but to think, not to exercise his sense of touch, but to draw conclusions, the schoolmaster, even at the present day, receives but slight assistance from systems of psychology, systems which, until recently, have consisted of little more than a somewhat arbitrary analysis and classification of states of consciousness. It can therefore scarcely be called weakness, on the part of Comenius, if he failed to solve the problem that still waits to be attacked, in the laboratory, by the special application to psychology of physiological methods, and, in the class-room, by the patient observation of teachers who are anxious to educate rather than to instruct.

It was his lack of a firm psychological basis and his

belief that at sixteen a boy might be subjected to much the same educational discipline as a child of six that led Comenius so entirely to overlook the great gulf that exists between the two ages, and made him so absolutely certain that he had, once and for all, solved the problem of education.

Into this train of thought he was to a large extent led by his habit of appealing to nature as a standard and of taking natural processes as models. It is true that to him Nature and the Deity are almost synonymous terms. "By the voice of Nature we understand the universal providence of God, which never ceases to work all in all things; that is to say, which continually developes each creature for the end to which it has been destined." But, in practice, Nature comes to mean the external processes that are to be seen in the growth of a tree or of an animal, and here it is that the fatal error is introduced, the error into which other writers on education have fallen, as well as Comenius. As long as the child is in the stage of "nutrition and growth," as long as his education consists of the training of organs of sense-perception, so long the appeal to nature is justified. But when a higher stage is reached, when the child becomes thoroughly self-conscious, a very different element is introduced. The work of the true educationist, far from furthering natural tendencies, frequently consists in counteracting them, in making a careful selection of qualities, in developing some and in hindering the growth of others, and this in accordance with an ideal to be found nowhere but in the mind, and to which Nature, in the ordinary sense of the word, has nothing to say. Here again we may reasonably excuse Comenius for going astray, when so recent a writer as Mr. Herbert Spencer has committed himself to the statement that "Nature illustrates to us in the simplest way the true theory and practice of *moral* discipline!"

For the rest, it is to practical schoolmasters that Comenius, writing as a practical schoolmaster, particularly recommends himself. If his work is not overloaded with psychology, it appeals all the more to men whose habit of mind leads them to action rather than to the analysis of mental phenomena. While there is scarcely a problem connected with education that is not discussed in the *Great Didactic*, the work never becomes academic, and the author never forgets that he is writing for the teacher in his class-room and not for the philosopher in his study.

The Great Didactic

of

John Amos Comenius

The Great Didactic

Setting forth

The whole Art of Teaching
all Things to all Men

or

A certain Inducement to found such Schools in all
the Parishes, Towns, and Villages of every
Christian Kingdom, that the entire
Youth of both Sexes, none
being excepted, shall

Quickly, Pleasantly, & Thoroughly

Become learned in the Sciences, pure in Morals,
trained to Piety, and in this manner
instructed in all things necessary
for the present and for
the future life,

in which, with respect to everything that is suggested,

Its Fundamental Principles are set forth from the essential
nature of the matter,
Its Truth is proved by examples from the several
mechanical arts,
Its Order is clearly set forth in years, months, days, and
hours, and, finally,
An easy and sure Method is shown, by which it can
be pleasantly brought into existence.

Let the main object of this, our Didactic, be as follows : To seek and to find a method of instruction, by which teachers may teach less, but learners may learn more ; by which schools may be the scene of less noise, aversion, and useless labour, but of more leisure, enjoyment, and solid progress ; and through which the Christian community may have less darkness, perplexity, and dissension, but on the other hand more light, orderliness, peace, and rest.

God be merciful unto us and bless us, and cause his face to
    shine upon us ;
That thy way may be known upon earth, thy saving health
    among all nations.—Psalm lxvii. 1, 2.

GREETING TO THE READER

[*The References are to notes at the end of the book*]

1. DIDACTIC signifies the art of teaching. Several men of ability, taking pity on the Sisyphus-labour of schools, have lately endeavoured to find out some such Art, but with unequal skill and unequal success.

2. Some merely wished to give assistance towards learning some language or other with greater ease. Others found ways of imparting this or that science or art with greater speed. Others suggested improvements of various kinds; but almost all proceeded by means of unconnected precepts, gleaned from a superficial experience, that is to say, *a posteriori*.

3. We venture to promise a GREAT DIDACTIC, that is to say, the whole art of teaching all things to all men, and indeed of teaching them with certainty, so that the result cannot fail to follow; further, of teaching them pleasantly, that is to say, without annoyance or aversion on the part of teacher or pupil, but rather with the greatest enjoyment for both; further of teaching them thoroughly, not superficially and showily, but in such a manner as to lead to true knowledge, to gentle morals, and to the deepest piety. Lastly, we wish to prove all this *a priori*, that is to say, from the unalterable nature of the matter itself, drawing off, as from a living source, the constantly flowing runlets, and bringing them together again into one concentrated stream, that we may lay the foundations of the universal art of founding universal schools.

4. The prospect which is here held out is indeed great and very desirable, though I can easily foresee that to many it will appear to be an idle dream rather than the exposition of a real possibility.

In the meantime let each one, whoever he may be, withhold his judgment until he knows the true nature of my proposition. He will then be at liberty not only to form his judgment, but also to make it public. For I cannot wish, and much less can I claim, to hurry along any one by persuasion so that he give his approval to an insufficiently established proposition ; but rather desire that each observer should naturally bring to bear on the matter, his own, and indeed his keenest senses (which should be dulled by no deceits of the imagination). This it is that I most earnestly demand and entreat.

5. The matter is indeed a serious one, and, as all should earnestly wish for the result, so should all, with united effort, carefully pass judgment on the means, since the salvation of the human race is at stake.

What better or what greater service could we perform for the state than to instruct and to educate the young? Especially at the present time and in the present condition of morals, when they have sunk so low that, as Cicero says, all should join to bridle them and keep them in check. It was Philip Melanchthon who remarked that to educate the young well was a greater feat than to sack Troy ; and in this connection we may note the saying of Gregory Nazianzen :[1] "To educate man is the art of arts, for he is the most complex and the most mysterious of all creatures."

6. Now to portray the art of arts is a troublesome matter, and calls for exceptional criticism ; and not that of one man alone, but of many ; since no individual is so keensighted that the greater part of any matter does not escape his observation.

7. With justice therefore I demand from my readers, and adjure all who shall see this undertaking, by the salvation of mankind : firstly, not to attribute it to indiscretion if

any one resolve not only to investigate so weighty a matter, but also to give promises; since this can only have the advantage of others as its object. Secondly, not to lose heart at once, if the first attempt do not succeed on the spot, and the longed-for result be not brought to full completion by us. For in any matter it is necessary that the seed should first sprout, and then raise itself gradually.

However incomplete, therefore, our essay may be, and however much it fall short of the goal at which we aim, the investigation itself will prove that it has reached a higher stage, and one lying nearer the goal than hitherto. Finally, I ask my readers to bring with them to their criticism as much attention and keenness as is befitting in matters of the greatest importance. It will be my first step to touch briefly on the circumstances that led to this essay and to enumerate the chief points that present any novelty; I can then with full confidence entrust the one to my reader's candour, the other to his further research.

8. This art of teaching and of learning was in former centuries to a great extent unknown, at any rate in that degree of perfection to which it is now wished to raise it, and on that account the world of culture and the schools were so full of toil and weariness, of weakness and deceits, that only those who were gifted with parts beyond the ordinary could obtain a sound education.

9. But recently it has pleased God to let the morning glow of a newly-rising age appear, in which He has inspired some sturdy men in Germany, who, weary of the errors of the present method of instruction, began to think out an easier and shorter way of teaching languages. This they did, the one after the other, and therefore some with greater, others with less success, as may be seen in the didactic works that they gave to the world.

10. I here allude to men like Ratke,[2] Lubin,[3] Helwig,[4] Ritter,[5] Bodin,[6] Glaum, Vogel,[7] Wolfstirn,[8] and he who deserves to be placed before them all, John Valentine Andreæ[9] (who in his golden writings has laid bare the diseases not only of the Church and the state, but also of

the schools, and has pointed out the remedies).   In France
too they set this stone in motion, since, in the year 1629,
Janus Cæcilius Frey[10] brought out a fine work on Didactic
(under the title, *A new and easy way to the goodly Sciences
and Arts, to Languages, and to Rhetoric*).

11. It is almost incredible what pleasure I found, and
how my pain over the decline of my native land and the
terribly oppressed state of all Germany was lightened whenever opportunity arose and I turned over the pages of these
writings.   For I began to hope that it was not without
purpose that the providence of the Almighty had allowed
it to come to pass that the decline of the old schools and
the foundation of new ones in harmony with new ideas
should take place at one and the same time.   For he who
intends to raise a new building, invariably levels the ground
beforehand and removes the less comfortable or ruined
houses.

12. This thought raised in me a joyful hope mingled with
pleasant emotion ; but I soon felt this vanish, and reflected
that it would be impossible to reconstruct such an important
institution from the very beginning.

13. As I wished for instruction on some points, and on
others wished, myself, to instruct my fellows, I applied by
letter first to one then to another of the above-mentioned
writers.   In vain, however, partly because some guarded
their ideas with great care, partly because the letters did
not reach those to whom they were directed, and therefore
remained unanswered.

14. Only one of them (the renowned J. V. Andreæ)
sent the friendly answer that he wished to be of some
assistance, and urged me to proceed with my efforts.
Stimulated by this, my spirit began to take more daring
flights, till at last my unbounded solicitude for the public
good led me to take the matter thoroughly in hand.

15. So, putting on one side the discoveries, thoughts,
observations, and admonitions of others, I began myself to
investigate the matter thoughtfully and to seek out the
causes, the principles, the methods, and the objects of the

art of teaching (*discentia* as they may be called after Tertullian).

16. This was the origin of my treatise, which, as I trust, developes the subject more thoroughly than has hitherto been done. It was first composed in my mother tongue for the use of my people, and afterwards on the advice of several men of standing translated into Latin, in order that, if possible, it might be of universal use.

17. For, as Lubin says in his Didactic, Charity bids us not to niggardly withhold from mankind what God has intended for the use of all, but to throw it open to the whole world.

For it is the nature of all true possessions that they can be shared by all; and that they advantage all more and more in proportion as they are shared by greater numbers.

18. It is also a law of human existence that if any know of assistance lying close at hand to those who are struggling he should not withhold it from them; especially in a case, as in the one before us, where the matter concerns not one but many, and not individuals merely but towns, provinces, kingdoms, and in short the whole human race.

19. Should there be any man who is such a pedant as to think that the reform of schools has nothing to do with the vocation of a Theologian, let him know that I was myself thoroughly penetrated with this idea. But I have found that the only way in which I can be freed from it is to follow God's call, and without digression to devote myself to that work to which the divine impulse directs me.

20. Christian readers, suffer me to speak with you confidentially! My more intimate friends know that I am a man of little ability and almost without literary training, but that, nevertheless, I lament the defects of the age, and make great endeavours to remedy these in any way that is possible, whether by means of my own discoveries or those of others (though this can only take place by the grace of God).

21. Therefore, if anything should find favour, it is not my work but His who is wont to win praise from the mouths

of children, and who in order to prove Himself faithful, earnest, and benign, gives to those who ask, opens to those who knock, and grants Himself to those who seek Him (Luke ii.), and whose good gifts to us we ought to pass on ungrudgingly to others.   As my Saviour knows, my heart is so simple that it makes no difference to me whether I teach or am taught, whether I exhort or am exhorted, whether I am the teacher of teachers, or the scholar of scholars.

22. And so, what the Lord permits me to observe, that give I forth for public use and as common property.

23. If any find anything better, let him follow my example, lest, having buried his talent in a napkin, he be accused of wantonness by our Lord, who wills that His servants put out to usury so that the talent which is given to each may win another talent (Luke xix.)

To seek what is great is noble, was ever noble, and ever will be noble.

What thou hast begun with God cannot remain without result.

DEDICATORY LETTER [1]

To all superiors of human society, to the rulers of states, the pastors of Churches, the parents and guardians of children, grace and peace from God the Father of our Lord Jesus Christ in the Holy Ghost.

God, having created man out of dust, placed him in a Paradise of desire, which he had planted in the East, not only that man might tend it and care for it, but also that he might be a garden of delight for his God.

For as Paradise was the pleasantest part of the world, so also was man the most perfect of things created. In Paradise each tree was delightful to look at, and more pleasant to enjoy than those which grew throughout the earth. In man, the whole material of the world, all the forms and the varieties of forms were, as it were, brought together into one in order to display the whole skill and wisdom of God. Paradise contained the tree of the knowledge of good and evil; man had the intellect to distinguish, and the will to choose between the good and the bad. In Paradise was the tree of life. In man was the tree of Immortality itself; that is to say, the wisdom of God, which had planted its eternal roots in man.

And so each man is, in truth, a Garden of Delights for his God, as long as he remains in the spot where he has been placed. The Church too, which is a collection of men devoted to God, is often in Holy Writ likened to a Paradise, to a garden, to a vineyard of God. But alas

[1] Following Lindner, I have slightly curtailed this Dedicatory Letter.

for our misfortune! We have at the same time lost the Paradise of bodily delight in which we were, and that of spiritual delight, which we were ourselves. We have been cast out into the deserts of the earth, and have ourselves become wild and horrible wildernesses. We were ungrateful for the gifts, both of the body and of the soul, with which God had so richly provided Paradise; with right therefore have we been deprived of them and been dowered with calamity.

But glory, praise, honour, and blessing for everlasting to our merciful God who abandoned us for a while but did not thrust us from Him for ever. . . . The garden of the Church, the delight of God's heart, blooms anew.

But does this new plantation of God succeed entirely according to His wishes? Do all the shoots grow successfully? Do all the newly-planted trees bring forth spikenard, crocus, cinnamon, myrrh, spices, and costly fruits? Do we hear the voice of God calling to His Church: I had planted thee a noble vine, wholly a right seed: how then art thou turned into the degenerate plant of a strange vine unto me? (Jeremiah ii. 21). Here we have the complaint of God that even this new plantation of Paradise is deteriorating. . . .

He who knows not that he is ill cannot heal himself; he who feels not his pain utters no sigh; he who sees not his danger does not start back, even though he be on the brink of an abyss; and so it is not to be wondered at that he who perceives not the wave of disorder which is sweeping over the human race and over the Church, does not lament the fact. But he who sees himself and others covered with countless wounds; he who remarks that the wounds and boils, both his own and other men's, fester ever more and more; and who knows that he, with others, stands in the midst of gulfs and precipices and wanders among snares, in which he sees one man after another being caught, it is hard for him not to be terrified, not to marvel, not to perish with grief.

For what part of us or of our concerns is in good condition? None. Everything lies overturned or in

shreds. With most men such a dulness of wit is pre-
dominant, instead of the understanding through which we
ought to be equal to the angels, that they know no more
about those things which are worthy of our attention than
do the beasts. Instead of the circumspection with which
those who are destined for eternity ought to prepare themselves for it, there reigns such forgetfulness, not only of
eternity but also of mortality, that most men give themselves
up to what is earthly and transient, yea, even to the death
that stands before them. Instead of the godly wisdom
through which it has been given to us to know, to honour,
and to enjoy the One who is the height of all goodness,
there has arisen a horrible shrinking from that God in
whom we live, move, and have our being, and a foolish
conjuration of His holy name. Instead of mutual love and
purity, reign hatred, enmity, war, and murder. Instead of
justice, we find unfairness, roguery, oppression, theft, and
rapine; instead of purity, uncleanliness and audacity of
thought, word, and deed; instead of simplicity and truth,
lying, deception, and knavery; instead of modesty, pride
and haughtiness between man and man.

But in spite of all this, there remains for us a twofold
comfort. First, that God keeps the eternal Paradise in
readiness for His chosen ones, and that there we shall find
a perfection, more complete and more durable than that
first one which we lost. Into this Paradise went Christ
(Luke xxiii. 43), thither was Paul caught up (2 Corinthians
xii. 4), and John saw its splendour with his own eyes (Rev.
i. 12; xxi. 10).

Another consolation consists in this, that here below also
God continually renews the Paradise of the Church, and
turns its deserts into a garden of delights. We have on
several occasions seen with what grandeur this has already
taken place: after the Fall, after the Flood, after the entrance
of the children of Israel into the land of Canaan, under
David and Solomon, after the return from Babylon and the
rebuilding of Jerusalem, after Christ's ascension into heaven
and the preaching of the Gospel to all nations, under

Constantine, and elsewhere. Perchance even now, after such a bloody war and after such devastation, the Father of mercy looks upon us graciously: how thankfully should we approach Him, and ourselves take care of our own interests, working by those ways and means which the most wise God, the Ordainer of all things, will show us.

The most useful thing that the Holy Scriptures teach us in this connection is this, that there is no more certain way under the sun for the raising of sunken humanity than the proper education of the young. Indeed Solomon, after he had gone through the whole labyrinth of human error and had mournfully recognised that perverseness could not be cured nor imperfections enumerated, turned at length to the young and adjured them to remember their Creator in the days of their youth, to fear Him, and to keep His commandments, for that this was the whole duty of man (Eccles. xii. 13). And in another place, "Train up a child in the way he should go, and when he is old he will not depart from it" (Proverbs xxii. 6). David also says, "Come, ye children, hearken unto me: I will teach you the fear of the Lord" (Psalm xxxiv. 11). The heavenly David himself, the true Solomon, the eternal Son of God who came down from heaven to turn us from sin, leads us on to the same path when He says, "Suffer the little children to come unto me, and forbid them not: for of such is the kingdom of God" (Mark x. 14), and said to us besides, "Verily I say unto you, Except ye be converted, and become as little children, ye shall not enter into the kingdom of heaven" (Matthew xviii. 3). What advice is this! Hear, all of you, and weigh carefully what the Lord and Master declares; how He announces that the little ones only are fit for the kingdom of God, that they are heirs of the kingdom and that only those who become as little children are to be admitted to share this inheritance. O dear children, may you rightly appreciate this goodly privilege! Just consider, we elders, who consider that we alone are men, but that you are apes, that we alone are wise, and that you lack sense, that we are eloquent, but you speechless—we, I say, are sent to learn our lessons from you! You are set over us as masters, you are to be our models and examples. If any one should wish to deliberate why God prizes children so highly, he will find no weightier reason than this, that children are simpler and more susceptible to the remedy which the mercy of God grants to the lamentable condition of men. For this reason it is that Christ commands us elders to become as little children, that is, to throw off the evil that we have gained from a bad education and from the evil examples of the world, and to return to our former condition of simplicity, gentleness, modesty, purity, and obedience. But, because nothing is harder than to lay aside our habits, it comes to pass that there is no more difficult task than for a badly-trained man to return to his former state. The tree remains as it grows, high or low, with straight or with crooked branches, and when it is full grown cannot be altered. The felloe, the piece of wood which has been bent to the shape of the wheel and has become hard in this position, breaks rather than be straightened, as experience teaches us. God also says the same of men who are accustomed to evil dealing: "Can the Ethiopian change his skin or the leopard his spots? then may ye also do good that are accustomed to do evil" (Jeremiah xiii. 23). From this it necessarily follows that, if the corruption of the human race is to be remedied, this must be done by means of the careful education of the young.

But in order to educate the young carefully it is necessary to take timely precautions that their characters be guarded from the corruptions of the world, that the seed of honour sown in them be brought to a happy growth by pure and continuous teaching and examples, and, lastly, that their minds be given over to the true knowledge of God, of man, and of nature, that they may grow accustomed to see in this light the light of God, and to love and to honour the Father of Light above all things.

If this take place, the truth of the Psalmist's words will be evident, "Out of the mouth of babes and sucklings hast thou ordained strength because of thine enemies, that thou mightest still the enemy and the avenger " (Psalm viii. 3).

For this reason has God given the little ones angels as guardians (Matthew xviii. 10), has placed their parents over them to take care of them, and bidden to bring them up in the nurture and admonition of the Lord (Ephesians vi. 4); and thus He solemnly bids all others, under penalty of eternal damnation, not to lead the young into sin through a bad example (Matthew xviii. 6, 7).

But how are we to carry this out when corruption is spreading so rapidly? In the time of the Patriarchs, since these holy men dwelt in seclusion from the world, and, in their own families, were not only fathers but priests, masters, and teachers as well, this was not such a difficult matter. For, after they had removed their children from intercourse with wicked men and had enlightened them by good and virtuous example, they brought them up by gentle admonition, encouragement, and, where necessary, by correction. God Himself is witness that Abraham did so, when He says: " For I know him, that he will command his children and his household after him, and they shall keep the way of the Lord to do justice and judgment" (Genesis xviii. 19). But now we dwell close together, the good and the bad are mingled, and the bad are many more than the good. The example of these men makes so powerful an impression on the young that the precepts for the practice of virtue, which we administer as an antidote against evil, have either no result at all or one that is inappreciable. But what must be the result if even these precepts are seldom delivered? There are few parents who are in the position to teach their children anything good, either because they have themselves never learned anything of the kind, or because their heads are full of other things; and thus education is neglected.

There are also few teachers who can bring good principles home to the young, and when one arises he is snatched up by some man in high position that he may busy himself with his children; the people get little advantage from him. Thus it comes to pass that the rest of the children grow up without the education that they need, like a forest which no one plants, waters, cuts, or keeps in order. Hence it is that we find unruly manners and customs in the world, in towns and in market-places, in houses and in men, for these both in body and soul are full of confusion. If Diogenes, Socrates, Seneca, or Solomon were to come to life again this day and visit us, they would find the world in the same state as formerly. Were God to address us from heaven He could only say as He said before : "They are all gone astray, they are all together become filthy: there is none that doeth good, no, not one " (Psalm xiv. 3). If, therefore, any man exist who can devise some plan, or who with tears, sighs, and entreaties can obtain from heaven a method by which some improvement may be made in the youth who are growing up, let him not hold his tongue, but rather let him advise, think, and speak. "Cursed be he that maketh the blind to wander out of the way," says God (Deuteronomy xxvii. 18). And cursed, therefore, is he who can free the blind from their error and does not do so. "Woe unto him who shall offend one of these little ones," says Christ (Matthew xviii. 6, 7). Woe also unto him who can prevent injury and does not. God wills not that the ass or the ox that strays through field and forest and sinks under its burden be deserted, but that it receive help, even if the helper do not know to whom it belongs, or if he know that it is his enemy's (Deuteronomy xxii. 1). Can it then please Him that we pass by without thought, and stretch out no helping hand, when we see the errors, not of beasts, but of intelligent beings, not of one or two, but of the whole world? Let this be far from us !

Cursed be he that doeth the work of the Lord deceitfully, and cursed be he that keepeth back his sword from blood (Jeremiah xlviii. 10). And yet we hope to remain guiltless while we thoughtlessly suffer the terrible Babylon of error that is ours ! Up, let him seize his sword who is girt with one, or who knows where one lies buried in its sheath! Let him demand the destruction of Babylon, that he be blessed by the Lord!

And so fulfil this command of the Lord with eagerness, ye rulers, ye servants of the Most High, and with the sword of righteousness banish the disorder with which the world is filled.

Busy yourselves, ye governors, ye faithful servants of Jesus Christ, and utterly destroy evil with the sword that is entrusted to you, with the two-edged sword of speech! Ye have seen that early youth is the best time to attack the evils of the human race; that the tree which is to thrive for ages is best planted when quite young; that Sion is most easily raised on the site of Babylon when the living building-stones of God, the young, are early broken, shaped, and fitted for the heavenly building. If we wish to have well-ordered and prosperous Churches, states, and households, thus and in no other way can we reach our goal.

But how to take this in hand and to carry it out with the desired result, this I will place before your eyes, I whose spirit the Lord has called to the work. See, hear, and mark its nature carefully, you to whom the Lord has given eyes to see, ears to hear, and minds to judge.

If a light, unseen before, be revealed to any, let him give God the glory and not grudge the illumination to the rising generation. But if he perceive any defect, even the smallest, in this light, let him complete and perfect it, or, that it may be perfected, let him recall the saying, "Many eyes are better than one."

Thus we shall mutually help one another to carry out the work of God with unanimity; thus we shall escape the curse which threatens those who neglect the Lord's work; thus we shall consult the welfare of the world's most precious possession, the young, as much as is possible; thus we shall shine with the brightness granted to those that turn others to righteousness (Daniel xii. 3).

May God have mercy on us, that we see the light! Amen.

THE USE OF THE ART OF TEACHING [11]

THAT the art of teaching be placed on a proper foundation is to the advantage—

1. Of parents, who up to this time have for the most part been uncertain how much to expect from their children. They hired tutors, besought them, strove to win them over by gifts, changed them, just as often in vain as with any result. But now that the method of teaching has been reasoned out with unerring accuracy, it will, with the assistance of God, be impossible that the desired result should not follow.

2. Of schoolmasters, the greater number of whom have been quite ignorant of their art, and who used therefore to wear themselves out when they wished to fulfil their duty, and to exhaust their strength in laborious efforts: or used to change their method, trying in turn first one plan then another—a course which involved a tedious waste of time and of energy.

3. Of students, who may master the sciences without difficulty, tedium, complaints, or blows, as if in sport and in merriment.

4. Of schools, which, when the method has been established, will be not only preserved continuously in full vigour, but increased without limit. For they will indeed become places of amusement, houses of delights and attractions, and since (on account of the infallibility of the method) each student, of whatever capacity, will become a doctor (of a higher or lower grade), it will never be

possible for a dearth of suitable school-teachers to arise, or for learning not to flourish.

5. Of states, according to the testimony of Cicero. With whom agrees that of Diogenes the Pythagorean (to be found in Stobæus [12]). For what is the foundation of the whole state? Surely, the development of the young. Since vines that have not been well cultivated will not bear good fruit.

6. Of the Church, since the proper organisation of schools alone can bring it about that the churches shall never lack learned doctors, and that learned doctors shall never lack suitable hearers.

7. And lastly, it is to the advantage of heaven that schools should be reformed for the exact and universal culture of the intellect, that those whom the sound of the divine trumpet is unable to stir up may be the more easily freed from darkness by the brilliancy of the divine light. For, although the Gospel be preached everywhere (and we hope that it will be preached to the ends of the earth), still the same thing is apt to happen as takes place in any meeting-place, tavern, or other tumultuous gathering of men, that not he alone is heard or gains particular attention who brings forward the best things, but that each one occupies with his own trifles the man near whom he happens to sit or to stand. Thus it comes to pass in the world. Though the ministers of the Word fulfil their duty with great zeal; though they talk, orate, exhort, testify, they none the less remain unheard by the greater part of mankind. For many never go to religious meetings except by chance; others come with their ears and eyes closed, and, as their minds are occupied with other matters, pay little attention to what is taking place. And lastly, if they do attend and grasp the purport of the sacred exhortation, they are not so greatly affected by it as they should be, since the accustomed sluggishness of their minds and the evil habits that they have acquired, blunt, bewitch, and harden them, so that they are unable to free themselves from their old custom. And thus they stick

fast in their habitual blindness and sin, as if bound so firmly by chains that none but God Himself could free them from their ingrained perverseness.   As one of the fathers has said, it is very near a miracle if an inveterate sinner be converted to repentance.   Now, as in other matters, so in this; where God supplies means, to ask for a miracle is to tempt Him.   Let us therefore consider it our duty to meditate on the means by which the whole Christian youth may be more fervidly stirred up to vigour of mind and love of heavenly things.   If we can attain this we shall see the kingdom of heaven spread more and more, as of old.

Let none therefore withdraw his thoughts, desires, strength, or resources from such a sacred undertaking.   He who has given the will, will also grant its fulfilment, and we ought without exception to demand this with good heart from the divine mercy.   For the salvation of man and the glory of the Most High is at stake.

Joh. Val. Andreæ.

P.S.—It is inglorious to despair of progress, and wrong to despise the counsel of others.

SUBJECTS OF THE CHAPTERS

CHAPTER I

MAN IS THE HIGHEST, THE MOST ABSOLUTE, AND THE MOST EXCELLENT OF THINGS CREATED

1. WHEN Pittacus [13] of old gave to the world his saying " Know thyself," the sentiment was received by the wise with so much approval, that, in order to impress it on the people, they declared that it had fallen from heaven, and caused it to be written in golden letters on the temple of the Delphic Apollo, where great assemblies of men used to collect. Their action was prudent and wise; but their statement was false. It was, however, in the interests of truth, and is of great importance to us.

2. For what is the voice from heaven that resounds in the Scriptures but " Know thyself, O man, and know Me." Me the source of eternity, of wisdom and of grace; thyself, My creation, My likeness, My delight.

3. For I have destined thee to be the companion of My eternity; for thy use I designed the heaven, the earth and all that in them is; to thee alone I gave all those things in conjunction, which to the rest of creation I gave but singly, namely, Existence, Vitality, Sense, and Reason. I have made thee to have dominion over the works of My hands. I have placed all things under thy feet, sheep and oxen and the beasts of the field, the fowl of the air and the fish of the sea, and I have crowned thee with glory and with honour (Psalm viii.) To thee, finally, lest anything should be lacking, I have given Myself in personal

communion, joining My nature to thine for eternity, and in this distinguishing thee from all created things, visible and invisible.   For what creature in heaven or in earth can boast that God was manifest in his flesh and was seen of angels (1 Tim. iii. 16), not, forsooth, that they might only see and marvel at Him whom they desired to see (1 Peter i. 12), but that they might adore God made manifest in the flesh, the son of God and of man (Hebrews i. 6; John i. 51; Matthew iv. 11).   Know therefore that thou art the corner-stone and epitome of my works, the representative of God among them, the crown of My glory.

4. Would that this were inscribed, not on the doors of temples, not on the title-pages of books, not on the tongues, ears, and eyes of all men, but on their hearts! Would that this could be done to all who undertake the task of educating men, that they might learn to appreciate the dignity of the task and of their own excellence, and might bring all means to bear on the perfect realisation of their divinity!

CHAPTER II

1. REASON itself dictates that such a perfect creature is destined to a higher end than all other creatures, that of being united with God, the culmination of all perfection, glory, and happiness, and of enjoying with Him absolute glory and happiness for ever.

2. Now although this is clear from Scripture, and we stedfastly believe that it is the truth, it will be no loss of time if we lightly touch on the various ways in which God has indicated that our destination lies beyond this life.

3. First, in the creation itself; for He did not simply command man to exist, as He did the rest of His creatures; but, after solemn consideration, He formed a body for him with His own fingers and breathed the soul into it from Himself.

4. Our nature shows that this life is not sufficient for us. For here we live a threefold life, the vegetative, the animal, and the intellectual or spiritual. Of these the action of the first is confined to the body, the second can extend itself to objects by the operation of the senses and of movement, while the third is able to exist separately, as is evident in the case of angels. So that, as it is evident that this, the last stage of life, is greatly overshadowed and hindered in us by the two former, it follows of necessity that there will be a future state in which it may be brought to perfection.

5. All our actions and affections in this life show that we do not attain our ultimate end here, but that everything connected with us, as well as we ourselves, has another destination. For whatever we are, do, think, speak, contrive, acquire, or possess, contains a principle of gradation, and, though we mount perpetually and attain higher grades, we still continue to advance and never reach the highest.

For in the beginning a man is nothing, and has been non-existent from eternity. It is from his mother's womb that he takes his origin. What then is a man in the beginning? Nothing but an unformed mass endowed with vitality. This soon assumes the outlines of a human body, but has, as yet, neither sense nor movement.

Later on it begins to move and by a natural process bursts forth into the world. Gradually the eyes, ears, and other organs of sense appear. In course of time the internal senses develope and the child perceives that he sees, hears, and feels. Then the intellect comes into existence by cognising the differences between objects; while, finally, the will assumes the office of a guiding principle by displaying desire for certain objects and aversion for others.

6. But in all these individual points of progress we find nothing but succession. For the intelligence that underlies matter makes itself seen by degrees, like a ray of dawn shining through the darkness of night, and, as long as life remains, there is a continual access of light, unless a man become utterly brutish. Thus our actions are at first weak, unformed and confused; then the virtues of the mind unfold themselves proportionately to the forces of the body, so that as long as we live (unless the greatest lethargy take possession of us and bury us alive) we are continually exercising our faculties.

In a worthy mind all these functions tend to a higher development, nor can we find any end of the things that we desire or wish to accomplish.

7. In whatever direction a man turns he may perceive

this experimentally. If any have an excessive desire for riches he will not find anything that can satisfy his greed, though he possess the whole world; as was evident in the case of Alexander. If any burn with desire for honour he will not be able to rest though the whole world adore him.

If any give himself over to pleasure, rivers of delight may bathe all his senses, but he becomes accustomed to them, and his appetite continues to desire one thing after another. If any apply his mind to the study of wisdom he will find no end; for the more a man knows, the more he realises his ignorance. Rightly did Solomon say that the eye could not grow tired of seeing or the ear of hearing.

8. Indeed, the examples of those who die teach us that death does not put the last touch to existence. For those whose life has been righteous rejoice that they are to enter on a better one; while those who are filled with love of the present life, seeing that they must leave it and migrate elsewhere, begin to tremble and to reconcile themselves with God and man, if by any chance this be still possible. And, although the body, broken down by pain, grows faint, the senses become clouded, and life itself slips away, the mind fulfils its functions more vividly than ever, as we see when a man circumspectly summons his family and heirs about his death-bed. So that he who sees a pious and wise man dying sees nothing but the structure of clay falling asunder; he who listens to him hears an angel's voice and cannot but confess that the dweller is only taking his departure while the house falls to ruin about him. Even the heathen understood this, so that the Romans, according to Festus,[14] called death *abitio*, and with the Greeks, οἴχεσθαι, which signifies "to go away," is frequently used instead of "to die" and "to perish." This can only be because by "death" nothing is understood but transition to another life.

9. This is all the more evident to us Christians, now that Christ, the Son of the living God, has been sent from

heaven to regenerate in us the image of God. For having been conceived of a woman He walked among men; then, having died, He rose again and ascended into heaven, nor had death any more dominion over Him. Now He has been called "our forerunner" (Hebr. vi. 20), "the firstborn among his brethren" (Rom. viii. 30), "the head over all things" (Ephes. i. 22), and the archetype of all who are to be formed in the image of God (Rom. viii. 29). As then, He did not visit this earth in order to remain on it, but that, when His course was run, He might pass to the eternal mansions; so we also, His companions, must pass on and must not make this our abiding-place.

10. To each of us, then, his life and his abiding-place is threefold. The mother's womb, the earth, and the heaven. From the first into the second he passes by nativity, and from the second into the third by death and resurrection. From the third he makes no move, but rests there for all eternity.

In the first stage we find life in its simplicity, with the commencement of movement and of feeling. In the second we have life, motion, sense, and the elements of intellect. In the third we find the full plenitude of all.

11. The first life is preparatory to the second, and the second to the third, while the third exists for itself and is without end. The transition from the first into the second and from the second into the third, is narrow and accompanied by pain; and in both cases some covering or surrounding must be laid aside (in the first case the after-birth, in the second the body itself), just as the egg-shell is discarded when a chicken is hatched. Thus the first and second abiding-places are like workshops in which are formed, in the first the body, for use in the following life; in the second the rational soul, for use in the life everlasting. In the third abiding-place the perfection and fruition of both will be realised.

12. Thus (to use them as a type) were the Israelites born in Egypt. Thence, through the passes of the

mountains and through the Red Sea, they were brought into the desert. They built temples, they learned the law, they fought with various tribes, and, at length, having with difficulty crossed the Jordan, they were made heirs of Canaan, the land flowing with milk and honey.

CHAPTER III

1. THAT this life, since its destination is elsewhere, is not (properly speaking) a life at all, but only the prelude to a real and everlasting existence, will be evident, firstly, from the witness of our own selves, secondly, from the world, and, thirdly, from the Holy Scriptures.

2. If we examine ourselves, we see that our faculties grow in such a manner that what goes before paves the way for what comes after. For example, our first life is in our mother's womb. But for the sake of what does it exist? of the life itself? Not at all. The process that here takes place is intended to form the embryo into the suitable abiding-place and instrument of the soul, for convenient use in the life on earth which follows. As soon as this preparation is finished we burst forth into the light because in this stage no further development is possible. In the same way, this life on earth is nothing but a preparation for eternity, and exists in order that the soul, through the agency of the body, may prepare for itself those things which will be of use in the future life. As soon as this is accomplished we go hence, because further undertakings are of no avail. Many of us, also, are snatched away unprepared or are hurled to destruction, just as abortive embryos are produced from the womb, destined not for life but for death. In each of which cases God,

it is true, gives His permission, but man is the guilty cause.

3. The visible world itself, from whatever point of view we regard it, bears witness that it has been created for no other end than that it may serve for the progeneration, the nutrition, and the training of the human race. For as it pleased God not to create all men at the same moment, as was done with the angels, but only a male and a female who should increase by generation ; and, as a sufficient length of time was necessary for this purpose, He granted some thousands of years. And in order that this period might not be confused, silent, and dark, He spread forth the heavens and placed in them the sun, the moon, and the stars, and commanded these, by circling round, to measure out the hours, the days, the months, and the years. Further, because the beings whose birth was contemplated were corporeal and needed a place to dwell in, space to breathe and move in, food to nourish them, and clothing to adorn them, He constructed in the lowest part of the firmament a solid substratum, the earth. Around this He poured the air, He irrigated it with waters, and bade plants and animals of various kinds to spring forth ; and this not only to supply necessary wants, but also to promote enjoyment. And because He had made man in His own image and had given him a mind, in order that its proper nutrition might not be wanting to that mind, He divided each class of creatures into many species, that this visible universe might be a continual mirror of the infinite power, wisdom, and goodness of God, and that by its contemplation man might be compelled to marvel at the Creator, moved to recognise Him, and enticed to love Him, when the might, the beauty, and the sweetness that lie invisible in the abyss of eternity shone out on all sides through these visible manifestations, and suffered themselves to be handled, seen, and tasted. Thus the world is nothing but our nursery, our nurturing place, and our school, and there is, therefore, a place beyond, whither we shall be transferred when we are

dismissed from the classes of this school and are sent to that university which is everlasting. Reason alone makes this truth manifest, but it is more plainly visible in the divine oracles.

4. God Himself testifies in Hosea that the heavens exist for the sake of the earth, the earth that it may produce corn, wine, and oil, and these in turn for man (Hosea ii. 21, 22). All things therefore, even time itself, exist for the sake of man. For no longer a duration of time will be granted than is necessary to fill up the number of the elect (Rev. vi. 11). As soon as this is accomplished the heavens and the earth will pass away and the place shall know them no more (Rev. xi. 1). For a new heaven and a new earth will appear, in which justice shall dwell (Rev. xxi. 1 ; 2 Peter iii. 13). And finally, the way in which the Scriptures speak of this life show that it is nothing but the preparation for that to come. For they call it a way, a progress, a gate, and an expectation, while us they call pilgrims, newcomers, sojourners, and lookers forward to another and lasting state (Gen. xlvii. 9 ; Psalm xxxix. 12 ; Job vii. 10 ; Luke xii. 33).

5. Now this we are taught by the facts themselves and by the manifest condition of all men. For what mortal has ever existed who, having been born, has not disappeared again from the earth, since we have been destined for eternity. This being the case, it follows that our state here is one of transition. Whence Christ says, "Therefore be ye also ready, for in an hour that ye think not the Son of Man cometh" (Matt. xxiv. 44). And this is the reason (as we learn from Scripture) that God calls some hence in early youth ; for He sees that they are ready, as was Enoch (Gen. v. 24 ; Wisdom iv. 14). Why, on the other hand, does He show such long-suffering toward the wicked? Because He does not wish that any should be overtaken unprepared, but that he should repent (2 Peter iii. 9). If, however, any man abuse the patience of God, He bids him be snatched away.

6. As, then, it is certain that our sojourn in our mother's

womb is a preparation for the life in the body, so certain is it that our sojourn in the body is a preparation for the life which shall follow this one, and shall endure for ever. Happy is he who leaves his mother's womb with limbs well formed! Happier a thousand times is the man who shall bear his soul hence in purity and cleanliness.

CHAPTER IV

THERE ARE THREE STAGES IN THE PREPARATION FOR
    ETERNITY: TO KNOW ONESELF (AND WITH ONESELF
    ALL THINGS); TO RULE ONESELF; AND TO DIRECT
    ONESELF TO GOD.

1. IT is evident, then, that the ultimate end of man is eternal
happiness with God. The subordinate ends, also, at which
we aim in this transitory life, are evident from the words of
the divine soliloquy which the Creator uttered when about
to make man. "Let us make man," He said, "in our
image, after our likeness; and let them have dominion
over the fish of the sea, and over the fowl of the air,
and over the cattle, and over all the earth, and over
every creeping thing that creepeth upon the earth" (Gen.
i. 26).

2. From which it is plain that man is situated among
visible creatures so as to be

(i)   A rational creature.

(ii) The Lord of all creatures.

(iii) A creature which is the image and the joy of its
Creator.

These three aspects are so joined together that they
cannot be separated, for in them is laid the basis of the
future and of the present life.

3. To be a rational creature is to name all things, and
to speculate and reason about everything that the world
contains, as we find it in Gen. ii. 19, or, in the words of

Solomon (Wisdom vii. 17), to know how the world was made and the operation of the elements; the beginning, ending, and midst of the times; the alterations of the turning of the sun, and the change of seasons; the circuits of years and the positions of stars; the natures of living things and the furies of wild beasts; the violence of winds and the reasonings of men; the diversities of plants and the virtues of roots; in a word, everything that is secret and that is manifest. To man belong the knowledge of handicrafts and the art of speaking, lest (as says the son of Sirach) anything should remain unknown, be it small or great, in any department of knowledge (Eccles. v. 12). For thus, if he know the properties of all things, will he be able to justify his title of " rational being."

4. To be the lord of all creatures consists in subjecting everything to his own use by contriving that its legitimate end be suitably fulfilled; in conducting himself royally, that is, gravely and righteously, among creatures (adoring only one above him, his Creator; recognising God's angels, man's fellow-servants, as his equals, and considering all other things as far beneath him). Thus will he preserve the dignity which has been granted to him. He should enslave himself to no creature, not even to his own flesh and blood; but should use all freely in his service, and not be ignorant where, when, how, and to what extent each may prudently be used, how far the body should be gratified, and how far our neighbour's interests should be consulted. In a word, he should be able to control with prudence his own movements and actions, external and internal, as well as those of others.

5. Finally, to be the image of God is to represent the perfection of his Archetype, who says Himself "Ye shall be holy, for I the Lord your God am holy " (Lev. xix. 2).

6. From this it follows that man is naturally required to be: (1) acquainted with all things; (2) endowed with power over all things and over himself; (3) to refer himself and all things to God, the source of all.

Now, if we wish to express these three things by three well-known words, these will be:

(i) Erudition.

(ii) Virtue or seemly morals.

(iii) Religion or piety.

Under Erudition we comprehend the knowledge of all things, arts, and tongues; under Virtue, not only external decorum, but the whole disposition of our movements, internal and external; while by Religion we understand that inner veneration by which the mind of man attaches and binds itself to the supreme Godhead.

7. In these three things is situated the whole excellence of man, for they alone are the foundation of the present and of the future life. All other things (health, strength, beauty, riches, honour, friendship, good-fortune, long life) are as nothing, if God grant them to any, but extrinsic ornaments of life, and if a man greedily gape after them, engross himself in their pursuit, occupy and overwhelm himself with them to the neglect of those more important matters, then they become superfluous vanities and harmful obstructions.

8. To illustrate the matter by an example. The time-piece (either the sun-dial or the mechanical clock) is an elegant and very necessary instrument for measuring time, and its essential excellence depends on the accurate joining together of all its parts. The case which is added, the chasings, the engravings, and the gildings are accessories which add something to its external appearance, but nothing to its utility. Were any to prefer a handsome clock to a good one, men would laugh at him for not realising in what the essential excellence of the object consisted. In the same way, the value of a horse consists in its strength, combined with spirit, speed, and promptness in obeying its rider's wishes. A flowing tail or one tied in a knot, hair combed and standing erect, gilded bits, gay coverings, and trappings of whatever kind, add decorative beauty, it is true, yet we call a man a fool if we see that he measures a horse's excellence by them.

Finally, a sound condition of health depends on the proper cooking of food, and òn our digestive organs being in good order.   To sleep softly, to dress well, and to fare delicately, add nothing to our health, but rather detract from it, and therefore a man is a fool who prefers dainties to wholesome viands.   But much more, and to his own damnation, is that man a fool who, wishing to be a man, gives more heed to the ornaments than to the essentials of human existence.   The Preacher, therefore, pronounces those ignorant and impious who think that our life is a pastime or a simple pursuit of wealth, and says that the praise and the blessing of God is very far from them (Wisdom xv. 12, 19).

9. It follows, therefore, that we advance towards our ultimate end in proportion as we pursue Learning, Virtue, and Piety in this world.

These three are undoubtedly the main issues of our life ; all else are side channels, hindrances, or ornamentations.

CHAPTER V

THE SEEDS OF THESE THREE (LEARNING, VIRTUE, AND
PIETY) ARE NATURALLY IMPLANTED IN US

1. By the word *nature* we mean, not the corruption which has
laid hold of all men since the Fall (on which account we are
naturally called the children of wrath, unable of ourselves
to have any good thoughts), but our first and original condition, to which, as to a starting-point, we must be recalled.
It was in this sense that Ludovicus Vives [15] said, "What
else is a Christian but a man restored to his own nature,
and, as it were, brought back to the starting-point from
which the devil has thrown him?" (Lib. i. *De Concordia
et Discordia*). In this sense, too, must we take the words
of Seneca, "This is wisdom, to return to nature and to the
position from which universal error (that is to say, the error
of the human race, originated by the first men) has driven
us," and again, "Man is not good but becomes so, as,
mindful of his origin, he strives toward equality with God.
No man who is viciously inclined ventures the ascent
towards the place whence he descended" (*Epist.* 93).

2. By the voice of nature we understand the universal
Providence of God or the influence of Divine Goodness
which never ceases to work all in all things; that is to
say, which continually developes each creature for the end
to which it has been destined. For it is a sign of the
divine wisdom to do nothing in vain, that is to say, without
a definite end or without means proportionate to that end.

Whatever exists, therefore, exists for some end, and has been provided with the organs and appliances necessary to attain to it. It has also been gifted with a certain inclination, that nothing may be borne towards its end unwillingly and reluctantly, but rather promptly and pleasantly, by the natural instinct that pain and death will ensue if any obstacle be placed in the way. And so it is certain that man also is naturally fitted for the understanding of facts, for existence in harmony with the moral law, and above all things for the love of God (since for these we have already seen that he is destined), and that the roots of these three principles are as firmly planted in him as are the roots of any tree in the earth beneath it.

3. In order, therefore, that we may thoroughly understand the saying of the son of Sirach, that Wisdom has placed everlasting foundations in man (Ecclesiasticus i. 14), let us examine the foundations of Wisdom, of Virtue, and of Piety, which have been laid in us, that we may see what a marvellous instrument of wisdom man is.

4. It is evident that man is naturally capable of acquiring a knowledge of all things, since, in the first place, he is the image of God. For an image, if it be accurate, necessarily reproduces the outlines of its archetype, as otherwise it will not be an image. Now omniscience is chief among the properties of God, and it follows that the image of this must be reflected in man. And why not? Man, in truth stands in the centre of the works of God and possesses a lucid mind, which, like a spherical mirror suspended in a room, reflects images of all things that are around it. All things that are around it, we say; for our mind not only seizes on things that are close at hand, but also on things that are far off, whether in space or in time; it masters difficulties, hunts out what is concealed, uncovers what is veiled, and wears itself out in examining what is inscrutable; so infinite and so unbounded is its power. If a thousand years were granted to man, in which, by grasping one thing after another, he might continually learn something fresh, he would still find some spot from which

13

the understanding might gain fresh objects of knowledge.

So unlimited is the capacity of the mind that in the
process of perception it resembles an abyss. The body is
enclosed by small boundaries; the voice roams within
wider limits; the sight is bounded only by the vault of
heaven; but for the mind, neither in heaven nor anywhere
outside heaven, can a boundary be fixed. It ascends as
far over the heavens above as below the depths beneath,
and would do so if they were even a thousand times more
vast than they are; for it penetrates through space with
incredible speed. Shall we then deny that it can fathom
and grasp all things?

5. Philosophers have called man a Microcosm or Epitome of the Universe, since he inwardly comprehends all
the elements that are spread far and wide through the
Macrocosm, or world at large; a statement the truth of
which is shown elsewhere. The mind, therefore, of a man
who enters this world is very justly compared to a seed
or to a kernel in which the plant or tree really does exist,
although its image cannot actually be seen. This is evident; since the seed, if placed in the ground, puts forth
roots beneath it and shoots above it, and these, later on,
by their innate force, spread into branches and leaves, are
covered with foliage, and adorned with flowers and fruit.
It is not necessary, therefore, that anything be brought to
a man from without, but only that that which he possesses
rolled up within himself be unfolded and disclosed, and
that stress be laid on each separate element. Thus Pythagoras used to say that it was so natural for a man to be
possessed of all knowledge, that a boy of seven years old,
if prudently questioned on all the problems of philosophy,
ought to be able to give a correct answer to each interrogation; since the light of Reason is a sufficient standard
and measure of all things. Still it is true that, since the
Fall, Reason has become obscure and involved, and does
not know how to set itself free; while those who ought to
have done so have rather entangled it the more.

6. To the rational soul, that dwells within us, organs of sense have been supplied, which may be compared to emissaries and scouts, and by the aid of these it compasses all that lies without. These are sight, hearing, smell, sound, and touch, and there is nothing whatever that can escape their notice. For, since there is nothing in the visible universe which cannot be seen, heard, smelt, tasted, or touched, and the kind and quality of which cannot in this way be discerned, it follows that there is nothing in the universe which cannot be compassed by a man endowed with sense and reason.

7. In addition to the desire for knowledge that is implanted in him, man is imbued not merely with a tolerance of but with an actual appetite for toil. This is evident in earliest childhood, and accompanies us throughout life. For who is there that does not always desire to see, hear, or handle something new? To whom is it not a pleasure to go to some new place daily, to converse with some one, to narrate something, or have some fresh experience? In a word, the eyes, the ears, the sense of touch, the mind itself, are, in their search for food, ever carried beyond themselves; for to an active nature nothing is so intolerable as ease and sloth. Even the fact that the ignorant admire learned men is but a sign that they feel the promptings of a certain natural desire. For they would wish themselves to be partakers of this wisdom, could they deem it possible. But, since they despair, they only sigh, and marvel at those whom they see in advance of them.

8. The examples of those who are self-taught show u most plainly that man, under the guidance of nature, can penetrate to a knowledge of all things. Many have made greater progress under their own tuition, or (as Bernard [16] says) with oaks and beeches for their teachers, than others have done under the irksome instruction of tutors. Does not this teach us that, in very truth, all things exist in man; that the lamp, the oil, the tinder, and all the appliances are there, and that if only he be sufficiently skilled to strike sparks, to catch them, and to kindle the

lamp, he can forthwith see and can reap the fullest enjoyment of the marvellous treasures of God's wisdom, both in himself and in the larger world; that is to say, can appreciate the numerical and proportional arrangement of the whole creation. Now, when the internal lamp is not lit, but the torches of strange opinions are carried round without, the effect must be as if lights were carried round a man shut up in a dark dungeon; the rays indeed penetrate the chinks, but the full light is unable to enter. Thus, as Seneca says: "The seeds of all arts are implanted in us, and God the master brings forth intellect from the darkness."

9. The things to which our minds may be likened teach the same lesson. For the earth (with which the Scriptures often compare our heart) receives seeds of every description. One and the same garden can be sown with herbs, with flowers, and with aromatic plants of every kind, if only the gardener lack not prudence and industry. And the greater the variety, the pleasanter the sight to the eyes, the sweeter the attraction to the nose, and the more potent the refreshment to the heart. Aristotle compared the mind of man to a blank tablet on which nothing was written, but on which all things could be engraved. And, just as a writer can write or a painter paint whatever he wishes on a bare tablet, if he be not ignorant of his art, thus it is easy for one who is not ignorant of the art of teaching to depict all things on the human mind. If the result be not successful, it is more than certain that this is not the fault of the tablet (unless it have some inherent defect), but arises from ignorance on the part of the writer or painter. There is, however, this difference, that on the tablet the writing is limited by space, while, in the case of the mind, you may continually go on writing and engraving without finding any boundary, because, as has already been shown, the mind is without limit.

10. Again, the comparison of our brain, the workshop of thought, to wax which either receives the impress of a seal, or furnishes the material for small images, is an apt one. For just as wax, taking every form, allows itself to be

modelled and remodelled in any desired way, so the brain, receiving the images of all things, takes into itself whatever is contained in the whole universe. This comparison throws a remarkable light on the true nature of thought and of knowledge. Whatever makes an impression on my organ of sight, hearing, smell, taste, or touch, stands to me in the relation of a seal by which the image of the object is impressed upon my brain. So true is this simile that when the object is removed from my eyes, my ears, my nostrils, or my hand, its image still remains before me; nor is it possible that it should not remain, unless my attention has wandered and the impression has been a weak one. For example, if I have seen or spoken to any one; if, when taking a journey, I have seen a mountain, a river, a field, a wood, or a town, or if I have read any-thing attentively in some author, all these things are im-printed on the brain, so that, as often as the recollection of them comes into my mind, the effect is the same as if I were actually seeing them with my eyes, hearing them with my ears, tasting them, or feeling them. And although of these impressions the brain places one before the other or receives some more distinctly and vividly than others, it still, in some way or other, receives, represents, and retains them all.

11. Here we have mirrored before us the marvellous wisdom of God, who was able to arrange that the small mass of our brains should be sufficient to receive so many thousands of images. For, if the particulars can be remembered of anything that any of us (and this applies particularly to men of learning) have, many years before, seen, heard, tasted, read, or collected by experience or by reasoning, it is evident that these details must be carried in the brain. Yet it is a fact that images of objects formerly seen, heard, or read of, of which thousands of thousands and many more exist, and which are daily multiplied as we daily see, hear, read, or experience something new, are all carefully stored up. What inscrutable wisdom and power of God lies here? Solomon wonders that all rivers

run into the sea, and that yet the sea is not full (Eccles. i. 7), and who will not marvel at this abyss of memory which exhausts all things, which gives all back again, and yet is never overfull or too void ?   In truth our mind is greater than the universe, since that which contains is necessarily greater than that which is contained.

12. Finally, the eye (or a mirror) resembles the mind in many ways.   If you hold anything before it, of whatever shape or colour, it will soon display a similar image in itself. That is to say, unless you are in the dark, or turn your back, or are too far off, at a distance greater than is fitting, or hinder the impression, or confuse it by movement; for in these cases it must be confessed that the result will be failure.   I speak, therefore, of what takes place naturally, when light is present and the object is suitably placed. Just as, then, there is no need for the eye to be compelled to open and look at any object, since, naturally thirsting for light, it rejoices to be fed by gazing, and suffices for all objects (provided that it be not confused by too many at once), and just as it can never be satiated by seeing, so does the mind thirst for objects, ever longs and yearns to observe, grasps at, nay, seizes on all information, and is indefatigable, provided that it be not surfeited with an excess of objects, and that they be presented to its observation one after the other, and in the proper order.

13. Even the heathen philosophers saw that a harmony of morals was necessary for man, although, being ignorant of that other light granted by heaven, which is the most certain guide to eternal life, they set up these sparks as torches; a vain endeavour.   Thus Cicero says: "The seeds of virtue are sown in our dispositions, and, if they were allowed to develope, nature herself would lead us to the life of the blest."   This goes rather too far !   "Now, however, from the time when we are brought forth to the light of day, we continually move in all wickedness, so that we almost seem to suck in faults with our nurse's milk" (*Tuscul.* iii.)   Thus the truth of the statement that the seeds of virtue are born with man is bound up with this two-

fold argument: (1) every man delights in harmony; (2) man himself, externally and internally, is nothing but a harmony.

14. That man delights in harmony and pursues it greedily, is obvious. For who does not take pleasure in a well-made man, an elegant horse, a beautiful portrait, or a charming picture? And what is the reason of this if not that the proportion of the parts and of the colours is a source of enjoyment? This pleasure of the eye is very natural. Again, who is not affected by music? and why? Because a harmony of voices makes a pleasing consonance. To whom does well-flavoured food not taste good? For the proper mixing of the flavours tickles the palate. Every man rejoices in moderate heat, in moderate cold, in the moderate inactivity or motion of the limbs. Why? if not because everything that is harmonised is congenial and lifegiving to nature, while everything that lacks moderation is hostile and harmful to her.

Even the virtues of others are a source of admiration to some people (for those devoid of them like them in others; though they may not imitate them, thinking good habits impossible to acquire when once vice has got the upper hand). Why then should not each man like them in himself? Surely we are blind if we do not recognise that we all have within us the roots of harmony.

15. Indeed, man is nothing but a harmony, both in respect of his body and of his mind. For, just as the great world itself is like an immense piece of clockwork put together with many wheels and bells, and arranged with such art that throughout the whole structure one part depends on the other, and the movements are perpetuated and harmonised; thus it is with man. The body is indeed constructed with wonderful skill. First of all comes the heart, the source of all life and action, from which the other members receive motion and the measurement of motion. The weight, the efficient cause of motion, is the brain, which by the help of the nerves, as of ropes, attracts and repels the other wheels or limbs, while the

variety of operations within and without depends on the commensurate proportion of the movements.

16. In the movements of the soul the most important wheel is the will; while the weights are the desires and affections which incline the will this way or that. The escapement is the reason, which measures and determines what, where, and how far anything should be sought after or avoided. The other movements of the soul resemble the less important wheels which depend on the principal one. Wherefore, if too much weight be not given to the desires and affections, and if the escapement, reason, select and exclude properly, it is impossible that the harmony and agreement of virtues should not follow, and this evidently consists of a proper blending of the active and the passive elements.

17. Man, then, is in himself nothing but a harmony, and, as in the case of a clock or of a musical instrument which a skilled artificer has constructed, we do not forthwith pronounce it to be of no further use if it become disorganised and corrupt (for it can be put to rights); thus, with regard to man, we may say that, no matter how disorganised by his fall into sin, he can, through the grace of God and by certain methods, be restored again to harmony.

18. That the roots of piety are present in man is shown by the fact that he is the image of God. For an image implies likeness, and that like rejoices in like, is an immutable law of nature (Eccles. xii. 7). Since, then, man's only equal is He in whose image he has been made, it follows that there is no direction in which he can be more easily carried by his desires than towards the fountain whence he took his origin; provided that he clearly understand the conditions of his existence.

19. The same thing is shown by the example of the moral philosophers, who, instructed by no word of God, but led by the blind instinct of nature, both acknowledged the Deity, venerated Him, and called upon His name, though they erred in the manner in which they put their

religion into practice. "All men have some conception of the gods, and all assign the highest place to a divine being," writes Aristotle (*De Cælo*, i. 3). Seneca also says: "The worship of the gods consists first in believing in them; then in acknowledging their majesty and their goodness, without which no majesty exists; then in recognising that it is they who preside over the world, include everything under their dominion, and act as guardians of the human race" (*Epist.* 96). How closely this resembles what the Apostle says (Hebrews xi. 6): "He that cometh to God must believe that he is, and that he is a rewarder of them that seek after him."

20. Plato also says: "God is the highest good, elevated high above all existence and above nature; towards which all creation strives" (*Timaeus*). And this is so true (that God is the highest good, which all things seek) that Cicero was able to say: "The first to teach us piety is nature" (*De Natura Deorum*, i.) And this is because (as Lactantius [17] writes, bk. iv. ch. 28): "We receive pardon on condition that we give just and due worship to the God who produced us. Him alone let us know and follow. By this chain of piety we have been bound and linked to God, and it is from this fact that religion derives its name."

21. It must be confessed that the natural desire for God, as the highest good, has been corrupted by the Fall, and has gone astray, so that no man, of his strength alone, could return to the right way. But in those whom God illumines by the Word and by His Spirit it is so renewed, that we find David exclaiming: "Whom have I in heaven but thee? And there is none on earth that I desire beside thee. My flesh and my heart faileth, but God is the strength of my heart and my portion for ever" (Psalm lxxiii. 25, 26).

22. Therefore, while we are seeking for the remedies of corruption, let none cast corruption in our teeth. For God will remove it through His Holy Ghost and by the intervention of natural means. For as Nebuchadnezzar, when human reason was taken from him and the soul of a

beast was his, yet retained the hope of returning to his
senses, and to his royal dignity as well, as soon as he
acknowledged that heaven was his superior (Daniel iv. 25),
so to us, who are trees rooted out of God's Paradise, the
roots are left, and these can germinate afresh when the rain
and the sun of God's grace are shed upon them.   Did not
God, soon after the Fall, and after the exile threatened to
us (the penalty of death), sow in our hearts the seeds of
fresh grace (by the promise of His blessed offspring)?   Did
He not send His Son to restore us to our former estate?

23. It is base, wicked, and an evident sign of ingrati-
tude, that we continually complain of our corrupt state,
but make no effort to reform it; that we bring forward
what the old Adam can work in us, but never experience
what the new Adam, Christ, can do.   The Apostle says
in his own name and in that of his Redeemer: "I can do
all things through him that strengtheneth me" (Phil. iv.
13).   If it be possible for a shoot grafted on a willow,
on a thorn, or on any other shrub, to germinate and bear
fruit, what would it not do if grafted on a stock similar to
itself?   See the argument of the Apostle (Romans xi. 24).
In addition, if God is able from these stones to raise up
children unto Abraham (Matthew iii. 9), why should He
not be able to excite to good works man, the son of God
from the first creation, adopted anew through Christ, and
born again through the Spirit of grace?

24. Ah! let us beware lest we neglect the grace of God,
which He is prepared to pour most liberally upon us.   For
if we, who are made one with Christ through faith, and dedicated to Him through the spirit of adoption, if we, I say,
deny that we, with our offspring, are fit for those things
which are of the kingdom of God, how was it that Christ
said of children that theirs was the kingdom of heaven?
or how can He refer us to them, bidding us to become as
little children, if we wish to enter into the kingdom of
heaven? (Matthew xviii. 3).

How is it that the Apostle pronounces the children of
Christians to be sacred (even where one only of the

parents is faithful), and says that they are not unclean (1 Cor. vii. 14). Even of those who have been implicated in the gravest crimes the Apostle dares to affirm : "Such were some of you ; but ye were washed, but ye were sanctified, but ye were justified in the name of the Lord Jesus Christ and in the Spirit of our God " (1. Cor. vi. 11). Can it therefore appear impracticable to any one, when we demand that the children of Christians (not the offspring of the old Adam but of the new, the sons of God, the little brothers and sisters of Christ) may be carefully trained, and declare that they are fit to receive in their hearts the seeds of eternity? We do not indeed demand fruit from a wild olive, but we come to the assistance of grafts freshly grafted on the tree of life, and help them to bear fruit.

25. We see, then, that it is more natural, and, through the grace of the Holy Spirit, easier for a man to become wise, honest, and righteous, than for his progress to be hindered by incidental depravity. For everything returns easily to its own nature, and this it is that the Scriptures say : " Truth is easily seen by those who love her, and can readily be found by those who seek her. She grants herself to the understanding, and those who wait before her door obtain her without trouble " (Wisdom vi. 13, 15). As the poet of Venusia says :

No one is so wild that he cannot be tamed,
If he patiently turn his ear to instruction and knowledge.

CHAPTER VI

IF A MAN IS TO BE PRODUCED, IT IS NECESSARY THAT HE BE FORMED BY EDUCATION

1. THE seeds of knowledge, of virtue, and of piety are, as we have seen, naturally implanted in us; but the actual knowledge, virtue, and piety are not so given. These must be acquired by prayer, by education, and by action. He gave no bad definition who said that man was a "teachable animal." And indeed it is only by a proper education that he can become a man.

2. For, if we consider knowledge, we see that it is the peculiar attribute of God to know all things by a single and simple intuition, without beginning, without progress, and without end. For man and for angels this is impossible, because they do not possess infinity and eternity, that is to say, divinity. It is enough for them to have received sufficient keenness of intellect to comprehend the works of God, and to gather a wealth of knowledge from them. As regards angels, it is certain that they also learn by perception (1 Peter i. 12; Ephes. iii. 10; 1 Kings xxii. 20; Job i. 6), and that their knowledge, like our own, is derived from experience.

3. Let none believe, therefore, that any can really be a man, unless he have learned to act like one, that is, have been trained in those elements which constitute a man. This is evident from the example of all things created, which, although destined for man, do not suit his uses until

fitted for them by his hands.   For example, stones have
been given to us as material with which to build houses,
towers, walls, pillars, etc.; but they are of no use until
they are cut and laid in their place by us.   Pearls and
precious stones destined to adorn man must be cut,
ground, and polished.   The metals, which are of vital use
in daily life, have to be dug out, melted, refined, and vari-
ously cast and hammered.   Till this is done they are of
less use to us than common earth.

From plants we derive food, drink, and medicines; but
first the herbs and grains have to be sown, hoed, gathered,
winnowed, and ground; trees have to be planted, pruned,
and manured, while their fruits must be plucked off and
dried; and if any of these things are required for medicine, or for building purposes, much more preparation is
needed.   Animals, whose essential characteristics are life
and motion, seem to be self-sufficing, but if you wish to
use them for the purposes for which they are suitable,
some training is necessary.   For example, the horse is
naturally suited for use in war, the ox for drawing, the ass
for carrying burdens, the dog for guarding and hunting,
the falcon and hawk for fowling; but they are all of little
use until we accustom them to their work by training.

4. Man, as far as his body is concerned, is born to
labour; and yet we see that nothing but the bare aptitude
is born in him.   He needs instruction before he can sit,
stand, walk, or use his hands.   Why, therefore, should it
be claimed for our mind that, of itself, it can exist in its
full development, and without any previous preparation;
since it is the law of all things created that they take their
origin from nothing and develope themselves gradually, in
respect both of their material and of the process of development?   For it is well known, and we showed in our
last chapter, that the angels, whose perfection comes very
near to that of the Almighty, are not omniscient, but make
gradual advances in their knowledge of the marvellous
wisdom of God.

5. It is evident, too, that even before the Fall, a school

in which he might make gradual progress was opened for man in Paradise. For, although the first created, as soon as they came into being, lacked neither the power of walking erect, nor speech, nor reason, it is manifest, from the conversation of Eve with the serpent, that the knowledge of things which is derived from experience was entirely wanting. For Eve, had she had more experience, would have known that the serpent is unable to speak, and that there must therefore be some deceit.

Much more, therefore, in this state of corruption must it be necessary to learn by experience, since the understanding which we bring with us is an empty form, like a bare tablet, and since we are unskilled to do, speak, or know anything; for all these faculties do but exist potentially and need development. And indeed this is much more difficult now than it can have been in the state of perfection, since not only are things obscure, but tongues also are confused (so that instead of one, many must now be learned, if a man for the sake of learning wish to hold communion with divers people, living and dead). The vernacular tongues also have become more complex, and no knowledge of them is born with us.

6. Examples show that those who in their infancy have been seized by wild animals, and have been brought up among them, have not risen above the level of brutes in intellect, and would not have been able to make more use of their tongues, their hands, and their feet than beasts can, had they not once more come into the society of men. I will give several instances. About the year 1540, in a village called Hassia, situated in the middle of a forest, a boy three years of age was lost, through the carelessness of his parents. Some years afterwards the country people saw a strange animal running about with the wolves, of a different shape, four-footed, but with a man's face. Rumour of this spread through the district, and the governor asked the peasants to try to catch it alive and bring it to him. This they did, and finally the creature was conveyed to the Landgrave at Cassel.

When it was taken into the castle it tore itself away, fled, and hid beneath a bench, where it glared fiercely at its pursuers and howled horribly. The prince had him educated and kept him continually in men's society, and under this influence his savage habits grew gentler by degrees; he began to raise himself up on his hind-legs and walk like a biped, and at last to speak intelligently and behave like a man. Then he related to the best of his ability how he had been seized and nurtured by the wolves and had been accustomed to go hunting with them. The story is found in M. Dresser's [18] work on *Ancient and Modern Education*, and Camerarius, [19] in his *Hours*, mentions the same case, and another one of a similar nature (bk. i. ch. 75).

Gulartius [20] also (in *Marvels of our Age*) says that the following occurred in France in 1563. Some nobles went hunting, and, after they had killed twelve wolves, at last caught in their nets something like a naked boy, about seven years old, with a yellow skin and curly hair. His nails were hooked like an eagle's, he was unable to speak, and could only utter wild shrieks. When he was brought into the castle he struggled so fiercely that fetters could scarce be placed on him; but after a few days of starvation he grew gentler, and within seven months had commenced to speak. He was taken round to various towns and exhibited, and his masters made much money out of him. At length a certain poor woman acknowledged him as her son. So true is Plato's remark (*Laws*, i. 6): "Man is the gentlest and most divine being, if he have been made so by true education; but if he have been subjected to none or to a false one he is the most intractable thing in the world."

7. Education is indeed necessary for all, and this is evident if we consider the different degrees of ability. No one doubts that those who are stupid need instruction, that they may shake off their natural dulness. But in reality those who are clever need it far more, since an active mind, if not occupied with useful things, will busy itself with what is useless, curious, and pernicious; and,

just as the more fertile a field is, the richer the crop of thorns and of thistles that it can produce, so an excellent intelligence becomes filled with fanciful notions, if it be not sown with the seeds of wisdom and of virtue; and, just as a mill-stone grinds itself away with noise and grating, and often cracks and breaks, if wheat, the raw material of flour, be not supplied to it, so an active mind, if void of serious things, entangles itself utterly with vain, curious, and noxious thoughts, and becomes the cause of its own destruction.

8. What are the rich without wisdom but pigs stuffed with bran? What are the poor who have no understanding of affairs but asses laden with burdens? What is a handsome though ignorant man but a parrot adorned with feathers, or, as has been said, a golden sheath in which there is a leaden dagger?

9. For those who are in any position of authority, for kings, princes, magistrates, pastors of churches, and doctors, it is as necessary to be imbued with wisdom as it is for a guide to have eyes, an interpreter to have speech, a trumpet to be filled with sound, or a sword to have an edge. Similarly, those in subordinate positions should be educated that they may know how to obey their superiors wisely and prudently, not under compulsion, with the obedience of an ass, but of their own free will and from love of order. For a rational creature should be led, not by shouts, imprisonment, and blows, but by reason. Any other method is an insult to God, in whose image all men are made, and fills human affairs with violence and unrest.

10. We see then that all who are born to man's estate have need of instruction, since it is necessary that, being men, they should not be wild beasts, savage brutes, or inert logs. It follows also that one man excels another in exact proportion as he has received more instruction. We may conclude this chapter with the words of the "Wise Man." "He who deems wisdom and discipline of no avail is wretched; his hopes (of attaining his desire) are vain, his labour is fruitless, and his work idle" (Wisdom iii. 11).

CHAPTER VII

A MAN CAN MOST EASILY BE FORMED IN EARLY YOUTH, AND
CANNOT BE FORMED PROPERLY EXCEPT AT THIS AGE

1. FROM what has been said it is evident that the circumstances of men and of trees are similar. For, as a fruit
tree (an apple, a pear, a fig, or a vine) is able to grow from
its own stock and of its own accord, while a wild tree will
not bring forth sweet fruits until it be planted, watered,
and pruned by a skilled gardener, so does a man grow of
his own accord into a human semblance (just as any
brute resembles others of his own class), but is unable to
develope into a rational, wise, virtuous, and pious creature,
unless virtue and piety are first engrafted in him. We
will now show that this must take place while the plants
are young.

2. From the human point of view there are six reasons
for this. First, the uncertainty of our present life. For that
we must leave it is certain, but when and how is uncertain.
And that any should be snatched away unprepared is a
danger greatly to be dreaded, since a man is thus doomed
eternally. For, just as a man must go through life without
a limb if he leave his mother's womb bereft of it, so, if,
when we leave this world, our minds have not been
moulded to the knowledge of and participation in God,
there will be no further opportunity given us. And therefore, as the matter is of such importance, the greatest haste
is necessary, lest any man be lost.

3. And although death be far off and a long life be assured, the formation of character should none the less begin early, because life must be spent not in learning but in acting. We should therefore be prepared for the actions of life as soon as possible, since we may be compelled to desist from action before we have learned our lesson properly. Indeed, if any wish to devote his life to learning, the multitude of objects which the Creator has placed before his happy gaze is infinite, and, if he chance to have a life like Nestor's, he will find his most useful occupation in discerning the treasures of divine wisdom that the Creator has provided, and in thus preparing for himself the bulwarks of a happy life. Man's senses, therefore, must be early brought to bear on the world that surrounds him, since throughout his whole life he has much to learn, to experience, and to accomplish.

4. It is the nature of everything that comes into being, that while tender it is easily bent and formed, but that, when it has grown hard, it is not easy to alter. Wax, when soft, can be easily fashioned and shaped; when hard it cracks readily. A young plant can be planted, transplanted, pruned, and bent this way or that. When it has become a tree these processes are impossible. New-laid eggs, when placed under a hen, grow warm quickly and produce chickens; when they are old they will not do so. If a rider wish to train a horse, a ploughman an ox, a huntsman a dog or a hawk, a bear-leader a bear for dancing, or an old woman a magpie, a raven, or a crow, to imitate the human voice, they must choose them for the purpose when quite young; otherwise their labour is wasted.

5. It is evident that this holds good with man himself. His brain, which we have already compared to wax, because it receives the images of external objects that present themselves to its organs of sense, is, in the years of childhood, quite wet and soft, and fit for receiving all images that come to it. Later on, as we find by experience, it grows hard and dry by degrees, so that things are less readily

impressed or engraved upon it. Hence Cicero's remark, "Boys pick up countless things with rapidity." In the same way it is only in the years of boyhood, when the muscles are still capable of being trained, that the hands and the other members can be trained to produce skilled work. If a man is to become a good writer, painter, tailor, smith, cabinet-maker, or musician, he must apply himself to the art from his early youth, when the imagination is active and the fingers flexible : otherwise he will never produce anything. If piety is to take root in any man's heart, it must be engrafted while he is still young ; if we wish any one to be virtuous, we must train him in early youth ; if we wish him to make great progress in the pursuit of wisdom, we must direct his faculties towards it in infancy, when desire burns, when thought is swift, and when memory is tenacious. "An old man who has still to learn his lessons is a shameful and ridiculous object ; training and preparation are for the young, action for the old " (Seneca, *Epist.* 36).

6. In order that man may be fashioned to humanity, God has granted him the years of youth, which are unsuitable for everything but education. While the horse, the ox, the elephant, and other beasts, mere animated masses, come to maturity in a few years, man alone scarcely does so in twenty or thirty. Now, if any imagine that this arises from chance or from some accidental cause or other, he surely betrays his folly. To all other things, forsooth, God has meted out their periods, while in the case of man alone, the lord of all, He allows them to be fixed by chance ! Or are we to suppose that nature finds it easier to complete the formation of man by slow processes ? Nature, who with no trouble can produce vaster bodies in a few months. We can only suppose, therefore, that the Creator, of deliberate intent, interposed the delay of youth, in order that our period of training might be longer ; and ordained that for some time we should take no part in the action of life, that, for the rest of our lives, and for eternity, we might be the more fitted to do so.

7. In man, that alone is lasting which has been imbibed

in early youth, as is clear from the same examples.   A jar, even though broken, preserves the odour with which it was imbued when new.   When a tree is young its branches spread out all round it, and remain in this position for hundreds of years, until it is cut down.   Wool is so tenacious of the colour with which it is first dyed, that it cannot be bleached.   The wooden hoop of a wheel, which has been bent into a curve, will break into a thousand pieces rather than return to straightness.   And similarly, in a man, first impressions cling so fast that nothing but a miracle can remove them.   It is therefore most prudent that men be shaped to the standard of wisdom in early youth.

8. Finally, it is most dangerous if a man be not imbued with the cleanly precepts of life from his very cradle.   For, when the external senses begin to fulfil their functions, the mind of man cannot remain at rest, and, if not engaged with what is useful, it occupies itself with the vainest and even with harmful things (a process which is assisted by the evil examples of a corrupt age), while later on, if it wish to unlearn what it has acquired, it finds this impossible or very difficult ; as we have already shown.   Hence the world is full of enormities which neither the civil magistrates nor the ministers of the Church are able to quell, since no serious attention is given to the source from which the evil flows.

9. If, then, each man have the welfare of his own children at heart, and if that of the human race be dear to the civil and ecclesiastical guardians of human affairs, let them hasten to make provision for the timely planting, pruning, and watering of the plants of heaven, that these may be prudently formed to make prosperous advances in letters, virtue, and piety.

CHAPTER VIII

THE YOUNG MUST BE EDUCATED IN COMMON, AND FOR THIS SCHOOLS ARE NECESSARY

1. HAVING shown that those plants of Paradise, Christian children, cannot grow up like a forest, but need tending, we must now see on whom this care should fall. It is indeed the most natural duty of parents to see that the lives for which they are responsible shall be rational, virtuous, and pious. God Himself bears witness that this was Abraham's custom, when He says: "For I have known him, to the end that he may command his children and his household after him, that they may keep the way of the Lord, to do justice and judgment" (Gen. xviii. 19). He demands it from parents in general, with this command: "And these words, which I command thee this day, shall be upon thine heart, and thou shalt teach them diligently unto thy children, and shall talk of them when thou sittest in thine house, and when thou walkest by the way, and when thou liest down, and when thou risest up" (Deut. vi. 7). By the Apostle also He says: "And ye fathers, provoke not your children to wrath, but nurture them in the chastening and admonition of the Lord" (Ephes. vi. 4).

2. But, since human occupations as well as human beings have multiplied, it is rare to find men who have either sufficient knowledge or sufficient leisure to instruct their children. The wise habit has therefore arisen of giving

over children, for their common education, to select persons, conspicuous for their knowledge of affairs and their soberness of morals. To such instructors of the young the name of preceptor, master, schoolmaster, or professor has been applied, while the places destined for this common instruction have been named schools, elementary schools, lecture-rooms, colleges, public schools, and universities.

3. On the authority of Josephus we learn that the patriarch Shem opened the first school, just after the flood. Later, this was called the Hebrew school. Who does not know that in Chaldæa, especially in Babylon, there were many schools, in which the arts, including astronomy, were cultivated? since, later on (in the time of Nebuchadnezzar), Daniel and his companions were instructed in the wisdom of the Chaldæans (Dan. i. 20), as was also the case with Moses in Egypt (Acts vii. 22). By the command of God, schools were set up in all the towns of the children of Israel; they were called synagogues, and in them the Levites used to teach the law. These lasted till the coming of Christ, and became renowned through His teaching and that of His Apostles. The custom of erecting schools was borrowed by the Romans from the Egyptians, the Greeks, and the Jews, and from the Romans it spread throughout their whole empire, especially when the religion of Christ became universal through the care of pious princes and bishops. History relates that Charlemagne, whenever he subjected any heathen race, forthwith ordained for it bishops and learned men, and erected churches and schools; and after him the other Christian emperors, kings, nobles, and magistrates have increased the number of schools so much that they are innumerable.

4. It is to the interest of the whole Christian republic that this Godly custom be not only retained but increased as well, and that in every well-ordered habitation of man (whether a city, a town, or a village), a school or place of education for the young be erected. This is demanded :—

5. (i) By the admirable method of transacting business which is in common use. For, as the head of a household makes use of various craftsmen when he has no leisure time to prepare what is necessary for his household economy, why should he make any difference in the case of education? When he needs flour, he goes to the miller; when flesh, to the butcher; when drink, to the inn-keeper; when clothing, to the tailor; when shoes, to the cobbler; when a house, a ploughshare, or a key, to the builder, the smith, or the lock-smith. Again, we have churches for religious instruction, and law courts and assembly rooms in which to discuss the causes of litigants and make weighty announcements to the assembled people; why not schools also for the young? Farmers do not feed their own pigs and cows, but keep hired herdsmen who feed them all at one time, while their masters, free from distraction, transact their own business. For this is a marvellous saving of labour, when one man, undisturbed by other claims on his attention, confines himself to one thing; in this way one man can be of use to many, and many to one man.

6. (ii) By necessity, because it is very seldom that parents have sufficient ability or sufficient leisure to teach their children. The consequence is that there has arisen a class of men who do this one thing alone, as a profession, and that by this means the advantage of the whole community is attained.

7. (iii) And although there might be parents with leisure to educate their own children, it is nevertheless better that the young should be taught together and in large classes, since better results and more pleasure are to be obtained when one pupil serves as an example and a stimulus for another. For to do what we see others do, to go where others go, to follow those who are ahead of us, and to keep in front of those who are behind us, is the course of action to which we are all most naturally inclined.

It is when the steed has rivals to surpass or leaders to follow,
That he runs his best.

Young children, especially, are always more easily led and ruled by example than by precept. If you give them a precept, it makes but little impression ; if you point out that others are doing something, they imitate without being told to do so.

8. (iv) Again, nature is always showing us by examples that whatever is to be produced in abundance must be produced in some one place. Thus, for instance, wood is produced in quantities in forests, grass in fields, fish in lakes, and metals in the bowels of the earth.

Specialisation, too, is carried to such an extent, that the forest which produces pines, cedars, or oaks, produces them in abundance, although other kinds of trees may be unable to grow there ; and, in the same way, land that produces gold does not produce other metals in like quantity. This truth can be seen much more plainly in our own bodies. It is very important that each limb share in the nourishment that is assimilated by the body. Its share, however, is not transmitted to each in its raw state, to be there digested and adapted; but there are certain fixed members, designed as workshops for the performance of this function, namely, to receive food for the use of the whole body, to heat it, to digest it, and, at length, to distribute nourishment to the other members. Thus, chyle is produced by the stomach, blood by the liver, vital spirit by the heart, and mental spirit by the brain : and these elements, when prepared, are properly diffused throughout all the limbs and preserve life in the whole body. And therefore, as workshops supply manufactured goods, churches supply piety, and law courts justice, why should not schools produce, purify, and multiply the light of wisdom, and distribute it to the whole body of the human community ?

9. (v) And, finally, we see the same tendency in the arts, if a rational procedure be used. When a tree cultivator, in his walks through woods and thickets, finds a sapling suitable for transplanting, he does not plant it in the same place where he finds it, but digs it out and places it in an orchard, where he cares for it in company with a hundred

others. And thus also, the man who breeds fishes for the kitchen, digs fish-ponds and allows thousands to multiply together. In these cases the larger the orchard the better grow the trees, and the larger the fish-pond the larger grow the fish. And therefore, as fish-ponds are dug for fish and orchards are laid out for fruit-trees, so also should schools be erected for the young.

CHAPTER IX

ALL THE YOUNG OF BOTH SEXES SHOULD BE SENT TO SCHOOL

1. THE following reasons will establish that not the children of the rich or of the powerful only, but of all alike, boys and girls, both noble and ignoble, rich and poor, in all cities and towns, villages and hamlets, should be sent to school.

2. In the first place, all who have been born to man's estate have been born with the same end in view, namely, that they may be men, that is to say, rational creatures, the lords of other creatures, and the images of their Creator. All, therefore, must be brought on to a point at which, being properly imbued with wisdom, virtue, and piety, they may usefully employ the present life and be worthily prepared for that to come. God Himself has frequently asserted that with Him there is no respect of persons, so that, if, while we admit some to the culture of the intellect, we exclude others, we commit an injury not only against those who share the same nature as ourselves, but against God Himself, who wishes to be acknowledged, to be loved, and to be praised by all upon whom He has impressed His image. In this respect the fervour of all men will increase in proportion to the flame of knowledge that has been kindled. For our love is in direct ratio to our knowledge.

3. Now we do not know to what uses divine providence has destined this or that man; but this is certain, that out

of the poorest, the most abject, and the most obscure, He has produced instruments for His glory. Let us, therefore, imitate the sun in the heavens, which lights, warms, and vivifies the whole earth, so that whatever is able to live, to flourish, and to blossom, may do so.

4. Nor is it any obstacle that some seem to be naturally dull and stupid, for this renders more imperative the universal culture of such intellects. The slower and the weaker the disposition of any man, the more he needs assistance, that he may throw off his brutish dulness and stupidity as much as possible. Nor can any man be found whose intellect is so weak that it cannot be improved by culture. A sieve, if you continually pour water through it, grows cleaner and cleaner, although it cannot retain the liquid; and, in the same way, the dull and the weak-minded, though they may make no advance in letters, become softer in disposition and learn to obey the civil magistrates and the ministers of the Church. There have, besides, been many instances in which those who are naturally stupid have gained such a grasp of the sciences as to excel those who were more gifted. As the poet truly says: "Industry overcomes all obstacles." Again, just as some men are strong as children, but afterwards grow sick and ailing, while others, whose bodies are sickly and undersized in youth, develope into robust and tall men; so it is with intellects. Some develope early, but soon wear out and grow dull, while others, originally stupid, become sharp and penetrating. In our orchards we like to have not only trees that bring forth early fruit, but also those that are late-bearing; for each thing, as says the son of Sirach, finds praise in its season, and at length, though late, shows that it has not existed in vain. Why, therefore, should we wish that in the garden of letters only one class of intellects, the forward and active, should be tolerated? Let none be excluded unless God has denied him sense and intelligence.

5. Nor can any sufficient reason be given why the weaker sex (to give a word of advice on this point in particular) should be altogether excluded from the pursuit

of knowledge (whether in Latin or in their mother-tongue). They also are formed in the image of God, and share in His grace and in the kingdom of the world to come. They are endowed with equal sharpness of mind and capacity for knowledge (often with more than the opposite sex), and they are able to attain the highest positions, since they have often been called by God Himself to rule over nations, to give sound advice to kings and princes, to the study of medicine and of other things which benefit the human race, even to the office of prophesying and of inveighing against priests and bishops. Why, therefore, should we admit them to the alphabet, and afterwards drive them away from books? Do we fear their folly? The more we occupy their thoughts, so much the less will the folly that arises from emptiness of mind find a place.

6. But let not all books be given to them indiscriminately, as they have been given to the young of the other sex (and indeed it is greatly to be deplored that more caution has not been displayed in this matter); but only those from which, by the due observation of God and of His works, true virtue and true piety can be learned.

7. And let none cast in my teeth that saying of the Apostle: "I permit not a woman to teach" (1 Tim. ii. 12), or that of Juvenal in the sixth satire: "See that thy lawful wife be not a chatterbox, that she express not the simplest matter in involved language, nor be deeply versed in history," or the remark of Hippolytus in Euripides: "I detest a blue-stocking. May there never be a woman in my house who knows more than is fitting for a woman to know. For 'tis in the wise especially that Cypris engenders the desire for evil." These opinions, I opine, stand in no true opposition to our demand. For we are not advising that women be educated in such a way that their tendency to curiosity shall be developed, but so that their sincerity and contentedness may be increased, and this chiefly in those things which it becomes a woman to know and to do; that is to say, all that enables her to look after her household and to promote the welfare of her husband and her family.

8. If any ask, "What will be the result if artisans, rustics, porters, and even women become lettered?" I answer, If this universal instruction of youth be brought about by the proper means, none of these will lack the material for thinking, choosing, following, and doing good things. All will know how the actions and endeavours of life should be regulated, within what limits we must progress, and how each man can protect his own position. Not only this, but all will regale themselves, even in the midst of their work and toil, by meditation on the words and works of God, and, by the constant reading of the Bible and other good books, will avoid that idleness which is so dangerous to flesh and blood. To sum up, they will learn to see, to praise, and to recognise God everywhere, and, in this way, to go through this life of care with enjoyment, and to look for the life to come with increased desire and hope. Does not such a condition of the Church represent to us the only paradise that it is possible to realise on this earth?

CHAPTER X

THE INSTRUCTION GIVEN IN SCHOOLS SHOULD BE UNIVERSAL

1. WE have already shown that every one ought to receive a universal education, and this at school. But do not, therefore, imagine that we demand from all men a knowledge (that is to say, an exact or deep knowledge) of all the arts and sciences. This would neither be useful of itself, nor, on account of the shortness of life, can it be attained by any man. For we see that each science is so vast and so complicated (as are physics, arithmetic, geometry, astronomy, or even agriculture and arboriculture) that it would occupy the lifetime of even the strongest intellects if they wished to master it thoroughly by investigation and experiment. Thus did Pythagoras devote himself to arithmetic, Archimedes to mechanics, Agricola to metallurgy,[21] and Longolius [22] (who spent his whole life in endeavouring to acquire a perfect Ciceronian style) to rhetoric. It is the principles, the causes, and the uses of all the most important things in existence that we wish all men to learn ; all, that is to say, who are sent into the world to be actors as well as spectators. For we must take strong and vigorous measures that no man, in his journey through life, may encounter anything so unknown to him that he cannot pass sound judgment upon it and turn it to its proper use without serious error.

2. We must, therefore, concentrate our energies on

obtaining that, throughout our whole lives, in schools and by the aid of schools: (i) our talents may be cultivated by study of the sciences and of the arts; (ii) languages may be learned; (iii) honest morals may be formed; (iv) God may be sincerely worshipped.

3. He spoke wisely who said that schools were the workshops of humanity, since it is undoubtedly through their agency that man really becomes man, that is to say (to refer to our previous analysis): (i) a rational creature; (ii) a creature which is lord over all creatures and also over himself; (iii) a creature which is the delight of his Creator. This will be the case if schools are able to produce men who are wise in mind, prudent in action, and pious in spirit.

4. These three principles, then, must be implanted in all the young in all schools, and this I shall prove, starting from the following fundamental points :—

(i) From the circumstances by which we are surrounded ;

(ii) From ourselves ;

(iii) From Christ the God-man, the most perfect example of our perfection.

5. Things themselves, as far as they concern us, can be divided into three classes only: (i) objects that we can observe, such as the heavens, the earth, and all that is in them ; (ii) objects that we can imitate, such as the marvellous order which pervades all things, and which man ought to imitate in his actions ; (iii) objects that we can enjoy, such as the grace of God and His manifold blessing here and for eternity. If man is to acquit himself creditably when brought into contact with this order of nature, he must be trained to know the things that are spread out for his observation in this marvellous amphitheatre, to do the things that it is right for him to do, and, finally, to enjoy those things of which the most benign Creator, treating him as a guest in His house, has, with liberal hand, given him the fruition.

6. If we consider ourselves, we see clearly that learning, virtue, and piety are of importance to all alike ; whether we

look at the essential being of the soul, or at the object of our creation and introduction into the world.

7. The soul in its essential elements consists of three potentialities, which recall the uncreated Trinity, and these are the intellect, the will, and the memory. The province of the intellect is to observe the differences between things, even down to the smallest details. The will concerns itself with choice—that is to say, with the choice of things that are advantageous and the rejection of those which are not. The memory stores up for future use all the things with which the intellect and the will have been busied, and reminds the soul of its dependence on God and of its duty; in which aspect it is also called conscience.

In order, then, that these faculties may rightly fulfil their offices, it is necessary that they be furnished with such things as may illumine the intellect, direct the will, and stimulate the conscience, so that the intellect may be acute and penetrating, the will may choose without error, and the conscience may greedily refer all things to God. Therefore, just as these faculties (the intellect, the will, and the conscience) cannot be separated, since they constitute the same soul, so it is impossible to separate those three ornaments of the soul, erudition, virtue, and piety.

8. Now, if we consider why we have been sent into the world, it will be evident from two points of view that the object is threefold, namely, that we may serve God, His creatures, and ourselves, and that we may enjoy the pleasure to be derived from God, from His creatures, and from ourselves.

9. If we wish to serve God, our neighbours, and ourselves, it is necessary for us to possess, with respect to God, piety; with respect to our neighbours, virtue; and with respect to ourselves, knowledge. These principles, however, are intimately connected, and a man, for his own advantage, should be not only learned, but also virtuous and pious; for that of his neighbour, not only virtuous, but also learned and pious; and for the glory of God, not only pious, but also learned and virtuous.

10. If we consider the happiness to which God has destined mankind, we find that He showed His intention clearly when creating man, since He introduced him into a world furnished with all good things; prepared for him, in addition, a paradise of delights; and, finally, arranged to make him a partner of His eternal happiness.

11. Now, by the term "happiness" we understand not the pleasures of the body (though these, since they consist of the vigour of good health, and of the enjoyment of food and of sleep, can only arise from the virtue of temperance), but those of the soul, which arise either out of the objects around us, or from ourselves, or, finally, from God.

12. The pleasure which arises out of things themselves, is the pleasure that a wise man experiences in speculation. For, wherever he betakes himself, whatever he observes, and whatever he considers, he finds everywhere such attractions, that often, as it were, snatched out of himself, he merges his identity in them. It is to this that the book of Wisdom refers: "The conversation of wisdom hath no bitterness; and to live with her hath no sorrow, but mirth and joy" (viii. 16). And a heathen philosopher says·: "There is nothing in life more pleasant than to seek out wisdom."

13. Pleasure in self is that very sweet delight which arises when a man, who is given over to virtue, rejoices in his own honest disposition, since he sees himself prompt to all things which the order of justice requires. This pleasure is far greater than the former one, according to the proverb "A good conscience is a perpetual feast."

14. Delight in God is the highest point to which pleasure can attain in this life, and is found when a man, feeling that God is eternally gracious to him, exults in His fatherly and immutable favour to such a degree that his heart melts with the love of God. He desires to know or to do nothing further, but, overwhelmed by God's mercy, he rests in peace and tastes the joys of eternal life. This is "the peace of God which passeth all understanding" (Phil. iv. 7), than which nothing more sublime can be desired or imagined.

These three principles, therefore, learning, virtue, and piety, are the three founts from which all the streams of the most perfect pleasures flow.

15. Lastly, God Himself, manifest in the flesh (that He might exhibit in Himself the perfection of all things), has taught by His example that these three elements must exist in each individual. For the Evangelist testifies that He advanced not only in stature, but also in wisdom and favour with God and man (Luke ii. 52). Here can be seen the blessed Trinity that adorns us. For what is wisdom but the knowledge of things as they are? What is it that brings us favour with men, if not amiability of character? What procures us the grace of God, if not the fear of the Lord, that is to say, inward, serious, and fervid piety? Let us, therefore, realise in ourselves that which we have seen in Jesus Christ, the absolute ideal of all perfection, the standard set up for us to imitate.

16. For this reason He said, "Learn of me" (Matt. xi. 29). And since this same Christ has been given to the human race as the most learned teacher, as the most holy priest, and as the most powerful king, it is evident that Christians should be formed on His model and should be enlightened through their intellects, sanctified through their consciences, and made powerful through their deeds (each in his own calling). Our schools, therefore, will then at length be Christian schools when they make us as like to Christ as is possible.

17. It is, therefore, an unhallowed separation if these three elements be not bound together as if by an adamantine chain. How wretched is the teaching that does not lead to virtue and to piety! For what is literary skill without virtue? He who makes progress in knowledge but not in morality (says an old proverb), recedes rather than advances. And thus, what Solomon said of the beautiful but foolish woman, holds good of the learned man who possesses not virtue: "As a jewel of gold in a swine's snout, so is a fair woman which is without discretion" (Prov. xi. 22). For, just as gems are set not in

lead but in gold, in which combination both are more beautiful, thus should knowledge be joined not to immorality but to virtue, when each will add adornment to the other. For the fear of the Lord, as it is the beginning and the end of wisdom, is also the coping-stone and crown of knowledge. The fear of the Lord is the beginning of wisdom (Prov. i. and elsewhere).

18. Since, therefore, a man's whole life depends on the instruction that he has received during boyhood, every opportunity is lost unless the minds of all are then prepared for every emergency that may arise in life. Just as in his mother's womb each man receives his full complement of limbs,—hands, feet, tongue, etc.—although all men are not to be artificers, runners, scribes, or orators; so at school all men should be taught whatever concerns man, though in after life some things will be of more use to one man, others to another.

CHAPTER XI

1. THIS confident heading may seem too presumptuous; but I challenge the facts themselves, and, while I constitute the reader as judge, will myself do nothing but summon witnesses. I call a school that fulfils its function perfectly, one which is a true forging-place of men; where the minds of those who learn are illuminated by the light of wisdom, so as to penetrate with ease all that is manifest and all that is secret (comp. Wisdom vii. 21), where the emotions and the desires are brought into harmony with virtue, and where the heart is filled with and permeated by divine love, so that all who are handed over to Christian schools to be imbued with true wisdom may be taught to live a heavenly life on earth; in a word, where all men are taught all things thoroughly.

2. But has any school either existed on this plane of perfection or held this goal in view; not to ask if any has ever reached it? Lest I should seem to chase Platonic ideas and to dream of perfection such as exists nowhere and cannot be hoped for in this life, I will point out by another argument that such schools ought to be and have never yet existed.

3. Dr. Luther, in his exhortation to towns of the empire on behalf of the erection of schools (A.D. 1525), asks for these two things, among others. Firstly, that schools may be founded in all cities, towns, and villages,

for the instruction of all the young of both sexes (the necessity of which we proved in chap. ix.), so that even peasants and artisans may, for two hours daily, receive instruction in useful knowledge, in morality, and in religion. Secondly, that an easier method of instruction may be introduced, so that students, instead of developing an antipathy towards learning, may be enticed by irresistible attractions, and that, as he says, boys may gain no less pleasure from study than from spending whole days in playing ball and amusing themselves. These are the views of Dr. Luther.

4. This is indeed a noble counsel, and worthy of such a man! But who does not see that matters have gone no farther than his wish? For where are those universal schools, where is that attractive method?

5. It is evident that nothing has been done, since in the smaller villages and hamlets no schools have been founded.

6. Where schools exist, they are not for the whole community, but only for the rich, since, owing to their cost, the poor cannot gain admission to them, except by some chance, such as pity on the part of some one. Among those excluded there are probably some excellent intellects, which are thus ruined and destroyed, to the great loss of the Church and of the state.

7. Further, the method used in instructing the young has generally been so severe that schools have been looked on as terrors for boys and shambles for their intellects, and the greater number of the students, having contracted a dislike for learning and for books, have hastened away to the workshops of artificers or to some other occupation.

8. On the other hand, those who remained at school (whether compelled to do so by parents and guardians, or influenced by the hope of obtaining some honourable position by means of their attainments, or drawn towards the liberal arts spontaneously and of their own nature) did not receive a serious or comprehensive education, but a preposterous and wretched one. For piety and virtue,

which form the most important element in education, were neglected more than anything else. In all the schools (and even in the universities, which ought to embody the greatest advances of human culture) these subjects held only a secondary place, so that for the most part, instead of tractable lambs, fiery wild asses and restive mules were produced; and instead of characters moulded to virtue, nothing issued from the schools but a spurious veneer of morality, a fastidious and exotic clothing of culture, and eyes, hands, and feet trained to worldly vanities. How few of these mannikins, who had for so long been polished by such a training in the languages and in the arts, realised that to the rest of the world they ought to be an example of temperance, charity, humility, humanity, gravity, patience, and continence!

The reason of this evidently is that the question of "virtuous living" is never raised in the schools. This is shown by the wretched discipline in nearly all schools, by the dissolute morals of all classes, and by the never-ceasing complaints, sighs, and tears of pious men. Can any one defend the condition in which our schools have been? An hereditary disease, sprung from our first parents, pervades all classes, so that, shut out from the tree of life, we direct our desires inordinately towards the tree of knowledge, and our schools also, permeated by this insatiable appetite, have hitherto pursued nothing but intellectual progress.

9. But with what method or with what success have they done even this? In truth, the only result achieved was the following. For five, ten, or more years they detained the mind over matters that could be mastered in one. What could have been gently instilled into the intellect, was violently impressed upon it, nay rather stuffed and flogged into it. What might have been placed before the mind plainly and lucidly, was treated of obscurely, perplexedly, and intricately, as if it were a complicated riddle.

10. In addition, though for the present we will pass

this over, the intellect was scarcely ever nourished by the actual facts, but was filled with the husks of words, with a windy and parrot-like loquacity, and with the chaff of opinions.

11. The study of the Latin language alone (to take this subject as an example), good heavens! how intricate, how complicated, and how prolix it was! Camp followers and military attendants, engaged in the kitchen and in other menial occupations, learn a tongue that differs from their own, sometimes two or three, quicker than the children in schools learn Latin only, though children have abundance of time, and devote all their energies to it. And with what unequal progress! The former gabble their languages after a few months, while the latter, after fifteen or twenty years, can only put a few sentences into Latin with the aid of grammars and of dictionaries, and cannot do even this without mistakes and hesitation. Such a disgraceful waste of time and of labour must assuredly arise from a faulty method.

12. On this subject the celebrated Eilhard Lubinus, professor in the University of Rostock, has with justice remarked: "When I consider the ordinary method of teaching boys in schools, it seems to me as if it had been laboriously devised with a view to make it impossible for teachers and pupils alike to lead or to be led to a knowledge of the Latin tongue, without great labour, great tedium, infinite trouble, and the greatest possible consumption of time. A state of things which I cannot think of without shuddering." And a little farther on: "After frequent consideration of these matters I find myself always led to the conclusion, that the entire system must have been introduced into schools by some evil and envious genius, the enemy of the human race." So says Lubinus, who is only one out of many authorities whom I could quote in my favour.

13. But what need is there of witnesses? How many of us there are who have left the schools and universities with scarcely a notion of true learning! I, unfortunate

man that I am, am one of many thousands, who have miserably lost the sweetest spring-time of their whole life, and have wasted the fresh years of youth on scholastic trifles. Ah, how often, since my mind has been enlightened, has the thought of my wasted youth wrung sighs from my breast, drawn tears from my eyes, and filled my heart with sorrow! How often has my grief caused me to exclaim:

Oh that Jupiter could bring back to me the years that are past and gone!

14. But these prayers are in vain. Bygone days will never return. None of us who is advanced in years can grow young again, commence his career anew, and, furnished with a better method, pursue it more successfully. Of this there is no question. One thing alone does remain, and that is to give those who come after us such advice as we can. By showing how it was that our masters led us into error we shall be able to point out the way in which such errors may be avoided.

CHAPTER XII

1. To cure deep-seated maladies is difficult and often well-nigh impossible. But if any one offer an efficacious remedy, does the sick man reject his services? Does he not rather wish to obtain aid as quickly as possible, and especially if he think that the physician is guided not by mere opinion but by solid reason? We, at any rate, in this our undertaking, have reached the point at which we must make plain (1) what we actually promise, and (2) on what principles we intend to proceed.

2. We promise, then, such a system of education that

(i) All the young shall be educated (except those to whom God has denied understanding).

(ii) And in all those subjects which are able to make a man wise, virtuous, and pious.

(iii) That the process of education, being a preparation for life, shall be completed before maturity is reached.

(iv) That this education shall be conducted without blows, rigour, or compulsion, as gently and pleasantly as possible, and in the most natural manner (just as a living body increases in size without any straining or forcible extension of the limbs; since if food, care, and exercise are properly supplied, the body grows and becomes strong, gradually, imperceptibly, and of its own accord. In the same way I maintain that nutriment, care, and exercise, prudently supplied to the mind, lead it naturally to wisdom, virtue, and piety).

(v) That the education given shall be not false but real, not superficial but thorough; that is to say, that the rational animal, man, shall be guided, not by the intellects of other men, but by his own; shall not merely read the opinions of others and grasp their meaning or commit them to memory and repeat them, but shall himself penetrate to the root of things and acquire the habit of genuinely understanding and making use of what he learns.

(vi) That this education shall be not laborious but very easy. The class instruction shall last only four hours each day, and shall be conducted in such a manner that one master may teach hundreds of pupils at the same time, with ten times as little trouble as is now expended on the teaching of one.

3. But who will have faith in these things before he see them? It is a well-known peculiarity of men that before a remarkable discovery is made they wonder how it can be possible, while after its achievement they are surprised that it was not discovered before. When Archimedes undertook for King Hiero to move down to the sea with one hand an immense ship that a hundred men were not able to stir, his proposal was received with laughter; but its accomplishment was viewed with stupefaction.

4. When Columbus suspected that there were new islands in the west, no one, with the exception of the King of Castille, was willing to hear him or give him any assistance towards making the experiment. It is related that his very companions on the voyage, in despair at their frequent disappointments, were within a little of throwing him into the sea and returning with their task unfulfilled. But, in spite of all, that vast new continent was discovered, and now we all wonder how it could have remained so long unknown. That well-known jest of Columbus illustrates the same point. For when, at a banquet, some Spaniards, who were envious that an Italian should have the glory of such a discovery, began to mock him, and

tauntingly said that the other hemisphere had been discovered not by skill but by chance, and could have been just as easily discovered by anybody else, he proposed an elegant problem. "How," he asked, "can a hen's egg, unsupported, be made to stand on its end?" When all had tried in vain to do this, he tapped the shell gently upon the table, cracked it, and in this way made it stand. The others laughed, and exclaimed that they could do the same thing. "No doubt you can, now that you have seen how it can be done," said he, "but how is it that no one could do it before me?"

5. I believe that the same thing would have happened if John Faust, the inventor of printing, had made it known that he possessed a method by which one man, within a week, could copy more books than ten of the fastest copyists could copy in a year in the ordinary way; that the books would be better written; that from beginning to end all the copies would be exactly similar; and that all would be absolutely free from errors provided that one copy had been corrected. Who would have believed him? Who would not have thought it a riddle, or a piece of vain and foolish boasting? And yet every child knows now that this is sober truth.

6. If Berthold Schwartz, the inventor of muskets, had addressed the archers with these words: "Your bows, your catapults, and your slings are of little worth. I will give you a weapon which, without any human force, by the agency of fire alone, will not only hurl forth stones and iron, but will propel them farther and with more certainty, so that they will strike, uproot, or lay low whatever comes in their way." Which of them would not have received him with laughter? So much is it the custom to consider everything new as marvellous and incredible.

7. Nor could the American Indians comprehend how one man is able to communicate his thoughts to another without the use of speech, without a messenger, but by simply sending a sheet of paper. Yet with us a man of the meanest intelligence can understand this.

Thus do the perplexities of one age afford amusement to the next.

8. I can easily see that this will happen to my new undertaking; in fact, I have already experienced it. Some people are certain to be indignant that there are men who find imperfections in the schools, books, and methods in use, and who dare to promise something unusual and extraordinary.

9. It would be easy for me to appeal to results as the most trustworthy witnesses (such confidence do I place in my God). But since I am writing this, not for the un-learned crowd, but for men of education, I must give demonstrative proof that it is possible to imbue all the young with knowledge, virtue, and piety, and to do so without that unpleasantness and difficulty continually experienced by the teachers, no less than by the learners, under the old system.

10. The one and sufficient demonstration is this: That each individual creature not only suffers itself to be easily led in the direction which its nature finds congenial, but is actually impelled towards the desired goal, and suffers pain if any obstacle be interposed.

11. A bird learns to fly, a fish to swim, and a beast to run without any compulsion. They do these things of their own accord as soon as they feel that their limbs are sufficiently strong. Water runs downhill of its own accord, and, in the same way, fire burns when fuel and a current of air are supplied; a round stone rolls down hill, while a square stone remains stationary; the eye and a mirror receive the impression of an object when there is sufficient light, and seeds sprout when their surroundings are suitably warm and damp. In fact, each of these things strives to fulfil the function for which it is naturally fitted, and does this more perfectly when assisted, no matter how slight the assistance may be.

12. Since then, as we saw in chap. v., the seeds of knowledge, of virtue, and of piety exist in all men (with the exception of monstrosities), it follows of necessity that

they need nothing but a gentle impulse and prudent guidance.

13. But, it is objected, it is not out of every piece of wood that a Mercury can be carved. I answer: But out of every human being, if he be not utterly corrupt, a man can be formed.

14. But our inner strength, some one will remark, has been weakened by the Fall. I reply, weakened, yes, but not extinguished. Even our bodily force, if it be in bad condition, can be restored to its natural vigour by walking, running, and artificial forms of exercise. For, although the first created were able to walk, speak, and think as soon as they came into existence, while we cannot do so unless taught by practice, it does not therefore follow that these things cannot be learned without perplexity, labour, and uncertainty. For, if we learn without very great difficulty to perform the functions of the body, such as eating, drinking, walking, and jumping, why should we not learn to perform those of the mind with similar ease, if the proper instruction be given? Again, in a few months a horse-trainer can teach a horse to trot, jump, run in a circle, and perform evolutions to signs given by a whip; a mere circus performer teaches a bear to dance, a hare to beat the drum, and a dog to plough, to wrestle, or to divine; a weak old woman can teach her parrot, her magpie, or her crow to imitate a human voice or a melody; and all these things can be taught in a short time, although they are contrary to nature. And shall not a man be easily taught those things to which nature, I will not say admits him, or leads him, but rather urges and impels him? The trainers of animals would laugh at any one who seriously brought forward this argument.

15. But it is objected that, owing to the difficulty of the subjects to be learned, all men cannot grasp them. I reply: What is that difficulty? Does there exist any body of such a dark colour that it cannot be reflected in a mirror, if placed conveniently in the light? Is there anything that cannot be painted on a canvas, provided that

the man who paints has learned the art of painting? Is
there any seed or root that the earth cannot receive and
bring to germination by its warmth, if the gardener understand when, where, and how it should be sown? Moreover, there is in the world no rock or tower of such a
height that it cannot be scaled by any man (provided he
lack not feet) if ladders are placed in the proper position
or steps are cut in the rock, made in the right place, and
furnished with railings against the danger of falling over.
It is true that very few scale the heights of wisdom, though
many start gaily on the journey, and that those who get any
distance do so at the cost of toil, loss of breath, weariness,
and giddiness; this, however, does not prove that there
is anything inaccessible to the human intellect, but only
that the steps are not well disposed, or are insufficient,
dangerous, and in bad repair—in other words, that the
method is complicated. It is an undoubted fact that any
man can attain any height that he may desire by means
of steps that are properly disposed, sufficient in number,
solid, and safe.

16. It will be urged, Some men have such weak
intellects that it is not possible for them to acquire
knowledge. I answer, It is scarcely possible to find a
mirror so dulled that it will not reflect images of some kind,
or for a tablet to have such a rough surface that nothing
can be inscribed on it. Again, if the mirror be soiled by
dirt or by spots, it must first be cleaned; if the tablet be
rough, it must be polished; both will then perform their
functions. In the same way, if teachers take sufficient
trouble, men will become polished, and finally all men will
understand all things (I stand firmly by my watchword
because my fundamental principles prove correct). There
is naturally a difference in intellects, and while those who
are slow may only be able to attain to one stage of
knowledge, the more gifted advance higher and higher,
from one object to another, and collect new observations
which are of great utility. Finally, though there may be
some intellects that do not admit of culture, just as knotty

wood is unsuitable for carving, even then my assertion will hold good for men of ordinary capacity, of whom, through God's grace, there is always a sufficiency. Indeed a man quite wanting in intellect is as rare a phenomenon as one who, from his birth, has lacked his full complement of limbs. For, in truth, blindness, deafness, lameness, and weakness seldom accompany a man from his cradle, but are caused by his own negligence; and thus it is with exceptional weakness of intellect.

17. A further objection is brought forward: With many not the capacity to learn but the inclination is lacking, and to compel these against their will is as unpleasant as it is useless. I answer: There is a story told of a philosopher who had two pupils, of whom one was idle and the other industrious. Both were sent away by their master; for one would not learn, though able to do so, while the other could not, though anxious to acquire knowledge. But how does the matter stand if it be shown that the teacher himself is the reason of the pupil's aversion to learning? Truly did Aristotle say that all men are born anxious to acquire knowledge, and that this is so we have seen in chapters v. and xi. In practice, however, the tender indulgence of parents hinders the natural tendency of children, and later on frivolous society leads them into idle ways, while the various occupations of city and court life, and the external circumstances which surround them, turn them away from their real inclinations. Thus it comes to pass that they show no desire to investigate what is unknown, and cannot concentrate their thoughts with ease. (For just as the tongue, when permeated with one flavour, judges another with difficulty, so the mind, when occupied with one subject, finds it hard to give its attention to another.) In these cases the external distraction must first be removed; nature will then assert itself with its original vigour, and the desire for knowledge will once more be apparent. But how many of those who undertake to educate the young appreciate the necessity of first teaching them how to acquire knowledge? The turner

shapes a block of wood with his axe before he turns it; the blacksmith heats iron before he hammers it; the cloth-weaver, before he spins his wool, first cleans, washes, cards, and fulls it; the shoemaker, before he sews the shoe, pre-pares, shapes, and smooths the leather; but who, I ask, ever thinks it necessary that the teacher, in the same way, should make his pupils anxious for information, capable of receiving instruction, and therefore ready for a many-sided education, before he begins to place knowledge before them? Teachers almost invariably take their pupils as they find them; they turn them, beat them, card them, comb them, drill them into certain forms, and expect them to become a finished and polished product; and if the result does not come up to their expectations (and I ask you how could it?) they are indignant, angry, and furious. And yet we are surprised that some men shrink and recoil from such a system. Far more is it matter for surprise that any one can endure it at all.

18. This is a suitable place in which to make a few remarks about differences of character. Some men are sharp, others dull; some soft and yielding, others hard and unbending; some eager after knowledge, others more anxious to acquire mechanical skill. From these three pairs of contradictory characters we get in all six distinct divisions.

19. In the first division must be placed those who are sharp-witted, anxious to learn, and easily influenced. These, more than all others, are suited for instruction. There is no need to provide them with what we may term a nutritive diet of knowledge, for, like goodly trees, they grow in wisdom of themselves. Nothing is needed but foresight; for they should not be allowed to hurry on too fast and thus to tire themselves out and wither away before their time.

20. Others are sharp-witted, but inclined to be slow and lazy. These must be urged on.

21. In the third place we have those who are sharp-witted and anxious to learn, but who at the same time are

perverse and refractory. These are usually a great source of difficulty in schools, and for the most part are given up in despair. If treated in the right way, however, they frequently develope into the greatest men. A good example of this type is Themistocles, the great Athenian general. As a youth he was very wild, so that his tutor said to him : "My boy, you will not develope into anything mediocre ; you will be either of great use or of great harm to your country." And later on, when people wondered at his strange character, he used to say, "Wild colts make the best horses, if only they are properly trained." Indeed, this was the case with Bucephalus, the horse of Alexander the Great. For, when Alexander saw that his father Philip was about to give away this unruly animal, which would suffer no rider on his back, he said : "What a magnificent horse these people are spoiling. They are unskilled and do not know how to treat it!" He forth-with took the horse in hand, and with marvellous skill (for he never used blows) he got it into such a condition that not only then but ever afterwards it carried him well, and no horse more noble or more worthy of his great master could be found in the whole world. Plutarch, who tells us this anecdote, remarks : "This story reminds us that many men of good parts are ruined by their teachers, who, in their inability to rule or to guide free men, treat them not as horses but as asses."

22. In the fourth place we have those who are flexible and anxious to learn, but who at the same time are slow and heavy. These can follow in the footsteps of the last-mentioned. But to render this possible the teacher must meet their weak natures half-way, must lay no heavy burden on them, must not demand anything excessive, but rather have patience, help them, strengthen them, and set them right, that they may not be disheartened. Though such pupils take longer to come to maturity, they will probably last all the better, like fruit that ripens late. And, just as the impression of a seal made in lead lasts a long time, though hard to make, so these men have more stable

characters than those who are more gifted, and do not easily forget what they have once learned. At school, therefore, they should be given every opportunity.

23. The fifth type are those who are weak-minded and at the same time lazy and idle. With these also a great improvement can be made, provided they are not obstinate. But great skill and patience are necessary.

24. Finally, we have those whose intellects are weak, and whose dispositions are perverse and wicked as well. These seldom come to any good. But, as it is certain that nature always provides some antidote for pernicious things, and that barren trees can be rendered fruitful if properly transplanted, we ought not to give up all hope, but should see if the perverseness, at least, cannot be combated and got rid of. It is only when this proves impossible that the twisted and knotted piece of wood may be cast aside, since it is useless to attempt to carve a Mercury out of it. "Barren land," says Cato, "should not be cultivated; nor even once ploughed." But an intellect of this kind, amenable to no treatment, can scarcely be found in a thousand, and this is a great proof of God's goodness.

25. The substance of these remarks is in harmony with the following saying of Plutarch: "For the characters of young children, no man is responsible; but it is in our power to make them virtuous by a proper training." Mark this well; he says "in our power." For the gardener can unfailingly train a struggling shoot into a tree, by using his skill in transplanting.

26. The four following reasons show that all the young, though of such different dispositions, may be instructed and educated by the same method.

27. Firstly: For all men the goal is the same, namely, knowledge, virtue, and piety.

28. Secondly: All men, though their dispositions may differ, possess the same human nature, and are endowed with the same organs of sense and of reason.

29. Thirdly: The differences of character are caused by nothing more than a superfluity or a lack of some of

the elements in the natural harmony, just as bodily diseases are nothing but abnormal states of wetness or dryness, of heat or cold. For example, what is sharpness of intellect but the fineness and rapid motion of the vital spirit in the brain, which passes through the sensory lobes with very great speed, and rapidly apprehends external objects? But if no obstacle be put in the way of this rapid motion, it dissipates the intellect and leaves the brain either weak or sluggish. Hence it is that so many precocious boys either die young or become stupid.

On the other hand, what is stupidity but a clammy viscosity of the humours of the brain, which can only be set in motion by constant suggestion? What are insolence and intractability but an excess of spirit and stubbornness, which must be tempered by discipline? What is slackness but a great lack of spirit which must be made good? Just as, then, the best remedies for bodily diseases are not those which try to put one extreme to flight by another (for this only makes the struggle greater), but those which seek to moderate all extremes, so that there shall not be too little on one side and too much on the other; so the best remedy against the errors of the human mind is a didactic method of such a kind that by its means excess and defect may be neutralised in the natural disposition, and that all the mental principles may be brought into harmony and into a pleasant agreement. Our method, therefore, is intended for intellects in which no element exists in an extreme form (and indeed these are always the most common), so that neither reins may be wanting to restrain active minds (that they may not wear themselves out before their time) nor spurs and goads to urge on the laggards.

30. Finally: Every excess or defect of disposition can be counteracted as long as it is not of old standing. In warfare, recruits are mixed with old soldiers; the weak and the strong, the sluggish and the active, fight under the same standard and obey the same orders as long as the battle continues. But, when the victory is gained, each pursues

the enemy as far as he is able, and takes as much booty as he wants. Thus it is in the camp of knowledge; the slow are mixed with the swift, the weak. with the quick-witted, the obstinate with the yielding, and are guided by the same precepts and examples as long as guidance is necessary. But, when school-days are over, each one must finish the remainder of his studies with what speed he can.

31. When I talk of admixture of intellects, I refer not so much to the spot where the instruction takes place as to the additional assistance that can be given to the pupil. For instance, if the teacher observe that one boy is cleverer than the rest, he can give him two or three stupid boys to teach; if he perceive one more trustworthy than the others, he may allow him to watch and to control those who have less character. Both will gain great advantage from this, provided that the teacher keep his eye on them, to see that everything is conducted as reason prescribes. But it is now time to have done with preliminaries, and to deal with the real subject of this treatise.

CHAPTER XIII

THE BASIS OF SCHOOL REFORM MUST BE EXACT ORDER IN ALL THINGS

1. WE find on investigation that the principle which really holds together the fabric of this world of ours, down to its smallest detail, is none other than order; that is to say, the proper division of what comes before and what comes after, of the superior and the subordinate, of the large and the small, of the similar and dissimilar, according to place, time, number, size, and weight, so that each may fulfil its function well. Order, therefore, has been called the soul of affairs. For everything that is well ordered preserves its position and its strength as long as it maintains its order; it is when it ceases to do so that it grows weak, totters, and falls. This may be seen clearly in instances taken from nature and from art.

2. Through what agency, I ask, does the world maintain its present condition? what is it that gives it its great stability? It is this, that each creature, obeying the command of nature, restrains its action within the proper limits; and thus, by careful observation of order in small details, the order of the universe is maintained.

3. Through what agency is the flux of time divided so accurately and so continuously into years, months, and days? Through none but the inflexible order of the vault of heaven.

4. What enables bees, ants, and spiders to do work of

such fineness that the mind of man finds it easier to marvel at than to imitate it? Nothing but their natural talent for harmoniously combining order, number, and mass in their constructions.

5. What is it that constitutes the human body such a marvellous instrument that it can perform almost countless functions, even though it have very few resources at its disposal? I mean, that with the few limbs it possesses, it can produce works whose complexity is so wondrous that nothing remains to be desired? It is without question the harmonious disposition of the limbs, and of their constituent parts, that brings this about.

6. What is it that makes it possible for a single mind to rule the whole body in which it dwells, and to direct so many operations at the same time? Nothing but the harmonious order in which the limbs are connected, and which enables them to obey the slightest hint given by the mind, and to set themselves in motion immediately.

7. How is it that a single man, a king or an emperor, can rule whole nations; that, although there are as many wills as there are individuals, all subordinate themselves to the service of that one man, and that, if his affairs go well, the affairs of each subject also must prosper? Again it is order that brings this about. Through its agency all are held together by the connecting bands of law and of obedience, so that some subjects are directly subordinate to and in immediate contact with the supreme ruler, while others in their turn are subordinate to these, and so on down to the meanest serf. The arrangement thus resembles a chain in which each link is intimately connected so that if the first be moved or remain at rest all the others will follow suit.

8. How was it that Hiero, unaided, could move a weight which hundreds of men had in vain tried to stir? Assuredly it was by means of a cleverly-devised machine, in which the cylinders, wheels, and other parts were arranged in such a way that when one worked on the other the force applied was much increased.

9. The terrible operations of artillery, by which walls are broken down, towers are shattered, and armies are laid low, depend on nothing but the proper arrangement of materials, so that the active is placed in close connection with the passive element; that is to say, on the proper mixing of saltpetre with sulphur (the coldest substance with the hottest), on the proper construction of the cannon, on its being skilfully loaded with powder and missiles, and, lastly, on its being correctly pointed at the objects to be hit. If one of these conditions be not properly fulfilled, the whole apparatus is useless.

10. How is it that the processes of printing, by which books can be multiplied quickly, neatly, and correctly, are properly carried out? Assuredly by means of order. The type must be cut, moulded, and polished, placed suitably in the type-boxes, and then arranged in the right order, while the paper must be prepared, damped, stretched, and placed under the press.

11. To take another example of mechanism. How is it that a carriage, a construction of wood and iron, can be so easily drawn by the horses that are fastened to it, and can be of such use for the conveyance of men and burdens? This is brought about by nothing but the skilful arrangement of wood and of iron in the wheels, the axle-trees, and the shafts. If one of these parts give way, the whole construction is useless.

12. How is it that men can trust themselves to the stormy sea in a construction made of a few pieces of wood? How is it that they make their way to the antipodes and return safe and sound? It is nothing but the proper combination of keel, mast, rudder, compass, etc., in the ship that enables them to do so. If any one of these fail in its action, they are in great danger of shipwreck or of foundering.

13. Finally, how is it that the machine for measuring time, the clock, which is nothing but a well-arranged and well-devised disposition of iron parts, moves harmoniously and evenly, and marks off minutes, hours, days, months,

and sometimes years? and this not only for the eyes but
for the ears as well, that it may give some sign at night
and to those at a distance? How is it that such an
instrument can wake a man out of sleep at a given hour,
and can strike a light to enable him to see? How is it
that it can indicate the quarters of the moon, the positions
of the planets, and the eclipses? Is it not a truly
marvellous thing that a machine, a soulless thing, can
move in such a life-like, continuous, and regular manner?
Before clocks were invented would not the existence of
such things have seemed as impossible as that trees could
walk or stones speak? Yet every one can see that they
exist now.

14. What is the hidden power that brings this to
pass? Nothing but the all-ruling force of order; that is
to say, the force derived from arranging all the parts
concerned according to their number, size, and importance, and in such a manner that each one shall perform
its own proper function as well as work harmoniously with
and assist the other parts whose action is necessary to
produce the desired result; that is to say, the size of each
part must be carefully regulated to suit that of the rest;
each part must fit properly into those which surround it;
and the general laws that regulate the equal distribution
of force to the several parts must be observed. In such
a case all the processes are more exact than in a living
body controlled by one mind. But if any part get out of
position, crack, break, become loose or bent, though it be
the smallest wheel, the most insignificant axle, or the tiniest
screw, the whole machine stops still or at least goes wrong,
and thus shows us plainly that everything depends on the
harmonious working of the parts.

15. The art of teaching, therefore, demands nothing
more than the skilful arrangement of time, of the subjects
taught, and of the method. As soon as we have succeeded
in finding the proper method it will be no harder to teach
school-boys, in any number desired, than with the help of
the printing-press to cover a thousand sheets daily with

the neatest writing, or with Archimedes' machine to move houses, towers, and immense weights, or to cross the ocean in a ship, and journey to the New World. The whole process, too, will be as free from friction as is the movement of a clock whose motive power is supplied by the weights. It will be as pleasant to see education carried out on my plan as to look at an automatic machine of this kind, and the process will be as free from failure as are these mechanical contrivances, when skilfully made.

16. Let us therefore endeavour, in the name of the Almighty, to organise schools in such a way that in these points they may bear the greatest resemblance to a clock which is put together with the greatest skill, and is cunningly chased with the most delicate tools.

CHAPTER XIV

THE EXACT ORDER OF INSTRUCTION MUST BE BORROWED FROM NATURE, AND MUST BE OF SUCH A KIND THAT NO OBSTACLE CAN HINDER IT.

1. LET us then commence to seek out, in God's name, the principles on which, as on an immovable rock, the method of teaching and of learning can be grounded. If we wish to find a remedy for the defects of nature, it is in nature herself that we must look for it, since it is certain that art can do nothing unless it imitate nature.

2. A few examples will make this clear. We see a fish swimming in the water; it is its natural mode of progression. If a man wish to imitate it, it is necessary for him to use in a similar manner the limbs that are at his disposal; instead of fins he must employ his arms, and instead of a tail, his feet, moving them as a fish moves its fins. Even ships are constructed on this plan; in the place of fins they must employ oars or sails, and in the place of a tail, the rudder. We see a bird flying through the air; it is its natural mode of progression. When Daedalus wished to imitate it, he had to take wings (large enough to carry such a heavy body) and set them in motion.

3. The organ of sound production in animals is a pipe consisting of muscular rings, provided at the top with the thyroid cartilage, as with a lid, and at the bottom with the lungs, as with a wind-bag.

On this model flutes, whistles, and other wind instruments are made.

4. It has been discovered that the substance that causes thunder in the clouds, and hurls down fire and stones, is saltpetre ignited in combination with sulphur. In imitation of this, gunpowder is now made out of sulphur and saltpetre. When this is ignited and fired from cannon, a mimic storm, with thunder and lightning, is produced.

5. It has been found that water always tends to preserve a level surface, even in vessels that communicate but are at some distance from one another. The experiment has been made of conducting water through pipes, and it has been found that it will rise from any depth to any height, provided that it originally fall from that height. This is an artificial arrangement, but it is also natural; for the exact mode in which the action takes place is artificial, but the law on which the action depends is natural.

6. The vault of heaven, on observation, has been found to revolve continuously, thus, by the various revolutions of the planets, producing the changes of the seasons which are so pleasant. In imitation of this an instrument has been devised, representing the daily revolution of the vault of heaven. It is composed of wheels arranged so that not only can one be driven by the other, but that all can be put into continuous motion. Now it was necessary to construct this instrument out of movable and immovable parts, as the universe itself is constructed, and consequently we find a solid pedestal, pillars, and circular rings, corresponding to the earth, the immovable element in the universe, while in place of the movable orbits in the heaven we have the various wheels. But because it was impossible to command any one wheel to turn round and to carry others with them (as the Creator gave the heavenly lights the power to move themselves, and others with them), the motive power has to be borrowed from nature, and a weight or a spring is used.

Either a weight is hung from the axle of the principal wheel, and by its tension causes the axle, the wheel to which it belongs, and the other wheels to turn; or a long strip of steel is forcibly bound round the axle, and by its endeavours to get free and straighten itself, makes the axle and the wheel turn round. In order that the rotation may not be too fast, but slow like that of the vault of heaven, other wheels are added, of which the last, driven by two teeth only, makes a clicking noise and is analogous to the change between the coming and the going light, or to that between day and night.   In addition to that part of the mechanism which gives the signal for the hours and the quarters, skilfully - devised triggers are added, which set it in motion at the right time, and then stop it again, just as nature, by the movement of the vault of heaven, allows winter, spring, summer, and autumn to come and to depart again at the right moment.

7. It is now quite clear that that order, which is the dominating principle in the art of teaching all things to all men, should be, and can be, borrowed from no other source but the operations of nature. As soon as this principle is thoroughly secured, the processes of art will proceed as easily and as spontaneously as those of nature. Very aptly does Cicero say: "If we take nature as our guide, she will never lead us astray," and also: "Under the guidance of nature it is impossible to go astray." This is our belief, and our advice is to watch the operations of nature carefully and to imitate them.

8. But some one may laugh at our expectations and may cast in our teeth the saying of Hippocrates: "Life is short, and art is long; opportunities are fleeting, experience is deceptive, and judgment is difficult." Here are five obstacles, the reasons why so few scale the heights of wisdom :—

(i) The shortness of life; through which so many are snatched away in youth before their preparations for life are finished.   (ii) The perplexing crowd of objects which

the mind has to grasp, and which makes the endeavour to
include all things within the limits of our knowledge, very
weary work. (iii) The lack of opportunities to acquire the
arts, or their rapid departure when they occur (for the
years of youth, which are the most suitable for mental
culture, are spent in playing, and the succeeding years,
in the present condition of mankind, bring far more
opportunities for worthless than for serious matters); or if
a suitable opportunity present itself, it vanishes before we
can grasp it. (iv) The weakness of our intellects and the
lack of sound judgment. The result of this is that we
get no farther than the outside shell, and never attain to
the kernel. (v) Finally, the circumstance that, if any wish
to grasp the true nature of things by patient observation
and experiments repeated as often as possible, the process
is too wearisome, and is at the same time deceptive and
uncertain (for instance, in such accurate observations the
most careful observer may make an error, and as soon
as one error creeps in, the whole observation becomes
worthless).

9. If all this be true, how can we dare hope for a
universal, sure, easy, and thorough road to learning? I
answer: Experience teaches us that this is true, but the
same experience teaches us also that the proper remedies
can be found. These things have been ordained thus by
God, the all-wise arranger of the universe, and are for our
good. He has given us a short span of life because, in
our present state of corruption, we should be unable to
employ a longer one profitably. For if we, who are born
and die, and with whom the end of life is but a few years
distant from the beginning, give ourselves up to folly:
what would we not do if we had hundreds or thousands
of years before us? God, therefore, has only wished to
grant as much time as He deemed sufficient preparation
for a better life. For this purpose life is long enough, if
only we know how to use it.

10. The diversity of objects has been equally ordained
by God for our advantage, that there might be no

lack of material to occupy, exercise, and educate our minds.

11. God permits opportunities to be fleeting, and only to be grasped by the fore-lock, that we may learn to seize them the very instant they present themselves.

12. Experience is deceptive in order that our attention may be excited, and that we may feel the necessity of penetrating to the essential nature of things.

13. Finally, judgment is difficult, in order that we may be urged on to eagerness and to continual effort, and that the hidden wisdom of God, which permeates all things, may, to our great satisfaction, become ever more apparent.

"If everything could be easily understood," says St. Augustine, "men would neither seek wisdom with keenness, nor find it with exultation."

14. We must therefore see in what way those obstacles which God's foresight has placed in our paths to make us keener and more energetic may, with God's aid, be set aside. This can only be attained—

(i) By lengthening our lives, that they may be sufficiently long for the scheme proposed.

(ii) By curtailing the subjects taught, that they may be proportionate to the duration of life.

(iii) By seizing opportunities, and not letting them slip away unused.

(iv) By unlocking the intellect, that it may grasp things with ease.

(v) By laying a foundation that is not to be shaken, and that will not deceive us, in the place of a tottering fabric of superficial observation.

15. We will therefore proceed, taking nature as our guide, to seek out the principles :—

(i) Of prolonging life.

(ii) Of curtailing the subjects, that knowledge may be acquired faster.

(iii) Of seizing opportunities, that knowledge may be acquired without fail.

(iv) Of unlocking the intellect, that knowledge may be easily acquired.

(v) Of sharpening the judgment, that knowledge may be thoroughly acquired.

To each of these points we shall devote a chapter. The question of curtailing the subjects of instruction will be treated of last.

CHAPTER XV

THE BASIS OF THE PROLONGATION OF LIFE

1. ARISTOTLE, as well as Hippocrates, has complained of the shortness of human life, and accuses nature of granting a long term of years to stags, ravens, and other animals, while she hems in by narrow boundaries the lives of men born to great responsibility. Seneca, however, opposes this view, and wisely says: "The life that we receive is not short, unless we make it so. We suffer from no lack of years, but carouse away those that are granted us. Life is long, if we do but know how to use it." And again: "Our lives are sufficiently long, and, if we order them well, allow us to bring the greatest undertakings to completion" (*De Brevitate Vitæ*, cc. i. and ii.)

2. If this be correct, and indeed it is very true, it is grossly culpable on our parts if our lives do not prove sufficiently long to bring great undertakings to completion, since the reason is that we waste our lives, partly by taking no care of them, so that they do not reach the natural limit, and partly by frittering them away on worthless objects.

3. A trustworthy authority (Hippolytus Guarino) [23] asserts, and gives good reasons for his assertion, that a man of the most delicate constitution, if he come into the world without any deformity, possesses enough vitality to carry him on to his sixtieth year; while a very strong man should attain to his hundredth year. If any die before this

age (it is, of course, well known that most men die as children, as youths, or in middle age), they are themselves to blame, since, by excesses, or by neglect of the natural demands of life, they have undermined their own health and that of their children, and have hastened their death.

4. The examples of men who, before middle age, have reached a point to which others could not attain in the course of a long life, prove that a short lifetime (*i.e.* one of fifty, forty, or thirty years) is sufficient to realise the highest aims, if only it be properly used. Alexander the Great died when he was thirty-three years old, and he was not only a master of all the sciences, but also conqueror of the world, which he had subdued less by sheer force than by the wisdom of his plans, and the rapidity with which he put them into execution. Giovanni Pico Mirandola,[24] who was even younger than Alexander when he died, attained by his philosophical studies such proficiency in all the departments of human knowledge, that he was considered the marvel of his age.

5. To take one more example, Jesus Christ, our Lord, remained only thirty-four years on earth, and in that time completed the task of Redemption. This He undoubtedly did to prove (for with Him every event has a mystic meaning) that whatever length of life a man may enjoy, it is sufficient to serve him as a preparation for eternity.

6. I cannot leave this question without quoting a golden saying of Seneca (out of his ninety-fourth letter): "I have," he says, "found many men who are just in their dealings with men, but few who are just in their dealings with God. We daily lament our fate; but what does it matter how soon we quit this world, since we must certainly quit it one day or other? Life is long if it be full, and it becomes full if the spirit exert its power on itself; if it learn the secret of self-control." And again: "I entreat of you, my Lucilius! let us strive that our lives, like earthly jewels, may be, not of great bulk, but of great weight"; and a little farther on: "Let us, therefore, deem that man one of the blest, who has used well the time allotted to him, no matter how

short it may have been. For he has seen the true light. He has not been one of the common herd; but has lived a full life, and has come to maturity." And again : "As a perfect man can exist in a small body, so can a perfect life be found in a short term of years. The duration of life is a purely accidental circumstance. Do you ask which is the path of life that reaches farthest? It is the path that leads to wisdom. He who attains wisdom, has reached not only the farthest, but also the highest goal."

7. Against this shortness of life, which is complained of, there are two remedies for us and for our children (and therefore for schools also). We must take all possible precautions that—

(i) Our bodies may be protected from disease and from death.

(ii) Our minds may be placed in such an environment that they can attain all knowledge.

8. The body must be protected from disease and from accidents, firstly, because it is the dwelling-place of the soul, which must leave this world as soon as ever the body is destroyed. If it fall into bad repair, and suffer damage in any of its parts, the soul, its guest, will have an inhospitable abode. Therefore, if we wish to dwell as long as possible in the palace of this world, into which we have been brought by God's grace, we must take wise forethought for the fabric of our bodies.

Secondly, this same body is not only intended to be the dwelling-place of the reasoning soul, but also to be its instrument, without which it could hear nothing, see nothing, say nothing, conduct no business, and could not even think. And since nothing exists in the mind that has not previously existed in the senses, the intellect takes the material of all its thoughts from the senses, and performs the operations of thought in a manner that may be termed "inner sensation," that is to say, by acting on the images of things that are brought before it. It follows, therefore, that, if the brain receive an injury, the imagination will be impaired, and that if an impression be made on the body, an impression will be made on the soul also. We may therefore unhesitatingly say that all should pray that they may have a sound mind in a sound body.

9. Our bodies are preserved in health and strength by a regular and moderate life, and on this we will make a few remarks from the medical point of view, taking a tree as illustration. In order to maintain its freshness, a tree needs three things: (1) a continuous supply of moisture; (2) copious transpiration; (3) an alternating period of rest and activity.

Moisture is necessary, because the tree would wither and dry up without it, but it must not be supplied in too great a quantity, as, if it be, it causes the roots to rot away. In the same way the body needs nourishment, because it wastes away from hunger and thirst without it; but it should not obtain a supply so large that the stomach is unable to digest it. The greater the moderation with which men partake of food, the easier they find its digestion. The generality of men pay but little attention to this law, and by taking too much food diminish their strength and shorten their lives. For death is caused by disease, disease by unwholesome juices, and these, in turn, by insufficient digestion. Insufficient digestion arises from over-nutrition, and takes place when the stomach is so full that it cannot digest, and is compelled to supply the various members of the body with semi-digested juices, and in this case it is impossible that diseases should not arise. As the son of Sirach says: " By surfeiting have many perished, but he that taketh heed prolongeth his life " (Ecclesiasticus xxxvii. 31).

10. In order that good health may be preserved, it is necessary that nourishment be not only moderate in quantity, but also simple in quality. When a tree is young and tender, the gardener does not water it with wine or with milk, but with the liquid that suits trees, namely water. Parents should therefore take care not to spoil their boys, particularly those who study, or ought to study,

by giving them dainties. Are we not told that Daniel and his companions, the youths of noble birth who had to apply themselves to the pursuit of wisdom, lived on a diet of pulse and water, and that they were found to be more capable and more active, and, what is of greater value, more intelligent, than all the other youths who ate of the king's meat? (Daniel i. 12 *sqq.*) But of these particulars we will speak in another place.

11. A tree must also transpire, and needs to be copiously refreshed by wind, rain, and frost; otherwise it easily falls into bad condition, and becomes barren. In the same way the human body needs movement, excitement, and exercise, and in daily life these must be supplied, either artificially or naturally.

12. Finally, a tree needs rest at stated periods, that it may not have to put forth branches, blossoms, and fruit perpetually, but may have some time to fulfil its inner functions, to develope sap, and in this way to strengthen itself. It was for this reason that God ordained that winter should follow summer, namely, to guarantee rest to all things that live on the earth, and even to the earth itself, since he commanded that the fields should lie fallow every seventh year (Lev. xxv.) In the same way He has ordained the night for man, and for other animals, in order that, by sleep and by resting their limbs, they may once more gather together the strength which the exertions of the day have dissipated. Even the smaller periods, such as the hours, are devised with a view to giving the body and the mind some relaxation; otherwise a strained and unnatural condition would set in. It is, therefore, useful to intersperse the labours of the day with recreation, amusements, games, merriment, music, and such-like diversions, and thus to refresh the inner and the outer senses.

13. He who observes these three principles (that is to say, eats moderately, exercises his body, and uses the relaxations supplied by nature) cannot fail to preserve his life and his health as long as possible. We naturally leave

out of consideration accidents that depend on a dispensation higher than ours.

We see then that a large portion of the good organisation of schools consists of the proper division of work and of rest, and depends on the disposition of studies, intervals to relieve the strain, and recreation.

14. This can be attained by the skilful disposition of the time devoted to study. Thirty years seem insignificant, and are easily dismissed from the tongue. But these years include many months, more days, and countless hours. In a single period of such duration much progress can be made, no matter how slow the process of advancement may be, provided it be continuous. We can see this in the growth of plants. It is impossible for the sharpest sight to perceive the process, since it takes place too gradually; but every month some increase is visible, and at the end of thirty years every one can see that the sapling has turned into a large and shady tree. The same holds good in the growth of our bodies. We do not see them growing, but only perceive that they have grown. So, too, with the acquisition of knowledge by the mind, as we learn from the well-known Latin couplet:

To a little add a little, and to that little yet a little more,
And in a short time you will pile up a large heap.

15. He who realises the natural strength of progress will easily understand this. From each bud a tree puts forth but one shoot yearly; but in thirty years the same tree will possess thousands of shoots, large and small, and leaves, blossoms, and fruit without number. Why then should it seem impossible to bring the activity of a man to any degree of intensity or fulness, and this in twenty or thirty years? Let us examine the matter more closely.

16. There are twenty-four hours in a day, and if, for the daily uses of life, we divide these into three parts, setting aside eight hours for sleep, and the same number for the external needs of the body (such as care of the health, meals, dressing and undressing, agreeable recrea-

tion, friendly converse, etc.), we have eight hours left for the serious work of life. We shall therefore have forty-eight working hours a week (setting aside the seventh day for rest). In one year this will amount to 2945 hours, and in ten, twenty, or thirty years to an immense number.

17. If, in each hour, a man could learn a single fragment of some branch of knowledge, a single rule of some mechanical art, a single pleasing story or proverb (the acquisition of which would require no effort), what a vast stock of learning he might lay by?

18. Seneca is therefore right when he says: "Life is long, if we know how to use it; it suffices for the completion of the greatest undertakings, if it be properly employed." It is consequently of importance that we understand the art of making the very best use of our lives, and to this point we will now direct our investigation.

CHAPTER XVI

THE UNIVERSAL REQUIREMENTS OF TEACHING AND OF
LEARNING; THAT IS TO SAY, A METHOD OF TEACHING
AND OF LEARNING WITH SUCH CERTAINTY THAT THE
DESIRED RESULT MUST OF NECESSITY FOLLOW.

1. EXCEPTIONALLY fine is that comparison made by our
Lord Jesus Christ in the gospel, "So is the kingdom of
God, as if a man should cast seed upon the earth; and
should sleep and rise night and day, and the seed should
spring up and grow, he knoweth not how. The earth beareth
fruit of herself; first the blade, then the ear, then the full
corn in the ear. But when the fruit is ripe, straightway
he putteth forth the sickle, because the harvest is come"
(Mark iv. 26).

2. The Saviour here shows that it is God who operates
in everything, and that nothing remains for man but to
receive the seeds of instruction with a devout heart; the
processes of growth and of ripening will then continue of
themselves, unperceived by him. The duty of the teachers
of the young, therefore, is none other than to skilfully scatter
the seeds of instruction in their minds, and to carefully water
God's plants. Increase and growth will come from above.

3. Is there any who denies that sowing and planting need
skill and experience? If an unpractised gardener plant
an orchard with young trees, the greater number of them
die, and the few that prosper do so rather through chance
than through skill. But the trained gardener goes to work

carefully, since he is well instructed, where, when, and how to act and what to leave alone, that he may meet with no failure. It is true that even an experienced man meets with failure occasionally (indeed it is scarcely possible for a man to take such careful forethought that no error can arise); but we are now discussing, not the abstract question of circumspection and chance, but the art of doing away with chance by means of circumspection.

4. Hitherto the method of instruction has been so uncertain that scarcely any one would dare to say: "In so many years I will bring this youth to such and such a point; I will educate him in such and such a way." We must therefore see if it be possible to place the art of intellectual discipline on such a firm basis that sure and certain progress may be made.

5. Since this basis can be properly laid only by assimilating the processes of art as much as possible to those of nature (as we have seen in the 15th chapter), we will follow the method of nature, taking as our example a bird hatching out its young; and, if we see with what good results gardeners, painters, and builders follow in the track of nature, we shall have to recognise that the educator of the young should follow in the same path.

6. If any think this course of action petty or commonplace, let him consider that from that which is of daily occurrence and universal notoriety and which takes place with good results in nature and in the arts (the teaching art excepted), we are seeking to deduce that which is less known and which is necessary for our present purpose. Indeed, if the facts from which we derive the principles that form the basis for our precepts are known, we can entertain hopes that our conclusions will be the more evident.

FIRST PRINCIPLE

7. *Nature observes a suitable time.*

For example: a bird that wishes to multiply its species, does not set about it in winter, when everything is stiff with cold, nor in summer, when everything is parched and withered by the heat; nor yet in autumn, when the vital force of all creatures declines with the sun's declining rays, and a new winter with hostile mien is approaching; but in spring, when the sun brings back life and strength to all. Again, the process consists of several steps. While it is yet cold the bird conceives the eggs and warms them inside its body, where they are protected from the cold; when the air grows warmer it lays them in its nest, but does not hatch them out until the warm season comes, that the tender chicks may grow accustomed to light and warmth by degrees.

8. *Imitation.*—In the same way the gardener takes care to do nothing out of season. He does not, therefore, plant in the winter (because the sap is then in the roots, preparing to mount and nourish the plant later on); nor in summer (when the sap is already dispersed through the branches); nor in autumn (when the sap is retiring to the · roots once more); but in spring, when the moisture is beginning to rise from the roots and the upper part of the plant begins to shoot. Later on, too, it is of great importance to the little tree that the right time be chosen for the various operations that are needful, such as manuring, pruning, and cutting. Even the tree itself has its proper time for putting forth shoots and blossoms, for growing, and for coming to maturity.

In the same manner the careful builder must choose the right time for cutting timber, burning bricks, laying foundations, building, and plastering walls, etc.

9. *Deviation.*—In direct opposition to this principle, a twofold error is committed in schools.

(i) The right time for mental exercise is not chosen.

(ii) The exercises are not properly divided, so that all advance may be made through the several stages needful, without any omission. As long as the boy is still a child he cannot be taught, because the roots of his understanding are still too deep below the surface. As soon as he becomes old, it is too late to teach him, because the intellect and the memory are then failing. In middle age it is difficult, because the forces of the intellect are dissipated over a variety of objects and are not easily concentrated. The season of youth, therefore, must be chosen. Then life and mind are fresh and gathering strength ; then everything is vigorous and strikes root deeply.

10. *Rectification.*—We conclude, therefore, that

(i) The education of men should be commenced in the springtime of life, that is to say, in boyhood (for boyhood is the equivalent of spring, youth of summer, manhood of autumn, and old age of winter).

(ii) The morning hours are the most suitable for study (for here again the morning is the equivalent of spring, midday of summer, the evening of autumn, and the night of winter).

(iii) All the subjects that are to be learned should be arranged so as to suit the age of the students, that nothing which is beyond their comprehension be given them to learn.

Second Principle

11. *Nature prepares the material, before she begins to give it form.*

For example : the bird that wishes to produce a creature similar to itself first conceives the embryo from a drop of its blood ; it then prepares the nest in which it is to lay the eggs, but does not begin to hatch them until the chick is formed and moves within the shell.

12. *Imitation.*—In the same way the prudent builder, before he begins to erect a building, collects a quantity of wood, lime, stones, iron, and the other things needful, in order that he may not have to stop the work later on from lack of materials, nor find that its solidity has been impaired. In the same way, the painter who wishes to produce a picture, prepares the canvas, stretches it on a frame, lays the ground on it, mixes his colours, places his brushes so that they may be ready to hand, and then at last commences to paint.

In the same way the gardener, before he commences operations, tries to have the garden, the stocks, the grafts, and the tools in readiness, that he may not have to fetch the necessary appliances while at work, and so spoil the whole operation.

13. *Deviation.* — Against this principle schools are offenders : firstly, because they take no care to prepare beforehand the mechanical aids such as books, maps, pictures, diagrams, etc., and to have them in readiness for general use, but at the moment that they need this or that, they make experiments, draw, dictate, copy, etc., and when this is done by an unskilled or careless teacher (and their number increases daily), the result is deplorable. It is just as if a physician, whenever he wishes to administer a medicine, had to wander through gardens and forests, and collect and distil herbs and roots, though medicaments to suit every case should be ready to his hand.

14. Secondly, because even in school-books the natural order, that the matter come first and the form follow, is not observed. Everywhere the exact opposite is to be found. The classification of objects is unnaturally made to precede a knowledge of the objects themselves, although it is impossible to classify, before the matter to be classified is there. I will demonstrate this by four examples.

15. (1) Languages are learned in schools before the sciences, since the intellect is detained for some years over the study of languages, and only then allowed to proceed to the sciences, mathematics, physics, etc. And yet things are essential, words only accidental ; things are the body, words but the garment ; things are the kernel, words the shells and husks. Both should therefore be presented to the intellect at the same time, but particularly the things, since they are as much objects of the understanding as are languages.

16. (2) Even in the study of languages the proper order is reversed, since the students commence, not with some author or with a skilfully-compiled phrase-book, but with the grammar ; though the authors (and in their own way

the phrase-books) present the material of speech, namely words, while the grammars, on the other hand, only give the form, that is to say, the laws of the formation, order, and combination of words.

17. (3) In the encyclopædic compilations of human knowledge, the arts are always placed first, while the sciences follow after; though the latter teach of the things themselves, the former how to manipulate the things.

18. (4) Finally: it is the abstract rules that are first taught and then illustrated by dragging in a few examples; though it is plain that a light should precede him whom it lights.

19. *Rectification.*—It follows, therefore, that in order to effect a thorough improvement in schools it is necessary:

(i) That books and the materials necessary for teaching be held in readiness.

(ii) That the understanding be first instructed in things, and then taught to express them in language.

(iii) That no language be learned from a grammar, but from suitable authors.

(iv) That the knowledge of things precede the knowledge of their combinations.

(v) And that examples come before rules.

Third Principle

20. *Nature chooses a fit subject to act upon, or first submits one to a suitable treatment in order to make it fit.*

For example: a bird does not place any object in the nest in which it sits, but an object of such a kind that a chicken can be hatched from it, that is to say, an egg. If a small stone or anything else falls into the nest, it throws it out as useless. But when the process of hatching takes place, it warms the matter contained in the egg, and looks after it until the chicken makes its way out.

21. *Imitation.*—In the same way the builder cuts down timber, of as good quality as possible, dries it, squares it,

and saws it into planks. Then he chooses a spot to build on, clears it, lays a new foundation, or repairs the old one so that he can make use of it.

22. In the same way, if the canvas or the surface do not suit his colours, the painter tries to make them more suitable, and, by rubbing them and polishing them, fits them for his use.

23. The gardener too (1) chooses from a fruit-bearing stock a shoot that possesses as much vitality as possible; (2) transplants it to a garden, and places it carefully in the earth; (3) does not burden it with a new graft unless he sees that it has taken root; (4) before he inserts the new graft, removes the former shoot, and even cuts a piece away round the stock in order that none of the sap may perform any function other than that of vivifying the graft.

24. *Deviation.*—Against this principle the schools are offenders: not because they include the weak of intellect (for in our opinion all the young should be admitted into the schools) but far more because:

(1) These tender plants are not transplanted into the garden, that is to say, are not entirely entrusted to the schools, so that none, who are to be trained as men, shall be allowed to leave the workshop before their training is complete.

(2) The attempt is generally made to engraft that noblest graft of knowledge, virtue and piety, too early, before the stock itself has taken root; that is to say, before the desire to learn has been excited in those who have no natural bent in that direction.

(3) The side-shoots or root-suckers are not removed before the grafting takes place; that is to say, the minds are not freed from all idle tendencies by being habituated to discipline and order.

25. *Rectification.*—It is therefore desirable:

(i) That all who enter schools persevere in their studies.

(ii) That, before any special study is introduced, the minds of the students be prepared and made receptive of it. (See the following chapter, Principle 2.)

(iii) That all obstacles be removed out of the way of schools.

"For it is of no use to give precepts," says Seneca, "unless the obstacles that stand in the way be removed." But of this we will treat in the following chapter.

Fourth Principle

26. *Nature is not confused in its operations, but in its forward progress advances distinctly from one point to another.*

For example: if a bird is being produced, its bones, veins, and nerves are formed at separate and distinct periods; at one time its flesh becomes firm, at another it receives its covering of skin or feathers, and at another it learns how to fly, etc.

27. *Imitation.*—When a builder lays foundations he does not build the walls at the same time, much less does he put on the roof, but does each of these things at the proper time and in the proper place.

28. In the same way a painter does not work at twenty or thirty pictures at once, but occupies himself with one only. For, though he may from time to time put a few touches to some others or give his attention to something else, it is on one picture and one only that he concentrates his energies.

29. In the same way the gardener does not plant several shoots at once, but plants them one after the other, that he may neither confuse himself nor spoil the operation of nature.

30. *Deviation.*—Confusion has arisen in the schools through the endeavour to teach the scholars many things at one time. As, for example, Latin and Greek grammar, perhaps rhetoric and poetic as well, and a multitude of other subjects. For it is notorious that in the classical schools the subject-matter for reading and for composition is changed almost every hour throughout the day. If this be not confusion I should like to know what is. It is just as if a shoemaker wished to make six or seven new

shoes at once, and took them up one by one in turn, only to lay them aside in a few minutes ; or as if a baker, who wished to place various kinds of bread in his oven, were to take them out again immediately, removing one kind as he put in another. Who would commit such an act of folly ? The shoemaker finishes one shoe before he begins another. The baker places no fresh bread in the oven until that already in it is thoroughly baked.

31. *Rectification.*—Let us imitate these people and take care not to confuse scholars who are learning grammar by teaching them dialectic, or by introducing rhetoric into their studies. We should also put off the study of Greek until Latin is mastered, since it is impossible to concentrate the mind on any one thing, when it has to busy itself with several things at once.

That great man, Joseph Scaliger,[25] was well aware of this. It is related of him that (perhaps on the advice of his father) he never occupied himself with more than one branch of knowledge at once, and concentrated all his energies on that one. It was owing to this that he was able to master not only fourteen languages, but also all the arts and sciences that lie within the province of man. He devoted himself to these one after the other with such success that in each subject his learning excelled that of men who had given their whole lives to it. And those who have tried to follow in his footsteps and imitate his method, have done so with considerable success.

32. Schools, therefore, should be organised in such a manner that the scholar shall be occupied with only one object of study at any given time.

FIFTH PRINCIPLE

33. *In all the operations of nature development is from within.*

For example : in the case of a bird it is not the claws, or the feathers, or the skin that are first formed, but the inner parts ; the outer parts are formed later, at the proper season.

34. *Imitation.*—In the same way the gardener does not insert his graft into the outer bark nor into the outside layer of wood, but making an incision right into the pith, places the graft as far in as it .will go.

In this way he makes the joint so firm that the sap cannot escape, but is forced right into the shoot, and uses all its strength in vivifying it.

35. So too, a tree, that is nourished by the rain of heaven and the moisture of the earth, assimilates its nutriment, not through its outer bark, but through the pores of its inmost parts.   On this account the gardener waters, not the branches, but the roots.   Animals also convey their food, not to their outer limbs, but to the stomach, which assimilates it and nourishes the whole body.   If, therefore, the educator of the young give special attention to the roots of knowledge, the understanding, these will soon impart their vitality to the stem, that is, to the memory, and finally blossoms and fruits, that is to say, a facile use of language and practical capacity will be produced.

36. *Deviation.*—It is on this point that those teachers fall into error who, instead of thoroughly explaining the subjects of study to the boys under their charge, give them endless dictations, and make them learn their lessons off by heart.   Even those who wish to explain the subject-matter do not know how to do so, that is to say, do not know how to tend the roots or how to engraft the graft of knowledge.   Thus they fatigue their pupils, and resemble a man who uses a club or a mallet, instead of a knife, when he wishes to make an incision in a plant.

37. *Rectification.*—It therefore follows

(i) That the scholar should be taught first to understand things, and then to remember them, and that no stress should be laid on the use of speech or pen, till after a training on the first two points.

(ii) That the teacher should know all the methods by which the understanding may be sharpened, and should put them into practice skilfully.

Sixth Principle

38. *Nature, in its formative processes, begins with the universal and ends with the particular.*

For example: a bird is to be produced from an egg. It is not the head, an eye, a feather, or a claw that is first formed, but the following process takes place. The whole egg is warmed; the warmth produces movement, and this movement brings into existence a system of veins, which mark in outline the shape of the whole bird (defining the parts that are to become the head, the wings, the feet, etc.) It is not until this outline is complete that the individual parts are brought to perfection.

39. *Imitation.*—The builder takes this as his model. He first makes a general plan of the building in his head, or on paper, or in wood. Then he lays the foundations, builds the walls, and lays on the roof. It is not until he has done this that he gives his attention to the small details that are necessary to complete a house, such as doors, windows, staircases, etc.; while last of all he adds ornamentation such as paintings, sculptures, and carpets.

40. An artist proceeds in the same way. He does not begin by drawing an ear, an eye, a nose, or a mouth, but first makes a charcoal sketch of the face or of the whole body. If he be satisfied that this sketch resembles the original, he paints it with light strokes of the brush, still omitting all detail. Then, finally, he puts in the light and shade, and, using a variety of colours, finishes the several parts in detail.

41. The procedure of the sculptor is the same. When he wishes to carve a statue, he takes a block of marble and shapes it roughly. Then he sets to work more carefully and outlines the most important features. Finally, he chisels the individual parts with the greatest accuracy and colours them artistically.

42. In the same way the gardener takes the most simple and universal part of a tree, namely, a shoot.

Later on, this can put forth as many branches as it possesses buds.

43. *Deviation.*—From this it follows that it is a mistake to teach the several branches of science in detail before a general outline of the whole realm of knowledge has been placed before the student, and that no one should be instructed in such a way as to become proficient in any one branch of knowledge without thoroughly understanding its relation to all the rest.

44. It follows also that arts, sciences, and languages are badly taught unless a general notion of the elements be first given. I remember well that, when we began to learn dialectic, rhetoric, and metaphysics, we were, at the very beginning, overburdened with long-winded rules, with commentaries and notes on commentaries, with comparisons of authors and with knotty questions. Latin grammar was taught us with all the exceptions and irregularities; Greek grammar with all its dialects, and we, poor wretches, were so confused that we scarcely understood what it was all about.

45. *Rectification.*—The remedy for this want of system is as follows : at the very commencement of their studies, boys should receive instruction in the first principles of general culture, that is to say, the subjects learned should be arranged in such a manner that the studies that come later introduce nothing new, but only expand the elements of knowledge that the boy has already mastered. Just as a tree, even if it live for a hundred years, puts forth no new branches, but only suffers those that already exist to develope and to spread.

(i) Each language, science, or art must be first taught in its most simple elements, that the student may obtain a general idea of it. (ii) His knowledge may next be developed further by placing rules and examples before him. (iii) Then he may be allowed to learn the subject systematically with the exceptions and irregularities; and (iv), last of all, may be given a commentary, though only where it is absolutely necessary. For he who has thoroughly mastered a subject from the beginning will have little need of a commentary, but will soon be in the position to write one himself.

SEVENTH PRINCIPLE

46. *Nature makes no leaps, but proceeds step by step.*

The development of a chicken consists of certain gradual processes which cannot be omitted or deferred, until finally it breaks its shell and comes forth. When this takes place, the mother does not allow the young bird to fly and seek its food (indeed it is unable to do so), but she feeds it herself, and by keeping it warm with her body promotes the growth of its feathers. When the chick's feathers have grown she does not thrust it forth from the nest immediately and make it fly, but teaches it first to move its wings in the nest itself or perching on its edge, then to try to fly outside the nest, though quite near it, by fluttering from branch to branch, then to fly from tree to tree, and later on from hill to hill, till finally it gains sufficient confidence to fly right out in the open. It is easy to see how necessary it is that each of these processes should take place at the right time; that not only the time should be suitable but that the processes should be graduated; and that there should be not graduation merely, but an immutable graduation.

47. *Imitation.*—The builder proceeds in the same manner. He does not begin with the gables or with the walls, but with foundations. When the foundations are laid he does not go on with the roof, but builds the walls. In a word, the order in which the several stages are combined depends on the relation that they mutually bear to one another.

48. The gardener likewise has to adopt the principle of graduation. The wild-stock must be found, dug up, transplanted, pruned, and cut; the graft must be inserted and the joint made firm, etc., and none of these processes can be omitted or taken in a different order. But, if these processes are carried out properly and in the right order,

it is scarcely possible, in fact it is impossible, for the result to be unsuccessful.

49. *Deviation.*—It is an evident absurdity, therefore, if teachers, for their own sake and that of their pupils, do not graduate the subjects which they teach in such a way that, not only one stage may lead on directly to the next, but also that each shall be completed in a given space of time. For unless goals are set up, means provided for reaching them, and a proper system devised for the use of those means, it is easy for something to be omitted or perverted, and failure is the result.

50. *Rectification.*—It follows therefore

(i) That all studies should be carefully graduated throughout the various classes, in such a way that those that come first may prepare the way for and throw light on those that come after.

(ii) That the time should be carefully divided, so that each year, each month, each day, and each hour may have its appointed task.

(iii) That the division of the time and of the subjects of study should be rigidly adhered to, that nothing may be omitted or perverted.

EIGHTH PRINCIPLE

51. *If nature commence anything, it does not leave off until the operation is completed.*

If a bird, urged by the impulse of nature, begin to sit on eggs, she does not leave off until she has hatched out the chickens. If she sat on them for a few hours only, the embryo in the egg would become cold and die. Even when the chickens are hatched she does not cease to keep them warm, but continues to do so until they have grown strong, are covered with feathers, and can endure the cold air.

52. *Imitation.*—The painter also, who has begun a picture, will produce his work best if he finish it without any interruption. For in this case the colours blend better and hold faster.

53. For this reason it is best to finish the erection of a building without any interruption ; otherwise the sun, the wind, and the rain spoil the work, the later additions will not be so firm, and on every side there will be cracks, weak spots, and loose joints.

54. The gardener too acts with wisdom, for when once he has begun to work at a graft he does not cease until the operation is completed. Since, if the sap dry in the stock or in the graft, owing to a delay in completing the process, the plant is ruined.

55. *Deviation.*—It is therefore injurious if boys are sent to school for months or years continuously, but are then withdrawn for considerable periods and employed otherwise; equally so if the teacher commence now one subject, now another, and finish nothing satisfactorily ; and lastly, it is equally fatal if he do not fix a certain task for each hour, and complete it, so that in each period his pupil can make an unmistakable advance towards the desired goal. Where such a fire is wanting, everything grows cold. Not without reason does the proverb say "Strike while the iron is hot." For if it be allowed to cool it is useless to hammer it, but it must once more be placed in the fire, and thus much time and iron are wasted. Since every time that it is heated, it loses some of its mass.

56. *Rectification.*—It follows therefore

(i) That he who is sent to school must be kept there until he becomes well informed, virtuous, and pious.

(ii) That the school must be situated in a quiet spot, far from noise and distractions.

(iii) That whatever has to be done, in accordance with the scheme of study, must be done without any shirking.

(iv) That no boys, under any pretext whatever, should be allowed to stay away or to play truant.

Ninth Principle

57. *Nature carefully avoids obstacles and things likely to cause hurt.*

For example, when a bird is hatching eggs it does not allow a cold wind, much less rain or hail, to reach them. It also drives away snakes, birds of prey, etc.

58. *Imitation.*—In the same way the builder, so far as is possible, keeps dry his wood, bricks, and lime, and does not allow what he has built to be destroyed or to fall down.

59. So, too, the painter protects a newly-painted picture from wind, from violent heat, and from dust, and allows no hand but his own to touch it.

60. The gardener also protects a young plant by a railing or by hurdles, that hares or goats may not gnaw it or root it up.

61. *Deviation.*—It is therefore folly to introduce a student to controversial points when he is just beginning a subject, that is to say, to allow a mind that is mastering something new to assume an attitude of doubt. What is this but to tear up a plant that is just beginning to strike root? (Rightly does Hugo say: "He who starts by investigating doubtful points will never enter into the temple of wisdom.") But this is exactly what takes place if the young are not protected from incorrect, intricate, and badly written books as well as from evil companions.

62. *Rectification.*—Care should therefore be taken

(i) That the scholars receive no books but those suitable for their classes.

(ii) That these books be of such a kind that they can rightly be termed sources of wisdom, virtue, and piety.

(iii) That neither in the school nor in its vicinity the scholars be allowed to mix with bad companions.

63. If all these recommendations are observed, it is scarcely possible that schools should fail to attain their object.

CHAPTER XVII

1. WE have already considered the means by which the educationist may attain his goal with certainty, we will now proceed to see how these means can be suited to the minds of the pupils, so that their use may be easy and pleasant.

2. Following in the footsteps of nature we find that the process of education will be easy

(i)   If it begin early, before the mind is corrupted.

(ii) If the mind be duly prepared to receive it.

(iii) If it proceed from the general to the particular.

(iv) And from what is easy to what is more difficult.

(v)   If the pupil be not overburdened by too many subjects.

(vi) And if progress be slow in every case.

(vii) If the intellect be forced to nothing to which its natural bent does not incline it, in accordance with its age and with the right method.

(viii) If everything be taught through the medium of the senses.

(ix) And if the use of everything taught be continually kept in view.

(x)   If everything be taught according to one and the same method.

These, I say, are the principles to be adopted if education is to be easy and pleasant.

3. *Nature begins by a careful selection of materials.*

For instance, for hatching a bird she selects fresh eggs and those that contain pure matter. If the formation of the chicken have already begun, it is in vain to expect any result.

4. *Imitation.* — The architect who wishes to erect a building, needs a clear plot of ground, and, if there be a house already standing there, he must pull it down before he can build the new one.

5. The artist, too, does his best work on a clean canvas. If it have already been painted on, or be dirty or rough, it must be cleaned or smoothed before he can use it.

6. For the preservation of precious ointments, empty jars must be procured, or those that are in use must be carefully cleansed of their contents.

7. The gardener, too, prefers to plant young trees, or, if he take them when too old, cuts off the branches in order that the sap may not be dissipated. For this reason Aristotle placed " privation " among the principles of nature, for he held that it was impossible to impress a new form on any material until the old one had been removed.

8. *Deviation.*—It follows from this : (1) That it is best to devote the mind to the pursuit of wisdom while it is still fresh, and before it has acquired the habit of dissipating its strength over a variety of occupations ; and that the later the education begins, the harder it will be for it to obtain a hold, because the mind is already occupied by other things. (2) That the result must be bad if a boy be instructed by several teachers at once, since it is scarcely possible for them all to use the same method, and, if they do not, the boy's mind is drawn first in one direction and then in another, and its development is thus hindered. (3) That it shows great lack of judgment if moral instruction be not made the first point when the education of children or of older boys is commenced ; since,

when they have been taught to control their feelings, they will be the more fit to receive other instruction. Horse-tamers keep a horse under absolute control with an iron bit, and ensure its obedience before they teach it its paces. Rightly does Seneca say : " First learn virtue, and then wisdom, since without virtue it is difficult to learn wisdom." And Cicero says : " Moral philosophy makes the mind fit to receive the seeds of further knowledge."

9. *Rectification.*—Therefore

(i) Education should be commenced early.

(ii) The pupil should not have more than one teacher in each subject.

(iii) Before anything else is done, the morals should be rendered harmonious by the master's influence.

SECOND PRINCIPLE

10. *Nature prepares its material so that it actually strives to attain the form.*

Thus the chicken in the egg, when sufficiently formed, seeks to develope itself still further, moves, and bursts the shell or breaks through it with its beak. After escaping from its prison, it takes pleasure in the warmth and nutriment provided by its mother, opens its beak expectantly and swallows its food greedily. It rejoices to find itself under the open sky, exercises its wings, and, later on, uses them with enjoyment; in a word, it displays a keen desire to fulfil all its natural functions, though throughout the whole process of development it advances step by step.

11. *Imitation.*—The gardener also must bring it about that the plant, properly provided with moisture and with warmth, take pleasure in its vigorous growth.

12. *Deviation.*—Therefore, those who drive boys to their studies, do them great harm. For what result can they expect? If a man have no appetite, but yet takes food when urged to do so, the result can only be sickness and vomiting, or at least indigestion and indisposition. On

the other hand, if a man be hungry, he is eager to take food, digests it readily, and easily converts it into flesh and blood. Thus Isocrates says: " He who is anxious to learn will also be learned." And Quintilian says: " The acquisition of knowledge depends on the will to learn, and this cannot be forced."

13. *Rectification.*—Therefore

(i) The desire to know and to learn should be excited in boys in every possible manner.

(ii) The method of instruction should lighten the drudgery of learning, that there may be nothing to hinder the scholars or deter them from making progress with their studies.

14. The desire to learn is kindled in boys by parents, by masters, by the school, by the subjects of instruction, by the method of teaching, and by the authority of the state.

15. By parents, if they praise learning and the learned in the presence of their children, or if they encourage them to be industrious by promising them nice books and clothes, or some other pretty thing ; if they commend the teachers (especially him to whom they entrust their sons) as much for their friendly feeling towards the pupils as for their skill in teaching (for love and admiration are the feelings most calculated to stimulate a desire for imitation); finally, if, from time to time, they send the child to him with a small present. In this way they will easily bring it about that the children like their lessons and their teachers, and have confidence in them.

16. By the teachers, if they are gentle and persuasive, and do not alienate their pupils from them by roughness, but attract them by fatherly sentiments and words ; if they commend the studies that they take in hand on account of their excellence, pleasantness, and ease ; if they praise the industrious ones from time to time (to the little ones they may give apples, nuts, sugar, etc.); if they call the children to them, privately or in the class, and show them pictures of the things that they must learn, or explain to them

optical or geometrical instruments, astronomical globes, and such-like things that are calculated to excite their admiration; or again, if they occasionally give the children some message to carry to their parents. In a word, if they treat their pupils kindly they will easily win their affections, and will bring it about that they prefer going to school to remaining at home.

17. The school itself should be a pleasant place, and attractive to the eye both within and without. Within, the room should be bright and clean, and its walls should be ornamented by pictures. These should be either portraits of celebrated men, geographical maps, historical plans, or other ornaments. Without, there should be an open place to walk and to play in (for this is absolutely necessary for children, as we shall show later), and there should also be a garden attached, into which the scholars may be allowed to go from time to time and where they may feast their eyes on trees, flowers, and plants. If this be done, boys will, in all probability, go to school with as much pleasure as to fairs, where they always hope to see and hear something new.

18. The subjects of instruction themselves prove attractive to the young, if they are suited to the age of the pupil and are clearly explained; especially if the explanation be relieved by a humorous or at any rate by a less serious tone. For thus the pleasant is combined with the useful.

19. If the method is to excite a taste for knowledge, it must, in the first place, be natural. For what is natural takes place without compulsion. Water need not be forced to run down a mountain-side. If the dam, or whatever else holds it back, be removed, it flows down at once. It is not necessary to persuade a bird to fly; it does so as soon as the cage is opened. The eye and the ear need no urging to enjoy a fine painting or a beautiful melody that is presented to them. In all these cases it is more often necessary to restrain than to urge on. The requisites of a natural method are evident from the preceding chapter and from the rules that follow.

In the second place, if the scholars are to be interested, care must be taken to make the method palatable, so that everything, no matter how serious, may be placed before them in a familiar and attractive manner; in the form of a dialogue, for instance, by pitting the boys against one another to answer and explain riddling questions, comparisons, and fables. But of this more in the proper place.

20. The civil authorities and the managers of schools can kindle the zeal of the scholars by being present at public performances (such as declarations, disputations, examinations, and promotions), and by praising the industrious ones and giving them small presents (without respect of person).

Third Principle

21. *Nature developes everything from beginnings which, though insignificant in appearance, possess great potential strength.*

For instance, the matter out of which a bird is to be formed consists of a few drops, which are contained in a shell, that they may be easily warmed and hatched. But these few drops contain the whole bird potentially, since, later on, the body of the chicken is formed from the vital principle which is concentrated in them.

22. *Imitation.*—In the same way a tree, no matter how large it may be, is potentially contained in the kernel of its fruit or in the shoot at the end of one of its branches. If one or the other of these be placed in the earth, a whole tree will be produced by the inner force that it contains.

23. *Terrible deviation.*—In direct opposition to this principle a terrible mistake is generally made in schools. Most teachers are at pains to place in the earth plants instead of seeds, and trees instead of shoots, since, instead of starting with the fundamental principles, they place before their pupils a chaos of diverse conclusions or the complete texts of authors. And yet it is certain that instruction rests on a very small number of principles, just as the earth is composed of four elements (though in diverse forms); and that from these principles (in accord-

ance with the evident limits of their powers of differentiation) an unlimited number of results can be deduced, just as, in the case of a tree, hundreds of branches, and thousands of leaves, blossoms, and fruits are produced from the original shoot. Oh! may God take pity on our age, and open some man's eyes, that he may see aright the true relations in which things stand to one another, and may impart his knowledge to the rest of mankind. With God's assistance I hope, in my *Synopsis of Christian Wisdom*, to give an earnest of my efforts to do so, in the modest hope that it may be of use to others whom God, in due season, may call to carry on the work.

24. *Rectification.*—In the meantime we may draw three conclusions:

(i) Every art must be contained in the shortest and most practical rules.

(ii) Each rule must be expressed in the shortest and clearest words.

(iii) Each rule must be accompanied by many examples, in order that the use of the rule may be quite clear when fresh cases arise.

Fourth Principle

25. *Nature advances from what is easy to what is more difficult.*

For example, the formation of an egg does not begin with the hardest part, the shell, but with the contents. These are at first covered by a membrane; it is not till later that the hard shell appears. The bird that learns to fly accustoms itself first to stand on its legs, then to move its wings gently, then to do so with more force until it can raise itself from the ground, and last of all gains sufficient confidence to fly through the air.

26. *Imitation.*—In the same way a carpenter's apprentice learns, first to fell trees, then to saw them into planks and fasten them together, and finally to build complete houses of them.

27. *Various Deviations.*—It is therefore wrong to teach the unknown through the medium of that which is equally unknown, as is the case :

(i) If boys who are beginning Latin are taught the rules in Latin.   This is just as if the attempt were made to explain Hebrew by Hebrew rules, or Arabic by Arabic rules.

(ii) If these same beginners are given as assistance a Latin-German instead of a German-Latin dictionary.   For they do not want to learn their mother-tongue by the aid of Latin, but to learn Latin through the medium of the language that they already know.   (On this error we will say more in chap. xxii.)

(iii) If boys are given a foreign teacher who does not understand their language.   For if they have no common medium through which they can hold communication with him, and can only guess at what he is saying, can anything but a Tower of Babel be the result ?

(iv) A deviation is made from the right method of teaching, if boys of all nations (*i.e.* French, German, Bohemian, Polish, or Hungarian boys) are taught in accordance with the same rules of grammar (those of Melanchthon or of Ramus,[26] for example), since each of these languages stands in its own particular relation to Latin, and this relation must be well understood if Latin is to be thoroughly taught to boys of these several nationalities.

28. *Rectification.*—These errors may be avoided

(i) If the teachers and their pupils talk the same language.

(ii) If all explanations are given in the language that the pupils understand.

(iii) If grammars and dictionaries are adapted to the language through the medium of which the new one is to be learned (that is to say, the Latin Grammar to the mother-tongue, and Greek Grammar to the Latin language).

(iv) If the study of a new language be allowed to proceed gradually and in such a way that the scholar learn first to understand (for this is the easiest), then to write (for here there is time for consideration), and lastly to speak (which is the hardest, because the process is so rapid).

(v) If, when Latin is combined with German, the German be placed first as the best known, and the Latin follow.

(vi) If the subject-matter be so arranged that the pupils get to know, first, that which lies nearest to their mental vision, then that which lies moderately near, then that which is more remote, and lastly, that which is farthest off. Therefore, if boys are being taught something for the first time (such as logic or rhetoric), the illustrations should not be taken from subjects that cannot be grasped by the scholars, such as theology, politics, or poetry, but should be derived from the events of every-day life. Otherwise the boys will understand neither the rules nor their application.

(vii) If boys be made to exercise, first their senses (for this is the easiest), then the memory, then the comprehension, and finally the judgment. In this way a graded sequence will take place; for all knowledge begins by sensuous perception; then through the medium of the imagination it enters the province of the memory; then, by dwelling on the particulars, comprehension of the universal arises; while finally comes judgment on the facts that have been grasped, and in this way our knowledge is firmly established.

Fifth Principle

29. *Nature does not overburden herself, but is content with a little.*

For instance, she does not demand two chickens from one egg, but is satisfied if one be produced. The gardener does not insert a number of grafts on one stock, but two at most, if he consider it very strong.

30. *Deviation.*—The mental energies of the scholar are therefore dissipated if he have to learn many things

at once, such as grammar, dialectic, rhetoric, poetic
Greek, etc., in one year (cf. the previous chapter, Prin
ciple 4).

Sixth Principle

31. *Nature does not hurry, but advances slowly.*

For example, a bird does not place its eggs in the fire
in order to hatch them quickly, but lets them develope
slowly under the influence of natural warmth. Neither
later on, does it cram its chickens with food that they may
mature quickly (for this would only choke them), but i
selects their food with care and gives it to them gradually
in the quantities that their weak digestion can support.

32. *Imitation.*—The builder, too, does not erect the
walls on the foundations with undue haste and then
straightway put on the roof; since, unless the foundations
were given time to dry and become firm, they would sink
under the superincumbent weight, and the whole building
would tumble down. Large stone buildings, therefore
cannot be finished within one year, but must have a
suitable length of time allotted for their construction.

33. Nor does the gardener expect a plant to grow
large in the first month, or to bear fruit at the end of the
first year. He does not, therefore, tend and water it
every day, nor does he warm it with fire or with quicklime
but is content with the moisture that comes from heaven
and with the warmth that the sun provides.

34. *Deviation.*—For the young, therefore, it is torture

(i) If they are compelled to receive six, seven, or eight
hours' class instruction daily, and private lessons in addition

(ii) If they are overburdened with dictations, with
exercises, and with the lessons that they have to commit
to memory, until nausea and, in some cases, insanity is
produced.

If we take a jar with a narrow mouth (for to this we
may compare a boy's intellect) and attempt to pour a
quantity of water into it violently, instead of allowing it to
trickle in drop by drop, what will be the result? Without

doubt the greater part of the liquid will flow over the side, and ultimately the jar will contain less than if the operation had taken place gradually. Quite as foolish is the action of those who try to teach their pupils, not as much as they can assimilate, but as much as they themselves wish ; for the faculties need to be supported and not to be overburdened, and the teacher, like the physician, is the servant and not the master of nature.

35. *Rectification.*—The ease and the pleasantness of study will therefore be increased :

(i) If the class instruction be curtailed as much as possible, namely to four hours, and if the same length of time be left for private study.

(ii) If the pupils be forced to memorise as little as possible, that is to say, only the most important things ; of the rest they need only grasp the general meaning.

(iii) If everything be arranged to suit the capacity of the pupil, which increases naturally with study and age.

Seventh Principle

36. *Nature compels nothing to advance that is not driven forward by its own mature strength.*

For instance, a chicken is not compelled to quit the egg before its limbs are properly formed and set; is not forced to fly before its feathers have grown ; is not thrust from the nest before it is able to fly well, etc.

A tree, too, does not put forth shoots before it is forced to do so by the sap that rises from the roots, nor does it permit fruit to appear before the leaves and blossoms formed by the sap seek further development, nor does it permit the blossoms to fall before the fruit that they contain is protected by a skin, nor the fruit to drop before it is ripe.

37. *Deviation.*—Now the faculties of the young are forced :

(i) If boys are compelled to learn things for which their age and capacity are not yet suited.

19

(ii) If they are made to learn by heart or do things that have not first been thoroughly explained and demonstrated to them.

38. *Rectification.*—From what has been said, it follows

(i) That nothing should be taught to the young, unless it is not only permitted but actually demanded by their age and mental strength.

(ii) That nothing should be learned by heart that has not been thoroughly grasped by the understanding. Nor should any feat of memory be demanded unless it is absolutely certain that the boy's strength is equal to it.

(iii) That nothing should be set boys to do until its nature has been thoroughly explained to them, and rules for procedure have been given.

EIGHTH PRINCIPLE

39. *Nature assists its operations in every possible manner.*

For example, an egg possesses its own natural warmth; but this is assisted by the warmth of the sun and by the feathers of the bird that hatches it. God, the father of nature, takes forethought for this. The newly-hatched chicken, also, is warmed by the mother as long as is necessary, and is trained by her in the various functions of life. This we can see in the case of storks, who assist their young by taking them on their backs and bearing them round the nest while they exercise their wings. In the same way nurses help little children. They teach them first to raise their heads and then to sit up; later on, to stand on their legs, and to move their legs preparatory to walking; then by degrees to walk and step out firmly. When they teach them to speak they repeat words to them and point to the objects that the words denote.

40. *Deviation.*—It is therefore cruelty on the part of a teacher if he set his pupils work to do without first explaining it to them thoroughly, or showing them how it should be done, and if he do not assist them in their first attempts; or if he allow them to toil hard, and

then loses his temper if they do not succeed in their endeavours.

What is this but to torture the young? it is just as if a nurse were to force a child to walk, while it is still afraid to stand on its legs, and beat it when it failed to do so. Nature's teaching is very different, and shows that we ought to have patience with the weak as long as their strength is insufficient.

41. *Rectification.*—From this it follows :

(i) That no blows should be given for lack of readiness to learn (for, if the pupil do not learn readily, this is the fault of no one but the teacher, who either does not know how to make his pupil receptive of knowledge or does not take the trouble to do so).

(ii) That the subjects that have to be learned by the pupils should be so thoroughly explained to them, that they can understand them as well as they understand their five fingers.

(iii) That, as far as is possible, instruction should be given through the senses, that it may be retained in the memory with less effort.

42. For example, the sense of hearing should always be conjoined with that of sight, and the tongue should be trained in combination with the hand. The subjects that are taught should not merely be taught orally, and thus appeal to the ear alone, but should be pictorially illustrated, and thus develope the imagination by the help of the eye. Again, the pupils should learn to speak with their mouths and at the same time to express what they say with their hands, that no study may be proceeded with before what has already been learned is thoroughly impressed on the eyes, the ears, the understanding, and the memory. With this object, it is desirable to represent pictorially, on the walls of the class-room, everything that is treated of in the class, by putting up either precepts and rules or pictures and diagrams illustrative of the subjects taught. If this be done, it is incredible how much it assists a teacher to impress his instruction on the

pupils' minds. It is also useful if the scholars learn to write down in their note-books or among their collections of idioms everything that they hear or read, since in this way the imagination is assisted and it is easier to remember them later on.

NINTH PRINCIPLE

43. *Nothing is produced by nature of which the practical application is not soon evident.* ·

For example, when a bird is formed it is soon evident that the wings are intended for flying and the legs for running. In the same way every part of a tree has its use, down to the skin and the bloom that surround the fruit.

Therefore

44. *Imitation.*—The task of the pupil will be made easier, if the master, when he teaches him anything, show him at the same time its practical application in every-day life. This rule must be carefully observed in teaching languages, dialectic, arithmetic, geometry, physics, etc. If it be neglected, the things that you are explaining will seem to`be monsters from the new world, and the attitude of the pupil, who is indifferent whether they exist or no, will be one of belief rather than of knowledge. When things are brought under his notice and their use is explained to him, they should be put into his hands that he may assure himself of his knowledge and may derive enjoyment from its application.

Therefore

45. Those things only should be taught whose application can be easily demonstrated.

TENTH PRINCIPLE

46. *Nature is uniform in all its operations.*

For instance, the production of all birds, and, indeed, of all living creatures, resembles that of any single bird which you may choose. It is only in the minor details that there are differences. So too in the case of plants, the development of one plant from its seed, the planting and the growth of a single tree, serve as illustrations of the way in which all the others, without exception, develope. One leaf on a tree resembles all the others, and in this respect does not change from year to year.

47. *Deviation.*—Differences of method, therefore, confuse the young, and make their studies distasteful to them, since not only do different teachers use different systems, but even individual teachers vary their method. For example, languages are taught in one way, dialectic in another, though both might be brought under the same method, in accordance with the harmony of the universe, and the universal and intimate relations that exist between objects and words.

48. *Rectification.*—Henceforth, therefore

(i) The same method of instruction must be used for all the sciences, the same for all the arts, and the same for all languages.

(ii) In each school the same arrangement and treatment should be adopted for all studies.

(iii) The class-books for each subject should, as far as is possible, be of the same edition.

In this way difficulties will be avoided and progress will be made easy.

CHAPTER XVIII

THE PRINCIPLES OF THOROUGHNESS IN TEACHING AND IN LEARNING

1. IT is a common complaint that there are few who leave school with a thorough education, and that most men retain nothing but a veneer, a mere shadow of true knowledge. This complaint is corroborated by facts.

2. The cause of this phenomenon appears on investigation to be twofold : either that the schools occupy themselves with insignificant and unimportant studies, to the neglect of those that are more weighty, or that the pupils forget what they have learned, since most of it merely goes through their heads and does not stick fast there. This last fault is so common that there are few who do not lament it. For if everything that we have ever read, heard, and mentally appreciated were always ready to hand in our memories, how learned we should appear ! We do, it is true, make practical use of much that we have learned, but the amount that we recollect is unsatisfactory, and the fact remains that we are continually trying to pour water into a sieve.

3. But can no cure be found for this ? Certainly there can, if once more we go to the school of nature, and investigate the methods that she adopts to give endurance to the beings which she has created.

I maintain that a method can be found by means of which each person will be enabled to bring into his mental consciousness not only what he has learned, but more as well; since he will recall with ease all that he has learned from teachers or from books, and, at the same time, will be able to pass sound judgment on the objective facts to which his information refers.

4. This will be possible:

(i) If only those subjects that are of real use be taken in hand.

(ii) If these be taught without digression or inter-ruption.

(iii) If a thorough grounding precede instruction in detail.

(iv) If this grounding be carefully given.

(v) If all that follows be based on this grounding, and on nothing else.

(vi) If, in every subject that consists of several parts, these parts be linked together as much as possible.

(vii) If all that comes later be based on what has gone before.

(viii) If great stress be laid on the points of resemblance between cognate subjects.

(ix) If all studies be arranged with reference to the intelligence and memory of the pupils, and the nature of language.

(x) If knowledge be fixed in the memory by constant practice.

We will now consider each of these principles in detail.

FIRST PRINCIPLE

5. *Nature produces nothing that is useless.*

For example, nature, when commencing to form a bird, does not give it scales, gills, horns, four feet, or any other organs that it cannot use, but supplies a head, a heart, wings, etc. In the same way a tree is not given ears, eyes, down, or hair, but bark, bast, wood, and roots.

6. *Imitation in the arts.*—In the same way no one who wishes to grow fruit in his fields, orchards, and gardens,

plants them with weeds, nettles, thistles, and thorns, but with good seeds and plants.

7. The builder, also, who wishes to erect a well-built house, does not collect straw, litter, dirt, or brushwood, but stones, bricks, oak planks, and similar materials of good quality.

8. *And in schools.*—In schools therefore

(i) Nothing should be studied, unless it be of undoubted use in this world and in the world to come,—its use in the world to come being the more important (Jerome reminds us that knowledge, that is to be of service to us in heaven, must be acquired on earth).

(ii) If it be necessary to teach the young much that is of value solely in this world (and this cannot be avoided), care must be taken that while a real advantage is gained for our present life, our heavenly welfare be not hindered thereby.

9. Why then pursue worthless studies? What object is there in learning subjects that are of no use to those who know them and the lack of which is not felt by those who do not know them? subjects, too, which are certain to be forgotten as time passes on and the business of life becomes more engrossing? This short life of ours has more than enough to occupy it, even if we do not waste it on worthless studies. Schools must therefore be organised in such a way that the scholars learn nothing but what is of value (the value and importance of recreation will be treated of in the right place).

SECOND PRINCIPLE

10. *When bodies are being formed, nature omits nothing that is necessary for their production.*

For example: in the formation of a bird, nature does not forget the head, the wings, the legs, the claws, the skin, or anything, in short, that is an essential part of a winged being of this kind.

11. *Imitation in schools.*—In the same way schools,

when they educate men, must educate them in every way, and suit them not only for the occupations of this life, but for eternity as well. Indeed it is with a view to the future life that all strenuous human effort should be undertaken.

12. Not the sciences alone, therefore, should be taught in schools, but morality and piety as well. Now a training in the sciences improves the understanding, the faculty of speech, and manual dexterity, so that everything that is of use can be suitably considered, discussed, and put into practice. If any one of these elements be omitted, a great gap is left, and, as result, not only is the education defective but the stability of the whole is endangered. Nothing can be stable unless all its parts are in intimate connection with one another.

Third Principle

13. *Nature does not operate on anything, unless it possess a foundation or roots.*

A plant does not shoot upwards before it has taken root, and would wither and die if it tried to do so. For this reason a clever gardener does not insert a graft unless he sees that the stock has taken root.

In the case of birds and of beasts we find, in the place of roots, the intestines (for in these the vitality is situated), and this part of the body is the first to be formed, being, as it were, the foundation of the rest.

14. *Imitation.*—In the same way an architect does not build a house without first laying a solid foundation, since otherwise the whole structure would soon fall down. Similarly an artist paints a foundation of colour before he puts in the fine shades ; otherwise the colours would easily crack and fade.

15. *Deviation.*—The laying of such a foundation for their instruction is neglected by those teachers (1) who take no trouble to make their pupils diligent and attentive, and (2) who do not begin by giving a general idea of the whole course of study, so that the pupils may realise how

much of the scheme projected is actually got through. For if the scholars perform their work without inclination, without attention, and without intelligence, how can any lasting result be expected?

16. *Rectification.*—Therefore

(i) Every study should be commenced in such a manner as to awaken a real liking for it on the part of the scholars, and this should be done by proving to them how excellent, useful, pleasant, and otherwise desirable it is.

(ii) A general notion of the language or art (consisting of a sketch, as slight as is possible, but yet embracing every branch of the subject in question) should be given to the pupil before the detailed consideration of the subject is proceeded with, in order that he may thus, at the very beginning, realise its aims, limits, and internal structure. For as the skeleton is the foundation of the whole body, so the general sketch of an art is the foundation of the whole art.

FOURTH PRINCIPLE

17. *Nature strikes her roots deep.*

Thus, the entrails of an animal are buried deep in its body. The deeper a tree strikes its roots, the firmer it will stand; while if the roots only just penetrate beneath the turf it is easily rooted up.

18. *Correction of the deviation.*—It follows, therefore, that the desire to learn should be thoroughly awakened in the pupils, and that the general conception of the subject should be thoroughly got into their heads. Until this has been carefully done a more detailed exposition of the art or language should not be attempted.

FIFTH PRINCIPLE

19. *Nature developes everything from its roots and from no other source.*

The wood, bark, leaves, flowers, and fruit of a tree come from the roots and from no other source. For although the rain may fall on the tree and the gardener may water it, the moisture must all be taken up through the roots, and then dispersed through the trunk, branches, boughs, leaves, and fruit. On this account the gardener, though he takes his graft from some other source, must let it into the stock in such a way that it may become incorporated with it, absorb moisture from its roots, and, nourished in this way, be capable of development. It is from the roots that a tree derives everything, and there is no necessity to supply leaves and branches from any other source. It is just the same when a bird is to be clothed with feathers. They are not taken from another bird, but grow from the innermost part of the body.

20. *Imitation in the arts.*—The prudent builder, too, erects a house in such a way that it can stand securely on its own foundations and can be supported by its own beams, without the need of any external props. For, if a building need external support, this is a proof of incompleteness and of a tendency to fall down.

21. When a man lays out a fishpond or a lake he finds a spring, and, by means of canals and pipes, conducts its water to his reservoir; but he does not allow water to flow in from any other source, nor does he use rain-water.

22. From this precept it follows that the proper education of the young does not consist in stuffing their heads with a mass of words, sentences, and ideas dragged together out of various authors, but in opening their understanding to the outer world, so that a living stream may flow from their own minds, just as leaves, flowers, and fruit spring from the buds on a tree, while in the following year a fresh bud is again formed and a fresh shoot, with its leaves, flowers, and fruit, grows from it.

23. *Terrible deviation in schools.*—Hitherto the schools have not taught their pupils to develope their minds like young trees from their own roots, but rather to deck themselves with branches plucked from other trees, and, like Æsop's crow, to adorn themselves with the feathers of other birds; they have taken no trouble to open the

fountain of knowledge that is hidden in the scholars, but
instead have watered them with water from other sources.
That is to say, they have not shown them the objective
world as it exists in itself, but only what this, that, or the
other author has written or thought about this or that
object, so that he is considered the most learned who best
knows the contradictory opinions which many men have
held about many things.   The result is that most men
possess no information but the quotations, sentences, and
opinions that they have collected by rummaging about in
various authors, and thus piece their knowledge together
like a patchwork quilt.   "Oh you imitators, you slavish
pack!" cries Horace.   A slavish pack indeed, and accustomed to carry burdens that are not their own.

24. But why, I ask you, do we allow ourselves to be
led astray by the opinions of other men, when what is
sought is a knowledge of the true nature of things?   Have
we nothing better to do than to follow others to their
cross-roads and down their by-ways, and to study attentively the deviation that each makes from the right path?
O brother mortals! let us hasten to the goal and give up
this idle wandering.   If our goal be firmly set before us, why
should we not hasten to it by the shortest road; why should
we use the eyes of other men in preference to our own?

25. The methods by which all branches of knowledge
are taught show that it really is the schools that are to
blame for this; that they really teach us to see by means
of the eyes of others, and to become wise by employing
their brains.   For these methods do not teach us to discover springs and conduct streams of water from them, but
place before us the water that has been drawn off from
various authors and teach us to return from these to the
springs.   For the dictionaries (at least so far as I know,
though perhaps with the exception of the one by Cnapius,[27]
but even in this one there are some things left to be
desired, as will be shown in chap. xxii.) do not teach
how to speak but only how to understand; the grammars
do not teach how to construct sentences but only how to

dissect them; and no vulgary gives any assistance towards joining the phrases skilfully together in conversation, or towards ringing changes on them, but only provides a haphazard collection of sentences. Scarcely any one teaches physics by ocular demonstration and by experiment, but only by quoting the works of Aristotle and of others. No one seeks to form the morals by working on the inward sources of action, but by purely external explanations and analysis of the virtues a superficial veneer of morality is given. This will be more evident when I come to the special methods of the arts and languages, but still more so, please God, when I give the outline of my Pansophia.

26. It is really to be wondered at that the men of former times did not understand this better, or that this error has not long since been rectified by those of the present day; since it is certain that we have here the actual reason why such slow progress has hitherto been made. Does the builder teach his apprentice the art of building by pulling down a house? Oh no; it is during the process of building a house that he shows him how to select his materials, how to fit each stone into its proper place, how to prepare them, raise them, lay them and join them together. For he who understands how to build will not need to be shown how to pull down, and he who can sew a garment together will be able to unrip it without any instruction. But it is not by pulling down houses or by unripping garments that the arts of building or of tailoring can be learned.

27. It is only too evident that the methods which are so faulty in this respect have not been rectified (1) since the education of many, if not of most men, consists of nothing but a string of names; that is to say, they can repeat the technical terms and the rules of the arts, but do not know how to apply them practically; (2) since the education of no man attains the position of universal knowledge that can give itself support, strength, and breadth, but is a heterogeneous compound of which one part is borrowed from one source and another from

another, whose elements are joined together on no logical principle, and which therefore bears no worthy fruit. For the knowledge that consists of the collected sayings and opinions of various authors resembles the tree which peasants erect when they make holiday, and which, though covered with branches, flowers, fruit, garlands, and crowns, cannot grow or even last, because its ornamentation does not spring from its roots, but is only hung on. Such a tree bears no fruit, and the branches that are attached to it wither and fall off. But a man who is thoroughly educated resembles a tree which grows from its own roots and is nourished by its own sap, and which, on that account, increases in size (and from day to day with more vigour), and puts forth leaves, blossoms, and fruits.

28. *Rectification.*—We arrive therefore at the following conclusion : men must, as far as is possible, be taught to become wise by studying the heavens, the earth, oaks, and beeches, but not by studying books ; that is to say, they must learn to know and investigate the things themselves, and not the observations that other people have made about the things. We shall thus tread in the footsteps of the wise men of old, if each of us obtain his knowledge from the originals, from things themselves, and from no other source. We may therefore lay it down as a law :

(i) That all knowledge should be deduced from the unchanging principles of the subject in question.

(ii) That no information should be imparted on the grounds of bookish authority, but should be authorised by actual demonstration to the senses and to the intellect.

(iii) That in dealing with any subject the analytic method should never be used exclusively ; in fact, preponderance should rather be given to the synthetic method.

SIXTH PRINCIPLE

29. *The more the uses to which nature applies anything, the more distinct subdivisions that thing will possess.*

For instance, the greater the number of joints into

which the limbs of any animal are divided, the more complex will be its movements, as we can see if we compare a horse with a snake. In the same way a tree stands more firmly and is more picturesque if its branches and roots spread out well and stand away from one another.

30. *Imitation.*—In the education of the young, care should be taken that everything that is taught be carefully defined and kept in its place, so that not only the teacher, but the pupil as well, may know exactly what progress he has made and what he is actually doing. It will also be of great assistance if all the books that are used in schools follow nature's example in this respect.

SEVENTH PRINCIPLE

31. *Nature never remains at rest, but advances continually ; never begins anything fresh at the expense of work already in hand, but proceeds with what she has begun, and brings it to completion.*

For instance, in the formation of the embryo, it is the feet, the head, and the heart that come first into existence, and these organs are not discarded but are perfected. A tree which is transplanted does not cast the branches that have previously grown upon it, but continues to provide them with sap and vitality, that with each successive year they may put forth more shoots.

32. *Imitation.*—In schools therefore

(i) All the studies should be so arranged that those which come later may depend on those that have gone before, and that those which come first may be fixed in the mind by those that follow.

(ii) Each subject taught, when it has been thoroughly grasped by the understanding, must be impressed on the memory as well.

33. For since, in this natural method of ours, all that precedes should be the foundation of all that comes after, it is absolutely essential that this foundation be thoroughly laid. For that only which has been thoroughly understood,

and committed to memory as well, can be called the property of the mind.

Truly does Quintilian say: "The acquisition of knowledge depends on the memory. Instruction is in vain if we forget what we hear or read." Ludovicus Vives also says: "The memory should be exercised in early youth, since practice developes it, and we should therefore take care to practise it as much as possible. Now, in youth, the labour is not felt, and thus the memory developes without any trouble and becomes very retentive." And in the *Introduction to Philosophy* he says: "The memory should not be permitted to rest, for there is no faculty that acts with greater readiness or developes more through action. Commit something to memory daily, for the more you commit to memory the more faithfully it will be retained, and the less, the less faithfully." The example of nature shows us that this is true. The more sap a tree sucks up, the stronger it grows, and, conversely, the stronger it grows, the more sap it pours through its fibres. An animal also developes in proportion to the strength of its digestion, and, conversely, the larger it grows the more nourishment it requires and the more it digests. This is the characteristic of every natural body that developes. In this respect, therefore, children should not be spared (though of course no over-pressure should be applied), for the foundations of unfailing progress will thus be laid.

Eighth Principle

34. *Nature knits everything together in continuous combination.*

For instance, when a bird is formed, limb is joined to limb, bone to bone, and sinew to sinew. So too in the case of a tree, the trunk is joined to the roots, the branches to the trunk, the young shoots to the branches, the buds to the shoots, and to these again the leaves, flowers, and fruits; so that, though there may be thousands of each, the whole constitutes one tree. So with a house, if it is to be durable, the walls must rest on the foundations, the ceilings and the roof upon the walls, and, in short, all the parts, from the largest to the smallest, must be connected and fitted together, so that they form a single house.

35. *Imitation.*—From this it follows :

(i) That the studies of a lifetime should be so arranged that they form an encyclopædic whole, in which all the parts spring from a common source and each is in its right place.

(ii) That everything taught should be supported by good reasons, so that no easy entrance may be given either for doubt or for forgetfulness.

Indeed these reasons are the nails, the clasps, and the clamps that hold an object fast in the memory and prevent it from fading away.

36. Now, to strengthen all information by giving reasons is equivalent to explaining things by their causes. That is to say, not only the nature of each object is pointed out but also the reason why it cannot be otherwise. For knowledge is nothing but the acquaintance with an object that we gain by mastering its causes. For instance, if the question arose whether it would be more correct to say *totus populus* or *cunctus populus*, and the teacher were merely to say "*cunctus populus* is the right phrase," but omitted to give any reason, the pupil would soon forget it. If, on the other hand, he were to say "*Cunctus* is a contraction for *conjunctus*,[28] and therefore *totus* should be used when the object denoted is homogeneous, *cunctus* when the conception is collective, as here," it is scarcely conceivable that the pupil could forget it, unless his intelligence were very limited. Again, if the grammatical question were to arise why we say *mea refert, tua refert,* but *ejus refert ;* that is to say, why we use the ablative (as it is supposed to be) in the first and second persons, but the genitive in the third person ; if I were to answer, that *refert* is a contraction for *res fert*, and that the phrases are therefore *mea res fert, tua res fert, ejus res fert* (or in their contracted form *mea refert, tua refert, ejus refert*), and that therefore *mea* and *tua* are not the ablative but the nominative, would not the pupil be stimulated to further efforts?

20

The scholars, therefore, should learn, and learn thoroughly, the etymology of all words, the reasons for all constructions, and the principles on which the rules for the various subjects of study have been formed (the principles of the sciences should in the first instance be impressed on the mind, not by merely giving the reasons, but by actual demonstration on the objects themselves).

This will prove most congenial to the pupils, and will therefore be of the greatest use in paving the way for the most thorough education possible; for their eyes will be opened to a remarkable extent, and they will acquire the habit of easily and naturally advancing from one thing to another.

37. In schools, therefore, everything should be taught through its causes.

NINTH PRINCIPLE

38. *Nature preserves a due proportion between the roots and the branches, with respect to both quality and quantity.*

The development of the branches above the earth is proportionate to that of the roots beneath. This could not be otherwise; for if the tree were only to grow upwards it would be unable to maintain its erect position, since it is the roots that help it to do so. If, on the other hand, it only grew downwards it would be useless, for it is the branches and not the roots that bear the fruit. With animals also there is a close connection between the external and the internal organs, for if the internal organs are healthy the external ones are so also.

39. *Imitation.*—The same holds good of education. It must first be applied to the inner roots of knowledge, and thus develope and gain strength, while at the same time care must be taken that it afterwards spread out into branches and foliage. That is to say, whenever instruction is given the pupil should be taught to apply his knowledge practically, as in the case of a language by speaking, and not merely to assimilate it mentally.

40. Therefore

(i) With every subject of instruction the question of its practical use must be raised, that nothing useless may be learned.

(ii) Whatever has been learned should be communicated by one pupil to the other, that no knowledge may remain unused. For in this sense only can we understand the saying : " Thy knowledge is of no avail if none other know that thou knowest." No source of knowledge, therefore, should be opened, unless rivulets flow from it. But of this will say more in the following principle.

Tenth Principle

41. *Nature becomes fruitful and strong through constant movement.*

Thus, when a bird hatches eggs, it does not only warm them, but, in order that they may be warmed equally on all sides, it turns them round daily (this can be easily observed in the case of geese, hens, and doves, since these hatch their eggs under our very eyes). When the chicken has broken through the shell it exercises itself by moving its beak, its limbs, and its wings, by stretching itself and raising itself from the ground, and by repeated attempts to walk and to fly, until it is sufficiently strong to do so.

The more a tree is buffeted by the winds, the faster it grows and the deeper it drives its roots. Indeed it is healthy for all plants to be stimulated by rain, storms, hail, thunder, and lightning, and for this reason those localities that are greatly exposed to storms of wind and of rain ought to produce harder wood than others.

42. *Imitation in the mechanical arts.*—In the same way the builder leaves the wind and the sun to make his buildings dry and firm. The smith also, who wishes to harden and temper his iron, places it repeatedly in the fire and in water, and thus, by alternating cold and heat, and by repeatedly softening the metal, ultimately renders it hard and durable.

43. From this it follows that education cannot attain to thoroughness without frequent and suitable repetitions of and exercises on the subjects taught. We may learn the most suitable mode of procedure by observing the natural movements that underlie the processes of nutrition in living bodies, namely those of collection, digestion, and distribution. For in the case of an animal (and in that of a plant as well) each member seeks for digestion food which may both nurture that member (since this retains and assimilates part of the digested food) and be shared with the other members, that the well-being of the whole organism may be preserved (for each member serves the other). In the same way that teacher will greatly increase the value of his instruction who

(i) Seeks out and obtains intellectual food for himself.

(ii) Assimilates and digests what he has found.

(iii) Distributes what he has digested, and shares it with others.

44. These three elements are to be found in the well-known Latin couplet :—

To ask many questions, to retain the answers, and to teach
    what one retains to others ;
These three enable the pupil to surpass his master.

Questioning takes place when a pupil interrogates his teachers, his companions, or his books about some subject that he does not understand. Retention follows when the information that has been obtained is committed to memory, or is written down for greater security (since few are so fortunate as to possess the power of retaining everything in their minds). Teaching takes place when knowledge that has been acquired is communicated to fellow-pupils or other companions.

With the two first of these principles the schools are quite familiar, with the third but little ; its introduction, however, is in the highest degree desirable. The saying,

" He who teaches others, teaches himself," is very true, not only because constant repetition impresses a fact indelibly on the mind, but because the process of teaching in itself gives a deeper insight into the subject taught. Thus it was that the gifted Joachim Fortius [29] used to say that, if he had heard or read anything once, it slipped out of his memory within a month ; but that if he taught it to others it became as much a part of himself as his fingers, and that he did not believe that anything short of death could deprive him of it. His advice, therefore, was that, if a student wished to make progress, he should arrange to give lessons daily in the subjects which he was studying, even if he had to hire his pupils. " It is worth your while," he says, " to sacrifice your bodily comfort to a certain extent for the sake of having some one who will listen while you teach, or, in other words, while you make intellectual progress."

45. This would certainly be of use to many and could easily be put into practice if the teacher of each class would introduce this excellent system to his pupils. It might be done in the following way: in each lesson, after the teacher has briefly gone through the work that has been prepared, and has explained the meanings of the words, one of the pupils should be allowed to rise from his place and repeat what has just been said in the same order (just as if he were the teacher of the rest), to give his explanations in the same words, and to employ the same examples, and if he make a mistake he should be corrected. Then another can be called up and made go through the same performance while the rest listen. After him a third, a fourth, and as many as are necessary, until it is evident that all have understood the lesson and are in a position to explain it. In carrying this out great care should be taken to call up the clever boys first, in order that, after their example, the stupid ones may find it easier to follow.

46. Exercises of this kind will have a fivefold use.

(i) The teacher is certain to have attentive pupils. For since the scholars may, at any time, be called up and asked to repeat what the teacher has said, each of them will be afraid of breaking down and appearing ridiculous before the others, and will therefore attend carefully and allow nothing to escape him.   In addition to this, the habit of brisk attention, which becomes second nature if practised for several years, will fit the scholar to acquit himself well in active life.

(ii) The teacher will be able to know with certainty if his pupils have thoroughly grasped everything that he has taught them.   If he finds that they have not, he will consult his own interest as well as that of his pupils by repeating his explanation and making it clearer.

(iii) If the same thing be frequently repeated, the dullest intelligences will grasp it at last, and will thus be able to keep pace with the others; while the brighter ones will be pleased at obtaining such a thorough grip of the subject.

(iv) By means of such constant repetition the scholars will gain a better acquaintance with the subject than they could possibly obtain by private study, even with the greatest diligence, and will find that, if they just read the lesson over in the morning and then again in the evening, it will remain in their memories easily and pleasantly.   When, by this method of repetition, the pupil has, as it were, been admitted to the office of teacher, he will attain a peculiar keenness of disposition and love of learning; he will also acquire the habit of remaining self-possessed while explaining anything before a number of people, and this will be of the greatest use to him throughout life.

47. Following out this idea, the scholars, when they meet one another after school hours, or when they go for walks together, should compare notes and discuss information that they have recently acquired, or should converse on anything new that attracts their attention.   It would be of great assistance, when a certain number of scholars meet for such discussion, if one of them (to be chosen either by lot or by vote) were to take the place of teacher, and control the proceedings.   If the scholar thus selected by his companions refuse the position, he should be severely reprimanded.   For, far from being rejected, such

opportunities of teaching and of learning should be sought after and competed for.

Of written exercises (a great help to progress) we will speak in our chapters on the Vernacular-School and on the Latin-School (chaps. xxvii. and xxviii.)

CHAPTER XIX

THE PRINCIPLES OF CONCISENESS AND RAPIDITY IN TEACHING

1. "BUT these projects are too wearisome and too comprehensive," many readers will here remark. "What a number of teachers and of libraries, and how much labour will be necessary in order that thorough instruction may be given in one subject!" I answer: This is undoubtedly so, and unless our labours are shortened the task will be no easy one; for this art of ours is as long, as wide, and as deep as the universe that has to be subdued by our minds. But who does not know that diffuse and difficult things can be brought into a small compass? who is ignorant that weavers can weave together a hundred thousand threads with the greatest rapidity, and can produce from these a great variety of stuffs? or that millers can grind thousands of grains with the greatest ease, and can separate the bran from the flour with great exactness and without any difficulty? Every one knows that engineers, without the slightest trouble and with comparatively small machines, can raise enormous weights, and that a weight of one ounce, if at a sufficient distance from the fulcrum of a lever, can counterbalance many pounds.

We see, therefore, that great achievements are more often a question of skill than of strength. Are learned men then to be the only people who do not know how to conduct their affairs with skill? Surely shame should

compel us to emulate the inventive spirit of other professions and find a remedy for the difficulties with which
schools have hitherto struggled.

2. It is impossible to find a remedy until we have discovered the diseases and their causes. What can it be
that has impeded the efforts of the schools and hindered
their success to such an extent that most men during their
whole stay at school do not traverse the whole range of
the sciences and arts, while some of them scarcely even
cross the threshold?

3. The causes of this are undoubtedly the following:
firstly, no fixed landmarks were set up, which might serve
as goals to be reached by the scholars at the end of each
year, month, or day, and there was a complete lack of
system.

4. Secondly, the roads that would infallibly lead to
these goals were not pointed out.

5. Thirdly, things that should naturally be associated
were not joined together, but were kept apart. For instance, the scholars in elementary schools were taught to
read, but were not given lessons in writing till some months
afterwards. In the Latin-School boys were allowed to
spend some years in learning words without any reference
to their meanings, so that their boyhood was wholly occupied by grammatical studies, and all philosophic interest
was reserved for a later period. In the same way the
scholars were only allowed to learn, never to teach, though
all these things (reading and writing, words and things,
learning and teaching) should be associated, just as, in
running, the raising of the feet is combined with the
setting of them on the ground again, or, in conversation,
listening is combined with answering, or, in playing ball,
throwing is combined with catching.

6. Fourthly, the arts and the sciences were scarcely
ever taught as part of an encyclopædic whole, but were
dealt out piece-meal. This has been the reason why, in
the eyes of the scholars, they seemed like a heap of wood
or of faggots, in which the exact connection and combining-

links can scarcely be discerned. Thus it came to pass that some grasped one fact, others another, and that none received a really thorough and universal education.

7. Fifthly, many different methods were employed. Each school and even each teacher used a different one. What was worse, teachers would use one method in one subject or language, and another in another, and, worst of all, even in one individual subject they varied their method, so that the scholar scarcely understood in what way he was expected to learn. This was the cause of the many delays that took place, and of the lassitude of the scholar, who had frequently no desire even to attempt new branches of study.

8. Sixthly, no method was known by which instruction could be given to all the pupils in a class at the same time; the individual only was taught. With a large number of pupils this must have been an impossible task for the teacher. The pupils also must have found it very wearisome and extremely irksome, if each had to go on preparing work until his turn arrived.

9. Seventhly, if there were several teachers, this was a fresh source of confusion; since each hour some new subject was introduced. Not to mention the fact that a diversity of teachers tends to distract the mind quite as much as a diversity of books.

10. Finally, both in school and out of it, the scholars had perfect freedom as regards the books they read, and the teachers gave them no assistance in their choice. For all were imbued with the idea that to read many authors afforded many opportunities of making progress, whereas such diversity produced nothing but distraction. It was not surprising, therefore, that very few mastered all the branches of study. The wonder was that any one was able to find his way out of such a labyrinth,—and indeed only the most gifted succeeded in doing so.

11. For the future, therefore, hindrances and delays of this sort must be set aside, and we must make straight for our goal, neglecting everything that is not of immediate service.

As the proverb says : "Where small means suffice, great should not be used."

12. Let us choose the sun for imitation, since it affords a striking example of the operations of nature. Its functions are laborious and almost unlimited (namely, to send forth its rays over the whole world and to supply all the elements, minerals, plants, and animals, of which countless species exist, with light, warmth, life, and strength), but it proves equal to them all, and every year fulfils the circle of its duties in the most admirable manner.

13. We will therefore examine its various principles of action, with reference to the above-mentioned desiderata of school management.

(i) The sun does not occupy itself with any single object, animal, or tree ; but lights and warms the whole earth at once.

(ii) It gives light to all things with the same rays ; covers all things with moisture by the same processes of evaporation and condensation ; it causes the same wind to blow on all things ; it puts all things in motion by the same warmth and cold.

(iii) It causes spring, summer, autumn, and winter to make their appearance in all lands at the same time. At the same time, through its agency, the trees grow green, blossom, and bear fruit (though naturally some do so earlier than others).

(iv) It always preserves the same order ; one day resembles another, one year resembles the next. It always operates on one object by the same method.

(v) It produces everything from its elementary form, and from no other source.

(vi) It produces in combination everything that ought to be combined ; wood with its bark and its core, a flower with its leaves, a fruit with its skin and its stalk.

(vii) It causes everything to develope through definite stages, so that one stage prepares the way for the next, and each stage follows naturally from the previous one.

(viii) Finally, it brings into existence nothing that is

useless, or destroys such an object if it be accidentally produced.

14. In imitation of this

(i) There should only be one teacher in each school, or at any rate in each class.

(ii) Only one author should be used for each subject studied.

(iii) The same exercise should be given to the whole class.

(iv) All subjects and languages should be taught by the same method.

(v) Everything should be taught thoroughly, briefly, and pithily, that the understanding may be, as it were, unlocked by one key, and may then unravel fresh difficulties of its own accord.

(vi) All things that are naturally connected ought to be taught in combination.

(vii) Every subject should be taught in definitely graded steps, that the work of one day may thus expand that of the previous day, and lead up to that of the morrow.

(viii) And finally, everything that is useless should be invariably discarded.

15. If these reforms could be introduced into schools, there is no doubt that the whole circle of the sciences might be completed with an ease that surpasses our expectation, just as the sun completes its circling course through the heavens every year.

Let us therefore get to work and see if these counsels can be carried into effect, and how the difficulties that hinder their realisation can be overcome.

FIRST PROBLEM

How can a single teacher teach a number of boys, no matter how great, at one time?

16. I maintain that it is not only possible for one teacher to teach several hundred scholars at once, but that it is also essential; since for both the teachers and their

pupils it is by far the most advantageous system. The larger the number of pupils that he sees before him the greater the interest the teacher will take in his work (just as the hands of a miner tremble with excitement when he discovers a rich vein of ore); and the keener the teacher himself, the greater the enthusiasm that his pupils will display. To the scholars, in the same way, the presence of a number of companions will be productive not only of utility but also of enjoyment (for it gives pleasure to all to have companions in their labours); since they will mutually stimulate and assist one another. Indeed for boys of this age emulation is by far the best stimulus. Again, if a teacher's class be small, this point or that may escape the ears of all his pupils. But if many hear him at once, each one grasps as much as he can, and then, when the lesson is repeated, all comes back into their minds again, since one mind has an invigorating effect on another and one memory on another. In short, as a baker makes a large quantity of bread by a single kneading of the dough and a single heating of the oven, as a brick-maker burns many bricks at one time, as a printer prints hundreds of thousands of books from the same set of type, so should a teacher be able to teach a very large number of pupils at once and without the slightest inconvenience. Do we not see that one trunk can support innumerable branches and supply them with sap, and that the sun is able to vivify the whole earth?

17. How is this to be done? Let us take our former examples, and watch the processes of nature. The trunk does not extend to the outermost branches, but remaining in its place supplies sap to the large ones that are in immediate connection with it, these pass it on to others, and these again in their turn to others, and so on until the smallest twigs have been reached. In the same way the sun does not illumine each individual tree, plant, or animal, but, sending forth its rays from on high, lights up half the world at once, and thus supplies each creature with light and warmth for its own use. We should here

notice that the sun's action may be assisted by the lie of the ground. Valleys and depressions, for instance, collect the rays and thus attain a higher degree of warmth.

18. If matters be arranged in the following manner, one teacher will easily be able to cope with a very large number of scholars. That is to say

(i) If he divide the whole body into classes, groups of ten, for example, each of which should be controlled by a scholar who is, in his turn, controlled by one of higher rank, and so on.

(ii) If he never give individual instruction, either privately out of school or publicly in school, but teach all the pupils at one and the same time. He should, therefore, never step up to any one scholar or allow any one of them to come to him separately, but should remain in his seat, where he can be seen and heard by all, just as the sun sends forth its rays over all things. The scholars, on the other hand, must direct their ears, eyes, and thoughts towards him and attend to everything that he tells them by word of mouth or explains by means of his hand or of diagrams. Thus, with a single blow, not one but many flies are killed.

19. (iii) With a little skill it will be possible to arrest the attention of the pupils, collectively and individually, and to imbue them with the notion that (as really is the case) the mouth of the teacher is a spring from which streams of knowledge issue and flow over them, and that, whenever they see this spring open, they should place their attention, like a cistern, beneath it, and thus allow nothing that flows forth to escape. The teacher also should take the greatest care never to speak unless all his pupils are listening, nor to teach unless they are all attending. In this connection that remark of Seneca's is very apposite : ("We should speak to none who is unwilling to listen.") Solomon also says : "Wisdom is before the face of him that hath understanding" (Prov. xvii. 24). That is to say, we should talk not to the winds but to the ears of men.

20. It is not solely by means of the leaders or of the other boys in charge, that attention can be awakened and retained. The teacher is himself the most important factor, and will succeed in his efforts if he observe eight rules.

(i) If, when he teaches, he take the trouble continually to introduce something that is entertaining as well as of practical use; for in this way the interest of the scholars will be excited and their attention will be arrested.

(ii) If, at the commencement of any new subject, he excite the interest of his pupils, either by placing it before them in an attractive manner or by asking them questions. These latter may either refer to what has preceded, and thus illustrate the connection between it and the subject in question, or to the new branch of study. For, if the scholar's ignorance of the subject be mercilessly exposed, he may be fired with a desire to master it and understand it thoroughly.

(iii) If he stand on an elevated platform, and, keeping all the scholars in his sight at once, allow none of them to do anything but attend and look at him.

(iv) If he aid their attention by appealing to the senses, especially to that of sight, whenever it is possible (as we have shown above, chap. xvii., in the third rule of the eighth Principle).

(v) If he occasionally interrupt his explanation with the words: Tell me (mentioning some boy), what have I just said? Repeat that sentence! Tell me; how have I reached this point? and remarks of a similar kind, the exact nature of which must depend on the class that he is teaching. If any pupil be found who is not paying attention, he should be reprimanded or punished on the spot. In this way the scholars will be made keen and attentive.

(vi) Similarly, if he ask one boy, and he hesitate, he should pass on to a second, a third, a tenth, or a thirtieth, and ask for the answer without repeating the question.

The result of this will be that all listen carefully to what is said to one of their number, and apply it to their own use.

(vii) If some of the boys cannot answer a question he should ask the whole class, and then, in the presence of the rest, praise those who answer best, that their example may serve to stimulate the others. If any pupil make a mistake he should be corrected, but at the same time the cause of the error (which a clever teacher will have no difficulty in discovering) should be made clear and the necessity for its recurrence obviated. It can scarcely be realised what an assistance to rapid progress this will be.

(viii) Finally, when the lesson is over, the scholars should be given leave to ask questions on any point that they wish explained, either in the present lesson or in a previous one. Private questioning should not be permitted. Each scholar who wishes to ask a question should either ask the teacher openly or get the leader of his division to do so (if this latter is unable to solve the difficulty himself). In this way the whole class will be benefited, and as much by the question as by the answer. If any scholar help to illustrate an important point by the intelligence of his questions, he should be commended, in order that the rest may thereby be incited to industry and keenness.

21. Such a daily training of the attention will not only be of momentary use to the young, but will stand them in good stead throughout their whole lives. For if this training last for some years, and they get into the habit of concentrating their minds on whatever is being done at the time, they will continue to do so of their own accord without any external pressure. If schools are organised on this principle, surely we may look forward to a considerable increase in the number of clever and intelligent men !

22. To this it may be objected that individual attention is necessary to see that each scholar keeps his books tidy, writes his exercises carefully, and learns his lessons

accurately, and that, if the class be large, this will take a
great deal of time. I answer: It is not necessary for the
teacher to hear the lessons or inspect the books of each
individual scholar; since he has the leaders of divisions to
assist him, and each of these can inspect the scholars in
his own division.

23. The teacher, as chief inspector, should give his
attention first to one scholar, then to another, more
particularly with the view of testing the honesty of those
whom he distrusts. For example, if the scholars have to
say a repetition lesson, he should call first on one pupil,
then on another, first one at the top of the class and then
one at the bottom, while all the rest attend. He may thus
ensure that each one be in readiness, since none can be
certain that he will not be examined. If the teacher observe
that a scholar begins his lessons without hesitation, and
feel convinced that he knows the rest equally well, he may
let another one go on, and if this one in turn seem well
prepared, may pass on to a third. In this way, by hearing
a few, he can rest assured that he has the whole class
under his control.

24. The same method should be pursued with dictations. One or more scholars should read out what has
been written, with the right punctuation and in a clear
voice, while the rest correct what they have written in
their books. The teacher should also himself examine the
books from time to time, and should punish any scholar
who has been doing his work carelessly.

25. The correction of written translations seems to
demand more time; but here also the same method may
be adopted with advantage. As soon as the leaders of
divisions have secured attention, one scholar should be
called upon to stand up and choose as his adversary any
other scholar that he pleases. As soon as this latter
stands up, the first scholar reads out his translation
sentence by sentence, while all the rest listen attentively,
the teacher in the meantime looking at the exercise to see
that it is properly written. At the end of each sentence

the scholar stops, and his adversary has the opportunity of pointing out any mistake that he may have perceived. Then other scholars in the division, and after them the whole class, may make criticisms on the rendering, and finally the teacher supplies any point that has been omitted.   While this is going on, the others correct the mistakes in their own exercises.   The adversary, however, should not do so, but should keep his own unaltered that he may submit it to the criticism of his companions.   As soon as the first sentence has been properly corrected, the next is taken, and so on until the exercise is finished. Then the adversary should read out his in the same way, while the original challenger takes care that he really reads his original translation and does not insert the corrections that have been made.   The individual words and phrases are then criticised as before.

After this, a second pair of adversaries is chosen, and the same procedure is repeated for as long as the time permits.

26. In this connection the leaders have two duties to perform.   Before the corrections begin they should see that all the scholars have their exercises ready, and while it is going on they should take care that each of them corrects his exercise when it contains the mistake that is under consideration.

27. The result of this will be

(i)   That the work of the teacher will be lightened.

(ii) That no scholar will be neglected.

(iii) That the scholars will attend better than formerly.

(iv) That what is said to one will be of equal advantage to all.

(v)   The differences in the mode of expression, that are certain to occur in so many different translations, will not only improve and strengthen the scholar's acquaintance with the subject-matter, but will also give him facility in using the language.

(vi) Finally, as soon as the first, second, and third pair have finished, it will frequently happen that the others have few or no mistakes left to correct. When this is the case, the remainder of the time may be devoted to the class in general, that those who are still uncertain about a passage may bring forward their difficulties, or those who think that their rendering is better than that which has been given may read it and receive criticism on it.

28. The method here suggested has been illustrated by an exercise in translation. Its application, however, is just as easy, if the exercise be one in style, rhetoric, logic, theology, or philosophy.

29. We have thus seen that one teacher can instruct a hundred scholars with as little labour as he would expend in teaching a few.

SECOND PROBLEM

How is it possible for all the scholars to be taught from the same books?

30. It is an undisputed fact that too many objects at once distract the attention. It will therefore be of immense advantage if the scholars be allowed to use no books but those that have been expressly composed for the class in which they are; and in this way it will always be possible to use with effect the order that was given to the worshippers in the temples of old, namely, "This shalt thou do." Since the less the eyes are distracted, the easier it is to concentrate the mind.

31. Secondly, if all the materials that are required for instruction, blackboards, inscriptions, first reading books, dictionaries, schematic diagrams of the arts, etc., be kept in constant readiness. For if (as is often the case) the teacher must prepare the exercise-books for the scholars, and write a model for them to copy, or if he have to dictate grammatical rules, the text of an author, or its translation, how much time is thereby lost! It is therefore necessary that sufficient quantities of all the books which are used in each class be kept in readiness, and that translations be supplied with those texts that are to be

translated into the mother-tongue. In this way the time that would otherwise have been employed in dictation, copying, and translating, can be used, and with far greater advantage, for explanation, repetition, and imitation.

32. There need be no fear that any concession is here being made to the teacher's idleness. For a preacher is considered to have done his duty if he read a text from the Bible, explain it, and point out its application, and it is a matter of indifference to his hearers whether he has himself translated the text from the original, or has used some standard translation; and in the same way it makes no difference to the scholars whether the teacher has arranged his own materials or whether some one else has done so for him. The important thing is that everything necessary be ready to hand, and that, under the teacher's direction, it be properly employed. It is indeed much better that everything of this nature be prepared before-hand, since, on the one hand, it will be freer from errors, and, on the other, more time will be left for the actual process of instruction.

33. For every school, therefore, books of this kind should be written,—in accordance with the rules already laid down for the attainment of ease, thoroughness, and economy of time,—and should constitute a complete, thorough, and accurate epitome of all the subjects of instruction. In short, they should give a true representation of the entire universe, which can thus be impressed upon the minds of the scholars. They should also, and this is a most important point, be written simply and clearly, and should give the scholars sufficient assistance to enable them, if necessary, to pursue their studies without the help of a teacher.

34. With this end in view it is desirable that they be written in the form of a dialogue. In this way (1) it is possible to suit the subject-matter and its exposition to the minds of the young, that neither may appear to them to be too full of difficulties. Nothing is more suited to inspire confidence than dialogue-form, and by means of it

the mind can be gradually led on to the desired goal. It is in this form that playwrights have expressed their views on the deterioration of morals, and have thereby admonished the people; in this form Plato wrote all his philosophical, and St. Augustine all his theological works, and Cicero also has employed it largely, thus coming down to the level of his readers. (2) Conversational form excites and retains the attention, while the alternation between question and answer, the various forms of expression and the amusing remarks that may be introduced, and even the changes that may be rung upon the *dramatis personæ*, all tend, not merely to counteract any antipathy to the subject, but even to create a keen desire to know more about it. (3) Instruction makes a far greater impression when given in this way. We remember an event better when we have seen it ourselves than when we have simply heard it narrated, and, in the same way, instruction that is given through the medium of a drama or of a dialogue stays in the heads of the scholars far better than if it be merely set forth by a teacher in the ordinary way, as may be proved by experience. (4) The greater part of our lives consists of friendly conversation, and it should therefore be easy to induce the young to acquire useful information, when they are at the same time learning to express themselves fluently and well. (5) Finally, dialogues of this kind act as a mild recreation, and may enliven the private gatherings of the students.

35. It is also desirable that the books used be of the same edition, so that they may be similar page for page and line for line. This is important both for the sake of reference and that the localisation of passages on certain pages may assist the memory.

36. It will also be of great use if an abstract of the contents of all the books used in the class be placed on the walls of the room. This should consist of the text, greatly abbreviated and condensed, or of illustrative pictures and reliefs, by means of which the senses, the memory, and the understanding may be daily exercised in con-

junction.   Not without purpose was it that, as the ancients relate, the walls of the temple of Æsculapius were covered with the precepts of the art of medicine, written there by Hippocrates himself.   This great theatre of the world, also, God has filled with pictures, statues, and living emblems of His wisdom, that He may instruct us by their means.   (Of these pictorial aids we will say more when we treat of the individual classes.)

THIRD PROBLEM

How is it possible for all the scholars in a school to do the same thing at one time ?

37. It is evident that it would be a useful arrangement if all the pupils in a class did the same lesson at one time, for in this way the teacher would have less trouble and the scholars greater advantage.   It is only when the attention of all is fixed on the same object, and when each tries in turn to correct the other, that keen rivalry can arise.   In every way the teacher must imitate a captain of recruits. This latter does not exercise each of his men separately, but leads out a whole company at once and shows them how to use their arms ; and even if he explain anything to one man apart, the remainder have to go through the same exercise in order that their attention may be retained.

The teacher should proceed on precisely similar lines.

38. Before he can do this it is necessary

(i) That the course of instruction commence at one definite time in each year, just as the influence of the sun on the vegetable world commences at one definite time, namely, in spring.

(ii) That the subjects of instruction be so divided that each year, each month, each week, each day, and even each hour may have a definite task appointed for it, since, if this be done, everything that is proposed will be completed with ease.   But of this we will say more in the proper place.

FOURTH PROBLEM

How is it possible to teach everything according to one and the same method ?

39. That there is only one natural method for all the sciences, and only one for all the arts and languages, will be shown in chaps. xx., xxi., and xxii. Any deviations that may be necessary are not important enough to constitute a fresh class, and are due less to peculiarities in the subject-matter than to the teacher himself, who must be guided by the ability, or the reverse, of his pupils and by the progress that they make in the actual languages or arts that he is teaching. The universal adoption of the natural method, therefore, will be as great a boon to scholars as a plain and undeviating road is to travellers It will be easier to point out special aberrations, if the universal principle be first laid down as indisputable.

FIFTH PROBLEM

How can many things be explained in a few words ?

40. To fill the minds of scholars with a dreary waste of books and of words is lost labour. For it is certain that a crust of bread and a mouthful of wine are more nutritious than a paunchful of trifle and of ragout, and that it is better to have a few gold pieces in one's purse than a hundred-weight of lead. Rightly does Seneca say of instruction : " Its administration should resemble the sowing of seed, in which stress is laid, not on quantity, but on quality." The conclusion, therefore, that we reached in chap. v. holds good : In man, the microcosm, everything is contained potentially. Bring light and he will straight-way see.

And indeed for men who are working in the dark the faintest glimmer of light is sufficient. It is therefore necessary to select or to write handbooks of the sciences and languages which are small in compass and practically arranged—cover the whole subject and contain a great deal of matter in a short space (Ecclesiasticus xxxii. 8)— that is to say, which place before the scholar the whole of the subject-matter by means of a small number of rules and definitions expressed in the simplest and clearest language, and sufficient in themselves to lead to more profound study.

Sixth Problem

How is it possible to do two or three things by a single operation ?

41. The example of nature shows that several things can be done at one time and by means of the same operation. It is an undoubted fact that a tree grows above the ground and beneath it at the same time, and that its wood, its bark, its leaves, and its fruit, all develope simultaneously. The same observation applies to animals, whose limbs all develope and grow stronger at the same time. Further, each limb performs several operations. The feet, for instance, not only support a man but also move him forwards and backwards in various ways. The mouth is not only the entrance to the body, but also serves as a masticator and as a trumpet that sounds whenever called upon to do so. With a single inspiration the lungs cool the heart, purify the brain, and assist in voice-production.

42. We find the same thing in the arts: (1) In the sun-dial, the single shadow cast by the gnomon points out the hour of the day, the sign of the zodiac in which the sun is moving, the length of the day and of the night, the day of the month, and several other things. (2) One pole serves to direct, to turn, and to hold back a carriage. (3) A good orator or writer instructs, excites, and pleases at the same time, even though his subject may make it difficult to combine these three elements.

43. The instruction of the young should be similarly organised, so that every activity may produce several results. It may be laid down as a general rule that each

subject should be taught in combination with those which are correlative to it; that is to say, words should be studied in combination with the things to which they refer; while reading and writing, exercises in style and in logical thought, teaching and learning, amusement and serious study, should be continually joined together.

44. Words, therefore, should always be taught and learned in combination with things, just as wine is bought and sold together with the cask that contains it, a dagger with its sheath, a tree with its bark, and fruit with its skin. For what are words but the husks and coverings of things? Therefore, when instruction is given in any language, even in the mother-tongue itself, the words must be explained by reference to the objects that they denote; and contrariwise, the scholars must be taught to express in language whatever they see, hear, handle, or taste, so that their command of language, as it progresses, may ever run parallel to the growth of the understanding.

The rule shall therefore run as follows:

The scholar should be trained to express everything that he sees in words, and should be taught the meaning of all the words that he uses. No one should be allowed to talk about anything that he does not understand, or to understand anything without at the same time being able to express his knowledge in words. For he who cannot express the thoughts of his mind resembles a statue, and he who chatters, without understanding what he says, resembles a parrot.

But we wish to train up *men*, and to do so as quickly as possible, and this end can only be attained when instruction in language goes hand in hand with instruction in facts.

45. From this it follows that we ought to exclude from our schools all books that merely teach words and do not at the same time lead to a knowledge of useful objects. We must bestow our labour on that which is of real importance, and, therefore (as Seneca says in his 9th Letter), must devote ourselves to the improvement of our understanding

rather than to the enlargement of our vocabulary. Any reading that is necessary can be got through quickly out of school-hours without tedious explanations or attempts at imitation; since the time thus spent could be better employed in the study of nature.

46. Exercises in reading and writing should always be combined. Even when scholars are learning their alphabet, they should be made to master the letters by writing them; since it is impossible to find a more agreeable method or one that will give them a greater incentive to work. For, since all children have a natural desire to draw, this exercise will give them pleasure, and the imagination will be excited by the twofold action of the senses. Later on, when they can read with ease, they should be made to exercise their powers on subject-matter that would in any case have to be learned, that is to say, something calculated to give them practical information or to instil morality or piety. The same plan may be adopted when they learn to read Latin, Greek, or Hebrew. It will be of great advantage to read and copy the declensions and conjugations over and over again, until, by this means, reading, writing, the meaning of the words, and the formation of the case-endings, have been thoroughly learned. In this case we have a fourfold result from a single exercise. A system of concentration that is of such vital importance should be applied to all branches of study, in order that, as Seneca says, what is learned by reading may be given form by writing, or that, as St. Augustine says of himself, we may write while we make progress and make progress while we write.

47. As a rule, no care is shown in the choice of the subjects that are given as exercises in style, and there is no connection between the successive subjects. The result is that they are exercises in style and nothing else, and have very little influence on the reasoning powers; indeed it frequently happens that, after much time and study have been devoted to them, they prove absolutely worthless and of no use for the business of life. Literary taste should therefore be taught by means of the subject-

matter of the science or art on which the reasoning powers of the class are being exercised. The teacher should tell his pupils stories about the originators of the subject and the times in which they lived, or should give them exercises in imitation based on the subject-matter, so that, by a single effort, notions of style may be imbibed, the reasoning powers may be improved, and, since either the teacher or the pupils are continually talking, the faculty of speech also may be exercised.

48. Towards the end of the 18th chapter I have shown that it is possible for the scholars to give instruction in the subject that they have just learned, and, since this process not only makes them thorough but also enables them to make progress more rapidly, it should not be overlooked in this connection.

49. Finally, it will be of immense use, if the amusements that are provided to relax the strain on the minds of the scholars be of such a kind as to lay stress on the more serious side of life, in order that a definite impression may be made on them even in their hours of recreation. For instance, they may be given tools, and allowed to imitate the different handicrafts, by playing at farming, at politics, at being soldiers or architects, etc. In spring they may be taken into the garden or into the country, and may be taught the various species of plants, vying with one another to see who can recognise the greater number. In this way they will be introduced to the rudiments of medicine, and not only will it be evident which of them has a natural bent towards that science, but in many the inclination will be created. Further, in order to encourage them, the mock titles of doctor, licentiate, or student of medicine may be given to those who make the greatest progress. The same plan may be adopted in other kinds of recreation. In the game of war the scholars may become field-marshals, generals, captains, or standard-bearers. In that of politics they may be kings, ministers, chancellors, secretaries, ambassadors, etc., and, on the same principle, consuls, senators, lawyers, or officials; since such pleasantries often

lead to serious things.   Thus would be fulfilled Luther's wish that the studies of the young at school could be so organised that the scholars might take as much pleasure in them as in playing at ball all day, and thus for the first time would schools be a real prelude to practical life.

SEVENTH PROBLEM

How are the subjects of study to be progressively graded ?

50. How this can be done, we have seen in the 5th, 6th, 7th and 8th Principles of the 16th chapter, and in the 5th, 6th and 7th Principles of the 18th chapter.   The important point is that suitable books should be written for the classical schools, and that these should embody hints to the teacher for their proper use, so that learning, morality, and piety may be led from one stage to another until they reach the highest.

EIGHTH PROBLEM

Of the removal and avoidance of obstructions.

51. Truly has it been said, that nothing is more useless than to learn and to know much, if such knowledge be of no avail for practical purposes ; and again, that not he who knows much is wise, but he who knows what is useful. The task of schools will therefore be rendered easier if the subjects taught be curtailed.   This can be done if omission be made

(i)   Of all unnecessary matter.

(ii) Of all unsuitable matter.

(iii) Of all minute detail.

52. Anything is unnecessary that is productive neither of piety nor of morality, and that is not essential for the cultivation of the mind.   Such are the names of heathen deities, the myths connected with them, and the religious observances of the ancients, as well as the productions of scurrilous and indecent poets and dramatists.   It may occasionally be necessary for the individual to read these things in private, but in the schools, where the founda-

tions of wisdom should be laid, nothing of the kind should be permitted. "What madness it is," says Seneca, "to learn so much trash, when time is so precious." Nothing, therefore, should be learned solely for its value at school, but for its use in life, that the information which a scholar has acquired may not vanish as soon as he leaves school.

53. Knowledge is unsuitable when it is uncongenial to the mind of this or that scholar. For there is as great a difference between the minds of men as exists between the various kinds of plants, of trees, or of animals; one must be treated in one way, and another in another, and the same method cannot be applied to all alike. It is true that there are men of great mental power who can compass every subject; but there are also many who find the greatest difficulty in mastering the rudiments of some things. Some display great ability for abstract science, but have as little aptitude for practical studies as an ass has for playing on the lyre. Others can learn everything but music, while others again are unable to master mathematics, poetry, or logic. What should be done in these cases? If we attempt to counteract a natural disinclination we are fighting against nature, and such effort is useless. For there will be either no result or one totally incommensurate with the energy expended. The teacher is the servant and not the lord of nature; his mission is to cultivate and not to transform, and therefore he should never attempt to force a scholar to study any subject if he see that it is uncongenial to his natural disposition; since it is more than probable that what is lacking in one direction will be compensated for in another. If one branch be cut off a tree, the others become stronger, because more vitality flows into them; and if none of the scholars be forced to study any subject against his will, we shall find no cases in which disgust is produced and the intelligence is blunted. Each one will develope in the direction of his natural inclinations (in accordance with the Divine will), and will serve God and man in his station in life, whatever that may be.

54. In the same way, if all minute and technical details (such as the species of plants and of animals, the various callings of mechanics, the names of all their tools and so forth) had to be learned, this would be a most wearisome and confusing task. In school-work it is sufficient if the wide classes that exist in nature, with their most important and most essential divisions, be made thoroughly clear. More specialised knowledge can easily be acquired later, as the opportunity arises.

Those who wish to win a speedy victory over the enemy, do not waste time in storming unimportant places, but go straight to the head-quarters of the war ; since it is certain that, if they can get the upper hand in a pitched battle, and capture the most important strongholds, all the others will surrender of their own accord. In the same way, if the principal points of any subject be mastered, the subsidiary details will be acquired with great ease. To this class of obstructions belong the voluminous dictionaries that contain every word in a language. For, since the greater number of them are never used, why should we force boys to learn them all, and thus overburden the memory ?

We have now treated of the saving of time and effort in teaching and in learning.

CHAPTER XX

1. WE must now collect together the scattered observations that we have made on the proper teaching of the
sciences, of the arts, of morality, and of piety.   By proper
teaching I mean teaching that combines ease, thoroughness, and rapidity.

2. Science, or the knowledge of nature, consists of an
internal perception, and needs the same accessories as the
external perception of the eye, namely, an object to observe, and light by which to observe it.   If these be given,
perception will follow.   The eye of the inner perception is
the mind or the understanding, the object is all that lies
within or without our apprehension, while the light is the
necessary attention.   But, as in the case of external perception a definite procedure is necessary in order to apprehend things as they are, so with internal perception a
certain method is necessary if things are to be presented
to the mind in such a way that it can grasp them and
assimilate them with ease.

3. The youth who wishes to penetrate the mysteries of
the sciences must carefully observe four rules :

(i)   He must keep the eye of his mind pure.

(ii) He must see that the object be brought near
to it.

(iii) He must pay attention.

(iv) He must proceed from one object to another in

accordance with a suitable method. For thus he wil
apprehend everything surely and easily.

4. Over the amount of ability that we possess we hav
no control, for God has portioned out this mirror of th
understanding, this inner eye, according to His will. Bu
it lies in our power to prevent it from growing dusty o
dim. By dust, I mean the idle, useless, and empty occu
pations of the mind. For our mind is in constant activity
like a continually running mill-stone, and is supplied by it
servants, the external senses, with material from every side
But unless the chief inspector, the reason, be continuall
on the watch, worthless material is supplied, such as chaff
straw, or sand, instead of corn or wheat. Thus it comes t
pass that, as in the case of a mill, every corner is filled witl
dust. This inner mill, therefore, the mind (which is als
a mirror) will be kept free from dust, if the young be kep
away from worthless occupations and be skilfully traine
to like worthy and useful things.

5. In order that the mirror may duly receive the image
of the objects, it is necessary that these latter be solid an
visible, and be also placed suitably before the eyes
Clouds and similar objects that possess little consistenc
make but a slight impression on a mirror, while object
that are not present make none at all. Those things
therefore, that are placed before the intelligence of th
young, must be real things and not the shadows of things
I repeat, they must be *things ;* and by the term I mear
determinate, real, and useful things that can make an im
pression on the senses and on the imagination. But the
can only make this impression when brought sufficientl
near.

6. From this a golden rule for teachers may be derived
Everything should, as far as is possible, be placed befor
the senses. Everything visible should be brought befor
the organ of sight, everything audible before that of hear
ing. Odours should be placed before the sense of smell
and things that are tastable and tangible before the sens
of taste and of touch respectively. If an object can make

an impression on several senses at once, it should be brought into contact with several, though with the limitations imposed in the seventh Principle of chap. viii.

7. For this there are three cogent reasons. Firstly, the commencement of knowledge must always come from the senses (for the understanding possesses nothing that it has not first derived from the senses). Surely, then, the beginning of wisdom should consist, not in the mere learning the names of things, but in the actual perception of the things themselves! It is when the thing has been grasped by the senses that language should fulfil its function of explaining it still further.

8. Secondly, the truth and certainty of science depend more on the witness of the senses than on anything else. For things impress themselves directly on the senses, but on the understanding only mediately and through the senses. This is evident from the fact that belief is at once accorded to knowledge derived from the senses, while an appeal is always made to them from *a priori* reasoning and from the testimony of others. We do not trust a conclusion derived from reasoning unless it can be verified by a display of examples (the trustworthiness of which depends on sensuous perception). No one could have such confidence in the testimony of another person as to disbelieve the experience of his own senses. Science, then, increases in certainty in proportion as it depends on sensuous perception. It follows, therefore, that if we wish to implant a true and certain knowledge of things in our pupils, we must take especial care that everything be learned by means of actual observation and sensuous perception.

9. Thirdly, since the senses are the most trusty servants of the memory, this method of sensuous perception, if universally applied, will lead to the permanent retention of knowledge that has once been acquired. For instance, if I have once tasted sugar, seen a camel, heard a nightingale sing, or been in Rome, and have on each occasion attentively impressed the fact on my memory, the incidents will

remain fresh and permanent. We find, accordingly, that children can easily learn Scriptural and secular stories from pictures. Indeed, he who has once seen a rhinoceros (even in a picture) or been present at a certain occurrence, can picture the animal to himself and retain the event in his memory with greater ease than if they had been described to him six hundred times. Hence the saying of Plautus: "An eye-witness is worth more than ten ear-witnesses." Horace also says: "What is entrusted to the fickle ears makes less impression on the mind than things which are actually presented to the eyes and which the spectator stores up for himself."

In the same manner, whoever has once seen a dissection of the human body will understand and remember the relative position of its parts with far greater certainty than if he had read the most exhaustive treatises on anatomy, but had never actually seen a dissection performed. Hence the saying, "Seeing is believing."

10. If the objects themselves cannot be procured, representations of them may be used. Copies or models may be constructed for teaching purposes, and the same principle may be adopted by botanists, geometricians, zoologists, and geographers, who should illustrate their descriptions by engravings of the objects described. The same thing should be done in books on physics and elsewhere. For example, the human body will be well explained by ocular demonstration if the following plan be adopted. A skeleton should be procured (either such an one as is usually kept in universities, or one made of wood), and on this framework should be placed the muscles, sinews, nerves, veins, arteries, as well as the intestines, the lungs, the heart, the diaphragm, and the liver. These should be made of leather and stuffed with wool, and should be of the right size and in the right place, while on each organ should be written its name and its function. If you take the student of medicine to this construction and explain each part to him separately, he will grasp all the details without any effort, and from that time forth will

understand the mechanism of his own body. For every branch of knowledge similar constructions (that is to say, images of things which cannot be procured in the original) should be made, and should be kept in the schools ready for use. It is true that expense and labour will be necessary to produce these models, but the result will amply reward the effort.

11. If any be uncertain if all things can be placed before the senses in this way, even things spiritual and things absent (things in heaven, or in hell, or beyond the sea), let him remember that all things have been harmoniously arranged by God in such a manner that the higher in the scale of existence can be represented by the lower, the absent by the present, and the invisible by the visible. This can be seen in the *Macromicrocosmus* of Robert Flutt,[30] in which the origin of the winds, of rain, and of thunder is described in such a way that the reader can visualise it. Nor is there any doubt that even greater concreteness and ease of demonstration than is here displayed might be attained.

12. So much of the presentation of objects to the senses. We must now speak of the light, the absence of which renders the presentation of objects to the eyes useless. This light of the teaching art is attention, and by its means the learner can keep his mind from wandering and can take in everything that is put before him. It is impossible for any man to see an object in the dark, or if his eyes be closed, no matter how near to him it may be; and in the same way, if you talk to one who is not attending, or show him anything, you will make no impression on his senses. This we can observe in the case of those who, while lost in thought, do not notice what is going on before their eyes. He, therefore, who wishes to show anything to another at night must provide light, and must polish the object so that it shines; and in the same way a master, if he wish to illumine with knowledge a pupil shrouded in the darkness of ignorance, must first excite his attention, that he may drink in information with a greedy mind.

How this can be done we have shown in the 17th chapter, and in the first Principle of the 19th chapter.

13. So much of the light. We will now speak of the mode in which objects must be presented to the senses, if the impression is to be distinct. This can be readily understood if we consider the processes of actual vision. If the object is to be clearly seen it is necessary: (1) that it be placed before the eyes; (2) not far off, but at a reasonable distance; (3) not on one side, but straight before the eyes; (4) and so that the front of the object be not turned away from, but directed towards, the observer; (5) that the eyes first take in the object as a whole; (6) and then proceed to distinguish the parts; (7) inspecting these in order from the beginning to the end; (8) that attention be paid to each and every part; (9) until they are all grasped by means of their essential attributes. If these requisites be properly observed, vision takes place successfully; but if one be neglected its success is only partial.

14. For instance, if any one wish to read a letter that has been sent him by a friend, it is necessary: (1) that it be presented to the eyes (for if it be not seen, how can it be read?); (2) that it be placed at a suitable distance from the eyes (for if it be too far off, the words cannot be distinguished); (3) that it be directly in front of the eyes (for if it be on one side, it will be confusedly seen); (4) that it be turned the right way up (for if a letter or a book be presented to the eyes upside down or on its side, it cannot be read); (5) the general characteristics of the letter, such as the address, the writer, and the date must be seen first (for unless these facts be known, the particular items of the letter cannot be properly understood); (6) then the remainder of the letter must be read, that nothing be omitted (otherwise the contents will not all be known, and perhaps the most important point will be missed); (7) it must be read in the right order (if one sentence be read here and another there, the sense will be confused); (8) each sentence must be mastered before the next is com-

menced (for if the whole be read hurriedly, some useful point may easily escape the mind); (9) finally, when the whole has been carefully perused, the reader may proceed to distinguish between those points that are necessary and those that are superfluous.

15. These points should be observed by those who teach the sciences, and may be expressed in nine very useful precepts.

(i) Whatever is to be known must be taught.

Unless that which is to be known be placed before a pupil, how is he to acquire a knowledge of it? Therefore let those who teach beware of concealing anything from their pupils, whether of intent, as do the envious and dishonest, or through carelessness, as is the case with those who perform their duties in a perfunctory manner. The two things necessary are honesty and hard work.

16. (ii) Whatever is taught should be taught as being of practical application in every-day life and of some definite use.

That is to say, the pupil should understand that what he learns is not taken out of some Utopia or borrowed from Platonic Ideas, but is one of the facts which surround us, and that a fitting acquaintance with it will be of great service in life. In this way his energy and his accuracy will be increased.

17. (iii) Whatever is taught should be taught straightforwardly, and not in a complicated manner.

This means that we must look straight at objects and not squint, for in that case the eyes do not see that at which they look, but rather distort and confuse it. Objects should be placed before the eyes of the student in their true character, and not shrouded in words, metaphors, or hyperboles. These devices have their use if the object be to exaggerate or to detract from, to praise or to blame what is already known. But when knowledge is being acquired they should be avoided and the facts should be set forth plainly.

18. (iv) Whatever is taught must be taught with reference

to its true nature and its origin; that is to say, through its causes.

This method of cognition is the best if the true nature of a fact is to be learned. For if its true nature be not made evident, this is not cognition but error. The true nature of a fact lies in the process that brought it into being. If it appear to contain elements not accounted for by that process, it is evident that there is some misapprehension. Now everything is brought into existence by its causes. Therefore to explain the causes of anything is equivalent to making a true exposition of that thing's nature, in accordance with the principles: "Knowledge consists in having a firm grip of causes," and "Causes are the guides of the understanding." Objects can thus be best, easiest, and most certainly cognised through a knowledge of the processes that produced them. If a man wish to read a letter he holds it as it was written, since it is a difficult thing to read a document that is inverted, or on its side, and in the same way, if a fact be explained by means of the process that gave it birth, it will be easily and surely understood. If, however, the teacher reverse the order of nature, he is certain to confuse the student. Therefore, the method employed in teaching should be based on the method of nature. That which precedes should be taken first, and that which follows last.

19. (v) If anything is to be learned, its general principles must first be explained. Its details may then be considered, and not till then.

The reasons for this have been given in chap. xvi. Principle 6. We give a general notion of an object when we explain it by means of its essential nature and its accidental qualities. The essential nature is unfolded by the questions *what? of what kind? and why?* Under the question *what?* are included the name, the genus, the function, and the end. Under the question *of what kind?* comes the form of the object, or the mode in which it is fitted to its end. Under the question *why?* the efficient or causal force by which an object is made suitable to its end. For example, did I wish to give a student a general notion of a man, I should say: Man is (1) the chief creation of God, and destined for dominion over other creatures ; (2) endowed with freedom of choice and action ; (3) and on that account provided with the light of reason, that he may direct his choice and his actions with wisdom. This is but a general notion of man, but it goes to the root of the matter and says everything about him that is essential. To these you may, if you like, add some of his accidental qualities, still keeping to generalities, and this must be done by asking the questions : *from what origin ? whence ? when ?* You may then proceed to his parts, the body and the soul. The nature of the body can be demonstrated through the anatomy of its organs ; that of the soul by examining the faculties of which it consists. All these points must be taken in their proper order.

20. (vi) All the parts of an object, even the smallest, and without a single exception, must be learned with reference to their order, their position, and their connection with one another.

Nothing exists in vain, and sometimes the strength of the larger parts depends on that of the smallest. Certain it is that in a clock, if one pin be broken or bent, or moved out of its place, the whole machine will stop. Similarly, in a living body, the loss of one organ may cause life to cease, and in a sentence it is often on the smallest words, such as prepositions and conjunctions, that the whole sense depends. Perfect knowledge of an object can therefore only be attained by acquiring a knowledge of the nature and function of each of its parts.

21. (vii) All things must be taught in due succession, and not more than one thing should be taught at one time.

The organ of vision is unable to take in two or three objects at one time (certain it is that he who reads a book cannot look at two pages at once, nay, cannot even see two lines, though they lie quite close together, nor two words, nor two letters, otherwise than successively) ; and in the

same way the mind can only grasp one thing at a time.
We should therefore make a distinct break in our progress
from one thing to another, that we may not overburden
the mind.

22. (viii) We should not leave any subject until it is
thoroughly understood.

Nothing can be done in a moment.   For every process
involves motion, and motion implies successive stages.
The pupil should therefore not pass on from any point in
a science until he has thoroughly mastered it and is
conscious that he has done so.   The methods to be employed are emphatic teaching, examination, and iteration,
until the desired result is attained.   This we have pointed
out in chap. xviii. Principle 10.

23. (ix) Stress should be laid on the differences which
exist between things, in order that what knowledge of
them is acquired may be clear and distinct.

Much meaning lies concealed in that celebrated saying :
" He who distinguishes well is a good teacher."   For too
many facts overwhelm a student, and too great a variety
confuses him.   Remedies must therefore be applied : in
the first case order, by means of which one thing may
be taken after another ; in the second, a careful consideration of the differences that exist in nature, that it may
always be evident in what respects one thing differs from
another.   This is the only method that can give distinct,
clear, and certain knowledge ; since the variety and actuality
of natural objects depend on their distinctive attributes,
as we have hinted in chap. xviii. Principle 6.

24. Now it is impossible that all teachers, when they
enter on their profession, should be possessed of the requisite skill, and it is therefore necessary that the sciences
which are taught in schools be mapped out in accordance
with the foregoing laws.   If this be done it will be difficult
for any teacher to miss his mark.   For, if the laws be
rigorously observed, it is beyond question that any man who
is once admitted into the royal palace and is allotted a
certain space of time can easily and without any trouble

master its whole contents, its pictures, statues, carpets, and other ornaments; and just as easy will it be for a youth who is admitted to the theatre of this world to penetrate with his mental vision the secrets of nature, and from that time forward to move among the works of God and of man with his eyes opened.

CHAPTER XXI

THE METHOD OF THE ARTS

1. "THEORY," says Vives, "is easy and short, but has no result other than the gratification that it affords. Practice, on the other hand, is difficult and prolix, but is of immense utility." Since this is so, we should diligently seek out a method by which the young may be easily led to the practical application of natural forces, which is to be found in the arts.

2. Art primarily requires three things: (1) A model or a conception; that is to say, an external form which the artist may examine and then try to imitate. (2) The material on which the new form is to be impressed. (3) The instruments by the aid of which the work is accomplished.

3. But when the instruments, the materials, and the model have been provided, three more things are necessary before we can learn an art: (1) a proper use of the materials; (2) skilled guidance; (3) frequent practice. That is to say, the pupil should be taught when and how to use his materials; he should be given assistance when using them that he may not make mistakes, or that he may be corrected if he do; and he should not leave off making mistakes and being corrected until he can work correctly and quickly.

4. With respect to these points eleven canons must be observed: six on the use of materials; three on guidance; and two on practice.

5. (i) What has to be done must be learned by practice.

Artisans do not detain their apprentices with theories, but set them to do practical work at an early stage; thus they learn to forge by forging, to carve by carving, to paint by painting, and to dance by dancing. In schools, therefore, let the students learn to write by writing, to talk by talking, to sing by singing, and to reason by reasoning. In this way schools will become work-shops humming with work, and students whose efforts prove successful will experience the truth of the proverb: "We give form to ourselves and to our materials at the same time."

6. (ii) A definite model of that which has to be made must always be provided.

This the student should first examine, and then imitate, as though he were following in the footsteps of a guide. For he who neither knows what has to be done nor how to do it, is unable to produce anything of himself, but must have a model placed before him. Indeed it is sheer cruelty to force any one to do what you wish, while he is ignorant what your wishes are; to demand, that is to say, that he form straight lines, right angles, or perfect circles, unless you first give him a ruler, a square, and a pair of compasses, and explain their use to him. Further, great care should be taken to provide in the school-room formulæ for or models of everything that has to be made, and these, whether drawings and diagrams, or rules and models, should be correct, definite, and simple; easy both to understand and to imitate. There will then be no absurdity in demanding of a man that he see, when provided with a light; that he walk, when he already stands on his feet; or that he use the tools that are already in his hands.

7. (iii) The use of instruments should be shown in practice and not by words; that is to say, by example rather than by precept.

It is many years since Quintilian said: "Through precepts the way is long and difficult, while through examples it is short and practicable." But alas, how little heed the ordinary schools pay to this advice. The very beginners in grammar are so overwhelmed by precepts, rules, exceptions to the rules, and exceptions to the exceptions, that for the most part they do not know what they are doing, and are quite stupefied before they begin to understand anything. Mechanics do not begin by drumming rules into their apprentices. They take them into the workshop and bid them look at the work that has been produced, and then, when they wish to imitate this (for man is an imitative animal), they place tools in their hands and show them how they should be held and used. Then, if they make mistakes, they give them advice and correct them, often more by example than by mere words, and, as the facts show, the novices easily succeed in their imitation. For there is great truth in that saying of the Germans, "A good leader finds a good follower." Very apposite, too, is the remark of Terence, "Do you go before; I will follow." This is the way, namely, by imitating, and without any laborious rules, that children learn to walk, to run, to talk, and to play. Rules are like thorns to the understanding, and to grasp their meaning needs both attention and ability, while even the dullest students are aided by example. No one has ever mastered any language or art by precept alone; while by practice this is possible, even without precept.

8. (iv) Practice should commence with the rudiments and not with ambitious works.

A carpenter does not begin by teaching his apprentice to build turrets, but first shows him how to hold the axe, to cut down trees, to shape planks, to bore holes, and to fasten beams together. A painter does not make his pupil commence by painting portraits, but teaches him how to mix colours, to hold the brush, and to make lines; then to attempt rough outlines, and so on. He who teaches a boy how to read explains to him, not the contents of the book, but the names and nature of the letters, and shows him how they can be joined together into syllables; then he proceeds to words, and then to sentences. In the same way the beginner in grammar should learn, first how to inflect single words, then how to join two together. Then he may advance to simple and compound sentences, and so on till he reach continuous prose. So too in dialectic. The student should first learn to distinguish things and the concepts of things by means of their genera and species; then to classify them afresh, with respect to some other common quality (for such links exist between all things); then to define and distribute them; then to estimate the value of the things and their concepts in combination, seeking out the what? the whence? and the why? and whether it be necessary or contingent. When he has had sufficient practice in this, he may proceed to ratiocination and seek how to draw conclusions from given premises, and finally he may essay discursive reasoning or the complete conduct of disputations. The same course may with advantage be followed in rhetoric. The student should first devote some time to the collection of synonyms, and may then learn to add epithets to nouns, verbs, and adverbs. He may then proceed to the use of antithesis, and later on to that of periphrasis. Then he may substitute figurative words for the originals, alter the order of the words for the sake of euphony, and adorn a simple sentence with all the figures of speech. Finally, when thoroughly versed in all these several points, and not sooner, he may proceed to the composition of a complete discourse. If any one advance step by step in any art, as here indicated, it is impossible that he should not make progress.

The basis of the foregoing was discussed in chap. xvii. Principle 4.

9. (v) Beginners should at first practise on a material that is familiar to them.

This rule we obtain from the 9th Principle of the 17th chapter, and from the 6th Corollary of the 4th Principle. Its meaning is that students should not be overburdened with matters that are unsuitable to their age, comprehension, and present condition, since otherwise they will spend their time in wrestling with shadows. For example,

when a Polish boy is learning to read or to write his letters
he should not be taught to do so from a book written in
Latin, Greek, or Arabic, but from one written in his own
language, that he may understand what he is doing.   Again,
if a boy is to understand the use of the rules of rhetoric,
the examples on which he is made to practise them should
not be taken from Virgil or from Cicero, or from theological,
political, or medical writers, but should refer to the objects
that surround him, to his books, to his clothes, to trees,
houses, and schools.   It will also be of use if the examples
that are taken to illustrate the first rule be retained,
although familiar, to illustrate the remainder.   In dialectic,
for example, a tree may be taken, and its genus, its species,
its relations to other objects, its characteristic peculiarities
and the logical definition and distribution of the term may
be treated of.   We may then proceed to the various ways
in which a statement may be made about a tree.   Finally,
we may show how, by a perfect train of reasoning, and by
taking the facts already ascertained as our starting-point,
we may discover and demonstrate other properties of a
tree.   In this way, if, in each case, the use of the rules be
illustrated by the same familiar example, the boy will easily
master their application to all other subjects.

10. (vi) At first the prescribed form should be imitated
with exactness.   Later on more freedom may be allowed.

A form will be expressed with more exactness in proportion as care is taken to make it resemble its original.   Thus
coins that are struck by one die are exactly like the die and
one another.   So also with books printed from metal type,
and with casts made in wax, plaster, or metal.   In all other
artistic operations, therefore, as far as is possible, any
imitation (at any rate the first) should be an exact copy of
its original, until the hand, the mind, and the tongue
gain more confidence, and can produce good imitations by
working freely on their own lines.   For instance, those who
learn writing take a thin and transparent sheet of paper,
place it over the copy that they wish to imitate, and thus
can easily form the letters that show through.   Or the

characters may be printed very faintly on a white page, so that the pupil may go over them with pen and ink, and in this way may easily acquire the habit of shaping them. The same thing holds good in style, if any construction or sentence extracted from a classic writer have to be imitated. If the original phrase be "Rich in possessions," the boy should be made to imitate it by saying, "Rich in coins," "Rich in moneys," "Rich in flocks," "Rich in vineyards." When Cicero says, "In the opinion of the most learned men, Eudemus easily holds the first place in astrology," this may be copied with very little alteration as "In the opinion of the greatest orators, Cicero easily holds the first place in eloquence," "In the opinion of the whole Church, St. Paul easily holds the first place in Apostleship." So too in logic, if the well-known dilemma be given : It is either day or night. But it is night; therefore it is not day; the boy may learn to imitate it by similarly opposing contradictory conceptions to one another. As, "He is either unlearned or learned. But he is unlearned; therefore he is not learned "; "Cain was either pious or impious, but he was not pious "; and so on.

11. (vii) The models of the objects that have to be produced must be as perfect as is possible, so that if any one exercise himself sufficiently in imitating them it will be possible for him to become perfect in his art.

It is impossible to draw straight lines with a curved ruler, and in the same way a good copy cannot be made from a bad model. Great care should therefore be taken that models be prepared of everything that is to be done in school, or indeed in life, and that these be exact, simple, and easy to imitate. They may be either models, pictures and drawings, or precepts and rules ; but all must be very short, very clear, self-evident, and absolutely correct.

12. (viii) The first attempt at imitation should be as accurate as possible, that not the smallest deviation from the model be made.

That is to say, as far as is possible. For whatever comes first is, as it were, the foundation of that which follows. If the foundation be firm, a solid edifice can be constructed upon it, but if it be weak this is impossible. According to the observations of physicians, the initial defects of digestion cannot be repaired later on, and similarly in any operation an error at the beginning vitiates all that follows. For this reason Timotheus the musician used to demand twice as large a fee from those pupils who had learned the rudiments of their art elsewhere, saying that his labour was twofold, as he had first to get them out of the bad habits that they had acquired, and then to teach them correctly. Those, therefore, who are learning any art should take care to make themselves masters of the rudiments by imitating their copies accurately. This difficulty once overcome, the rest follows of itself, just as a city lies at the mercy of foes when its gates are broken in. All haste should be avoided, lest we proceed to advanced work before the elementary stages have been mastered. He goes fast enough who never quits the road, and a delay which is caused by obtaining a thorough grip of first principles is really no delay, but an advance towards mastering what follows with ease, speed, and accuracy.

13. (ix) Errors must be corrected by the master on the spot ; but precepts, that is to say the rules, and the exceptions to the rules, must be given at the same time.

Hitherto we have urged that the arts be taught rather by example than by precept: we now add that precepts and rules must be given as well, that they may guide the operations and prevent error. That is to say, the less obvious points of the model should be clearly explained, and it should be made evident how the operation should begin, what it should aim at, and how that aim can be realised. Reasons should also be given for each rule. In this way a thorough knowledge of the art, and confidence and exactness in imitating, will be attained.

But these rules should be as short and as simple as possible, since we do not want to grow gray while acquiring them. When once mastered they should be of perpetual use, even when laid aside, just as knee-bands are of use to a child who is learning to walk, and, though they are afterwards discarded, the advantage derived from them remains.

14. (x) The perfect teaching of art is based on synthesis and analysis.

We have already shown (chap. xviii. Principle 5) by examples taken from nature and the workshop that in this relation synthesis is more important. The following points in addition will show that synthetic exercises should generally come first: (1) We should always commence with what is easy, and our own efforts are easier to understand than those of other people. (2) Writers take pains to conceal the artifices by which their results are obtained, so that at first the student finds difficulty in understanding what he sees, or fails to do so altogether. This difficulty would be removed if he began by practising on his own attempts, which are void of artifice. (3) The chief thing aimed at should be given the chief place in practice, and our real aim is to accustom the student of art to produce original work, and not merely to copy what is placed before him (see chapter xviii. Principle 5).

15. For all this, the accurate analysis of the work of others must not be neglected. It is only by continually traversing it that we get to know a road, its by-paths, and its cross-roads. Besides, the variety that exists in nature is so great that it is impossible for rules to cover it or for one mind to master it. Many processes require many rules to express them, and these we can only learn if we analyse and study, and by imitation and emulation put ourselves in a position to produce similar results.

16. It is our wish then that in each art complete and exact models or examples of everything that can be produced in that art be supplied to the student. Precepts also and rules should be given him to help him to carry out the processes, to guide his efforts at imitation, to show him how to avoid making faults, and to correct them when made. Then other and different models should be given him, and these he should learn to classify and compare

with the models that he has already used, and by copying a model that is like one previously used to produce work that resembles the original.   After this, the finished works of other artists (who must be well known) may be examined and analysed in accordance with the models and rules that are already familiar.   In this way the student will learn to employ the rules with greater ease, and will acquire the art of concealing his art.   Only after a course of exercises of this kind will he be in the position to criticise artistic productions, whether his own or those of others.

17. (xi) These exercises must be continued until artistic production becomes second nature.

For it is practice, and nothing else, that produces an artist.

CHAPTER XXII

THE METHOD OF LANGUAGES

1. LANGUAGES are learned, not as forming in themselves a part of erudition or wisdom, but as being the means by which we may acquire knowledge and may impart it to others.

It follows, therefore, (1) that not all languages should be learned, for this would be impossible; nor many, for this would be useless and would waste time that might be devoted to the acquisition of practical information; but only those that are necessary. Now necessary languages are these: the vernacular, for use at home, and the languages of the adjoining countries, for the sake of holding intercourse with neighbours. Thus for the Poles, German would be necessary; for others, the Hungarian, Wallachian, or Turkish languages. For the reading of serious books Latin is also advisable, as it is the common language of the learned. For philosophers and physicians, Greek and Arabic; and for theologians, Greek and Hebrew.

2. Not all these languages should be learned thoroughly, but only so far as is necessary.

It is not necessary to speak Greek or Hebrew as fluently as the mother-tongue, since there are no people with whom we can converse in those languages. It suffices to learn them well enough to be able to read and understand books written in them.

3. The study of languages, especially in youth, should be joined to that of objects, that our acquaintance with

the objective world and with language, that is to say, our knowledge of facts and our power to express them, may progress side by side.   For it is men that we are forming and not parrots, as has been said in chap. xix. Principle 6.

4. From this it follows, firstly, that words should not be learned apart from the objects to which they refer ; since the objects do not exist separately and cannot be apprehended without words, but both exist and perform their functions together.   It was this consideration that led me to publish the *Janua Linguarum ;* in which words, arranged in sentences, explain the nature of objects, and, as it is said, with no small success.

5. Secondly, that the complete and detailed knowledge of a language, no matter which it be, is quite unnecessary, and that it is absurd and useless on the part of any one to try to attain it.   Not even Cicero (who is considered the greatest master of the Latin language) was acquainted with all its details, since he confessed that he was ignorant of the words used by artisans ; for he had never mixed with cobblers and labourers, so as to see their handiwork and hear the technical terms that they used.   Indeed what object could he have had in learning such terms ?

6. Those who have expanded my *Janua* have paid no attention to this, but have stuffed it with uncommon words and with matter quite unsuited to a boy's comprehension.   A *Janua* should remain a *Janua*, and anything further should be reserved for a future time. This is especially the case with words which either never occur, or which, if met with, can easily be looked up in subsidiary books (such as vocabularies, lexicons, herbaries, etc.) It was for this reason that I discontinued my *Latinitatis Posticum* (into which I was introducing obsolete and unusual words).

7. In the third place it follows that the intelligence as well as the language of boys should preferably be exercised on matters which appeal to them, and that what appeals to adults should be left for a later stage.   They waste their time who place before boys Cicero and other great writers.

For, if students do not understand the subject-matter, how can they master the various devices for expressing it forcibly? The time is more usefully spent on less ambitious efforts, so devised that the knowledge of the language and the general intelligence may advance together and step by step. Nature makes no leap, and neither does art, since it imitates nature. We must teach boys to walk before we give them lessons in dancing; to ride on a hobby-horse before we set them on a charger; to prattle before they speak, and to speak before they deliver orations. It was Cicero who said that he could teach no one to deliver orations who had not first learned how to talk.

8. As regards the plurality of tongues, our method, which we will reduce to eight rules, will render the acquisition of the various languages an easy matter.

9. (i) Each language must be learned separately.

First of all the mother-tongue must be learned, and then the language that may have to be used in its place, I mean that of the neighbouring nation (for I am of opinion that modern languages should be commenced before the learned ones). Then Latin may be learned, and after Latin, Greek, Hebrew, etc.

One language should always be learned after, and not at the same time as, another; since otherwise both will be learned confusedly. It is only when they have been thoroughly acquired that it is of use to compare them by means of parallel grammars, dictionaries, etc.

10. (ii) Each language must have a definite space of time allotted to it.

We should take care not to convert a subsidiary study into a chief one, or to waste on the acquisition of words the time in which we might gain a knowledge of things. The mother-tongue, since it is intimately connected with the gradual unfolding of the objective world to the senses, necessarily requires several years (I should say eight or ten, or the whole of childhood, with a part of boyhood). We may then proceed to the other modern languages, each of which can be sufficiently mastered in one year.

Latin can be learned in two years, Greek in one year, and Hebrew in six months.

11. (iii) All languages are easier to learn by practice than from rules.

That is to say, by hearing, reading, re-reading, copying, imitating with hand and tongue, and doing all these as frequently as is possible. Cf. the preceding chapter, canons i. and xi.

12. (iv) But rules assist and strengthen the knowledge derived from practice.

This we have treated of in the previous chapter, canon ii. We speak more especially of the learned languages which we are compelled to learn from books, though we do not exclude modern languages. For Italian, French, German, Bohemian, and Hungarian can be, and indeed have already been, reduced to rules.

13. (v) The rules to which languages are reduced should be grammatical and not philosophic.

That is to say, they should not inquire into the causes and antecedents of words, phrases, and sentences, or seek to find out why this or that construction is necessary, but should simply state what is correct and how the constructions should be made. The subtler investigation into the causes and connecting links, the similarities and dissimilarities, the analogies and anomalies that exist in things and in words, is the business of the philosopher, and does but delay the philologist.

14. (vi) In writing rules for the new language the one already known must be continually kept in mind, so that stress may be laid only on the points in which the languages differ.

To call attention to points that they possess in common is not merely useless, but actually harmful, since the mind is terrified by the semblance of greater prolixity and irregularity than really exist. For instance, in Greek grammar there is no need to repeat the definitions of nouns, verbs, cases, and tenses, or rules of syntax which convey nothing new, and which may be considered as already familiar. Those only need be included in which the usage of Greek differs from that of Latin, which is already known. In this way Greek grammar may be reduced to a few pages, and will thus be both clearer and easier.

15. (vii) The first exercises in a new language must deal with subject-matter that is already familiar.

Otherwise the mind will have to pay attention to words and to things at the same time, and will thus be distracted and weakened. Its efforts should therefore be confined to words, that it may master them easily and quickly. Such subject-matter might very well be the Catechism, or Biblical history, or in fact anything that is sufficiently familiar. (Being short, my *Vestibulum* and *Janua* might be used; though these are more suitable to commit to memory, while the subjects suggested above are fit for constant reading on account of the constant recurrence of the same words, which will thus grow familiar and impress themselves on the memory.)

16. (viii) All languages, therefore, can be learned by the method.

That is to say, by practice, combined with rules of a very simple nature that only refer to points of difference with the language already known, and by exercises that refer to some familiar subject.

17. *Of the languages that should be learned carefully.*

As we said at the commencement of the chapter, all languages need not be learned with equal accuracy. The mother-tongue and Latin are the most worthy of attention, and we should all master them thoroughly. This course of language-study may be divided into four ages—

The first		babbling infancy		indistinctly
The second		ripening boyhood	in which	correctly
The third	age is	maturer youth	we learn to speak	elegantly
The fourth		vigorous manhood		forcibly

18. Gradation of this kind is the only true principle.

On any other system everything falls into confusion and disorder, as we have most of us experienced. But through these four grades all who wish to learn languages may pass with ease if the proper materials for teaching languages have been provided; that is to say, suitable school-books for the pupils and hand-books to assist the teacher, both of which should be short and methodical.

19. The school-books, suited to the several ages, should be four in number—

(i) The *Vestibulum*.
(ii) The *Janua*.
(iii) The *Palatium*.
(iv) The *Thesaurus*.

20. The *Vestibulum* should contain the materials for a child's conversation—a few hundred words, arranged in sentences, to which are added the declensions of nouns and the conjugations of verbs.

21. The *Janua* should contain all the common words in the language, about 8000 in number. These should be arranged in short sentences embodying descriptions of natural objects. To this there should be subjoined some short and clear grammatical rules, giving accurate directions for writing, pronouncing, forming, and using the words of the language.

22. The *Palatium* should contain diverse discourses on all matters, expressed in a varied and elegant style, with marginal references to the authors from which the several phrases are borrowed. At the end there should be given rules for altering and paraphrasing sentences in a thousand different ways.

23. The *Thesaurus* will be the name given to the classic writers who have written on any matter with serious intent and in a good style, with the addition of rules relating to the observation and collection of noteworthy passages and to the accurate translation (a most important matter) of idioms. Of these authors, some should be chosen to read in school; of others, a catalogue should be

formed, so that if any one desire to look up any subject in the authors who have written on it, he may be able to find out who they are.

24. By subsidiary books are meant those by whose help the school-books may be used with greater speed and with more result.

For the *Vestibulum* a small vocabulary, both Vernacular-Latin and Latin-Vernacular, should be provided.

For the *Janua* an etymological Latin-Vernacular dictionary, giving the simple words, their derivatives, their compounds, and the reason for the meanings attached.

For the *Palatium* a phraseological dictionary in the Vernacular, in Latin (and if necessary in Greek), forming a compendium of the various phrases, synonyms, and periphrases that occur in the *Palatium*, with references to the places where they are to be found.

Finally, for the completion of the *Thesaurus*, a comprehensive lexicon (Vernacular-Latin and Latin-Greek) which shall embrace, without exception, every point in each language. This should be carried out in a scholarly and accurate manner, care being taken that fine shades of meaning in the several languages be made to correspond, and that suitable parallels be found for idioms. For it is not probable that there exists any language so poor in words, idioms, and proverbs that it could not furnish an equivalent for any Latin expression, if judgment were used. At any rate, accurate renderings could be devised by any one who possessed sufficient skill in imitating, and in producing a suitable result from suitable material.

25. No such comprehensive dictionary has hitherto been produced. A Polish Jesuit, G. Cnapius, has, it is true, done good service to his countrymen by his work entitled *A Thesaurus of Polish, Latin, and Greek ;* but in this work there are three defects. Firstly, the collection of vernacular words and phrases is incomplete. Secondly, he has not observed the order that we suggested above, since individual, figurative, and obsolete words are not arranged under separate headings, though in this way the

peculiarities, the elegances, and the resources of both languages equally would be illustrated. For he has given a number of Latin renderings for each word and phrase of Polish, while according to my plan only one, but that an exact equivalent, should be given. In this way, my dictionary would be of great service to those translating books from Latin into the vernacular, and *vice versa*. Thirdly, in Cnapius' *Thesaurus* there is a great lack of method in the arrangement of examples. These should not be carelessly heaped together. First, simple illustrations, drawn from history, should be given, then more ambitious ones taken from the orators, then the more complex and uncommon usages of poets, and finally the uses that are obsolete.

26. But a detailed account of this comprehensive dictionary must be left for another time, as must also the further particulars of the *Vestibulum*, the *Janua*, the *Palatium*, and the *Thesaurus*, by means of which languages can be acquired with unfailing accuracy. Of these it will be fitting to speak when we deal with the several classes in detail.

CHAPTER XXIII

THE METHOD OF MORALS

1. So far we have discussed the problem of teaching and learning the sciences and the arts with greater readiness. We should, however, bear in mind the remark of Seneca (*Epist.* 89): "We ought not to learn these things, but rather to have learned them." They are, indeed, nothing but a preparation for more important matters, and as he says, "our beginnings, and not our completed works." What then is our true work? It is that study of wisdom which elevates us and makes us steadfast and noble-minded —the study to which we have given the name of morality and of piety, and by means of which we are exalted above all other creatures, and draw nigh to God Himself.

2. We must therefore see how this art of instilling true virtue and piety may be elaborated on a definite system, and introduced into schools, that we may with justice be able to call them the "forging-places of humanity."

3. The art of shaping the morals is based upon the following sixteen fundamental rules:

(i) All the virtues, without exception, should be implanted in the young.

For in morality nothing can be omitted without leaving a gap.

4. (ii) Those virtues which are called cardinal should be first instilled; these are prudence, temperance, fortitude, and justice.

In this way we may ensure that the structure shall not be built up without a foundation, and that the various parts shall form a harmonious whole.

5. (iii) Prudence must be acquired by receiving good instruction, and by learning the real differences that exist between things, and the relative value of those things.

A sound judgment on matters of fact is the true foundation of all virtue. Well does Vives say: "True wisdom consists in having a sound judgment, and in thus arriving at the truth. Thus are we prevented from following worthless things as if they were of value, or from rejecting what is of value as if it were worthless; from blaming what should be praised, and from praising what should be blamed. This is the source from which all error arises in the human mind, and there is nothing in the life of man that is more disastrous than the lack of judgment through which a false estimate of facts is made. Sound judgment," he proceeds, "should be practised in early youth, and will thus be developed by the time manhood is reached. A boy should seek that which is right and avoid that which is worthless, for thus the practice of judging correctly will become second nature with him."

6. (iv) Boys should be taught to observe temperance in eating and in drinking, in sleeping and in waking, in work and in play, in talking and in keeping silence, throughout the whole period of their instruction.

In this relation the golden rule, "Nothing in excess," should be dinned into their ears, that they may learn on all occasions to leave off before satiety sets in.

7. (v) Fortitude should be learned by the subduing of self; that is to say, by repressing the desire to play at the wrong time or beyond the proper time, and by bridling impatience, discontent, and anger.

The principle which underlies this is that we should accustom boys to do everything by reason, and nothing under the guidance of impulse. For man is a rational animal, and should therefore be led by reason, and, before action, ought to deliberate how each operation should be performed, so that he may really be master of his own actions. Now, since boys are not quite capable of such a deliberate and rational mode of procedure, it will be a great advance towards teaching them fortitude and self-control if they be forced to acquire the habit of performing the will of another in preference to their own, that is to say, to obey their superiors promptly in everything. "Those who train horses aright," says Lactantius, "first teach them to obey the reins," and he who wishes to instruct boys should commence by accustoming them to obey his orders. We may indeed cherish a hope that the turmoil with which the world is overwhelmed will be replaced by a better condition of affairs, if, in early youth, men learn to yield to one another and to be guided by reason in all that they do.

8. (vi) The young should learn to practise justice by hurting no man, by giving each his due, by avoiding falsehood and deceit, and by being obliging and agreeable.

Boys must be trained to act in this way, as we said above, by the method prescribed in the following canons.

9. (vii) The kinds of fortitude that are especially necessary to the young are frankness and endurance of toil.

For since life must be spent in intercourse with others and in action, boys must be taught to look men in the face and to meet honest toil without flinching. Otherwise they may become recluses and misanthropes, or idlers and cumberers of the earth. Virtue is practised by deeds and not by words.

10. (viii) Frankness is acquired by constant intercourse with worthy people, and by behaving, while in their presence, in accordance with the precepts that have been given.

Aristotle educated Alexander in such a manner that, when twelve years of age, he could suit himself to every kind of society, to that of kings, of the ambassadors of kings and of nations, of learned and unlearned men, of townsmen, of countrymen, and of artisans, and could ask suitable questions or give suitable answers on any subject that arose in conversation. In order that the young who are subjected to our comprehensive scheme of education may learn to imitate this, rules for conversation should be written, and the practice of them, by daily inter-course with tutors, schoolfellows, parents, and servants, should be insisted upon; masters also should take great care to correct any tendency to carelessness, forwardness, boorishness, or coarseness.

11. (ix) Boys will learn to endure toil if they are con-tinually occupied, either with work or with play.

It makes no difference what is done, or why it is done, if only the boy be occupied. Much can be learned in play that will afterwards be of use when the circumstances demand it. It is by working, therefore, that we must learn how to work, just as we learn how to act by acting (as we saw above); and in this way the continued occupations of mind and body, in which, at the same time, all over-pressure must be avoided, will produce an industrious disposition, and make a man so active that sluggish ease will be intolerable to him. Then will be seen the truth of Seneca's words: "It is toil that nourishes noble minds."

12. (x) The cognate virtue of justice, or promptness and willingness to serve others, must be diligently cultivated in the young.

The abominable vice of selfishness is inherent in our corrupt nature, and through it each man thinks of nothing but his own welfare, and troubles his head about no one else. This is a great source of confusion in life, since all are occupied with their own affairs and neglect the common good. The true object of life must therefore be diligently instilled into the youth, and they must be taught that we are born not for ourselves alone, but for God and for our neighbour, that is to say, for the human race.

Thus they will become seriously persuaded of this truth and will learn from their boyhood to imitate God, the angels, the sun, and the more noble of things created, that is to say, by desiring and striving to be of service to as many as possible. Thus will the good fortune of private and of public life be assured, since all men will be ready to work together for the common good, and to help one another. And they actually will do so if they have been properly taught.

13. (xi) Virtue must be inculcated at a very early stage before vice gets possession of the mind.

For if you do not sow a field with good seed it will produce nothing but weeds of the worst kind. But if you wish to subdue it, you will do so more easily and with a better hope of success if you plough it, sow it, and harrow it in early spring. Indeed, it is of the greatest importance that children be well trained in early youth, since a jar preserves for a long time the odour with which it has been imbued when new.

14. (xii) The virtues are learned by constantly doing what is right.

We have seen in chaps. xx. and xxi. that it is by learning that we find out what we ought to learn, and by acting that we learn to act as we should. So then, as boys easily learn to walk by walking, to talk by talking, and to write by writing, in the same way they will learn obedience by obeying, abstinence by abstaining, truth by speaking the truth, and constancy by being constant. But it is necessary that the child be helped by advice and example at the same time.

15. (xiii) Examples of well-ordered lives, in the persons of their parents, nurses, tutors, and school-fellows, must continually be set before children.

For boys are like apes, and love to imitate whatever they see, whether good or bad, even though not bidden to do so; and on this account they learn to imitate before they learn to use their minds. By "examples," I mean living ones as well as those taken from books; in fact, living ones are the more important because they make a stronger impression. And therefore, if parents are worthy and careful guardians of domestic discipline, and if tutors are chosen with the greatest possible care, and are men of exceptional virtue, a great advance will have been made towards the proper training of the young in morals.

16. (xiv) But, in addition to examples, precepts and rules of conduct must be given.

In this way imitation will be supplemented and strengthened (on this point the reader may refer to our remarks in chap. xxi. canon ix.) Rules of life should therefore be collected from Holy Scripture and from the sayings of wise men, and should deal with questions such as : "Why should we strive against envy?" "With what arms should we fortify ourselves against the sorrows and the chances of life?" "How should we observe modera- tion in joy?" "How should anger be controlled?" "How should illicit love be driven out?" and similar questions, according to the age of the pupil.

17. (xv) Children must be very carefully guarded from bad society, lest they be infected by it.

For, owing to our corrupt nature, evil clings to us readily. The young must therefore be carefully shielded from all sources of corruption, such as evil society, evil conversation, and worthless books (for examples of vice, whether they make their entrance through the eyes or through the ears, are poison to the mind). And finally, sloth should be guarded against, lest through idleness the young be led to evil deeds or contract a tendency to indolence. The important thing is that they be kept continually employed either with work or with play. Idle- ness should never be permitted.

18. (xvi) Since it is impossible for us to be so watchful that nothing evil can find an entrance, stern discipline is necessary to keep evil tendencies in check.

For our enemy Satan is on the watch not only while we sleep, but also while we wake, and as we sow good seed in the minds of our pupils he contrives to plant his own weeds there as well, and sometimes a corrupt nature brings forth weeds of its own accord, so that these evil dispositions must be kept in check by force. We must therefore strive against them by means of discipline, that is to say, by using blame or punishment, words or blows, as the occasion demands. This punishment should always be administered on the spot, that the vice may be choked as soon as it shows itself, or may be, as far as is possible, torn up by the roots. Discipline, therefore, should ever be watchful, not with the view of enforcing application to study (for learning is always attractive to the mind, if it be treated by the right method), but to ensure cleanly morals.

But of discipline we will treat more particularly in chap. xxxi.

CHAPTER XXIV

THE METHOD OF INSTILLING PIETY

1. PIETY is the gift of God, and is given us from on high by our counsellor and guide, the Holy Spirit. But, since the Holy Spirit usually employs natural agencies, and has chosen parents, teachers, and ministers who should faithfully plant and water the grafts of Paradise (1 Cor. iii. 6-8), it is right that these should appreciate the extent of their duties.

2. We have already explained what we mean by piety, namely, that (after we have thoroughly grasped the conceptions of faith and of religion) our hearts should learn to seek God everywhere (since He has concealed Himself with His works as with a curtain, and, invisibly present in all visible things, directs all, though unseen), and that when we have found Him we should follow Him, and when we have attained Him should enjoy Him. The first we do through our understanding, the second through our will, and the third through the joy arising from the consciousness of our union with God.

3. We seek God by noticing the signs of His divinity in all things created. We follow God by giving ourselves up completely to His will, both to do and to suffer whatever shall have seemed good to Him. We enjoy God by so acquiescing in His love and favour that nothing in heaven or on earth appears to us more to be desired than God Himself, that nothing appears pleasanter to think of, and

nothing sweeter than to sing His praises; thus our hearts are joined to His in love.

4. The sources from which we can draw this exaltation are three, and the manner in which we can draw from them is threefold.

5. These sources are Holy Writ, the world, and ourselves. The first is the Word of God, the second is His handiwork, and the third is inspired by Him. There is no doubt that we can derive the knowledge and the love of God from the Scriptures. The very heathen testify that piety can be derived from the world and from the wise contemplation of the marvellous works of God contained in it; for they, by nothing but the contemplation of the world, were brought to revere the Godhead. This is shown by the examples of Socrates, Plato, Epictetus, Seneca, and others. But still, in the case of these men, to whom no special revelation from on high had been given, this feeling of love was imperfect, and wrongly directed. That those who seek to gain a knowledge of God from His word as well as from His works are filled with the deepest love for Him, is shown by the instances of Job, Elihu, David, and other pious men.

6. The manner of drawing piety from these sources is threefold: meditation, prayer, and examination.

"These three," says Luther, "make a theologian; but indeed they are essential to make a true Christian."

7. Meditation is the constant, attentive, and devoted consideration of the works, the words, and the goodness of God; the thoughtful acknowledgment that it is from the good-will of God alone (either active or permissive) that all things come, and that all the counsels of the divine will attain their end in the most marvellous ways.

8. Prayer is the frequent, or rather the continual, yearning after God, and the supplication that He may sustain us in His mercy and guide us with His Spirit.

9. Examination is the continual testing of our progress in piety, and may come from ourselves or from others. Under this head come human, devilish, and divine temptations. For men should examine themselves to see if they

are faithful, and do the will of God; and it is necessary that we should be tested by other men, by our friends, and by our enemies. This is the case when those who are set over others are vigilant and attentive, and, by open or by secret scrutiny, try to find out what progress has been made; or when God places an adversary by our side to teach us to find our refuge in Him, and to show us how strong our faith is. Finally, Satan himself is sent by God, or comes against us of his own accord, that the state of our hearts may be made evident.

These three modes, therefore, must be instilled into the Christian youth, that they may learn to raise their hearts to Him who is the first and the last of all things, and may seek rest for their souls in Him alone.

10. The special method is contained in twenty-one rules.

(i) Care should be taken to instil piety in early childhood.

For not to put off such instruction is advantageous, and to put it off is dangerous, since it is only reasonable to begin with what naturally comes first, and is the most important. But what is more important than piety? What else is profitable for all things, having promise of the life which now is, and of that which is to come? (1 Tim. iv. 8). This is the one thing needful (Luke x. 42), to seek the Kingdom of God, since all things shall be added to him who does so (Matt. vi. 33). To postpone this is hazardous, since, unless the mind be imbued with the love of God when young, it is easy for a silent contempt of the Godhead and for profanity to make their entrance, and when once they have done so, it is difficult, if not impossible, to dislodge them. Thus the prophet, complaining of the horrible impiety of his people, says that there are none left whom God can teach, save "them that are weaned from the milk and drawn from the breasts," that is to say, the young (Isaiah xxviii. 9), and another prophet says that it is impossible to convert to well-doing those that are accustomed to do evil (Jeremiah xiii. 23).

11. (ii) Therefore, as soon as children can use their eyes, their tongues, their hands, and their feet, let them learn to look towards heaven, to stretch their hands upwards, to utter the names of God and of Christ, to bend the knee before His unseen majesty, and to revere it.

It is not so difficult to teach these things to children as those imagine, who, not realising how important it is for us to tear ourselves away from Satan, from the world, and from ourselves, pay little consideration to a matter of such gravity. At first the children will not understand the true nature of what they are doing, since their intelligence is still weak ; but what is of importance is that they learn to do that which subsequent experience will teach them to be right. For, when they have got into the habit of acting as they should, it will be easier to explain to them why such conduct is good, and how it is best carried out. God has commanded to consecrate all first-fruits to Him ; why not, therefore, the first-fruits of our thoughts, of our utterances, of our movements, and of our actions ?

12. (iii) While it is still possible to influence boys, it is of great importance to impress upon them that we are not here for the sake of this life, but are destined for eternity ; that our life on earth is only transitory, and serves to prepare us for our eternal home.

This can easily be taught by the examples of infants, boys, youths, and old men who are daily snatched away by death. These facts should be diligently impressed on the young, that they may realise how very transitory our life on earth is.

13. (iv) They should also be taught that our only business on earth should be to prepare for the next world.

For it would be foolish to pay attention to those things which will be taken from us, and to neglect those things which will accompany us into eternity.

14. (v) They should then be taught that the life to which men go when they leave this earth, is twofold : either a blessed life with God, or a wretched one in hell, and that both are everlasting.

This may be demonstrated by the example of Lazarus and the rich man ; for the soul of the former was carried away by angels into heaven, while that of the latter was carried by devils into hell.

15. (vi) And that those are thrice happy, who order their conduct in such a way that they are found worthy to stand in God's presence.

For apart from God, the source of light and of life, there is nothing but darkness, terror, agony, and everlasting death that knows no end ; so that it were better that they had never been born, who stray from God and cast themselves into the pit of eternal destruction.

16. (vii) But that those who have communed with God on earth, will go to Him after death.

As did Enoch and Elias, both while living, and others also (Gen. v. 24).

17. (viii) That those commune with God who keep Him continually before their eyes, fear Him, and fulfil His word.

And that this is the whole duty of man (Eccles. xi. 13), to which Christ referred when He said, " There is but one thing needful " (Luke x. 42). This is what Christians should ever have on their lips and in their hearts, lest, like Martha, they be too much engrossed with the cares of this life.

18. (ix) They should, therefore, acquire the habit of referring to God all that they see, hear, touch, do, and endure on earth.

Instances of this should be given. Those, for instance (it may be pointed out), who devote themselves to letters and a life of contemplation, should do so with but one object in view, namely, that they may see in everything the power, the wisdom, and the goodness of God, that they may be filled with love for Him, and may unite themselves so fast to Him in love that they can never be torn away. Those, again, who are engaged in practical pursuits, such as agriculture or mechanics, these have to seek bread and the necessaries of life ; but they should do so merely that they may live in decent comfort, and should strive to live thus solely that they may be enabled to serve God with a quiet and cheerful spirit, and that, by serving Him and proving acceptable to Him, they may be united with Him eternally. Those who have other ends in view deviate from God's will and from God Himself.

19. (x) From the very outset they should learn to find their chief occupation in those things that lead directly to God: in reading the Scriptures, in religious ceremonies, and in other good works.

For the perusal of the Scriptures renews and fosters our acquaintance with God, religious ceremonies create a link between God and man, and good works strengthen this link, for they show that we really observe the Word of God. These three should be seriously commended to all who are destined to lead a Godly life (as are all the Christian youth, dedicated to God through baptism).

20. (xi) The Holy Scriptures must be the Alpha and the Omega of Christian schools.

Hyperius [31] said that a theologian was born of the Scriptures, and we may find this observation at greater length in the Apostle Peter, who says that the sons of God are born of incorruptible seed, through the Word of God that liveth and abideth (1 Peter i. 23).

In Christian schools, therefore, God's Book should rank before all other books; that, like Timothy, all the Christian youth may, from boyhood, know the sacred writings which are able to make them wise unto salvation (2 Tim. iii. 15), and may be nourished in the words of the faith (1 Tim. iv. 6). On this subject Erasmus has written well in his *Paraclesis, or Exhortation to the Study of Christian Philosophy.* "The Holy Scripture" (he says) "is equally suitable to all, is within the capacity of little ones, nourishes them with milk, cherishes them, sustains them, and does all for them until they grow up in Christ. But, while it can be comprehended by the lowest intelligences, it is none the less an object of wonder to the highest. There is no age, no sex, no rank of life to which it is unsuitable. The sun is not more the common property of mankind than is the teaching of Christ. It rejects none

save those who hold themselves at a distance." He continues, "Would that it were translated into all languages,
that it might be known by the Turks and the Saracens,
and by the Scotch and the Irish as well. Many would
mock, it is true, but some would be won over. Would
that the ploughman might sing it at his plough, that the
weaver might repeat it at his loom, that the traveller
might beguile the tedium of the journey by its sacred story,
and that the conversations of Christians were taken from
its pages; for our daily conversation represents our true
character. Let each one get and read as much of Holy
Writ as he can. Let him who is behind not envy him
who is in front. Let him who is in front beckon forward
him who is behind, and despise him not. Why do we
confine to a few the book that contains the faith of all ?"
And near the end, "May all whom we have dedicated to
Christ in baptism be imbued with His teaching while in
the arms of their parents and among the caresses of their
nurses. For that which the mind first drinks in, sinks
deepest and remains longest. Let our first babbling be of
Christ, and let our infancy be modelled upon His Evangelists, which should be set before boys in such a way that
they may like them. In these studies they should be
trained, until by a silent increase they develope into men,
whose strength is in Christ. Happy is he whom death
snatches away while engaged on this study. Let us all,
therefore, drink in God's Word with our whole hearts, let
us embrace it, let us die while occupied with it, let us be
converted into it, since our morals are so intimately connected with our studies." In his *Compendium of Theology*
also he says : "In my opinion, it would not be a waste of
time to learn the Holy Book off by heart, even though we
did not understand it, as says St. Augustine."

Christian schools, therefore, should resound not with
Plautus, not with Terence, not with Ovid, not with Aristotle, but with Moses, David, and Christ, and methods
should be devised by which the Bible may be given to
children dedicated to God (for all the children of Christians

are holy) (1 Cor. vii. 14) as a means of learning their A B C; for thus they would grow familiar with it. For as language is made up of the sounds and the symbols of letters, thus is the whole structure of religion and piety formed out of the elements of Holy Scripture.

21. (xii) Whatever is learned from Scripture should convey a lesson of faith, charity, and hope.

These are the three noblest dispositions, and to these everything that God has seen good to reveal to us in His Word has reference. For He reveals some things to us that we may believe them, others He commands us that we may do them, and others again He promises that we may expect them from His mercy, both in this and in the future world. In the whole Bible nothing occurs that cannot be brought under one of these heads. All, therefore, should be taught to understand and to read intelligently what God has revealed.

22. (xiii) Faith, charity, and hope should be taught for practical use.

From the very beginning it is necessary to form practical and not theoretical Christians, if we wish to form true Christians at all. For religion is a real thing and not a reflection of reality, and should prove its reality by the practical results that it produces, just as a seed that is planted in good earth soon germinates. Hence the Scripture requires a "working faith" (Gal. v. 6), calls faith apart from works "barren" (James ii. 20), and asks for a "living hope" (1 Peter i. 3). Hence the constant injunction, that things are revealed from on high that we should do them. Christ also says: "If ye know these things, blessed are ye if ye do them" (John xiii. 17).

23. (xiv) Faith, charity, and hope will be taught in a practical manner, if boys and all men are taught to believe implicitly in all that God reveals, to do all that He commands, and to expect all that He promises.

It should be carefully impressed on the young that, if they wish the Word of God to supply them with divine strength, they should bring to it a humble and devoted heart, prepared to submit itself to God on all occasions, and actually doing so at the time. The sunlight reveals nothing to him who refuses to open his eyes, nor can a banquet satisfy him who refuses to eat; and in the same way the divine light supplied to our minds, the rules given for our actions, and the happiness promised to those who fear God, are all in vain unless they are received with prompt faith, earnest charity, and firm hope. Thus Abraham, the father of the faithful, trusted the Word of God and believed things incredible to the reason; obeyed the commands of God, no matter how hard they were (when bidden leave his native land and sacrifice his son); and hoped for things that seemed impossible, trusting in the promises of God—which living and active faith was counted to him for righteousness. All, therefore, who devote themselves to God, should be taught to fulfil these duties in their own persons.

24. (xv) Whatever is taught to the young in addition to the Scriptures (sciences, arts, languages, etc.) should be taught as purely subordinate subjects. In this way it will be made evident to the pupils that all that does not relate to God and to the future life is nothing but vanity.

Socrates is praised by the ancients because he turned philosophy from its barren and thorny speculations and brought it to bear on the province of morals. The Apostles professed to recall Christians from the thorny questions of the law and to lead them to the sweet charity of Christ (1 Tim. i. 5 *seq.*), and in the same way many modern theologians urge us to leave confused controversies, that destroy the Church far more than they build it up, and to attend to our own consciences and the practice of piety. O that God would have pity on us, that we might find some universal method by which all that occupies the mind of man might be brought into relation with God, and that we might learn to convert the business of this life, in which all mankind is immersed, into a preparation for the life to come! This would, indeed, be a sacred ladder on which our minds might mount to the eternal protector of all things, to the source of true happiness.

25. (xvi) All should be taught to reverence God both inwardly and outwardly. For inward without outward reverence tends to grow faint, while outward without inward reverence degenerates into hypocrisy.

The outward worship of God consists in conversing about Him, in preaching and hearing His Word, in adoring Him on bended knee, in singing His praises in hymns, and in attending to the Sacraments and the other services of the Church, public and private. The inward worship of God consists of continual meditation on the divine presence, of fearing and loving God, of abnegation and resignation of self, and of the ready will to do or to suffer all that God desires. These two forms of worship must be joined together, and not torn asunder; not only because it is right that God should be glorified in our bodies and in our minds, which belong to Him (1 Cor. vi. 20), but also because they cannot be separated without danger. Outward ceremonies without inward truth are an abomination to God, who says: "Who demands these things from you?" (Isaiah i.), "for He is a spirit and must be worshipped in spirit and in truth" (John iv.) But, since we are not merely spirits but have bodies and senses as well, it is necessary for our senses to be outwardly stimulated, that we may inwardly do what is right in spirit and in truth. On this account God, though He lays more stress on inward worship, ordained outward ceremonies and wishes them to be observed. Christ freed the worship of the New Testament from ceremony and taught that God should be worshipped in spirit and in truth, yet He Himself bent His head when He prayed to His Father, and continued His prayer for nights together; used to attend religious meetings, heard and questioned the doctors of the law, preached the Word, and sang hymns. Therefore, when we educate the young, we should educate them thoroughly, externally and internally, since otherwise we may produce either hypocrites, that is to say, superficial, fraudulent, and false worshippers

of God, or fanatics, who delight in their own visions, and
through their contempt of outward form undermine the
Church, or, finally, lukewarm Christians, in whom the
stimulus of external or the reality of internal worship is
wanting.

26. (xvii) Boys should be carefully habituated to the
outward works which are commanded by God, that they may
know that it is true Christianity to express faith by works.

Such works are the exercise of temperance, justice,
pity, and patience, which should continually occupy our
attention. "For, unless our faith brings forth such fruit
it is manifestly dead" (James ii.) But it must be living if
it is to bring us salvation.

27. (xviii) They should also learn to distinguish carefully
the objects of the blessings and of the judgments of God,
that they may make a good use of them.

Fulgentius [32] (Letter II. to Gallas) divides the blessings of
God into three classes. According to him, some are to
last for ever, others are to help us to attain eternity, while
others are only for the use of this present life. Of the first
kind are the knowledge of God, the joy of the Holy Spirit,
and the love of God that fills our hearts. Of the second
kind are faith, hope, and compassion for our neighbours.
Of the third kind are health, riches, friends, and the other
external goods that of themselves make us neither happy
nor unhappy.

In the same way the judgments or chastisements of God
are of three kinds. Some (whom God wishes to spare in
the life everlasting) are seized on earth and are tortured
that they may be purified and whitened (Dan. xi. 35; Rev.
vii. 14), as was the case with Lazarus. Others are spared
here that they may be punished in eternity, as was the Rich
Man. While the punishments of others begin here and
are continued in eternity, as is the case with Saul,
Antiochus, Herod, Judas, etc.

Men, therefore, must be taught to distinguish all these
from one another, that they may not be deceived by the
good things of the flesh and give precedence to what is

transitory, that they may realise that present ills are less to be feared than hell-fire, and "that they should not fear those who can only kill the body and have no further power, but Him who can destroy the body and can also thrust the soul down to hell" (Luke xii.)

28. (xix) They should also be told that the safest path of life is the path of the Cross; that Christ the King of Life has trodden it before us, and invites to it and leads along it those whom He loves best.

The mystery of our salvation was consummated on the Cross and depends on the Cross; for by it the old Adam was slain that the new Adam, fashioned after God's image, might live. Those, therefore, whom God loves, He chastises and crucifies with Christ, that when they rise with Christ He may set them on His right hand in heaven. Now, though this lesson of the Cross tells the power of God to save those who believe, to the flesh it is foolishness and an offence (1 Cor. i. 18). It is therefore very necessary to teach this lesson to Christians with great care, that they may understand that they cannot be the disciples of Christ unless they deny themselves, bear the Cross of Christ on their shoulders (Luke xiv. 26), and are prepared throughout their whole lives to follow God wherever He may lead them.

29. (xx) Care must be taken that, while all this is being taught, no conflicting examples come in the way.

That is to say, the boys must not hear or see blasphemies, perjuries, or other acts of impiety, but, whichever way they turn, should encounter nothing but reverence for the Deity, observance of religion, and conscientiousness. Evil conduct, also, whether at home or at school, should always be severely punished, and, if the punishment for profanity be always greater than for offences against Priscian [33] or for other faults, it will be impressed upon them that the former error is the more important to guard against.

30. (xxi) In this corrupt state of the world and of human nature we never make as much progress as we ought, or, if we do advance, are filled with complacency and spiritual pride, through the depravity of our flesh.

Now this is a very great danger (for God resists the proud), and therefore all Christians should be taught in their youth that our endeavours and our works are of no avail, unless Christ, the Lamb of God who takes away the sins of the world, help us with His perfection. On Him we must call and Him we must trust.

We shall thus have finally placed the hope of our salvation in safety, when we have laid the burden on Christ, the corner-stone. For He is the culminating point of all perfection in heaven and on earth, and is the one and only originator and guardian of our faith, our charity, our hope, and our salvation. For this reason God sent Him from heaven that He might become Immanuel (or God in man) and unite all men in God, and that, living with purity in the life which He had assumed, He might give men the example of a divine life; that by His innocent death He might expiate the sins of the world in His person, and might wash us clean with His blood; that He might show His victory over death by His resurrection, and ascending into heaven might send the Holy Ghost, the pledge of our salvation; and that He might thus rule us and preserve us, and, finally, take us to Himself, that we may be with Him and see His glory.

31. Thus to the eternal Saviour of all men, with the Father and the Holy Ghost, be praise, and honour, and blessing, and glory, for evermore. Amen.

32. It remains to draw up a detailed method for the several classes.

CHAPTER XXV

IF WE WISH TO REFORM SCHOOLS IN ACCORDANCE WITH
THE LAWS OF TRUE CHRISTIANITY, WE MUST REMOVE
FROM THEM BOOKS WRITTEN BY PAGANS, OR, AT ANY
RATE, MUST USE THEM WITH MORE CAUTION THAN
HITHERTO.[34]

1. RESISTLESS necessity compels us to treat at length a
subject which we have touched on in the previous chapter.
If we wish our schools to be truly Christian schools, the
crowd of Pagan writers must be removed from them.
First, therefore, we will set forth the reasons which underlie
our views, and then the method of treating these ancient
writers so that, in spite of our caution, their beautiful
thoughts, sayings, and deeds may not be lost to us.

2. Our zeal in this matter is caused by our love of God
and of man; for we see that the chief schools profess
Christ in name only, but hold in highest esteem writers
like Terence, Plautus, Cicero, Ovid, Catullus, and Tibullus.
The result of this is that we know the world better than
we know Christ, and that, though in a Christian country,
Christians are hard to find. For with the most learned
men, even with theologians, the upholders of divine
wisdom, the external mask only is supplied by Christ,
while the spirit that pervades them is drawn from Aristotle
and the host of heathen writers. Now this is a terrible
abuse of Christian liberty, a shameless profanation, and a
course replete with danger.

3. Firstly, our children are born for heaven and are reborn through the Holy Ghost.   They must therefore be educated as citizens of heaven, and their chief instruction should be of heavenly things, of God, of Christ, of the angels, of Abraham, of Isaac, and of Jacob.   This instruction should take place before any other, and all other knowledge should be shielded from the pupil; firstly, because of the uncertainty of life, that no one may be snatched away unprepared, and secondly, because first impressions are the strongest, and (if they are religious impressions) lay a safe foundation for all that follows in life.

4. Secondly, God, though He made provision of every kind for His chosen people, gave them no school other than his own Temple, where He Himself was the Master, we were the pupils, and his oracles were the subject taught.   For thus He speaks by Moses: " Hear, O Israel, the Lord our God is one God: and thou shalt love the Lord thy God with all thine heart, and with all thy soul, and with all thy might.   And these words, which I command thee this day, shall be upon thine heart; and thou shalt teach them diligently unto thy children, and shalt talk of them when thou sittest in thine house, and when thou walkest by the way, and when thou liest down, and when thou risest up " (Deut. vi. 4).   And by Isaiah: " I am the Lord thy God, which teacheth thee to profit, which leadeth thee by the way that thou shouldst go " (xlviii. 17); and again, " Should not a people seek unto their God ? "   Christ also says: " Search ye the Scriptures " (John v. 39).

5. God has shown by the following words that His voice is the brightest light for our understanding, the most perfect law for our actions, and the surest support for our weakness.   " Behold, I have taught you statutes and judgments !   Keep therefore and do them; for this is your wisdom and your understanding in the sight of the peoples, which shall hear all these statutes and say: Surely this great nation is a wise and understanding

people" (Deut. iv. 5, 6). To Joshua, also, He speaks thus : "This book of the law shall not depart out of thy mouth, but thou shalt meditate therein day and night. For then thou shalt make thy way prosperous and thou shalt have good success" (Jos. i. 8). By David also He says: "The precepts of the Lord are right, rejoicing the heart: the commandment of the Lord is pure, enlightening the eyes" (Psalm xix. 8). Finally, the Apostle bears witness "that every scripture inspired of God is profitable for teaching, etc., that the man of God may be complete" (2 Tim. iii. 16, 17). The wisest of men (by this I mean truly enlightened Christians) have made the same assertion. Chrysostom has said : "What it is needful to know, and what it is not needful to know, *that* we can learn from the Scriptures." And Cassiodorus [35] says : "The Scriptures are a heavenly school, a guide through life, the only true source of information. To search for the true meaning of them should occupy the student's whole time, and leave him no leisure to be led astray by philology."

6. God expressly forbade His chosen people to have anything to do with the learning or the customs of the heathen : "Learn not the way of the nations" (Jer. x. 2); and again, "Is it because there is no God in Israel that ye go to inquire of Baalzebub the God of Ekron? (2 Kings i. 3); "Should not a people seek unto their God? on behalf of the living should they seek unto the dead? To the law and to the testimony! if they speak not according to this word, surely there is no morning for them" (Isaiah viii. 19, 20). And why? Surely because "all wisdom cometh from the Lord, and is with him for ever. To whom else hath the root of wisdom been revealed?" (Ecclesiasticus i. 1, 6); "Although they have seen light and dwelt on the earth, the way of knowledge have they not known. Nor understood the paths thereof, etc. It hath not been heard of in Chanaan, neither hath it been seen in Theman. The Agarenes that seek wisdom upon earth, the authors of fables and searchers out of understanding, have not known the way

of wisdom.   But he that knoweth all things knoweth it
and hath found out all the way of knowledge and hath
given it unto Jacob his servant and Israel his beloved"
(Baruch iii. 20, 21, 22, 23, 32, 36, 37); "He hath not
dealt so with any nation, and as for his judgments, they
have not known them" (Psalm cxlvii. 20).

7. Whenever His people went aside from His laws to
the snares of man's imagination, God used to blame not
only their folly in forsaking the fountain of wisdom (Baruch
iii. 12), but the twofold evil that they had committed,
in forsaking Him, the fountain of living waters, and hewing
them out broken cisterns that could hold no water (Jer.
ii. 13).   Through the agency of Hosea He complained
also that His people held too much intercourse with other
nations, saying: "Though I write for him my law in ten
thousand precepts, they are counted as a strange thing"
(Hos. viii. 12).   But, I ask, is not this what those
Christians are doing who hold heathen books in their
hands night and day, while of the sacred Word of God
they take no account, as if it did not concern them?
And yet, as God bears witness, it is no vain thing, but our
very life (Deut. xxxii. 47).

8. Therefore the true Church and the true worshippers
of God have sought for no teaching other than the Word
of God, from which they have drawn the true and heavenly
wisdom that is superior to all earthly knowledge.   Thus
David says of himself: "Thy commandments make me
wiser than mine enemies," and "I have more understanding than all my teachers, for thy testimonies are my
meditation" (Psalm cxix. 98, 99).   Similarly Solomon,
the wisest of mortals, confesses: "The Lord giveth
wisdom; out of his mouth cometh knowledge and understanding" (Prov. ii. 6).   The son of Sirach also testifies
(in the prologue to his book) that his wisdom is drawn
from the law and the prophets.   Hence the exultation of
the righteous when they see light in the light of God
(Psalm xxxvi. 9); "O Israel, happy are we: for things that
are pleasing to God are made known unto us" (Baruch

vi. 4). "Lord, to whom shall we go? thou hast the words of eternal life" (John vi. 68).

9. The examples of all ages show us that it has been an occasion for stumbling whenever the Church has turned aside from the fountain of Israel. Of the Jewish Church, sufficient is known from the lamentations of the Prophets. As regards the Christian Church, we learn from history that a pure faith lasted as long as the Gospel, and nothing else, was preached by the Apostles and their successors. But as soon as the heathen entered the Church in numbers, and the ardour that existed at first grew cold, pagan books were read, at first in private and then in public, and the result was a great confusion of doctrine. The key of knowledge was lost by the very men who boasted that they alone possessed it, and from that time opinions without number were substituted for the articles of faith. Then did strife arise, whose end is not yet visible; charity grew cold, and piety disappeared. And thus, under the name of Christendom, paganism came into existence again, and still reigns supreme. For the threat of the Lord Jehovah had to be fulfilled: "If they speak not according to the Word of God, surely there is no morning for them" (Isaiah viii. 20). "Therefore the Lord hath poured out upon them the spirit of sleep, and hath closed their eyes, that all vision might become unto them as the words of a book that is sealed," because they worshipped God in accordance with the teaching of man (Isaiah xxix. 10, 11, 13, 14). O, how truly in their case is fulfilled what the Holy Spirit says of the heathen philosophers: "They became vain in their reasonings, and their senseless heart was darkened" (Rom. i. 21). In short, if the Church is to be purified from uncleanness, there is only one way, and that is to put aside all the seductive teaching of man and return to the pure springs of Israel, and thus to give over ourselves and our children to the teaching and guidance of God and of His word. Thus at last will the prophecy come to pass, "And all thy children shall be taught of God" (Isaiah liv. 13).

10. Indeed our dignity as Christians (who have been made sons of God and heirs of the kingdom of heaven through Christ) does not permit us to degrade ourselves and our children by allowing them to have an intimate acquaintance with pagan writers, and to read them with such approval. We do not choose parasites, fools, or buffoons, but serious, wise, and pious men as tutors for the sons of our kings and princes. Should we not blush, therefore, when we confide the education of the sons of the King of Kings, of the brothers of Christ and heirs of eternity, to the jesting Plautus, the lascivious Catullus, the impure Ovid, that impious mocker at God, Lucian, the obscene Martial, and the rest of the writers who are ignorant of the true God? Those who, like them, live without the hope of a better life, and wallow in the mire of earthly existence, are certain to drag down to their own level whoever consorts with them. Christians, we have carried our folly far enough! Let us pause here. God calls us to better things, and it is good to obey His call. Christ, the eternal Wisdom of God, has opened a school for the sons of God in His own house; in which the supreme control is exercised by the Holy Spirit, and the professors and masters are the Prophets and the Apostles, all endowed with true wisdom, and all holy men, who, by their teaching and example, point out the way of truth and of salvation; where the pupils are the elect of God, the first-fruits of men, ransomed by God and by the Lamb; where the inspectors and guardians are the angels and archangels, the principalities and powers in heaven (Eph. iii. 10); and where true wisdom, which is of use to us in this world and the next, is taught on all subjects that the mind of man can grasp. For the mouth of God is the fountain from which all the streams of wisdom flow; the countenance of God is the torch from which the rays of true light are scattered; the Word of God is the root from which spring the shoots of true wisdom. Happy are they, therefore, who look on the face of God, listen to His words, and receive His sayings in their hearts. For this is the only

true and infallible way to attain the true and eternal wisdom.

11. Nor can we omit all mention of the earnestness with which God forbade His people to have anything to do with the works of the heathen, and of the consequences that followed their disregard of His injunction : " The Lord will consume those nations from thy sight. But the graven images of their gods shall ye burn with fire. Thou shalt not covet the silver or gold that is on them, nor take it unto thee, lest thou be snared therein, for it is an abomination to the Lord thy God ; and thou shalt not bring àn abomination into thine house, and become a devoted thing like unto it " (Deut. vii. 22, 25, 26). And again : "When the Lord thy God shall cut off the nations from before thee, take heed to thyself that thou be not ensnared to follow them, after that they be destroyed from before thee, and that thou inquire not after their gods, saying, How do these nations serve their gods ? But what thing soever I command you, that shall ye observe to do ; thou shalt not add thereto, nor diminish from it " (Deut. xii. 29). After their victory Joshua reminded them of this, and advised them to remove the idols (Jos. xxiv. 23) ; but they did not obey him, and these heathen productions became a snare for them, so that they continually fell into idolatry until both kingdoms were overthrown. Should not we, therefore, take warning by their example, and avoid their error ?

12. "But books are not idols," some one will say. I reply : They are the works of the heathen, whom God has destroyed from before the face of His Christian people, as He did of old. Nay, they are more dangerous than idols. For these only led away those who were fools at heart (Jer. x. 14), while books deceive even the wisest (Col. ii. 8). The former were works of men's hands (as God used to say when chiding the folly of the idolaters), the latter are the works of the human understanding. The former dazzled the eyes by the brilliancy of their gold and silver, the latter blind the intelligence by the plausibility of their

carnal wisdom.   Do you still deny that pagan books are
idols?   What was it that led the Emperor Julian away
from Christ?   What was it that so undermined the understanding of Pope Leo X. that he believed the history of
Christ to be 'a mere fable?   Under what influence did
Cardinal Bembo [36] dissuade Sadoleto from reading the
Bible (saying that such folly was unsuitable for so great a
man)?   What is it that in these days leads so many learned
Italians and others towards Atheism?   Would that there
were none in the reformed Church of Christ who have
been drawn away from the Scriptures by Cicero, Plautus,
and Ovid, writers that reek of death.

13. But it may be said : The abuse must be attributed
not to the things, but to the persons.   There are pious
Christians to whom no harm is done by reading pagan
authors.   The Apostle replies : "We know that no idol is
anything in the world : howbeit in all men there is not
that knowledge (that is to say, the power of discerning).
Take heed lest this liberty of yours become a stumbling-
block to the weak " (1 Cor. viii. 4, 7, 9).

Now God in His mercy preserves many from destruction,
and there is no excuse for us if, knowingly and willingly,
we have anything to do with such snares (I mean the
divers inventions of the human mind or of Satan's cunning), since it is certain that some, nay most men, are
unhinged by them and are led into Satan's net.   Let us
rather obey God and not bring idols into our house, nor
set up Dagon by the Ark of the Covenant, nor mingle the
wisdom that is from on high with that which is earthly,
bestial, and devilish, nor give any occasion for stirring up
the anger of God against our sons.

14. Of a precisely similar nature was the event that
Moses uses as an illustration.   Nadab and Abihu, the sons
of Aaron, and young priests (in ignorance of their duty),
filled their censers with common, instead of with sacred,
fire.   For this they were smitten with fire by God, and
died (Levit. x. 1).   Now what are the children of Christians
but a holy priesthood to offer up spiritual sacrifices to

God? (1 Peter ii. 5). If we fill their censers, their minds, with strange fire, are we not handing them over to the anger of God? For to a Christian soul all is strange, and should be strange, that has any other source than the Holy Spirit; and of such a kind are the ravings of the heathen philosophers and poets, as the Apostle bears witness (Rom. i. 21, 22; Col. ii. 8, 9). Not without reason did Jerome call poetry the wine of devils; since it intoxicates the incautious and sends them to sleep, and, while they sleep, plies them with monstrous opinions, dangerous temptations, and the foulest desires. We should therefore be on our guard against these philtres of Satan.

15. If we do not obey the wise counsels of God, the Ephesians will stand in judgment against us, for they, as soon as the light of divine wisdom shone upon them, burnt all their curious books, since these were henceforth useless to them as Christians (Acts xix. 19). The modern Greek Church also, although there exist the most excellent philosophical and poetical works, written by the Greeks of old, who were reputed the wisest of men, has forbidden its followers to read them under pain of excommunication. The result of this is that, although with the invasion of barbarism they have fallen into great ignorance and superstition, God has hitherto preserved them from being carried away by anti-Christian error. In this matter, therefore, we ought to imitate them, that (greater stress being laid on the reading of Scripture) the heathen darkness, which still remains, may be removed, and that in the light of God we may see light (Psalm xxxvi. 9). "O house of Jacob, come ye, and let us walk in the light of the Lord" (Isaiah ii. 5).

16. Let us now see by what reasonings the mind of man rebels against these injunctions, and winds about like a snake, seeking to avoid the necessity of obeying the Faith and serving God. The arguments used are as follows:

17. (i) Great wisdom is to be found in the philosophers, the orators and the poets. I answer: Those are worthy of darkness who turn away their eyes from the light. Twilight is as mid-day to the owl, but animals, that are

accustomed to light, think otherwise. O foolish men who look for light in the darkness of the human reason! Lift up your eyes on high. The true light comes from heaven, from the Father of Light! Any light that is visible in human efforts arises from a few sparks that seem to shine because of the darkness that surrounds them; but what are a few sparks to us, in whose hands a blazing torch has been placed (the effulgent word of God)? If men investigate natural phenomena, they do but set the glass to their lips, without touching the wine; while in the Scriptures the Ruler of the Universe Himself recounts the mysteries of His works, and explains the nature of things created, visible and invisible. When the philosophers talk of morals, they are like birds that have been caught with quicklime, for they make great efforts to move without making any advance. But the Scriptures contain true descriptions of the virtues, with keen exhortations that pierce to the marrow. When pagan writers wish to teach piety, they merely teach superstition, since they are not imbued with the true knowledge of God or of His will. "For, behold, darkness shall cover the earth, and gross darkness the peoples: but the Lord shall arise upon thee, and his glory shall be seen upon thee" (Isaiah lx. 2). Now the sons of light should be at liberty to journey to the sons of darkness, that, having seen what a difference there is, they may rejoice the more in the path of light, and may feel compassion for the darkness of their neighbours; but to wish to exalt their glimmer above our own light is intolerable, and an insult to God and to our souls. "Of what advantage is it," says Isidor,[37] "to be learned in human doctrine, and know nothing of divine? to follow perishable inventions, and despise heavenly mysteries? If we love the Scriptures we must avoid those books that outwardly are eloquent and well written, but inwardly lack wisdom." What a condemnation of such books! They are husks without kernels. Such was also the opinion of Philip Melanchthon: "What do the best philosophers teach but self-confidence and self-love? Cicero in his *De Finibus* estimates each kind of virtue with reference to self-love. How much pride and haughtiness there is in Plato! It seems to me that a self-sufficient character must inevitably imbibe faulty instincts from the ambition that pervades his writings. The teaching of Aristotle is nothing but one long struggle to prove himself worthy of a good place among the writers on practical philosophy" (*System of Theology*).

18. (ii) Again it is said: If they do not teach theology rightly, at any rate they teach philosophy, and this cannot be learned from the sacred writings, that have been given us for our salvation. I answer: The Word of God most high is the fountain of wisdom (Ecclesiasticus i. 5). True philosophy is nothing but the true knowledge of God and of His works, and this cannot be learned better than from the mouth of God Himself. For this reason St. Augustine, praising the Holy Scripture, says: "Here is philosophy, since the cause of everything that exists is in the Creator. Here are ethics, since a good and honest life can only be formed if those things are loved which ought to be loved, that is to say, God and our neighbour. Here is logic, since truth, the light of the rational soul, is God Himself. Herein is the salvation of the state; for the state can never be well guarded, or rest on a foundation of confidence and peace, unless the common good be loved, and this, in its highest and truest sense, is God." Recently, too, it has been pointed out by many that the foundations of all the sciences and philosophic arts are contained in Scripture, and more truly than elsewhere, so that the part played by the Holy Spirit in our education is indeed wonderful. For, though its first object is to instruct us in things invisible and eternal, it nevertheless unfolds the laws of nature and of art at the same time, teaching us how to reason wisely on all subjects and how to apply our reason in a practical manner. Yet of all this there is but a trace in the works of the pagan philosophers. A writer on theology has said that the marvellous wisdom of Solomon consisted in bringing the law of God into the families, the schools, and the public places,

and there is no reason why the wisdom of Solomon, that is to say, true and heavenly wisdom, should not once more be ours, if we give our children the Word of God instead of pagan books, and thus supply them with counsels for all the chances of life.   Our object, therefore, should be to have in our homes that which can make us wise, even in that external or worldly wisdom that we call philosophy.   Those were luckless times when the children of Israel had to go down to the Philistines to polish each man his plough, his mattock or his axe, because there was no smith in the land of the Israelites (1 Sam. xiii. 19, 20).   But it is surely not necessary that the resources of the Israelites should always be limited in this way; especially as the arrangement was a bad one, for the following reason: the Philistines supplied the Israelites with harrows, but on no account would they supply them with swords that might be used against themselves.   From the pagan philosophers, in the same way, you can get the well-known syllogisms and flowers of speech, but from this source you will find it impossible to procure swords and spears with which to combat impiety and superstition.   Let us then hope for the times of David and of Solomon, when the Philistines were laid low but Israel reigned and rejoiced in its good fortune.

19. (iii) But, for the sake of style, students of Latin should read Terence, Plautus, and similar writers. I answer: Are we to bring our children into ale-houses, cook-shops, taverns, and other dens of iniquity, in order that they may learn how to speak?   For, I ask you, is it not into such unclean places that Terence, Plautus, Catullus, Ovid, and the rest of them lead our young?   What do they set before them but jesting, feasting, drunkenness, amours, and deceits, from which Christians should avert their eyes and ears, even if they encounter them by chance?   Is the natural man not depraved enough, that it is necessary to bring to him and to show to him all manner of wickedness, and, as it were, to seek out opportunities to hurl him to destruction?   But it will be said: "The matter in those authors is not all bad."   I answer: Evil sticks far more

readily than good, and it is therefore a very dangerous practice to send the young to a spot where good and evil occur in combination. If we wish to poison any one, we do not give him poison alone, but mix it with some pleasant drink, the presence of which does not interfere with the action of the poison. This is precisely the way in which these men-destroyers of old mixed their hellish poisons with cunning inventions and with elegance of style; and are we to remain conscious of their devices and not strike the potion from their hands?

Some one else may object: "They are not all lascivious writers. Cicero, Virgil, Horace, and others are serious and earnest." I answer: None the less they are blind pagans, and turn the minds of their readers from the true God to other gods and goddesses (Jove, Mars, Neptune, Venus, Fortune, etc.), though God has said to His people: "Make no mention of the name of other gods, neither let it be heard out of thy mouth" (Exodus xxiii. 13). Then what a chaos of superstitions, of false opinions, of earthly desires at variance with one another, is to be found in these writers! The spirit with which they fill their readers must be very different from that of Christ. Christ calls us from the world, they plunge us into the world. Christ teaches self-abnegation, they teach self-love. Christ teaches us to be humble, they to be magnanimous. Christ demands meekness, they inculcate self-assertion. Christ bids us be simple as doves, they show us how to turn an argument in a thousand different ways. Christ urges us to modesty, they spend their time in mocking others. Christ loves those who believe easily, they prefer those who are suspicious, argumentative, and obstinate. To conclude briefly and in the words of the Apostle: "What communion hath light with darkness? and what concord hath Christ with Belial? or what portion hath a believer with an unbeliever?" (2 Cor. vi. 15). Rightly does Erasmus say: "Bees avoid withered flowers; and no book, the contents of which are impure, should be opened." And again: "It is safest to sleep on clover, for it is said that no serpents lurk in it, and on the same principle we should confine ourselves to those books in which no poison is to be feared."

20. Moreover, what attraction have these pagan authors that is not to be found in our sacred writers? Are they the only people who understand the elegances of style? The most perfect master of language is he who gave it to us, the Holy Spirit. His words are sweeter than honey and more piercing than a two-edged sword; more active than the fire that liquefies metals, and weightier than a hammer which grinds rocks to powder, for they tell us of God. Is it heathen writers alone who relate marvellous events? Our Scriptures are full of events that are truer and far more wonderful. Are they the only authors who can fashion figures of speech, and riddling sayings, or write passages that are forcible and pithy? Our Scriptures are full of such passages. Leprous is his imagination who prefers Abana and Pharphar, rivers of Damascus, to Jordan and the waters of Israel (2 Kings v. 12). Blind is the eye to which Olympus, Helicon, and Parnassus seem more beautiful than Sinai, Sion, Hermon, Tabor, and Olivet. Deaf is the ear to which the lyre of Orpheus, of Homer, or of Virgil sounds sweeter than David's lute. Corrupt is the palate to which Nectar, Ambrosia, and the Castalian springs taste better than celestial Manna and the fountains of Israel. Perverse is the heart that finds more pleasure in the names of the gods, the goddesses, the muses, and the graces than in the adorable names of Jehovah, of Christ the Saviour, and of the Holy Ghost. Blind is the hope that wanders through the Elysian fields in preference to the gardens of Paradise. With them all is romance, a mere shadow of truth, while with us all is reality and the very essence of truth.

21. But it will be said: These writers contain elegances of speech and moral sentiments that are worthy of our adoption. Is not this a sufficient reason for sending our children to them? Should we not spoil the Egyptians

and strip them of their raiment?   Does not God bid us do so? (Exodus iii. 22).   It is the right of the Church to usurp all the possessions of the heathen.   I answer: When Manasseh and Ephraim wished to seize the land of the heathen, the men alone advanced; the women and children stayed behind in safety (Joshua i. 14). We should do the same.   Men of wisdom and judgment, steadfast in the faith, should go forward and disarm these pagan writers; the young should not be exposed to danger.   What if our youths were killed or wounded or taken prisoner?   How many, alas, has pagan philosophy already drawn away from Christ and given over to Atheism!   The safest plan, therefore, is to send armed men to deprive those accursed by heaven of their gold, silver, and precious things, and to distribute them among the heirs of God.   O that God would stir up some heroic spirit to cull those flowers of elegance from the vast deserts in which they grow, and plant them in the garden of Christian philosophy, that nothing be lacking there.

22. Finally, if any pagan writers are to be countenanced, let them be Seneca, Epictetus, Plato, and similar teachers of virtue and honesty; since in these comparatively little error and superstition are to be found.   This was the opinion of the great Erasmus, who advised that the Christian youth be brought up on the Holy Scriptures, but added: "If they have anything to do with profane literature, let it be with those books that approximate most closely to the Scriptures" (*Compendium of Theology*).   But even these books should not be given to the young until their Christian faith is well assured; and in any case careful editions should be issued in which the names of the gods and the general tone of superstition should be removed.   For it is on the condition that their heads be shaved and their nails pared, that God allows heathen maidens to be taken to wife (Deut. xxi. 12).   Let there be no misunderstanding.   We do not absolutely prohibit Christians from reading heathen writings, since to those who believe Christ has given the power of taking up serpents, and drinking deadly things

with impunity (Mark xvi. 18); but the sons of God, whose faith is yet weak, should not be exposed to these serpents, and to give them the opportunity of drinking such poison would indeed be rash. Great caution should therefore be used, and this is what we urge. The Spirit of Christ has said that the children of God should be nourished by the spiritual milk that is without guile (1 Peter ii. 2 ; 2 Tim. iii. 15).

23. But those who thus incautiously aid the cause of Satan and oppose that of Christ have yet another argument. "The Holy Scriptures," they say, "are too hard for the young, and therefore some other books must be given them to read until their judgment is mature."

I answer : This is the language of those who err and know not the Scriptures nor the power of God, as I will show in three ways : firstly, there is a well-known story told of Timotheus the celebrated musician, that whenever he took a fresh pupil he asked him if he had already learned the rudiments with another master. If he answered in the negative he took him at a moderate price ; if in the affirmative he charged twice as much. For he said that those who had already learned give him twice as much trouble, as he had first to cure them of their bad habits, and then to teach them the right way to play. Now, our master, and that of the human race, is Jesus Christ, and we are forbidden to go to any other (Matt. xvii. 5, and xxiii. 8). He it was who said : "Suffer the little children to come unto me, and forbid them not " (Mark x. 14), and shall we, contrary to His will, lead them elsewhere ? Are we afraid that Christ's task will be too light, and that He will teach them His ways too easily ? And are we therefore to take them through the cook-shops and taverns, and give them to Christ to reform when thoroughly corrupt ? This is a terrible proposal for the unhappy and innocent boys ; for either they will have to spend their whole lives in laboriously getting rid of the habits they have acquired, or they will be altogether rejected by Christ, and given over to the tuition of Satan. Is not that which has been consecrated to Moloch an abomination to God? Let the Christian magistrates and the heads of the Churches—by God's mercy I implore it—take steps to prevent Christian boys, born in Christ and consecrated through baptism, from being offered up to Moloch.

24. The cry that the Scriptures are too difficult to be understood by children, is altogether false. Does God not know how to suit His Word to our understanding? (Deut. xxxi. 11, 12, 13). Does not David say that the law of the Lord gives wisdom to little ones (N.B. *to little ones*)? Does not Peter say that the Word of God is milk for the newborn babes of God, given to them that they may grow thereby unto salvation (1 Peter ii. 2)? The Word of God, therefore, is the sweetest and best milk for the new-born children of God. Why oppose God on this point? Especially since pagan learning needs teeth to masticate it; yes, and often breaks them. Therefore the Holy Spirit, through David, invites the little ones into His school: "Come, ye children, hearken unto me; I will teach you the fear of the Lord" (Psalm xxxiv. 11).

25. Lastly, that the Scriptures contain passages of great profundity is perfectly true; but they are of such a kind that, while elephants sink to the bottom, lambs can swim with ease in them, to quote the words of St. Augustine when he wished to lay stress on the difference between the wise of the world who rush into Scriptural criticism presumptuously and Christ's little ones who approach God's Word in a humble and meek spirit. Besides, what need is there to begin with difficult passages? We can proceed step by step. First, we should embark upon the Catechism, and then keep in shallow water by teaching Scripture history, moral sentences, and the like, that can be easily understood, but which at the same time lead to the weightier matters that follow. And finally, when our pupils are fit for it, we can introduce them to the mysteries of the Faith. Thus, knowing the sacred writings from their infancy, they will be the more easily preserved from worldly corruption, and will be made wise unto salvation through

faith which is in Christ Jesus (2 Tim. iii. 15). For, if a man give himself up to God, sit at the feet of Christ, and listen to the wisdom that comes from on high, it is impossible that the Spirit of Grace should not fill him, kindle within him the light of true reason, and point out the true path of salvation.

26. I pass over the fact that those authors who are placed before Christian boys instead of the Bible (Terence, Cicero, Virgil, etc.), possess the very defects that are attributed to the Scriptures, since they are difficult and not suited to the young. It was not for boys that they wrote, but for men of mature judgment, accustomed to the theatre and the law-courts, and it therefore goes without saying that they can be of no advantage to any one else. One thing at any rate is certain, that he who has reached man's estate will derive more profit from reading Cicero once than if he had learned his entire works off by heart when a boy, and that such studies should therefore be deferred to a suitable season, and then only approached by those to whom they will be of use, if indeed they are of use to any one.

Of far greater importance is the point that has already been mentioned, namely, that the task of Christian schools is to form citizens, not for the world, but for heaven, and that they should accordingly be supplied with masters who are better acquainted with heavenly than with earthly things.

27. Let us conclude, therefore, with the angelic words: "In the place wherein the highest beginneth to show his city, there can no man's building be able to stand" (2 Esdras x. 54). As God wishes us to be trees of righteousness, the planting of the Lord, that He may be glorified (Isaiah lxi. 3), we should not allow our children to be shrubs in the plantation of Aristotle, or of Plato, or of Plautus, or of Cicero, or of any author whose works they may chance to read: "Every plant, which my heavenly Father planted not, shall be rooted up" (Matt. xv. 13); "Tremble therefore, ye who cease not to murmur, and to exalt yourselves against the knowledge of God" (2 Cor. x. 5).

CHAPTER XXVI

OF SCHOOL DISCIPLINE

1. THERE is a proverb in Bohemia, "A school without discipline is like a mill without water," and this is very true.
For, if you withdraw the water from a mill, it stops, and,
in the same way, if you deprive a school of discipline, you
take away from it its motive power. A field also, if it be
never ploughed, produces nothing but weeds; and trees,
if not continually pruned, revert to their wild state and
bear no fruit. It must not be thought, however, that we
wish our schools to resound with shrieks and with blows.
What we demand is vigilance and attention on the part of
the master and of the pupils. For discipline is nothing
but an unfailing method by which we may make our
scholars, scholars in reality.

2. As regards discipline, therefore, it is advisable that
the educator of youth know its object, its subject-matter,
and the various forms which it may assume, since he will
then know why, when, and how, systematised severity is
to be used.

3. We may start with the incontestable proposition that
punishment should be employed towards those who err.
But it is not because they have erred that they should be
punished (for what has been done cannot be undone), but
in order that they may not err again in the future. Discipline should therefore be free from personal elements,
such as anger or dislike, and should be exercised with such

26

frankness and sincerity of purpose, that even the pupils may feel that the action taken is for their good, and that those set over them are but exercising paternal authority. They will thus regard it in the same light as a bitter draught prescribed for them by the doctor.

4. Now no discipline of a severe kind should be exercised in connection with studies or literary exercises, but only where questions of morality are at stake. For, as we have already shown, studies, if they are properly organised, form in themselves a sufficient attraction, and entice all (with the exception of monstrosities) by their inherent pleasantness. If this be not the case, the fault lies, not with the pupil, but with the master, and, if our skill is unable to make an impression on the understanding, our blows will have no effect. Indeed, by any application of force we are far more likely to produce a distaste for letters than a love for them. Whenever, therefore, we see that a mind is diseased and dislikes study, we should try to remove its indisposition by gentle remedies, but should on no account employ violent ones. The very sun in the heavens gives us a lesson on this point. In early spring, when plants are young and tender, he does not scorch them, but warms and invigorates them by slow degrees, not putting forth his full heat until they are full-grown and bring forth fruit and seeds. The gardener proceeds on the same principle, and does not apply the pruning-knife to plants that are immature. In the same way a musician does not strike his lyre a blow with his fist or with a stick, nor does he throw it against the wall, because it produces a discordant sound ; but, setting to work on scientific principles, he tunes it and gets it into order. Just such a skilful and sympathetic treatment is necessary to instil a love of learning into the minds of our pupils, and any other procedure will only convert their idleness into antipathy and their lack of interest into downright stupidity.

5. If, however, some stimulus be found necessary, better means than blows can be found. Sometimes a few severe words or a reprimand before the whole class is very effica-

cious, while sometimes a little praise bestowed on the others has great effect. "See how well so-and-so attends! See how quickly he sees each point! While you sit there like a stone!" It is often of use to laugh at the backward ones. "You silly fellow, can't you understand such a simple matter?" Weekly, or at any rate monthly, contests for the first place in class may also be introduced, as we have shown elsewhere. Great care, however, should be taken that these experiments do not degenerate into a mere amusement, and thus lose their force; since, if they are to act as a stimulus to industry, they must be backed on the part of the pupil by a love of praise and a dislike of blame or of losing his place in class. It is therefore absolutely essential that the master be always in the room, that he throw a good deal of energy into his work, and that he scold the idlers and praise the hard-working boys before the whole class.

6. Only in the case of moral delinquencies may a severer discipline be used: (1) as, for instance, in the case of impiety of any kind, such as blasphemy, obscenity, or any other open offence against God's law. (2) In the case of stubbornness and premeditated misbehaviour, such as disobeying the master's orders, or the conscious neglect of duty. (3) In the case of pride and disdain, or even of envy and idleness; as, for example, if a boy refuse to give a schoolfellow assistance when asked to do so.

7. For offences of the first kind are an insult to God's majesty. Those of the second kind undermine the foundation of all virtue, namely, humility and obedience. While those of the third kind prevent any rapid progress in studies. An offence against God is a crime, and should be expiated by an extremely severe punishment. An offence against man is iniquitous, and such a tendency should be promptly and sternly corrected. But an offence against Priscian is a stain that may be wiped out by the sponge of blame. In a word, the object of discipline should be to stir us up to revere God, to assist our neighbours, and to perform the labours and duties of life with alacrity.

8. The sun in the heavens teaches us the best form of discipline, since to all things that grow it ministers (1) light and heat, continuously; (2) rain and wind, frequently; (3) lightning and thunder, but seldom; although these latter are not wholly without their use.

9. It is by imitating this that the master should try to keep his pupils up to their work.

(1) He should give them frequent examples of the conduct that they should try to imitate, and should point to himself as a living example. Unless he does this, all his work will be in vain.

(2) He may employ advice, exhortation, and sometimes blame, but should take great care to make his motive clear and to show unmistakably that his actions are based on paternal affection, and are destined to build up the characters of his pupils and not to crush them. Unless the pupil understands this and is fully persuaded of it, he will despise all discipline and will deliberately resist it.

(3) Finally, if some characters are unaffected by gentle methods, recourse must be had to more violent ones, and every means should be tried before any pupil is pronounced impossible to teach. Without doubt there are many to whom the proverb, "Beating is the only thing that improves a Phrygian," applies with great force. And it is certain that, even if such measures do not produce any great effect on the boy who is punished, they act as a great stimulus to the others by inspiring them with fear. We should take great care, however, not to use these extreme measures too readily, or too zealously, as, if we do, we may exhaust all our resources before the extreme case of insubordination which they were intended to meet, arises.

10. In short, the object of discipline should be to confirm those who are being trained up for God and for the Church, in that disposition which God demands in His sons, the pupils in the school of Christ, so that they may rejoice with trembling (Psalm ii. 11), and looking to their own salvation may rejoice always in the Lord (Phil. ii. 4 and 10),

that is to say, that they may love and reverence their masters, and not merely allow themselves to be led in the right direction, but actually tend towards it of their own accord.

This training of the character can only be accomplished in the above-mentioned ways : by good example, by gentle words, and by continually taking a sincere and undisguised interest in the pupil. Sudden bursts of anger should only be used in exceptional circumstances, and then with the intention that renewed good feeling shall be the result.

11. For (to give one more example) did any one ever see a goldsmith produce a work of art by the use of the hammer alone? Never. It is easier to cast such things than to beat them out, and, if any excrescence have to be removed, it is not by violent blows that the artificer gets rid of it, but by a series of gentle taps, or by means of a file or a pair of forceps ; while he completes the operation by polishing and smoothing his work. And do we believe that irrational force will enable us to produce intelligent beings, images of the living God ?

12. A fisherman, too, who catches fish in deep waters with a drag-net, not only fastens on pieces of lead to sink it, but also attaches corks to the other end of it, that it may rise to the surface of the water. In the same way whoever wishes to ensnare the young in the nets of virtue, must, on the one hand, humble and abase them by severity, and, on the other, exalt them by gentleness and affection. Happy are the masters who can combine these two extremes ! Happy are the boys who find such masters !

13. Here we may quote the opinion which that great man, Eilhard Lubinus, doctor of theology, has expressed on the reform of schools in the preface to his edition of the New Testament in Greek, Latin, and German—

"The second point is this: the young should never be compelled to do anything, but their tasks should be of such a kind and should be set them in such a way that they will do them of their own accord, and take pleasure in them. I am therefore of opinion that rods and blows, those weapons of slavery, are quite unsuitable to freemen, and should never be used in schools, but should be reserved for boys of an abnormal and servile disposition. Such boys are easily recognised and must be removed from the school at once, on account both of the sluggishness of their disposition and of the depravity that is generally found in conjunction with it. Besides, any knowledge that they may acquire will be employed for wicked purposes, and will be like a sword in the hands of a madman. There are, however, other kinds of punishment suitable for boys who are free-born and of normal disposition, and these we may employ."

CHAPTER XXVII

OF THE FOURFOLD DIVISION OF SCHOOLS, BASED ON AGE
AND ACQUIREMENTS

1. ARTISANS are accustomed to fix certain limits of time for
the training of an apprentice (two, three, or seven years),
according to the ease or difficulty of the trade. Within
these limits a complete training can be had, and those
apprentices who have completed the course become,
first, journeymen, and then master-workmen. The same
system must be adopted in school organisation, and
distinct periods of time must be mapped out for the
acquirement of arts, sciences, and languages respectively.
In this way we may cover the whole range of human
knowledge within a certain number of years, and may
possess true learning, true morality, and true piety by the
time we leave the forging-places of humanity.

2. In order that this goal may be reached, the whole
period of youth must be devoted to the cultivation of the
intellect (and by this we do not mean that one art only,
but that all the liberal arts and all the sciences should
be acquired). The process should begin in infancy and
should continue until the age of manhood is reached; and
this space of twenty-four years should be divided into well-
defined periods. In this we must follow the lead of
nature. For experience shows that a man's body continues to grow up to his twenty-fifth year, and that after
this it only increases in strength; and we must conclude

that this slow rate of increase has been accorded to man by the forethought of God (for the larger bodies of animals attain their full growth in a few months, or in a couple of years at most) that he may have the more time to prepare himself for the duties of life.

3. The whole period, therefore, must be divided into four distinct grades: infancy, childhood, boyhood, and youth, and to each grade six years and a special school should be assigned.

I. For infancy		The mother's knee.
II. For childhood	the school	The Vernacular-School.
III. For boyhood	should be	The Latin-School or Gymnasium.
IV. For youth		The University and travel.

A Mother-School should exist in every house, a Vernacular-School in every hamlet and village, a Gymnasium in every city, and a University in every kingdom or in every province.

4. These different schools are not to deal with different subjects, but should treat the same subjects in different ways, giving instruction in all that can produce true men, true Christians, and true scholars; throughout graduating the instruction to the age of the pupil and the knowledge that he already possesses. For, according to the laws of this natural method, the various branches of study should not be separated, but should be taught simultaneously, just as the various parts of a tree increase together at every period of its growth.

5. The difference between these schools is threefold. Firstly, in the earlier schools everything is taught in a general and undefined manner, while in those that follow the information is particularised and exact; just as a tree puts forth more branches and shoots each successive year, and grows stronger and more fruitful.

6. Secondly, in the Mother-School the external senses should be exercised and taught to distinguish the objects that surround them. In the Vernacular-School, the internal senses, the imagination and the memory, in combination

with their cognate organs, should be trained, and this by reading, writing, painting, singing, counting, measuring, weighing, and committing various things to memory. In the Latin-School the pupil should be trained to understand and pass judgment on the information collected by the senses, and this by means of dialectic, grammar, rhetoric, and the other sciences and arts that are based on principles of causation. Finally, to the University belong those subjects that have special relation to the will, namely, the faculties, of which theology teaches us to restore harmony to the soul; philosophy, to the mind; medicine, to the vital functions of the body; and jurisprudence, to our external affairs.

7. Our faculties are best developed in the following manner. The objects should first be placed before the organs of sense on which they act. Then the internal senses should acquire the habit of expressing in their turn the images that result from the external sensation, both internally by means of the faculty of recollection, and externally with the hand and tongue. At this stage the mind can begin to operate, and, by the processes of exact thought, can compare and estimate all objects of knowledge. In this way an acquaintance with nature and a sound judgment may be obtained. Last of all, the will (which is the guiding principle in man) makes its power felt in all directions. To attempt to cultivate the will before the intellect (or the intellect before the imagination, or the imagination before the faculty of sense perception) is mere waste of time. But this is what those do who teach boys logic, poetry, rhetoric, and ethics before they are thoroughly acquainted with the objects that surround them. It would be equally sensible to teach boys of two years old to dance, though they can scarcely walk. Let our maxim be to follow the lead of nature in all things, to observe how the faculties develope one after the other, and to base our method on this principle of succession.

8. A third difference between the schools is this. The Mother-School and the Vernacular-School embrace all the

young of both sexes. The Latin-School gives a more thorough education to those who aspire higher than the workshop; while the University trains up the teachers and learned men of the future, that our churches, schools, and states may never lack suitable leaders.

9. These four classes of schools may be compared to the four seasons of the year. The Mother-School recalls the gentle spring, filled with the varied scent of flowers. The Vernacular-School represents the summer that spreads before our eyes its full ears and early fruit. The Latin-School corresponds to autumn, for here the fruit in the fields and vineyards is collected and stored away in the granaries of our mind. And last of all, the University may be compared to the winter, when we prepare for various uses the fruit already collected, that we may have sufficient to sustain us for the rest of our lives.

10. Our method of education may also be compared to the various stages in the growth of a tree. The boys who are six years of age and are tenderly cared for by their parents are like shoots that have been carefully planted, have taken root, and are beginning to put forth buds. At twelve years of age they are like a young tree that is covered with branches and buds, though it is as yet uncertain how these will develope. At eighteen years of age, youths well instructed in languages and arts are like trees covered with blossoms that are pleasant to see and to smell, and at the same time give promise of fruit. And finally, at twenty-four or twenty-five years of age, young men, who have been thoroughly educated at a university, resemble a tree covered with fruit that can be plucked and used when it is required.

But we must now examine the several stages in detail.

CHAPTER XXVIII

SKETCH OF THE MOTHER-SCHOOL

1. It is when it first comes into being that a tree puts forth the shoots that are later on to be its principal branches, and it is in this first school that we must plant in a man the seeds of all the knowledge with which we wish him to be equipped in his journey through life. A brief survey of the whole of knowledge will show the possibility of this, and this survey can easily be made if we bring everything under twenty headings.

2. (i) Metaphysic (as it is called) should certainly be our starting-point, since the first conceptions that children have are general and confused. They see, hear, taste, and touch, but are ignorant of the exact object of their sensations. They commence, therefore, by learning the general concepts: something, nothing, it is, it is not, thus, otherwise, where, when, like, unlike, etc., and these are nothing but the prime concepts of metaphysic.

3. (ii) In physics, a boy, during the first six years of his life, can be brought to know what are water, earth, air, fire, rain, snow, frost, stone, iron, trees, grass, birds, fishes, oxen, etc. He may also learn the names and uses of the members of his body, or at any rate of the external ones. At this age these things are easily learned, and pave the way for natural science.

4. (iii) A boy learns the elements of optics when he begins to distinguish and to call by their names light, dark-

ness, and shade, and to know the difference between the principal colours, white, black, red, etc.

5. (iv) The rudiments of astronomy will consist in knowing what is meant by the heavens, the sun, the moon, and the stars, and in watching their rising and their setting daily.

6. (v) We know the elements of geography when we learn the nature of mountains, valleys, plains, rivers, villages, citadels, or states, according to the situation of the place in which we are brought up.

7. (vi) The basis of chronology is laid, if the boy understand what is meant by an hour, a day, a week, or a year; or what summer and winter are; or the signification of the terms "yesterday," "the day before yesterday," "to-morrow," "the day after to-morrow," etc.

8. (vii) The commencement of history consists in recollecting and reporting what has recently happened, or how this or that person has carried out this or that matter; though this exercise should only relate to some incident in the child's life.

9. (viii) The seeds of arithmetic will be planted if the child understand what is meant by "much" and "little," can count up to ten, can see that three are more than two, and that one added to three makes four.

10. (ix) He will possess the elements of geometry if he know what we mean by "large" and "small," "long" and "short," "broad" and "narrow," "thick" and "thin"; what we signify by a line, a cross, or a circle, and how we measure objects in feet and yards.

11. (x) The elements of statics will have been learned if the children see objects weighed in scales, or acquire the power of telling the approximate weight of objects by weighing them in their hands.

12. (xi) They will receive a training in mechanics if they are permitted or are actually taught to employ their hands continually; for instance, to move something from one place to another, to arrange something else in one way or another, to construct something, or to pull something to

pieces, to make knots or to undo them, and so forth; the very things that children of this age love to do. As these actions are nothing but the efforts of an active mind to realise itself in mechanical production, they should not be hindered, but rather encouraged and skilfully guided.

13. (xii) The elements of the process of reasoning, namely dialectic, are learned when the child observes that conversations are carried on by means of question and answer, and himself acquires the habit of asking and answering questions. He should, however, be taught to ask sensible questions and to give direct answers, and also not to wander from the point at issue.

14. (xiii) The grammar of childhood consists in learning to speak the mother-tongue correctly, that is to say, in pronouncing with distinctness the letters, syllables, and words.

15. (xiv) The beginnings of rhetoric consist in imitating the figures of speech that occur in family conversation, but more especially in the appropriate use of gesture, and in inflecting the voice so as to suit the words; that is to say, the voice should be raised on the last syllables of words, in asking questions, and lowered in answering them. This and similar points are acquired naturally, but a little instruction is of great assistance if any mistakes are made.

16. (xv) Children may get some notion of poetry by learning a number of verses off by heart, for preference those that contain some moral sentiment.

17. (xvi) They will take their first steps in music by learning easy hymns and psalms. This exercise should form part of their daily devotions.

18. (xvii) The rudiments of economics are acquired when the child learns the names of the various members of a family, that is to say, what is meant by the terms father, mother, maid-servant, man-servant, etc.; or the various parts of a house, as hall, kitchen, bedroom, stable; or the names of domestic utensils, as table, plate, knife, broom, etc.

19. (xviii) It is not so easy to give a foretaste of politics, as at this age the understanding is only sufficiently developed to take in household affairs. Some attempt, however, may be made. It may be pointed out, for instance, that, in a state, some men meet together in a council-chamber and are called councillors, and that of these some are called members, others ministers, others lawyers, and so forth.

20. (xix) But it is of morals (ethics), in particular, that the foundations should be solidly laid, for to a well-educated youth we wish the practice of virtue to be second nature. For instance,

(1) Temperance should be practised by never over-filling the stomach, and by never taking more food than is necessary to appease hunger and thirst.

(2) Cleanliness should be practised at meals, and in the treatment of clothes, dolls, and toys.

(3) Reverence should be shown by the child to his superiors.

(4) Obedience to both commands and prohibitions should always be willing and prompt.

(5) Truth should always be religiously observed. False-hood and deceit should never be permitted, whether in jest or in earnest (for jests of this kind may degenerate into a serious evil).

(6) They will learn justice if they never touch, take, keep, or hide anything that belongs to any one else, if they annoy no one, and envy no one.

(7) It is of greater importance that they learn to practise charity, so that they may be ready to give alms to those whom need compels to ask for them. For love is the especial virtue of Christians. Christ bids us practise it; and, now that the world is growing aged and cold, it is greatly to the interest of the Church to kindle in men's hearts the flame of love.

(8) Children should also be taught to occupy themselves continually, either with work or with play, so that idleness may become intolerable to them.

(9) They should be taught to speak but little and to refrain from saying all that rises to their lips, nay, even to *maintain absolute silence* when the occasion demands it; that is to say, when others are speaking, when any distinguished person is present, and when the circumstances demand silence.

(10) It is also important that they learn patience in infancy, since this will be of use to them throughout their whole lives. In this way the passions may be subdued before they acquire strength, while reason, and not impulse, will gain the upper hand.

(11) Politeness and readiness to help others is a great ornament of youth, and, indeed, of every age. This also should be learned in the first six years, that our youths may lose no opportunity of rendering services to those whom they meet.

(12) Nor must we omit to train them in good manners, that they may do nothing stupidly or boorishly. To this end they should learn the manners of polite society; such as how to shake hands, how to make a modest request when they want anything, and how to bend the knee and kiss the hand gracefully when returning thanks for a kindness.

21. (xx) Finally, by the time they are six years old, boys should have made considerable progress in religion and piety; that is to say, they should have learned the heads of the Catechism and the principles of Christianity, and should understand these and live up to them as far as their age permits. Thus, by realising that the Deity is ever present, by seeing God around them, and by fearing Him as the just avenger of the wicked, they will be prevented from committing any sinful act; while by loving, reverencing, and praising in Him the just recompenser of the righteous, and by seeking for His compassion in life and in death, they will be led to omit no righteous act that they think may please Him, will acquire the habit of living as if they were in God's presence, and (as the Scripture saith) will walk with God.

22. We shall thus be able to apply to Christian children the words that the Evangelist uses of Christ Himself: " He advanced in wisdom and stature, and in favour with God and men " (Luke ii. 52).

23. We have now described the limits and the tasks of the Mother-School.[38] It is impossible to give a more detailed account, or a time-table stating how much work should be done in each year, month, and day (as is both possible and desirable in the Vernacular-School and in the Latin-School), for two reasons : firstly, because it is not possible for parents, who have their household duties to occupy them, to proceed as methodically as a schoolmaster can, whose sole occupation is to instruct youth ; secondly, because, in respect of intellect and teachableness, some children develope much sooner than others. Some children of two years old can speak with ease, and display great intelligence, while others are scarcely equal to them when five years old. With this early education, therefore, all detail must be left to the prudence of the parent.

24. Assistance, however, may be given in two ways. In the first place, a hand-book should be written for parents and nurses, that they may have their duties in black and white before their eyes. This hand-book should contain a brief description of the various subjects in which the children should be educated, and should state the occasions that are most suitable for each, and with what words and what gestures it is best to instil them. Such a book with the title, " Informatory of the Mother-School," has still to be written by me.

25. The other aid to study in the Mother-School is a picture-book which should be put straight into the child's hands. At this age instruction should mainly be carried on through the medium of sense-perception, and, as sight is the chiefest of the senses, our object will be attained if we give the children pictures of the most important objects in physics, optics, astronomy, geometry, etc., and these may be arranged in the order of the subjects of knowledge that we have just sketched. In this book should be depicted

mountains, valleys, trees, birds, fishes, horses, oxen, sheep, and men of varied age and height. Light and darkness also should be represented, as well as the heavens with the sun, moon, stars, and clouds, while to these the principal colours should be added. Articles connected with the house and the workshop, such as pots, plates, hammers, pincers, etc., should not be omitted. State functionaries should be represented; the king with his sceptre and crown, the soldier with his arms, the husbandman with his plough, the waggoner with his waggon, and the post-cart going at full speed; while over each picture should be written the name of the object that it represents, as "house," "ox," "dog," "tree," etc.

26. This picture-book will be of use in three ways: (1) It will assist objects to make an impression on the mind, as we have already pointed out. (2) It will accustom the little ones to the idea that pleasure is to be derived from books. (3) It will aid them in learning to read. For, since the name of each object is written above the picture that represents it, the first steps in reading may thus be made.

CHAPTER XXIX

SKETCH OF THE VERNACULAR-SCHOOL

1. IN chap. ix. I demonstrated that all the young of both sexes should be sent to the public schools, I now add that they should first be sent to the Vernacular-School. Some writers hold the contrary opinion. Zepper[39] (*Pol.* bk. i. ch. 7) and Alsted[40] (*Scholastic*, ch. 6) would persuade us that only those boys and girls who are destined for manual labour should be sent to the Vernacular-School, while boys whose parents wish them to receive a higher education should be sent straight to the Latin-School. Moreover, Alsted adds: "Some will doubtless disagree with me, but the system that I propose is the one which I would wish adopted by those whose educational interests I have most at heart." From this view my whole didactic system forces me to dissent.

2. (i) The education that I propose includes all that is proper for a man, and is one in which all men who are born into this world should share. All therefore, as far as is possible, should be educated together, that they may stimulate and urge on one another.

(ii) We wish all men to be trained in all the virtues, especially in modesty, sociability, and politeness, and it is therefore undesirable to create class distinctions at such an early age, or to give some children the opportunity of considering their own lot with satisfaction and that of others with scorn.

(iii) When boys are only six years old, it is too early to determine their vocation in life, or whether they are more suited for learning or for manual labour. At this age, neither the mind nor the inclinations are sufficiently developed, while, later on, it will be easy to form a sound opinion on both. In the same way, while plants are quite small, a gardener cannot tell which to hoe up and which to leave, but has to wait until they are more advanced. Nor should admission to the Latin-School be reserved for the sons of rich men, nobles, and magistrates, as if these were the only boys who would ever be able to fill similar positions. The wind blows where it will, and does not always begin to blow at a fixed time.

3. (iv) The next reason is that my universal method has not as its sole object the Latin language, that nymph on whom such unbounded admiration is generally wasted, but seeks a way by which each modern language may be taught as well (that every spirit may praise the Lord more and more). This design should not be frustrated by the complete and arbitrary omission of the Vernacular-School.

4. (v) To attempt to teach a foreign language before the mother-tongue has been learned is as irrational as to teach a boy to ride before he can walk. To proceed step by step is of great importance, as we have seen in chap. xvi. Principle 4. Cicero declared that he could not teach elocution to those who were unable to speak, and, in the same way, my method confesses its inability to teach Latin to those who are ignorant of their mother-tongue, since the one paves the way for the other.

5. (vi) Finally, what I have in view is an education in the objects that surround us, and a brief survey of this education can be best obtained from books written in the mother-tongue, which embody a list of the things that exist in the external world. This preliminary survey will render the acquisition of Latin far easier, for it will only be necessary to adapt a new nomenclature to objects that are already known; while to the knowledge of actual facts may

be added by degrees that of the causes which underlie those facts.

6. Proceeding, therefore, on the basis of my fourfold division of schools, we may define the Vernacular-School as follows. The aim and object of the Vernacular-School should be to teach to all the young, between the ages of six and twelve, such things as will be of use to them throughout their whole lives. That is to say:

(i) To read with ease both print and writing in their mother-tongue.

(ii) To write, first with accuracy, then with speed, and finally with confidence, in accordance with the grammatical rules of the mother-tongue. These rules should be written in a popular form, and the boys should be exercised in them.

(iii) To count, with ciphers and with counters, as far as is necessary for practical purposes.

(iv) To measure spaces, such as length, breadth, and distance, with skill.

(v) To sing well-known melodies, and, in the case of those who display especial aptitude, to learn the elements of advanced music.

(vi) To learn by heart the greater number of the psalms and hymns that are used in the country. For, if brought up in the praise of God, they will be able (as the Apostle says) to exhort one another with psalms and hymns and spiritual songs, singing to God from their hearts.

(vii) Besides the Catechism they should know the most important stories and verses in the Bible, and should be able to repeat them word for word.

(viii) They should learn the principles of morality, which should be drawn up in the shape of rules and accompanied by illustrations suitable to the age and understanding of the pupils. They should also begin to put these principles into practice.

(ix) They should learn as much economics and politics as is necessary to enable them to understand what they see daily at home and in the state.

(x) They should also learn the general history of the world; its creation, its fall, its redemption, and its preservation by God up to the present day.

(xi) In addition, they should learn the most important facts of cosmography, such as the spherical shape of the heavens, the globular shape of the earth suspended in their midst, the tides of the ocean, the shapes of seas, the courses of rivers, the principal divisions of the earth, and the chief kingdoms of Europe; but, in particular, the cities, mountains, rivers, and other remarkable features of their own country.

(xii) Finally, they should learn the most important principles of the mechanical arts, both that they may not be too ignorant of what goes on in the world around them, and that any special inclination towards things of this kind may assert itself with greater ease later on.

7. If all these subjects have been skilfully handled in the Vernacular-School, the result will be that those youths who begin the study of Latin or who enter on agriculture, trade, or professional life will encounter nothing which is absolutely new to them; while the details of their trades, the words that they hear in church, and the information that they acquire from books, will be to them nothing but the more detailed exposition or the more particular application of facts with which they are already acquainted. They will thus find themselves all the fitter to use their understanding, their powers of action, and their judgment.

8. To attain this result we employ the following means :—

(i) All the children in the Vernacular-School, who are destined to spend six years there, should be divided into six classes, each of which, if possible, should have a class-room to itself, that it may not hinder the others.

(ii) Specially prepared books should be supplied to each class, and these should contain the whole subject-matter of the literary, moral, and religious instruction prescribed for the class. Within these limits no other books should be needed, and, by their aid, the desired result should infallibly be obtained.   They should embody a complete grammar of the mother-tongue, in which should be comprised the names of all the objects that children of this age can understand, as well as a selection of the most common phrases in use.

9. These class-books should be six in number, corresponding to the number of the classes, and should differ, not in their subject-matter, but in their way of presenting it. Each should embrace all the above-mentioned subjects; but the earlier ones should treat of them in a general manner, choosing their better known and easier features; while those which come later should draw attention to the less known and more complex details, or should point out some fresh way of treating the subject, and thus excite interest and attention.   The truth of this will soon be evident.

10. Care must be taken to suit all these books to the children for whom they are intended; for children like whimsicality and humour, and detest pedantry and severity. Instruction, therefore, should ever be combined with amusement, that they may take pleasure in learning serious things which will be of genuine use to them later on, and that their dispositions may be, as it were, perpetually enticed to develope in the manner desired.

11. The titles of these books should be of such a kind as to please and attract the young, and should at the same time express the nature of their contents.   Suitable names might be borrowed from the nomenclature of a garden, that sweetest possession of youth.   Thus, if the whole school be compared to a garden, the book of the lowest class might be called the violet-bed, that of the second class the rose-bed, that of the third the grass-plot, and so on.

12. Of the matter and form of these books I will speak in greater detail elsewhere.   I will only add that, as they are written in the mother-tongue, the technical terms of the arts should also be expressed in the vernacular, and not in Latin or Greek.   For (1) we wish the young to

make progress with as little delay as possible. Now foreign terms must necessarily be explained before they are understood, and, even when explained, are not properly understood, but are thought to have no meaning apart from their technical signification. In addition, they are difficult to remember. On the other hand, if the vernacular terms are used, it is only necessary to point out the object designated by each term. In this way we wish to remove all delays and difficulties from the path of this elementary instruction. (2) Besides this, we wish to cultivate and improve the vernacular languages, and this is to be done, not by imitating the French, who incorporate Greek and Latin words that the people cannot understand (for which practice Stevin blames them), but by expressing our meaning in terms which can be understood by everybody. Stevin [41] gave the same advice to the Belgians (*Geog.* bk. i.), and carried it into effect in his work on mathematics.

13. But it may be objected that all languages are not rich enough to supply suitable equivalents for Greek and Latin terms; that even if this were done, the learned would not relinquish their use; and, lastly, that those boys who are going to learn Latin had better begin at this stage, and so avoid the necessity of learning fresh technical terms later on.

14. I reply: If any language be obscure, or insufficient to express necessary ideas, this is the fault, not of the language, but of those who use it. The Romans and Greeks had originally to form the words that are now in use, and these words seemed so obscure and so rude that their authors were uncertain if they could ever serve as a vehicle for thought. But now that they are universally accepted they prove sufficiently expressive. As an illustration of what I mean, take the terms "essence," "substance," "accident," "quality," "quantity," etc. No language, therefore, need lack words unless men lack industry.

15. As for the second objection; let the learned retain their own terms. We are now seeking a way by which the

common people may be led to understand and take an interest in the liberal arts and sciences ; and with this end in view we must not speak in a language that is foreign to them, and that is in itself artificial.

16. And lastly, those boys who have to learn Latin later on will find it no disadvantage to know the technical terms in their mother-tongue, nor will it prove any hindrance to them that they praised God in their own language before doing so in Latin.

17. The third requisite is an easy method of introducing these books to the young, and of this we will give a brief sketch in the following rules :

(i) The class lessons should not exceed four daily, of which two should be before mid-day, and two after. The remaining hours of the day may profitably be spent in domestic work (especially among the poor), or in some form of recreation.

(ii) The morning should be devoted to the exercise of the intellect and the memory, the afternoon to that of the hand and the voice.

(iii) In the morning the master shall read over the lesson for the hour several times, while the whole class attends, and shall explain anything that needs explanation in simple language, and in such a way that it cannot but be understood. He shall then bid the boys read it in turn, and while one reads it in a clear voice the rest should attend and follow in their books. If this be continued for half an hour, or longer, the clever boys and at last even the stupid ones will try to repeat by heart what they have just read. For the tasks that are set must be short ; not too long for an hour's lesson, or too hard for the boys to understand.

(iv) No fresh work should be done in the afternoon, but the lessons done in the morning should be repeated. The pupils should transcribe portions of their printed books, and should compete with one another to see who can best remember the morning's lesson, or who is most proficient in writing, in singing, or in counting.

18. Not without reason do we recommend that all the pupils copy their printed books as neatly as they can. (1) The manual exercise of copying will help to impress on their minds the matter copied. (2) If the practice be made a daily one, it will teach them to write well, quickly, and accurately, and this will be of the greatest use in the further prosecution of their studies, and in conducting the affairs of life. (3) This will be the surest proof to parents that their children are not wasting their time at school, and will enable them to judge how much progress they are making.

19. We have no space to go into further particulars at present, and will only touch on one more point. If any boys are to learn foreign languages, they should learn them now, at about the age of ten, eleven, or twelve, that is to say, *between* the Vernacular-School and the Latin-School. The best way is to send them to the place where the language that they wish to learn is spoken, and in the new language to make them read, write, and learn the class-books of the Vernacular-School (the subject-matter of which is already familiar to them).

CHAPTER XXX

SKETCH OF THE LATIN-SCHOOL

1. In this school the pupils should learn four languages and acquire an encyclopædic knowledge of the arts. Those youths who have completed its whole curriculum should have had a training as:

(i) Grammarians, who are well versed in Latin and in their mother-tongue, and have a sufficient acquaintance with Greek and Hebrew.

(ii) Dialecticians, who are well skilled in making definitions, in drawing distinctions, in arguing a point, and in solving hard questions.

(iii) Rhetoricians or orators, who can talk well on any given subject.

(iv) Arithmeticians, and (v) geometricians; both on account of the use of these sciences in daily life, and because they sharpen the intellect more than anything else.

(vi) Musicians, both practical and theoretical.

(vii) Astronomers, who have, at any rate, mastered the rudiments, such as the knowledge of the heavenly bodies, and the calculation of their movements, since without this science it is impossible to understand not only physics but also geography and a great part of history.

2. The above are commonly known as the seven liberal arts, a knowledge of which is demanded from a doctor of philosophy. But our pupils must aim higher than this, and in addition must be:

(viii) Physicists, who know the composition of the earth, the force of the elements, the different species of animals, the powers of plants and of minerals, and the structure of the human body, and who, besides knowing these things, can apply them to the various uses of life. Under this head is thus comprised a part of medicine, of agriculture, and of other mechanical arts.

(ix) Geographers, who are well acquainted with the external features of the earth, and know the seas, the islands that are in them, the rivers, and the various kingdoms.

(x) Chronologers, who can fix periods of time, and trace the course of the centuries from the beginning of the world.

(xi) Historians, who possess a fair knowledge of the history of the human race, of the chief empires, and of the Church, and who know the various customs and fortunes of races and of men.

(xii) Moralists, who can draw fine distinctions between the various kinds of virtue and of vice, and who can follow the one and avoid the other. This knowledge they should possess both in its general form and in its special application to the life of the family, of the state, and of the Church.

(xiii) Finally, we wish them to be theologians, who, besides understanding the principles of their faith, can also prove them from the Scriptures.

3. When this course is finished, the youths, even if they have not a perfect knowledge of all these subjects (indeed at their age perfection is impossible, since experience is necessary to complete the theoretical knowledge that they have acquired, and the sea of learning cannot be exhausted in six years), should, at any rate, have laid a solid foundation for any more advanced instruction that they may receive in the future.

4. For the curriculum of six years, six distinct classes will be necessary, the names of which, starting from the lowest, might be as follows :—

(i)   The Grammar class.
(ii) The Natural Philosophy class.
(iii) The Mathematical class.

(iv) The Ethics class.
(v)   The Dialectic class.
(vi) The Rhetoric class.

5. I presume that no one can raise any objection to my placing grammar first, since it is the key of all knowledge ; but to those who are always guided by custom it may seem strange that I have placed real studies before dialectic and ethics.   No other arrangement, however, is possible. It has already been shown that the study of facts must precede that of their combinations, that matter logically precedes its form, that this is the only method by which sure and rapid progress can be made, and that we must therefore learn our facts by observation before we can either pass a sound judgment on them, or enunciate them in well-turned phrases.   A man may have the whole apparatus of logic and of eloquence at his fingers' ends, but of what value can his investigation or his proof be, if he be ignorant of the objects with which he is dealing ?   It is as impossible to talk sensibly about matters with which we are not acquainted as it is for a virgin to bring forth a child. Things exist in themselves, and are quite independent of their relation to thought and to speech.   But thought and speech have no meaning apart from things, and depend entirely upon them.   Unless it refers to definite objects, speech is nothing but sound without sense, and it is there- fore absolutely necessary to give our pupils a thorough preliminary training in real studies.

6. Though many have held the contrary opinion, it has been conclusively shown by learned writers that the study of natural philosophy should precede that of ethics.

Lipsius,[42] in his *Physiology*, bk. i. chap. i., writes as follows :—

"I am distinctly in agreement with the distinguished authorities who hold that natural philosophy should come first.   Its study is productive of great pleasure, stimulates and retains the attention, and forms a suitable introduc- tion to ethics."

7. It is open to argument whether the Mathematical

class should or should not precede the Natural Philosophy class. It was with the study of mathematics that the ancients commenced the investigation of nature, for which reason they gave them the name of " The Sciences "; while Plato forbade those who were ignorant of geometry to enter his Academy. Their reasons for holding this view are easy to understand, since the sciences that deal with number and quantity make a special appeal to the senses, and are therefore easy to grasp; besides, they make a powerful impression on the imagination, and thus prepare the mind for studies of a more abstract nature.

8. All this is very true, but we have some other considerations to take into account: (1) In the Vernacular-School we advised the education of the senses, and the development of the mind through their means, and as our pupils have by this time been through a course of arithmetic they can scarcely be considered quite ignorant of mathematics. (2) Our method advances step by step. Before proceeding to complex problems of magnitude, we should deal with bodies in the concrete, and thus prepare our minds to grasp more abstract notions. (3) The curriculum of the Mathematical class, as drawn up by us, embodies most of the arts, and these cannot be thoroughly mastered without some knowledge of natural philosophy. But indeed, if others suggest a different order, and justify their preference by theoretical or practical reasons, I have no wish to gainsay them. My own view is opposed to theirs, and I have given my reasons for it.

9. As soon as a fair knowledge of Latin has been acquired (by the aid of the *Vestibulum* and the *Janua*, which are to be used in the first class), the pupils should be instructed in the science of first principles, commonly called metaphysics (though in my opinion it should be called prophysics or hypophysics, that is to say, antenatural or sub-natural). For this science embraces the primary and the most important principles of existence, dealing with the essential hypotheses on which all things depend, their attributes, and their logical differences; and

includes the most general definitions, axioms, and laws of nature. When these are known (and by my method the task is an easy one), it will be possible to learn particulars and details with little effort, since, in a way, they will already be familiar, and nothing will be necessary but the application of general principles to particular instances. Immediately after this grounding in first principles, which should not occupy more than three months (for they will be speedily learned, being principles of pure reason and easily grasped by the mind), we may proceed to deal with the visible universe, that the marvels of nature (already set forth in the prophysic) may be demonstrated more and more clearly by particular examples. This will be supplied by the Natural Philosophy class.

10. From the essential nature of things we proceed to the more exact investigation of their accidental properties, and this we call the Mathematical class.

11. The pupils must next investigate man himself, viewed as a free agent and as the lord of creation. They must learn to notice what things are in our power, what are not, and how everything must submit to the inflexible laws of the universe.

This they will learn in the fourth year, in the Ethics class. But this must not consist of an historical course or of a mere statement of facts, as in the Vernacular-School. The reasons which underlie each fact must be given, that the pupils may acquire the habit of concentrating their attention on cause and effect. All controversial matter, however, must be carefully excluded from these first four classes, since we wish this to be reserved for the fifth class that follows.

12. In the Dialectic class, after a brief training in the laws of reasoning, the pupils should go over the whole field of natural philosophy, mathematics, and ethics, and carefully investigate any weighty points that are usually discussed by learned men. This gives an opportunity for explaining the cause and the nature of the controversy, for distinguishing between the thesis and the antithesis,

and for showing by what arguments, real or plausible, either may be controverted. The mistakes of the opposite side should then be exposed, and the cause of error and the fallacy of the arguments employed should be clearly shown; while, if there be an element of truth on both sides, the conflicting arguments may be reconciled. The utility of this process will be great, as it will not only comprise the recapitulation of facts already known, and illustrate those that are less familiar, but will at the same time teach the art of reasoning, of investigating what is unknown, and explaining what is obscure, of simplifying ambiguity, limiting statements that are too general, defending the truth with the weapons of truth, unmasking falsehood, and setting in order facts that are confused.

13. Last of all comes the Rhetoric class. In this the pupils should be taught to make an easy and profitable use of all that they have hitherto learned, and here it will be seen that they have learned something and have not spent their time in vain. For, in accordance with the saying of Socrates, "Speak, that I may see your character," we must train them to speak well, now that we have taught them to think accurately.

14. Therefore, after a preliminary training in the shortest and simplest rules of oratory, they should proceed to put these into practice by imitating the best masters. They should, however, not confine themselves to the subjects that they have already studied, but should traverse the whole field of truth, of existence, of human life, and of divine wisdom; that if they know anything which is true, good, pleasant, or useful they may be able to express it in suitable language, or, if necessary, to hold a brief for it. For this purpose they will at this stage be supplied with a mental furniture that is by no means to be despised, namely, a varied acquaintance with the facts of nature, and a good stock of words, of phrases, and of historical knowledge.

15. But of this we can speak more fully elsewhere; that is to say, if it be necessary, since the details will work

themselves out in practice. We will only touch on one point further. An acquaintance with history is the most important element in a man's education, and is, as it were, the eye of his whole life. This subject, therefore, should be taught in each of the six classes, that our pupils may be ignorant of no event which has happened from ancient times to the present day; but its study must be arranged in such a way that it lighten their work instead of increasing it, and serve as a relaxation after their severer labours.

16. Our idea is that each class should have its own hand-book, dealing with some special branch of history; for example:

In class i. An epitome of Biblical history.
          ii. Natural history.
          iii. The history of art and of inventions.
          iv. The history of morals.
          v. The history of customs, treating of the habits of different nations.
          vi. The general history of the world and of the principal nations; but especially of the boys' native land, dealing with the whole subject tersely and comprehensively.

17. As regards the special method to be employed, I will make only one remark. The four hours of daily class instruction should be arranged as follows: the two morning hours should be devoted (as soon as morning prayer has been held) to the science or the art that forms the special subject of the class. Of the afternoon hours the first should be given to history, and, in the second, the pupils should be made to exercise style, declamation, and the use of their hands, in accordance with the requirements of the class.

CHAPTER XXXI

OF THE UNIVERSITY

1. OUR method does not really concern itself with University studies, but there is no reason why we should not state our views and our wishes with regard to them. We have already expressed our opinion that the complete training in any of the sciences or faculties should be reserved for the University.

2. Our ideal scheme is as follows:

(i) The curriculum should be really universal, and provision should be made for the study of every branch of human knowledge.

(ii) The methods adopted should be easy and thorough, that all may receive a sound education.

(iii) Positions of honour should be given only to those who have completed their University course with success, and have shown themselves fit to be entrusted with the management of affairs.

We will briefly give some details on each of these points.

3. If its curriculum is to be universal, the University must possess (1) learned and able professors of all the sciences, arts, faculties, and languages, who can thus impart information to all the students on any subject; (2) a library of well-selected books for the common use of all.

4. The studies will progress with ease and success if, firstly, only select intellects, the flower of mankind, attempt them. The rest had better turn their attention to more

suitable occupations, such as agriculture, mechanics, or trade.

5. Secondly, if each student devote his undivided energies to that subject for which he is evidently suited by nature. For some men are more suited than others to be theologians, doctors, or lawyers, just as others have a natural aptitude for and excel in music, poetry, or oratory. This is a matter in which we are apt to make frequent mistakes, trying to carve statues out of every piece of wood, and disregarding the intention of nature. The result is that many enter on branches of study for which they have no vocation, produce no good results in them, and attain to greater success in their subsidiary pursuits than in those that they have chosen.

A public examination, therefore, should be held for the students who leave the Latin-School, and from its results the masters may decide which of them should be sent to the University, and which should enter on the other occupations of life. Those who are selected will pursue their studies, some choosing theology, some politics, and some medicine, in accordance with their natural inclination and with the needs of the Church and of the state.

6. Thirdly, those of quite exceptional talent should be urged to pursue all the branches of study, that there may always be some men whose knowledge is encyclopædic.

7. Care should be taken to admit to the University only those who are diligent and of good moral character. False students, who waste their patrimony and their time in ease and luxury, and thus set a bad example to others, should not be tolerated. Thus, if there is no disease, there can be no infection, and all will be intent upon their work.

8. We said that every class of author should be read in the University. Now this would be a laborious task, but its use is great, and it is therefore to be hoped that men of learning, philologers, philosophers, theologians, physicians, etc., will render the same service to students as has been rendered to those who study geography by geo-

graphers. For these latter make maps of the provinces, kingdoms, and divisions of the world, and thus present to the eye huge tracts of sea and land on a small scale, so that they can be taken in at a glance. Painters, also, produce accurate and life-like representations of countries, cities, houses, and men, no matter of what size the originals may be. Why, therefore, should not Cicero, Livy, Plato, Aristotle, Plutarch, Tacitus, Gellius, Hippocrates, Galen, Celsus, Augustine, Jerome, etc., be treated in the same way and epitomised? By this we do not allude to the collections of extracts and flowers of rhetoric, that are often met with. These epitomes should contain the whole author, only somewhat reduced in bulk.

9. Epitomes of this kind will be of great use. In the first place it will be possible to obtain a general notion of an author when there is no time to read his works at length. Secondly, those who (following Seneca's advice) wish to confine themselves to the works of one writer (for different writers suit different dispositions), will be able to take a rapid survey of all and to make their choice in accordance with their tastes. Thirdly, those who are going to read the authors in their entirety will find that these epitomes enable them to read with greater profit, just as a traveller is able to take in the details of his journey with greater ease, if he have first studied them on a map. Finally, these abstracts will be of great use to those who wish to make a rapid revision of the authors that they have read, as it will help them to remember the chief points, and to master them thoroughly.

10. Summaries of this kind may be issued both separately (for the use of poor students and those who are not in the position to read the complete works) and bound up with the complete works, that those who wish to read them may get an idea of the subject-matter before they begin.

11. As regards academic exercises, I imagine that public debates, on the model of a Gellian society, should be of great assistance. Whenever a professor delivers lectures on any subject, works which treat of that subject,

and these the best that exist, should be given to the students for their private reading. Then the morning lecture of the professor should serve as the subject for an afternoon debate, in which the whole class may join. One student may ask a question about some point that he does not understand, and may point out that in the author which he has been studying he has found an opinion, backed by reasonable arguments and opposed to that of the professor. Any other student may then rise (some forms of order being observed), and may answer the question raised ; while others may then decide if the point has been properly argued. Finally the professor, as president, may terminate the discussion. In this way, the private reading of each student will be of use to the whole class, and the subject will be so impressed on their minds that they will make real progress in the theory and practice of the sciences.

12. This practice of dissertation may be the means of fulfilling my third wish, that public posts of honour be given to none but the worthy. This result will be obtained if the appointment to these posts depend not on the decision of one man, but on the unanimous opinion of all. Once a year, therefore, the University should be visited by commissioners appointed by the king or by the state, just as the Latin-School is examined by its masters. The industry of the professors and students can thus be tested, and the most diligent of the latter should receive a public recognition of merit by having the degree of doctor or of master conferred upon them.

13. It is most important that everything be conducted with perfect fairness, and therefore, instead of allowing the academic degree to be won by a disputation, the following plan should be adopted. The candidate (or several at once) should be placed in the midst. Then men of the greatest knowledge and experience should question him and do all they can to find out what progress he has made, both in theory and in practice. For example, they may examine him on the text of the Scriptures, of Hippocrates,

of the Corpus Juris, etc.; asking him where such and such a passage occurs, and how it agrees with some other passage? if he knows of any writer who holds a different opinion, and who that writer is? What arguments he brings to bear, and how the contradictory views may be reconciled? with other similar questions. A practical examination should then follow. Various cases of conscience, of disease, and of law should be submitted to the candidate, and he should be asked what course of action he would pursue, and why? He should thus be examined with regard to a number of cases, until it is evident that he has an intelligent and thorough grasp of his subject. Surely, students who knew that they were to be publicly examined with such severity, would be stimulated to great industry.

14. There is no need to say anything about travel (to which we assigned a place in this last period of six years, or at its conclusion), except to remark that we are at one with Plato, who forbade the young to travel until the hotheadedness of youth had passed away, and they were sufficiently versed in the ways of the world to do so with advantage.

15. It is scarcely necessary to point out how useful a School of Schools or Didactic College would be, in whatever part of the world it were founded. Even if it be vain to hope for the actual foundation of such a college, the desired result might still be brought about, existing institutions being left as they are, if learned men would work together, and in this way seek to promote the glory of God. These men should make it the object of their associated labours to thoroughly establish the foundations of the sciences, to spread the light of wisdom throughout the human race with greater success than has hitherto been attained, and to benefit humanity by new and useful inventions; for, unless we wish to remain stationary or to lose ground, we must take care that our successful beginnings lead to further advances. For this no single man and no single generation is sufficient, and it is therefore essential that the work be carried on by many, working together

and employing the researches of their predecessors as a starting-point.　This Universal College, therefore, will bear the same relation to other schools that the belly bears to the other members of the body; since it will be a kind of workshop, supplying blood, life, and strength to all.

16. But we must return to our subject and say what remains to be said about our schools.

CHAPTER XXXII

OF THE UNIVERSAL AND PERFECT ORDER OF INSTRUCTION

1. WE have now spoken at length on the necessity of reforming schools and on the methods by which this reformation can be effected. It will not be amiss if we give a brief summary of our ideals and of the means we have proposed for their realisation.

2. Our desire is that the art of teaching be brought to such perfection that there will be as much difference between the old system and the new, as there is between the old method of multiplying books by the pen and the new method introduced by the printing-press; that is to say, the art of printing, though difficult, costly, and complicated, can reproduce books with greater speed, accuracy, and artistic effect, than was formerly possible; and, in the same way, my new method, though its difficulties may be somewhat alarming at first, will produce a greater number of scholars and will give them a better education as well as more pleasure in the process of acquiring it, than did the old lack of method.

3. It is easy to imagine how impracticable the first attempts of the inventor of printing must have appeared, in comparison with the simple use of the pen; but the event showed of what great use the invention was. For, firstly, by means of a printing-machine two youths can now produce more copies of a book than could have been written by two hundred in the same time.

Secondly, manuscript copies differ in the number and size of their pages, and the individual lines do not correspond to one another; while printed copies are as like to their original as one egg is like to another, and this is a great advantage.

Thirdly, it is impossible to tell if manuscripts are correct without revising them and comparing them accurately with the original, and this is a laborious and wearisome task. But in the case of printed books the correction of one proof ensures the accuracy of thousands of copies. This would seem incredible to any one unacquainted with printing, but is nevertheless true.

Fourthly, only firm and stiff paper is suitable to write on, but printing is possible on thin and flimsy paper, or on linen.

Finally, it is possible for men who are unable to write to be the most excellent printers; since it is not with their fingers that they carry out the operation, but by means of skilfully arranged type that cannot err.

4. Similar results might be obtained if this new and comprehensive method of teaching were properly organised (for as yet the universal method exists only in expectation and not in reality), since (1) a smaller number of masters would be able to teach a greater number of pupils than under the present system. (2) These pupils would be more thoroughly taught; (3) and the process would be refined and pleasant. (4) The system is equally efficacious with stupid and backward boys. (5) Even masters who have no natural aptitude for teaching will be able to use it with advantage; since they will not have to select their own subject-matter and work out their own method, but will only have to take knowledge that has already been suitably arranged and for the teaching of which suitable appliances have been provided, and to pour it into their pupils. An organist can read any piece of music from his notes, though he might not be able to compose it or to sing or play it from memory; and a school-master, in the same way, should be able to teach anything, if he have

before his eyes the subject-matter and the method by which it should be taught.

5. Pursuing this analogy to the art of printing, we will show, by a more detailed comparison, the true nature of this new method of ours, since it will thus be made evident that knowledge can be impressed on the mind, in the same way that its concrete form can be printed on paper. In fact, we might adapt the term "typography" and call the new method of teaching "didachography." But this conception we will analyse at length.

6. The art of printing involves certain materials and processes. The materials consist of the paper, the type, the ink, and the press. The processes consist of the preparation of the paper, the setting up and inking of the type, the correction of the proof, and the impression and drying of the copies. All this must be carried out in accordance with certain definite rules, the observance of which will ensure a successful result.

7. In didachography (to retain this term) the same elements are present. Instead of paper, we have pupils whose minds have to be impressed with the symbols of knowledge. Instead of type, we have the class-books and the rest of the apparatus devised to facilitate the operation of teaching. The ink is replaced by the voice of the master, since this it is that conveys information from the books to the minds of the listener; while the press is school-discipline, which keeps the pupils up to their work and compels them to learn.

8. Any kind of paper can be used, but the cleaner it is, the better it will receive the impress of the type. In the same way, our method can deal with any class of intelligence, but succeeds best with talented pupils.

9. There is a great analogy between the type and the class-books (that our method requires). Firstly, the type have to be cast and polished, before books can be printed; and in the same way the necessary apparatus must be provided before we can begin to use the new method.

10. A considerable quantity of type is required to

print a whole work, and the same thing holds good of class-books and teaching apparatus; since it is irritating, tedious, and fatal to good teaching to begin and then to· be compelled to leave off through lack of the proper appliances.

11. A well-managed printing-press is supplied with all kinds of type, and is thus equal to every demand that can be made upon it; and, similarly, our class-books must contain everything necessary for a thorough education, that there may be no one who by their aid cannot learn whatever should be learned.

12. The type are not left in confusion, but are neatly arranged in boxes that they may be ready to hand when needed. Similarly, our class-books do not present their subject-matter to the pupil in a confused mass, but split it up into sections, allotting so much to a year, a month, a day, and an hour.

13. Only those type which are needed at the minute are taken from the type-cases; the rest remain undisturbed. Similarly, no books but those intended for his class should be given to a boy; others would only confuse and distract him.

14. Finally, type-setters use a straight edge which helps them to arrange the words in lines, and the lines in columns, and prevents any part from getting out of place. In the same way the instructors of the young should have some standard or model to aid them in their work; that is to say, guide-books should be written for their use, and these should tell them what to do on each occasion, and should preclude the possibility of error.

15. There will, therefore, be two kinds of class-books, those that contain the subject-matter and are intended for the pupils, and guide-books to assist the teacher to handle his subject properly.

16. As we have already remarked, it is the voice of the teacher that corresponds to the ink used in printing. If it be attempted to use type when they are dry, nothing but a faint and evanescent mark is made on the paper, in

contrast to the firm and almost indelible impression that results when they have been inked. Similarly, the instruction that boys receive from books, those dumb teachers, is obscure and imperfect, but when it is supplemented by the voice of the teacher (who explains everything in a manner suitable to his hearers), it becomes vivid and makes a deep impression on their minds, so that they really understand what they learn and are conscious that they understand it. Again, printing-ink differs from writing-ink, since it is made, not with water, but with oil (indeed, those who want a very superior ink, use the finest oil and the best charcoal); and, similarly, the voice of a teacher who can teach persuasively and clearly should sink like oil into the pupils' minds and carry information with it.

17. Finally, the function of the press in printing is performed in schools by discipline, which is in itself sufficiently powerful to ensure that no pupil shirk his studies. Every sheet of paper that is to form part of a book must pass through the press (hard paper needing more, and soft paper less pressure); and, similarly, whoever wishes to learn at a school must be subjected to its discipline. There are three grades of discipline: firstly, perpetual watchfulness; for since we can never put implicit faith in the diligence or innocence of boys (are they not Adam's brood?) we must keep them continually under our eyes. Secondly, blame, by which those who leave the beaten path must be recalled to the way of reason and obedience. Finally, punishment, which must be employed if exhortation have no effect. All discipline, however, must be used with prudence and with no other object than to induce the pupils to do all their work well.

18. I said that certain processes were necessary, and that these had to be carried out in a certain definite manner. This point deserves a brief investigation.

19. If a certain number of copies of a book is to be printed, that number of sheets is taken at once and printed from the same block, and from each successive block, from the beginning to the end of the book, the same number of

sheets, and neither more nor less, is printed ; since otherwise some copies of the book would be imperfect. In the same way, our didactic method lays it down as an essential condition that the whole school be given over at one and the same time to the teaching of one master, that from beginning to end all the scholars be subjected to a graduated course of instruction, and that none be allowed to enter after the session has once begun, or to leave before it is finished. In this way it will be possible for one master to teach a large number of pupils, and for all the pupils to learn every branch of knowledge thoroughly. It will therefore be necessary for all the public schools to open and to close at the same time (it suits our method best if the schools open in autumn rather than in spring), in order that the task allotted to each class may be completed each year, and that all (except those wanting in intellect) may be brought up to a certain standard at the same time, and may enter the next class together. This is an exact analogy of the method used in printing when all the copies of the first page are printed first, then those of the second page, and so on.

20. The better class of books are divided into chapters, columns, and paragraphs, and have spaces on their margins and between their lines. Similarly, our didactic method must have its periods of toil and of rest, with definite spaces of time set apart for honest recreation. The tasks are mapped out for each year, month, day, and hour, and if these divisions are duly observed no class can fail to reach the necessary standard at the end of the session. There are excellent reasons why the hours of public instruction should not exceed four daily, of which two should be before, and two after mid-day. On Saturday the two afternoon hours may be remitted, and the whole of Sunday should be devoted to divine service, so that we have thus twenty-two hours weekly and (making allowance for the holidays) about a thousand hours yearly. How much might be taught and learned in this time, were it only methodically employed !

21. As soon as the type has been set up, the paper is flattened out and laid ready to hand, that nothing may impede the process of printing. Similarly, a teacher should place his pupils in front of him that he may see them and be seen by all. This we have already shown in chap. xix. Problem 1.

22. The paper is damped and softened, that it may be better fitted to receive the impression of the type. Similarly the pupils in a school must continually be urged to attend, as we have already explained.

23. When this has been done, the type are inked, that a distinct impression may be taken from them. Similarly, the teacher makes the lesson vivid by means of his voice, reading it over and explaining it, that all may understand.

24. The paper is then put into the press, one piece after the other, that the metal type may impress their form on each and every sheet. Similarly, the teacher, after he has explained a construction, and has shown by examples how easily it can be imitated, asks individual pupils to reproduce what he has said, and thus show that they are not merely learners, but actually possessors of knowledge.

25. The printed sheets are then exposed to the wind and are dried. Similarly, in school, the intellects of the pupils are exposed to the bracing influences of repetition, examination, and emulation, until it is certain that the lesson has been thoroughly learned.

26. When they have passed through the press, the printed sheets are all taken and arranged in order, that it may be seen if the copies are complete and without defects, and are therefore fit to be bound, sold, and used. The same function is performed in schools by the examination at the end of the year, when the progress of the pupils, and the thoroughness and comprehensiveness of their training, are investigated by the inspectors ; the object being that these latter may certify that the subjects appointed have been properly learned.

27. So far we have confined ourselves to generalities, reserving our detailed investigation for a more suitable

occasion. For the present it is sufficient to have shown that our discovery of didachography, or our universal method, facilitates the multiplication of learned men in precisely the same way that the discovery of printing has facilitated the multiplication of books, those vehicles of learning, and that this is greatly to the advantage of mankind, since " the multitude of the wise is the wisdom of the world " (Wisdom vi. 24). And, since our desire is to increase the sum of Christian wisdom, and to sow the seeds of piety, of learning, and of morality in the hearts of all who are dedicated to God, we may hope for the fulfilment of the divine prophecy : "The earth shall be full of the knowledge of God, as the waters cover the sea " (Isaiah xi. 9).

CHAPTER XXXIII

OF THE THINGS REQUISITE BEFORE THIS UNIVERSAL METHOD CAN BE PUT INTO PRACTICE

1. THERE is no one, I imagine, who, after a careful examination of the question, will not perceive how blessed would be the condition of Christian kingdoms and states if they were supplied with schools of the kind that we desire. We must therefore see what is necessary in order that these speculations may not remain speculations, but may be realised in some definite form. Not without reason does John Cæcilius Frey express his surprise and indignation that throughout so many centuries no one has ventured to reform the barbarous customs of our schools and universities.

2. For more than a hundred years much complaint has been made of the unmethodical way in which schools are conducted, but it is only within the last thirty that any serious attempt has been made to find a remedy for this state of things. And with what result? Schools remain exactly as they were. If any scholar, either privately or in school, embarked on a course of study, he found himself a butt for the mockery of the ignorant or the malevolence of the ill-disposed, or finally, being unable to obtain any assistance, found his endeavour too laborious, and gave it up. Thus all efforts have hitherto been in vain.

3. We must therefore seek and find some way by which, with God's assistance, motive power may be supplied to

the machine that is already sufficiently well constructed, or at any rate can be constructed on the foundations which exist, if the obstacles and hindrances that have hitherto been present be wisely and firmly removed.

4. Let us isolate and examine these obstacles.

(i) There is a great lack of methodical teachers who could take charge of public schools and produce the results that we have in view (indeed, with regard to my *Janua* which is already used in schools, a man of great judgment has written to me complaining that in most places one thing is lacking, namely, suitable men to use it).

5. (ii) But even if teachers of this kind existed, or if they could all perform their task with ease by using time-tables and forms all ready prepared for them, how would it be possible to support them in each village and town, and in every place where men are born and brought up in Christ?

6. (iii) Again, how can it be arranged that the children of the poor shall have time to go to school?

7. (iv) The opposition of pedants, who cling to old ways and despise everything that is new, is greatly to be dreaded, but for this some remedy can easily be found.

8. (v) There is one factor which by its absence or its presence can render the whole organisation of a school of no avail or can aid it in the highest degree, and that is a proper supply of comprehensive and methodical class-books. Since the invention of printing, it has been an easy matter to find men who are able and willing to make use of it, who will supply the funds necessary for the printing of good and useful books, and who will purchase books of this kind. Similarly, if the subsidiary apparatus necessary for comprehensive teaching were provided, it would be easy to find men to employ it.

9. It is evident, therefore, that the success of my scheme depends entirely upon a suitable supply of encyclopædic class-books, and these can be provided only by the collaboration of several original-minded, energetic, and learned men. For such a task transcends the strength of one man, and especially of one who is unable to devote his whole

time to it, or who may be imperfectly acquainted with some of the subjects that must be included in the comprehensive scheme. Moreover, if absolute perfection be desired, one lifetime is not sufficient for the completion of the work, which must therefore be entrusted to a collegiate body of learned men.

10. But it is impossible to call such a body into existence unless it be supported and financed by some king or state, while to ensure success a quiet and secluded spot and a library are necessary. In addition, it is essential that no one offer any opposition to such a goodly plan for glorifying the Creator and benefiting the human race, but rather that all prepare to work in harmony with the grace of God, which will be communicated to us more liberally through these new channels.

11. Therefore let your zeal blaze forth when ye hear this wholesome counsel. O dearest parents of children, into whose charge God has entrusted His most precious treasures, those made in His own image, may ye never cease to entreat the God of Gods that these efforts may have a successful issue, and by your prayers and solicitations to work upon the minds of powerful and learned men. In the meantime, bring up your children piously in the fear of God, and thus prepare the way for that more universal education of which we have spoken.

12. Do you also, O instructors of the young, whose task it is to plant and water the tender grafts of paradise, pray with all earnestness that these aids to your labours may be perfected and brought into daily use as soon as possible. For since ye have been called that "ye may plant the heavens and lay the foundations of the earth" (Isaiah li. 16), what can be more pleasing to you than to reap as rich a harvest as possible from your labour? Therefore, let your heavenly calling, and the confidence of the parents who entrust their offspring to you, be as a fire within you, and give you and those who come under your influence no rest until the whole of your native land is lit up by this flaming torch.

13. Ye men of learning, to whom God has given wisdom and keen judgment that ye may be able to criticise such matters as these and improve them by your counsels, see that ye delay not to assist the sacred fire with your sparks, nay, rather with your torches and with your fans. Let all consider that saying of our Christ: "I came to cast fire upon the earth; and what will I if it is already kindled?" (Luke xii. 49). If He wish His fire to burn, woe unto him who, when he has the opportunity of bringing fuel to the flames, contributes nothing but the smoke of envy, malevolence, and opposition. Remember the reward that He promises to His good and faithful servants who employ the talents entrusted to them in such a way that they gain others, and the threats that He utters against the slothful who bury their talents in the earth (Matt. xxv. 25). Therefore, let not your own knowledge suffice you, but use all your strength to further the instruction of others. Be guided by the example of Seneca, who says: "I wish to communicate all that I know to others"; and again: "If knowledge were given me on the condition that I should keep it to myself and not share it with others, I should refuse it" (*Epist.* 27). Do not, therefore, withhold instruction and wisdom from the Christian people, but rather say with Moses: "Would God that all the Lord's peoples were prophets!" (Num. xi. 29). The reformation of the Church and of the state is comprised in the proper instruction of the young; and shall we, who know this, stand idle, while others put their hand to the work?

14. May we all, with one accord, be moved to promote such a worthy object in every possible manner by advising, warning, exhorting, reforming, and in every way furthering the work for God and for posterity. And let no one think that he is not called upon to act in the matter. For though a man may be naturally unsuited to be a schoolmaster, or may be fully engaged by his duties as a clergyman, a politician, or a physician, he makes a great mistake if he think that he is on that account exempt from the common task of school-reform. If he wish to prove his devotion to

his calling, to him who calls him, and to those to whom he is sent, he is bound not only to serve his God, his Church, and his country, but also to train up others to do so after him. Socrates has been praised because he employed his time in educating the young instead of holding some public office. "It is of more use," said he, "to train men who can govern, than to govern oneself."

15. O learned scholars, I beseech you not to despise these suggestions because they originate with one less learned than yourselves. Remember the saying of Chrysippus: "Many a market-gardener has spoken to the point. Perchance an ass may know what you do not." And of Christ: "The wind bloweth where it listeth, and ye hear its voice, but know not whence it comes or whither it goes." In the sight of God I protest that it is not by any overweening confidence in myself, or by a desire for fame or for personal advantage, that I am impelled to advertise these ideas of mine. It is the love of God and the wish to improve the condition of humanity that goad me on, and will not suffer me to keep silence when my instinct tells me what should be done. Therefore, if any oppose my efforts, and hinder the realisation of my ideas instead of aiding it, let him be assured that he is waging war, not against me, but against God, against his own conscience, and against nature, whose will it is that what is for the common good be given over for the use of all men.

16. To you also I appeal, Theologians, since it is in your power to be the greatest assistance or the greatest obstacle to my designs. If you choose the latter course, the saying of Bernhard will be fulfilled: "That Christ has no bitterer enemies than His followers, and especially those who hold the first place among them." But let us hope that your actions will be worthier, and more suited to your calling. Remember that our Lord charged Peter to feed not only His sheep but also His lambs, enjoining him to take especial care of the latter (John xxi. 15). This is a reasonable injunction, since shepherds find it easier to feed sheep than to feed lambs, which have still to be moulded

by the discipline of the flock and the staff of the herdsman. Surely a man betrays his ignorance if he prefer unlettered hearers! What goldsmith does not try to procure the very purest gold? What shoemaker does not try to obtain the finest leather? Let us likewise be children of light and wise in our generation, and let us pray that schools may supply us with as many educated hearers as possible.

17. And suffer not envy to enter into your hearts, O servants of the living God, but rather lead others to that charity that envies not, seeks not its own advantage, and thinks no evil. Let no envious thoughts arise if others originate schemes that have never entered into your minds, but be content to learn from others; in order that (as Gregory says) all, being full of faith, may praise God, and may be instrumental in spreading the truth.

18. But to you, in particular, do I direct my prayers, ye rulers and magistrates, who, in God's name, preside over human affairs. To you, as to Noah, it has been entrusted from on high to build an ark for the preservation of the Word of God in this terrible deluge of disasters (Gen. vi.) It is your duty, as it was that of the princes of old, to aid in the building of the sanctuary, and to see that no obstacle be placed in the way of the artificers whom the Lord has filled with His Spirit and has taught to devise ingenious plans (Exod. xxxvi.) You, like David and Solomon, should summon architects to build the temple of the Lord, and should supply them with the necessary materials (1 Kings vi. ; 1 Chron. xxix.) You are those centurions whom Christ will love if you have loved His little ones, and erected schools for them (Luke vii. 5).

19. For Christ's sake, for the sake of our children's salvation, I beseech you to listen to me. This is a weighty question, and concerns the glory of God and the salvation of mankind. Well do I know how much you love your country. If a man came to you and promised to tell you how all your towns might be fortified at a slight cost, how all your youths might be instructed in the art of warfare, how your rivers might be made navigable and be filled

with merchant-vessels, in short, how your state might be brought to a higher pitch of prosperity and security, you would give, not only your careful attention, but your heartiest thanks as well, to him who showed such solicitude for your welfare. And now, what is far more important than any of these things has been shown you, namely, the real and never-failing method by which a supply of such men may be secured, men who, by discoveries such as I have indicated, can be of immense service to their country. With truth did the sainted Luther write, when exhorting the cities of Germany to found schools: "Where one ducat is expended in building cities, fortresses, monuments, and arsenals, one hundred should be spent in educating one youth aright, since, when he reaches manhood, he may induce his fellows to carry out useful works. For a good and wise man is the most precious treasure of a state, and is of far more value than palaces, than heaps of gold and of silver, than gates of bronze and bars of iron." Solomon also is of the same opinion (Eccles. ix. 13). If then we acknowledge that no expense should be spared in order to give one youth a thorough education, what can we say when the gate is opened to the universal education of all, and to an unfailing method by which the understanding may be developed? when God promises to shower His gifts upon us? when our salvation seems so near at hand that His glory dwells with us on earth?

20. Open wide your gates, O princes, that the King of glory may come in (Psalm xxiv.) Give to the Lord glory and honour, ye sons of the mighty. May each one of you be like David, who sware unto the Lord, and vowed unto the mighty one of Jacob: "Surely I will not come unto the tabernacle of my house, nor go up into my bed ; I will not give sleep to mine eyes, or slumber to mine eyelids ; until I find out a place for the Lord, a tabernacle for the Mighty One of Jacob" (Psalm cxxxii.) Stay not to consider the expense. Give to the Lord, and He will repay you a thousandfold. He who says, "The silver is mine and the gold is mine" (Haggai ii. 9), can demand this as a

right, yet of His mercy He adds (when exhorting the people
to build His temple) : " Prove me now forthwith if I will
not open you the windows of heaven, and pour you out
a blessing that there shall not be room enough to receive
it " (Mal. iii. 10).

21. Do Thou, therefore, O Lord our God, give each one
of us a joyful heart to serve Thy glory as best he may.
For Thine is the grandeur, the power, the glory, and the
victory.   All that is in heaven and in earth is Thine.
Thine, O Lord, is the kingdom ; Thou art over all princes.
Thine are the riches, and Thine is the glory, the might,
and the power; Thou canst glorify and magnify whatso-
ever Thou pleasest.   For what are we, who have but
received Thy gifts from Thy hands ?   We are but strangers
in Thy sight as were our fathers.   Our life on earth is but
a shadow and passes away.   O Lord our God, all that we
do to the honour of Thy name, comes from Thee.   Give
to Thy Solomons a perfect heart that they may do all that
tends to Thy glory (1 Chron. xxix.)   Strengthen, O God,
that which Thou hast wrought for us (Psalm lxviii. 28).
Let Thy work appear unto Thy servants, and Thy glory
upon their children.   And let the beauty of the Lord our
God be upon us ; and establish Thou the works of our
hands upon us (Psalm xc. 16).   In Thee, O Lord, have I
trusted, let me never be confounded.   Amen.

NOTES

1. GREGORY NAZIANZEN.—A Father of the Church in the fourth century. He was renowned for his eloquence, which he employed in combating the Arian heresy.

2. WOLFGANG RATICH or RATKE (born at Wilster in 1571, died at Erfurt in 1635).—One of the immediate forerunners of Comenius in school reform. He enjoyed the patronage of Count Ludwig of Anhalt-Köthen, through whose liberality he was enabled to found a six-class school at Köthen, in accordance with his didactic principles. He also undertook the reorganisation of the schools at Augsburg, Weimar, Magdeburg, and Rudolfstadt. The lack of success that attended his efforts was due to his quarrelsome disposition and to his utter inability to establish a *modus vivendi* with his colleagues and assistants. For his Principles, see Intr. II. p. 136.

3. EILHARD LUBIN (born in 1565, in the Duchy of Oldenburg; died in 1621).—Professor of Poetry and Theology at the University of Rostock. His *Didactic*, quoted by Comenius in sec. 17 of his introduction, has not been preserved.

4. CHRISTOPHER HELWIG (1581-1617).—Professor of Theology, of Greek, and of Oriental Languages in the University of Giessen. He was one of the Commissioners who examined Ratke's didactic method in 1612.

5. FRANCISCUS RITTER.—This may possibly have been a clergyman and mathematician of some repute in the Palatinate in the early seventeenth century. Morhof mentions him under the name Franciscus Ridderus (*Polyhistor*, i. 1. 16).

6. JOHANNES BODINUS (1530-1596).—A lawyer at Toulouse, author of a treatise, *Methodus ad facilem historiarum cognitionem.*

7. VOGEL.—Probably Ezechiel Vogel, a schoolmaster at Göttingen, and author of a work, *Ephemerides linguæ Latinæ*, in which he shows how a boy, by working two hours daily, may learn Latin in one year.

8. Glaum ; Wolfstirn.—Of the owners of these names I have been unable to obtain any information.

9. John Valentine Andreæ.—Court-preacher at Stuttgart, where he died in 1654. He was a considerable power in the Church and in the school-room.

10. Janus Cæcilius Frey.—A German physician residing at Paris, where he died of the plague in 1631. On educational questions he wrote several books, remarkable for their sound common-sense.

11. This section is signed with Andreæ's name, but cannot have been written by him, as in the original Bohemian version of the *Great Didactic* it appears in a considerably altered form. Possibly the last sentence is quoted from one of Andreæ's works.

12. Stobæus.—A native of Stobi in Macedonia, where he lived about 500 A.D., and composed an Anthology of extracts from as many as 500 Greek authors.

13. Pittacus of Mitylene.—One of the seven wise men of Greece. Lived about 600 B.C.

14. Sextus Pompeius Festus.—A Roman grammarian who lived towards the end of the fourth century A.D.

15. John Ludovic Vives.—One of the great pedagogues of the sixteenth century. Was born at Valencia in 1492 ; professed the "Humanities" at Louvain and was afterwards invited by Henry VIII. to England, where he became the tutor of the Princess Mary. His best known works on education are : *De ratione studii puerilis epistolæ duæ ; De tradendis disciplinis sive de institutione Christiana ; De institutione fœminæ Christianæ ; Introductio ad Sapientiam.*

16. Bernhard.—Abbot of Clairvaux in 1115. A man of great ecclesiastical and political influence, and one of the instigators of the Third Crusade.

17. Lactantius.—For some years tutor to a son of the Emperor Constantine. Converted to Christianity in middle life, he wrote a voluminous treatise, *Divinarum institutionum libri vii.* ; a plea for Christianity, intended for pagans who had received a philosophic education. He died about 330 A.D.

18. Matthew Dresser (1536-1607).—Was successively Professor of Greek at Erfurt, Professor of Rhetoric at Jena, Rector of the school at Meissen, and Professor of Greek and Latin at Leipzig.

19. Liebhard Camerarius.—A renowned sixteenth century scholar and editor of the classics. Sympathised with the Reformation and was . a friend of Melanchthon's. Died in 1574.

20. Gulartius.—Nothing appears to be known of this scholar or his works.

21. GEORGE AGRICOLA (born in Saxony, 1490).—The founder of the modern school of mineralogy and metallurgy. Mining in Germany owed much to his researches, which were considered authoritative as late as the eighteenth century.

22. CHRISTOPHER LONGOLIUS (1488-1522).—Born at Mecheln and resident in Paris. A renowned classic of his day. Died at Padua.

23. HIPPOLITUS GUARINO.—Lived in the first half of the seventeenth century. Was town physician at Speyer.

24. JOHN PICO MIRANDOLO (1463-1494).—In early youth gave evidence of remarkable ability. When fourteen years old went to Bologna, where he studied canon law and philosophy. His memory was so retentive that if 20,000 words were repeated to him once, he could reproduce them in the same order. He published 900 theses and challenged the learned men of the whole world to dispute with him on any one of them. Accused of heresy, he was acquitted by Pope Innocent VIII. He died at Florence.

25. JOSEPH JUSTUS SCALIGER.—Flourished in France at the end of the sixteenth and beginning of the seventeenth centuries. Possessed a marvellous knowledge of the classics and of oriental languages. His learning was more than equalled by his vanity and quarrelsomeness.

26. PIERRE DE LA RAMÉE.—Professor of Mathematics and Humanity at the University of Paris in the middle of the sixteenth century. Was killed in the Massacre of St. Bartholomew, August 24th, 1572.

27. GREGORY CNAPIUS (1574-1638).—A Polish Jesuit, Professor of Oratory, Mathematics, and Theology. Was author of a *Thesaurum Polono-Latino-Græcum.*

28. Not *conjunctus* but *convinctus* is now the generally accepted derivation of *cunctus.*

29. JOACHIM FORTIUS or RINGELBERG (died in 1536).—Born at Antwerp and brought up at the court of Maximilian I. A man of varied talent, and a voluminous author, he attained success as a mathematician, a philologist, a painter, and an etcher.

30. ROBERT FLUTT (1574-1637).—Born at Milgate in Kent. Travelled in France, Spain, Italy, and Germany, and finally settled in London, where he practised medicine. On physics he had the most fantastic notions, and imagined that the root principles of chemistry were to be found in the Bible. Was author of a *Meteorologica Cosmica.*

31. ANDREAS HYPERIUS (1511-1564).—A member of the Reformed Church, born at Ypres. He studied at Paris and lectured there on Dialectic and Rhetoric, afterwards becoming Professor of Theology at Marburg.

32. FULGENTIUS.—A Catholic Bishop who lived about 500 A.D.

He defended the views of the Orthodox Church against the Arian and Pelagian heresies.

33. PRISCIAN.—A grammarian who lived and taught at Constantinople in the sixth century. His Latin Grammar was the basis for much of the grammatical instruction of the middle ages.

34. *Expulsion of pagan books.*—It is difficult to reconcile Comenius' denunciation of the classics in this chapter with his introduction of them into his scheme elsewhere. In this phase of mind he does but return to the distrust displayed by the Church for the new learning introduced by the Renaissance. It is curious to note that no stress is laid on the Utilitarian and "pressure-of-other-subjects" argument now so frequently made use of. Comparatively recently (1850 and 1851) two French writers, the Abbé Gaume and Bastiat, have condemned the use of the classics in schools from a point of view very similar to that of Comenius. Gaume in a pamphlet, *Le ver rongeur*, maintained that all literature prior to Christ's coming was devoid of morality, and that the Fathers should be read in preference to Latin writers of the golden age. Bastiat, in a curious book entitled *Baccalauréat et Socialisme*, objects to any study that will introduce school-boys to a people who, like the Romans, lived by robbery and oppression. "Cette nation," he declares, "s'est fait une politique, une morale, une religion, une opinion publique conforme au principe brutal qui la conserve et la développe. La France ayant donné au clergé le monopole de l'éducation, celui-ci ne trouve rien de mieux à faire que d'envoyer toute la jeunesse française chez ce peuple, vivre de sa vie, s'inspirer de ses sentiments, s'enthousiasmer de ses enthousiasmes, et respirer ses idées comme l'air."

35. CASSIODORUS (died 562 A.D.)—Held high office under Theodoric and his successor. After the fall of the Goths he retired into seclusion and employed himself in writing works of a philosophic nature on grammar and orthography.

36. PIETRO BEMBO.—A renowned Italian Cardinal in the sixteenth century. Was secretary to Pope Leo X., and wrote with elegance in both Latin and Italian.

37. ISIDORUS (died 635 A.D.)—Bishop of Seville. Was a student of the classics in an age when they were generally neglected. Compiled a kind of encyclopædia entitled *Originum sive Etymologiarum libri xx.*

38. *Sketch of the Mother-School.*—It is interesting to observe the development or rather the application at the present day of Comenius' ideas on infant education. The following extracts from the French code of 1887 reflect the Comenian spirit very markedly :—

"L'école maternelle n'est pas une école au sens ordinaire du mot ;

elle forme le passage de la famille à l'école, elle garde la douceur affec-
tueuse et indulgente de la famille, en même temps qu'elle initie au
travail et à la régularité de l'école." . . . "Une bonne santé ; l'ouïe,
la vue, le toucher déjà exercés par une suite graduée de ses petits jeux
et de ses petites expériences propres à l'éducation des sens ; des idées
enfantines, mais nettes et claires, sur les premiers éléments de ce qui
sera plus tard l'instruction primaire ; un commencement d'habitudes et
de dispositions sur lesquelles l'école puisse s'appuyer pour donner plus
tard un enseignement régulier ; le goût de la gymnastique, du chant, du
dessin, des images, des récits ; l'empressement à écouter, à voir, à observer, à imiter, à questionner, à répondre ; une certaine faculté d'attention entretenue par la docilité, la confiance et la bonne humeur ;
l'intelligence éveillée enfin et l'âme ouverte à toutes les bonnes impressions morales ; tels doivent être les résultats de ces premières années
passées à l'école maternelle, et, si l'enfant qui en sort arrive à l'école
primaire avec une telle préparation, il importe peu qu'il y joigne
quelques pages de plus ou de moins du syllabaire."

39. WILLIAM ZEPPER.—A preacher at Herborn at the close of the
sixteenth and beginning of seventeenth centuries.

40. JOHN HENRY ALSTED.—See Intr. I. p. 4, and Intr. II. p. 137.

41. SIMON STEVIN (died 1633).—The author of numerous mathematical works and an inspector of dams in Holland.

42. JUSTUS LIPSIUS (born 1574).—Resided at Louvain, where he
wrote works of a philosophical nature. His learning and his literary
style are greatly praised by Morhof.

APPENDIX

14. 1623. The Labyrinth of the World and the Paradise of the Heart. Amsterdam, 1663. [C.]

15. 1623. The orphan's plight. That is to say, abandonment by all friends, protectors, and helpers. Lissa, 1634. [C.]

16. 1625. Centrum securitatis. Lissa, 1633. [C.]

17. 1625. The Revelations and Visions of Christopher Kotter. [C.]

18. 1626. The Psalms of David. A version in Czech. Vienna, 1661.

19. 1628-32. The Didactic of John Amos Comenius. Prague, 1849. [C.]

The Latin version, under the title *Didactica Magna*, was published at Amsterdam in 1657.

20. 1628. Informatorium of the Mother-School. Prague, 1858. [C.]

The Latin version, under the title : Schola Infantiæ, sive de provida Juventutis primo sexennio Educatione. Amsterodami, 1657.

German version by Comenius. Lissa, 1633.

21. 1628. Vernaculæ Scholæ Classis sex Libelli.

22. 1628. J. A. Comenii Janua Linguarum Reserata. Sive Seminarium Linguarum et Scientiarum Omnium. Hoc est Compendiosa Latinam (et quamlibet aliam) Linguam, una cum Scientiarum, Artiumque omnium fundamentis, perdiscendi Methodus ; sub Titulis centum, Periodis autem mille, comprehensa. 1st edition pub. by Comenius in 1633. Published in Greek and Latin at Oxford as late as 1800. And in Latin, German, and Czech at Prague in 1874.

23. 1629. De veris et falsis prophetis. Written in Czech and translated into Latin for inclusion in Lux in Tenebris.

24. 1630. Praxis Pietatis ; The practice of true Piety. [C.] Lissa, 1631.

25. 1630. Funeral oration over Esther Sadowska (written in German).

26. 1631. Grammatica latina legibus vernaculæ concinnata.

27. 1631. Concordance of the Holy Scriptures. (Burnt at Lissa.)

28. 1631. Evangelistarum Harmonia.

29. 1632. Historia fratrum Bohemorum.

30. 1632. Manual of the Holy Scriptures. Written for the Bohemian Church. [C.]

31. 1632. History of the sufferings, the death, the burial, and the resurrection of Jesus Christ ; compiled from the four Evangelists. [C.]

32. 1632. Historia Persecutionum Ecclesiæ Bohemicæ. Jam inde a primordiis conversionis suæ ad Christianismum, hoc est, Anno 894 ad Annum usque 1632. Ferdinando secundo Austriaco regnante, In qua Inaudita hactenus Arcana Politica consilia, artes, præsentium bellorum veræ causæ et judicia horrenda exhibentur. Nunc primum edita cum duplici Indice. A.D. 1648. Translated into Czech and published at Lissa in 1655.

33. 1632. Haggæus Redivivus. Sorrowful exhortation, in God's name, of Christian rulers, of God's ministers, and of all nations. [C.]

34. 1632. Short sketch of the reorganisation of schools in the Kingdom of Bohemia. [C.]

35. 1632. The Basis and Duration of the two Churches, the true and the false; of which the true Church, founded in Paradise through the name of Jesus Christ, will endure to the end of the World. [C.]

36. 1632. Some questions that concern the Unity of Bohemian Brethren. First printed in 1878. [C.]

37. 1632-3. Physicæ ad lumen divinum reformatæ synopsis philodidactorum et theodidactorum censuræ exposita. Lipsiæ, 1633.

38. 1632. Astronomia ad lumen Physicum reformanda.

39. 1632-3. The wisdom of the Forefathers set forth as a mirror for their Descendants. First printed in 1849. [C.]

40. 1633. Januæ Linguarum Reseratæ Vestibulum, Quo Primus ad Latinam Linguam aditus Tirunculis paratur. Many editions. Latest in 1867.

41. 1634. Suggestions for a new edition of the Chant-Book. [C.]

42. 1634. Conatuum Comenianorum Præludia. Oxoniæ, 1637.

43. 1635. Leges Illustris Gymnasii Lesnensis.

44. 1635. Account of a tractate hostile to the Unity, by Samuel Martin, and refutation of the same. Lissa, 1636. [C.]

45. 1636. XXI. Sermons. Of the mysteries of Death and of Resurrection. Lissa, 1636. [C.]

46. 1636. The Mirror of Good Government. Funeral oration over Count Raphael of Lissa. Lissa, 1636. (Composed in German.)

47. 1637. J. A. Comenii Faber Fortunæ sive Ars consulendi ipsi sibi. Amsterodami, 1657.

48. 1637. The Way of Peace; that is to say, the only true and unfailing means by which God's Church can be preserved in Harmony, Concord, and Love. Lissa, 1637. [C.]

49. 1637. De Quæstione Utrum Dominus Jesus Propriâ Virtute a mortuis Resurrexit. Ad Melchiorem Schefferum Socinistam, breve ac solidum Joh. A. Comenii Responsum. Amstelodami apud Joannem Janssonium 1659.

50. 1637. De Sermonis Latini Studio, Per Vestibulum, Januam, Palatium, et Thesauros Latinitatis, quadripartito gradu plene absolvendo, Didactica Dissertatio. Lissa, 1637.

51. 1638. Diogenes Cynicus Redivivus, sive De compendiose Philosophando. Ad Scholæ ludentis exercitia olim accommodatus, nunc autem luci datus. Authore J. A. Comenio. Amstelodami, 1658.

52. 1638. Abrahamus Patriarcha. Scena repræsentatus anno 1641 in Januario, sub examen Scholæ publicum. Amstelodami. Anno 1661.

53. 1638. Conatuum Pansophicorum Dilucidatio. In gratiam censorum facta. Londini, 1639.

54. 1639. A Dextris et Sinistris, hoc est pro fide in Christum, Deum-Hominem cum Marcioniticis deliriis (Humanitatem Christi abnegantibus) Lucta. Amsterodami, 1662.

55. 1640. De Christianorum Uno Deo, Patre, Filio, Spiritu. Fides antiqua, Contra Novatores. Amstelodami, 1659.

56. 1640 (?). Janua Rerum reserata, hoc est Sapientia prima (quam vulgo Metaphysicam vocant) ita Mentibus hominum adaptata ut per eam in totam Rerum Ambitum Omnemque interiorem Rerum Ordinem Et in omnes intimas rebus Coæternas Veritates Prospectus pateat Catholicus Simulque ut eadem omnium humanorum Cogitationum, Sermonum, Operum, Fons et Scaturigo, Formaque ac Norma esse appareat. Authore J. A. Comenio. Lugduni Batavorum. Apud Hæredes Jacobi Heeneman. Anno 1681.

57. 1641. Via Lucis. Hoc est, Rationabilis disquisitio, quomodo Intellectualis animorum Lux, Sapientia, tandem sub Mundi vesperam per omnes mentes et gentes feliciter spargi possit. Amstelodami, 1688.

58. 1641-3. J. A. Comenii Pansophiæ Diatyposis Ichnographica et Orthographica delineatione. Totius futuri operis amplitudinem, dimensionem, usus adumbrans. Amsterodami, 1645.

59. 1643. Irenica quædam scripta Pro pace Ecclesiæ.

60. 1643. Calendarium Ecclesiasticum.

61. 1644. Judicium de Judicio Valeriani Magni Mediolanensis, Super Catholicorum et Acatholicorum Credendi Regula, sive Absurditatum Echo. Amstelodami, 1644.

62. 1644-6. Linguarum Methodus Novissima Fundamentis Didacticis solide superstructa. 1648.

63. 1645. Jo. Amos Comenii Eccl. Boh. Episcopi, De Rerum Humanarum Emendatione Consultatio Catholica. 2nd ed. Halle, 1702.

64. 1645. Judicium Ulrici Neufeldii de Fidei Catholicæ Regula Catholica, Ejusque Catholico Usu ad Valerianum Magnum Omnesque Catholicos. 1645.

65. 1645. Regulæ Vitæ Sapientis, harmonicæ, tranquillæ, actuosæ, negotiis obrutæ, liberaliter otiosæ, peregrinantis denique. 1645.

66. 1645. Pansophiæ dogmaticæ, Latinis olim decretoriæ, nunc systematicæ vulgo dictæ delineatio juxta diatyposin J. A. Comenii.

67. 1646. Christianismus reconciliabilis reconciliatore Christo. Hoc est quam facile Christiani si vere ac serio Christiani esse velint, non discordare possint, tam clara ut Sol meridie est demonstratio.

68. 1648. Independentia æternarum Confusionum Origo Spectamini Venerabilis Nationalis Synodi in Nomine Christi Londini in Anglia congregatæ subjecta Anno 1648.

69. 1649. Of the casting out of the dumb and other devils. A sermon delivered at Lissa. 1649. [C.]

70. 1649. Index plenus vocum Germanicarum.

71. 1649. Johannis Lasitii, nobilis Poloni Historiæ de Origine Et Rebus gestis Fratrum Bohemicorum Liber Octavus, qui est De Moribus et Institutis eorum. Ob præsentem rerum statum seorsim editus. Anno 1649.

72. 1649. Manuductio in viam pacis ecclesiasticæ.

73. 1649. Funeral Oration over Paul Fabrik. [C.]

74. 1650. Syntagma rerum, conceptuum, et verborum.

75. 1650. The Will of the Dying Mother; in which she divides among her sons and heirs the treasures entrusted to her by God. Lissa, 1650. [C.]

76. 1650. Schola Pansophica. Hoc est, Universalis Sapientiæ Officina, ab annis aliquot ubi ubi gentium erigi optatæ: Nunc autem Auspiciis Illustrissimi Domini D. Sigismundi Racocis de Felseovadas Saros-Pataki Hungarorum feliciter erigenda. 1651.

77. 1651. De reperta ad Authores Latinos prompte legendos et clare intellegendos Facili Brevique Via, Schola Latina, Tribus Classibus divisa. Amsterodami, 1657.

78. 1651-2. Eruditionis Scholasticæ Pars Tertia. Atrium Rerum et Linguarum Ornamenta exhibens. In usum Scholæ Patakinæ editum. Anno 1652.

79. 1651. J. A. Komensky's The Art of Preaching. Prague, 1823. [C.]

80. 1651. Primitiæ laborum Scholasticorum. 1651.

81. 1651-2. Laborum Scholasticorum in Illustri Patakino Gymnasio continuatis.

82. 1652. Joachimi Fortii Ringelbergii De Ratione Studii Liber Vere Aureus. Des. Erasmi Roterodami. De Ratione Studii. Edited by Comenius, with an Introduction.

83. 1653. Fortius Redivivus, sive de pellenda Scholis ignavia.

84. 1653. Præcepta Morum. In usum Juventutis collecta. Anno 1653.

85. 1653. Leges Scholæ bene ordinatæ.

30

86. 1653. Orbis sensualium pictus. Hoc est, Omnium fundamentalium in Mundo rerum et in Vita actionum, Pictura et Nomenclatura. Nuremberg, 1658.

87. 1653. Animæ sanctæ Æterna Regna cum Triumpho ingredientis Beatum Satellitium. Anno 1653. Addressed to Laurence de Geer on the death of his father.

88. 1654. Schola Ludus seu Encyclopædia viva, h. e. Januæ Linguarum praxis comica. Patak, 1656.

89. 1654. J. A. Comenii Lexicon Atriale Latino-Latinum Simplices et nativas rerum nomenclationes e Janua Linguæ Latinæ jam notas, in elegantes varie commutare docens. Amstelodami, 1658.

90. 1654. Laborum Scholasticorum Patakini obitorum Coronis, Sermone valedictorio, ad Scholam Patakinam, ejusque solertes D. D. Scholarchas et Visitatores, Generosorumque Reverendorum magnam panegyrin, habito imposita. Anno 1654.

91. 1654. Gentis felicitas Speculo exhibita iis, qui num felices sint et quomodo fieri possint, cognoscere velint. 1659.

92. 1654-7. Lux in Tenebris. Hoc est Prophetiæ Donum quo Deus Ecclesiam Evangelicam (in Regno Bohemiæ et incorporatis Provinciis) sub tempus horrendæ ejus pro Evangelio persequutionis extremæque dissipationis ornare, ac paterne solari dignatus est. Submissis de statu Ecclesiæ in Terris, præsenti et mox futuro, per Christophorum Cotterum Silesium, Christinam Poniatovam Bohemam, et Nicolaum Drabicium Moravum, Revelationibus vere divinis, ab anno 1616 usque ad annum 1656 continuatis. Quæ nunc e Vernaculo in Latinum fideliter translatæ in Dei gloriam, afflictorum solatia, aliorumque salutarem informationem ipsius Oraculi jussu in lucem dantur. Anno 1657.

93. 1655. The struggle with God in prayer, followed by Resignation to His Will in death as in life. A sermon preached at Lissa on Sept. 24th; at the close of a day of great danger. 2nd ed. Halle, 1765. [C.]

94. 1655. Panegyricus Carolo Gustavo Magno Svecorum, Gothorum, Vandalorumque Regi, incruento Sarmatiæ Victori, et quaquâ venit Liberatori, Pio, Felici, Augusto. Heroi afflictis in solatia, Regibus in exemplum, nato. Lugduni Batavorum, 1656.

95. 1655-6. Evigila Polonia.

96. 1656. Enoch; or, Of the continual intercourse of believers with God. 1656. [C.]

97. 1656. The Gift of Long Life. A sermon preached at the burial of Wacslaw Lochar, Consenior of the Moravian Church at Lissa. [C.]

98. 1656. Materiarum Pansophicarum Sylva, Definitionum scil.

omnium rerum et Axiomatum (supra 20 annos magnâ diligentiâ Congestatus) thesaurus. Burnt at Lissa.

99. 1656. Sapientia Bis et Ter Oculata, Aliud in alio acute videns, aliudque per aliud potenter demonstrans. Burnt at Lissa.

100. 1656. Lesnæ Excidium, Anno 1656 in Aprili factum, fide historica narratum.

101. 1657. Parvulis parvulus, Omnibus Omnia. Hoc est Vestibuli Lat. Linguæ Auctarium. Voces Latinas primitivas construi, cœptas, et in Sententiolas breves redactas, exhibens. Amsterdami, 1657.

102. 1657. J. A. Comenii pro Latinitate Januæ Linguarum suæ, illiusque praxeos Comicæ, Apologia. Amstelodami, 1657.

103. 1657. J. A. Comenii Opera Didactica Omnia, ab anno 1627 ad 1657 continuata. Amsterodami, Anno 1657.

104. 1658. Janua sive Introductorium in Biblia Sacra. Norimbergæ, 1658.

105. 1658. Novi Testamenti Epitome, Typorum Diversitate Res, Verba, Phrases, Atque Sententias Exhibens. Norimbergæ, 1658.

106. 1659. Disquisitiones de Caloris et Frigoris natura, in prodromum novæ editionis Physicæ ad lumen divinum restituendæ. Amstelodami, 1659.

107. 1659. Book of Chants for the Bohemian Church. Amsterdam, 1659. [C.]

108. 1659. Vindicatio Famæ et conscientiæ Johannis Comenii a Calumniis Nicolai Arnoldi. Lugduni Batavorum, 1659.

109. 1659. Historia Revelationum Christophori Kotteri, Christinæ Poniatoviæ, Nicolai Drabicii et quæ circa illas varie acciderunt, usque ad earundem Anno 1657 publicationem, et post publicationem. 1659.

110. 1659. Cartesius cum sua naturali Philosophia a Mechanicis eversus. Amsterodami, 1659.

111. 1660. The mournful cry of the Shepherds, terror-struck by God's anger, to their perishing and scattered flocks. Amsterdam, 1660. [C.]

112. 1660. De bono Unitatis et ordinis disciplinæque et obedientiæ. Amst. 1660.

113. 1660. De Irenico Irenicorum. Hoc est : Conditionibus Pacis a Socini Secta reliquo Christiano Orbi oblatis, ad omnes Christianos facta Admonitio A. Johan. Amos Comenio. Amsterodami, Anno 1660.

114. 1661. Theologia Naturalis. A Raymundo de Sabunde ante duo secula conscriptus, nunc autem Latiniore stylo in compendium redactus. Amst. 1661.

115. 1661. Catechism for young Bohemians. Amst. 1661. [C.]

116. 1661. J. A. Comenio de Iterato Sociniano Irenico Iterata ad Christianos Admonitio. Amst. 1661.

117. 1661. Socinismi Speculum uno intuitu quidquid ibi creditur aut non creditur, exhibens. Amst. 1661.

118. 1662. Johan. Amos Comenii Admonitio Tertia. I. Ad D. Zwickerum ut impios suos adversus Christum et Christianam fidem impetus temperet; II. ad Christianos ut tandem evigilent. Amst. 1662.

119. 1662. Confession of the Beliefs, Teaching, and Religion of the Unity of the Bohemian Brethren. Amst. 1662. [C.]

120. 1662. De rerum humanarum Emendatione Consultationis Catholicæ Pars Secunda Panaugia. Ubi de accendenda Mentibus ante omnia Luce quadam universali, in qua omnes, Omnia, Omnino videri possint, consultatur.

121. 1662. The Moral Teaching of Cato the Wise, translated into Bohemian. Amst. 1662. [C.]

122. 1663. Renuntiatio Mundi. Amst. 1663.

123. 1663. Revelationum Divinarum, in usum Seculi nostri quibusdam nuper factarum, Epitome. 1663.

124. 1664-7. Lux e Tenebris. Tenebris, humanarum abominationum, Divinarumque plagarum. Lux, Divinarum Consolationum, glorioseque reflorescentis Ecclesiæ.

125. 1667. Petrus Serarius : Responsio ad Exercitationem Paradoxam Anonymi cujusdam Cartesianæ Sectæ Discipuli qua Philosophiam pro infallibili S. Literas interpretandi normâ Orbi Christiano obtrudit. Amst. 1667.

126. 1669. Unum Necessarium, Scire Quid Sibi sit Necessarium ; in Vita et Morte, et post Mortem. Quod non Necessariis Mundi Fatigatus et ad Unum Necessarium Sese Recipiens, Senex J. A. Comenius, Anno ætatis suæ 77, Mundo expendendum offert. Amst. 1668.

127. 1669. De Zelo sine scientia et charitate, Admonitio Fraterna J. A. Comenii ad D. Samuelem Maresium : Pro minuendis odiis et ampliandis favoribus. Amst. 1669.

Printed by R. & R. Clark, Limited, *Edinburgh.*

ALGEBRA. An Elementary Text-Book for the Higher Classes of Secondary Schools and for Colleges. By G. CHRYSTAL, M.A., LL.D., Professor of Mathematics in the University of Edinburgh.
PART I. Third Edition. Price 10s. 6d. PART II. With Index. Price 12s. 6d.

ASTRONOMY, A History of, during the Nineteenth Century. By AGNES M. CLERKE. Third Edition, revised and enlarged. In one vol., demy 8vo. Illustrated. Price 12s. 6d.

BOTANY, an Introduction to Structural (Flowering Plants). By D. H. SCOTT, M.A., F.R.S., Honorary Keeper of the Jodrell Laboratory, Royal Gardens, Kew. Second Edition. Crown 8vo. Illustrated with 183 figures. Price 3s. 6d.

CHEMICAL THEORY, an Introduction to. By ALEXANDER SCOTT, M.A., D.Sc., Jacksonian Demonstrator in the University of Cambridge. Crown 8vo. Price 5s.

DYNAMICS. By P. G. TAIT, M.A., Professor of Natural Philosophy in the University of Edinburgh. Crown 8vo. Price 7s. 6d.

ELECTRICITY, Electrometer, Magnetism, and Electrolysis. By Prof. CHRYSTAL and W. N. SHAW. 4to. Illustrated. Price 5s.

FISHES, Introduction to the Study of. With Index. By ALBERT C. L. G. GÜNTHER. Illustrated with 320 Wood Engravings. Demy 8vo. 720 pp. Price 12s. 6d.

FUNGI, Introduction to the Study of. Their Organography, Classification, and Distribution. For the Use of Collectors. By M. C. COOKE, M.A., LL.D. Demy 8vo. Illustrated. Price 14s.

LIGHT. Second Edition. By Prof. TAIT. Crown 8vo. Price 6s.

LOGIC. The Process of Argument. A Contribution to Logic. By ALFRED SIDGWICK. Crown 8vo. Price 5s.

MAMMALS, Introduction to the Study of. By Sir W. H. FLOWER, K.C.B., and R. LYDEKKER. Illustrated with 357 Wood Engravings. Demy 8vo. Price 12s. 6d.

MATTER, Properties of. Third Edition. By Prof. TAIT. Crown 8vo. Price 7s. 6d.

MICROSCOPIC FOAMS AND ON PROTOPLASM, Investigations on. By Prof. O. BÜTSCHLI. Translated from the German by E. A. MINCHIN, B.A. Oxon. Demy 8vo. Illustrated with 12 Lithographic Plates. Price 18s. net.

MINERALOGY, Elements of. By Prof. JAMES NICOL. Second Edition, revised and enlarged. Crown 8vo. Price 7s. 6d.

PHILOSOPHY, Early Greek. By JOHN BURNET, M.A., Professor of Greek, University of St. Andrews. Demy 8vo. Price 10s. 6d.

POLITICAL ECONOMY, Principles of. By J. SHIELD NICHOLSON, M.A., Professor of Political Economy in the University of Edinburgh. Vol. I., Demy 8vo. Price 15s.

THEOLOGY, A Manual of. By THOMAS B. STRONG, M.A. Crown 8vo. Price 5s.

ZOOLOGY of the Invertebrata. A Text-Book for Students. By A. E. SHIPLEY, M.A., Fellow and Assistant Tutor of Christ's College, and Demonstrator of Comparative Anatomy in the University of Cambridge. Demy 8vo. Illustrated. Price 18s. net.

LONDON: A. & C. BLACK, SOHO SQUARE.

RECTORIAL ADDRESSES

DELIVERED AT THE UNIVERSITY OF ST. ANDREWS

SIR WILLIAM STIRLING-MAXWELL TO THE
MARQUIS OF BUTE (1863-1893)

EDITED, WITH AN INTRODUCTION, BY

WILLIAM KNIGHT, LL.D.
PROFESSOR OF MORAL PHILOSOPHY IN THE UNIVERSITY

Demy 8vo. Price 10s. 6d.

EARLY GREEK PHILOSOPHY

BY

JOHN BURNET, M.A.
PROFESSOR OF GREEK IN THE UNIVERSITY OF ST. ANDREWS

Demy 8vo. Price 10s. 6d.

EDINBURGH SKETCHES

AND

MEMORIES

BY

DAVID MASSON, M.A., LL.D.
EMERITUS PROFESSOR OF ENGLISH LITERATURE IN THE
UNIVERSITY OF EDINBURGH

Demy 8vo. Price 10s. 6d.

MEMORIALS OF EDINBURGH

IN THE

OLDEN TIME

BY THE LATE
SIR DANIEL WILSON, LL.D.

2 Vols. Medium Quarto. Price 25s.

LONDON : A. & C. BLACK, SOHO SQUARE.

THE REMAINS OF ANCIENT ROME

BY

J. H. MIDDLETON, M.A., LL.D.

DIRECTOR OF THE SOUTH KENSINGTON MUSEUM

With 102 Wood Engravings and 4 Coloured Plans

2 Vols. Post 8vo. Price 25s.

STUDIES OF THE GREEK POETS

BY THE LATE
JOHN ADDINGTON SYMONDS

New and Enlarged Edition, with a Chapter on Herondas

2 Vols. Post 8vo. Price 25s.

ABBOTSFORD AND ITS TREASURES

BY

THE HON. MRS. MAXWELL SCOTT OF ABBOTSFORD

Illustrated by WILLIAM GIBB

Royal Quarto. Price £2 : 12 : 6 net.

THE TRAGEDY OF FOTHERINGAY

FOUNDED ON THE JOURNAL OF D. BOURGOING, PHYSICIAN TO
MARY QUEEN OF SCOTS, AND ON UNPUBLISHED
MS. DOCUMENTS

Illustrated with Three Photogravures and Four Illustrations
not hitherto Published

BY

THE HON. MRS. MAXWELL SCOTT OF ABBOTSFORD

Square 8vo. Price 12s. 6d. net.

LONDON : A. & C. BLACK, SOHO SQUARE.

www.ingramcontent.com/pod-product-compliance
Lightning Source LLC
Chambersburg PA
CBHW022016050726
47499CB00004BA/1022

* 9 7 8 1 5 2 8 7 0 5 4 1 7 *